Multimodal Film Analysis

D1826476

Routledge Studies in Multimodality

Edited by Kay L. O'Halloran, *National University of Singapore*

Multimodal Film Analysis

How Films Mean

**John A. Bateman and
Karl-Heinrich Schmidt**

Routledge
Taylor & Francis Group
NEW YORK   LONDON

First published 2012
by Routledge
711 Third Avenue, New York, NY 10017

Simultaneously published in the UK
by Routledge
2 Park Square, Milton Park, Abingdon, Oxfordshire OX14 4RN

First issued in paperback 2014

Routledge is an imprint of the Taylor and Francis Group, an informa company

© 2012 Taylor & Francis

The right of John A. Bateman and Karl-Heinrich Schmidt to be identified
as authors of this work has been asserted by them in accordance with
sections 77 and 78 of the Copyright, Designs and Patents Act 1988.

Typeset in Sabon by IBT Global.

All rights reserved. No part of this book may be reprinted or reproduced or
utilised in any form or by any electronic, mechanical, or other means, now
known or hereafter invented, including photocopying and recording, or in
any information storage or retrieval system, without permission in writing
from the publishers.

Trademark Notice: Product or corporate names may be trademarks or
registered trademarks, and are used only for identification and explanation
without intent to infringe.

Library of Congress Cataloging-in-Publication Data
Bateman, John A.
   Multimodal film analysis : how films mean / John A. Bateman and
Karl-Heinrich Schmidt.
      p. cm. — (Routledge studies in multimodality)
   Includes bibliographical references and index.
   1. Motion pictures—Philosophy.   2. Motion pictures—Semiotics.
I. Schmidt, Karl-Heinrich.   II. Title.
   PN1995.B2953 2012
   791.4301—dc23
   2011033715

ISBN: 978-0-415-88351-1 (hbk)
ISBN: 978-0-415-75443-9 (pbk)

In memory of

Joyce L. Bateman, 10th July 1930 – 6th January 2011

Charlotte Edith Schmidt, 7th September 1922 – 4th June 2011

Contents

1 Analysing film

"I wanted to understand the ways in which a film pre-arranges its reception and pre-figures its spectator." (Casetti, 1998: xvii)

"Start with this question, which I think is one of the most fascinating we can ask: What enables us to understand films?" (David Bordwell, May 2011, `http://www.davidbordwell.net/essays/commonsense.php`)

The quotations above express in a nutshell the task we will be taking on in this book. In common with many other authors over the years, we will be concerned with how a sequence of moving images can be constructed in ways that guide its viewers to entertain certain lines of interpretation rather than others. A fairly widespread proposal for how this works—one spanning some otherwise quite diverse theoretical positions—is that understanding film may be a capacity that is not particularly concerned with film at all, but rather forms part and parcel of a more general 'sense-seeking' behaviour in humans. This, after all, would explain why films appear to be much more broadly and readily comprehensible than, for example, texts written in some particular natural language.

Somewhat in contrast to this—or rather, as we set out in more detail below, *complementary* to this—we will be arguing that films are constructed in ways that guide interpretation *even prior* to handing over the task of understanding to some viewer's 'common sense'. Films appear to more or less directly inform viewers which pieces of information have to be brought together, which not, and when. It is only this 'pre-structuring', we suggest, that keeps common sense from running wild—after all, many things might be compatible with what is shown, but films do not often leave their viewers guessing about which lines of interpretation to follow and which not. And even when films *do* do this, the effect is not achieved by chance—here again the structuring of the film has to be such that lines of interpretation are quite deliberately not closed off, remaining open and potentially relevant for understanding.

To reveal mechanisms of this kind, we need to drill rather more deeply into the foundations of film. This brings into play a range of further accompanying assumptions and theoretical positions concerning the nature of 'film', of 'interpretation', of 'viewers' and of much else besides. Our main task in this chapter will therefore be to indicate our own orientation to these issues, setting out the direction that the rest of the book will follow.

We also need to address one further question before we get started. Given that there are so many books now available which claim to tell us how to understand films, one might reasonably ask why we need another one! Our answer to this relies on the fact that we are *not* going to present here yet another overview of the resources that film provides, its historical development, its contexts of production and so on. Although these are all important components of an understanding of cinema and film, our emphasis in this book lies elsewhere. We will be taking for granted a broad understanding of film that is already quite sophisticated. Although we briefly introduce important terms that we take from film theory when they occur and give pointers to where the interested reader can best find further information if necessary, we will be assuming that the reader already has at least some familiarity with the more or less 'standard' ways of describing films. We then seek to move beyond this by developing a detailed analytic framework that is significantly more supportive of systematic and empirically-grounded investigations of the filmic medium.

In many cases, the analyses we provide will be consistent with high quality insightful analyses produced by more traditional means. They will, however, be reached in a way that is held more tightly to specifiable aspects of the filmic material than is usual in film analysis. One important consequence of, and motivation for, such an approach is that it also becomes possible to rule out bad, or mistaken analyses more easily—that is, our method will constrain analysis so that the analysis is more reliable and trustworthy, giving us better criteria for the evaluation of proposals and competing hypotheses. This is one of the chief requirements for any approach that is to support empirical investigations, which in our view is itself an indispensable precondition for a more robust state of the art.

A good indication both of the scope of our inquiry and of our reasons for believing that a foundation of the kind we propose is necessary can be drawn from David Bordwell's book length critique of film criticism *Making Meaning* (Bordwell, 1989). Bordwell, one of the leading film analysts of our times, argues for a distinction between *film comprehension* and *film interpretation* (Bordwell, 1989: 8–9). The former, film comprehension, is intended to pick out meanings that are in some sense 'explicitly' recoverable from the work analysed; the latter are further inferences made by the analyst in order to reveal more abstract, 'implicitly' made meanings. Similar distinctions are made across the board in the study of interpretation regardless of medium; Todorov (1990), for example, distinguishes for the case of literary works 'signified facts', understood solely on the basis of the 'language in which the text is written', from 'symbolised facts', interpretations which 'vary from subject to subject' and which necessarily involve considerations of cultural and individual context. Entire literatures have grown up around this question of whether meaning is 'in the text', 'in the hearer', 'in the author' or some complex mixture of these.

Pursuing these notions for film, Bordwell sees explicitly recoverable meanings as ranging from specific events and character actions portrayed within the story up to general statements made on the basis of these specifics, potentially with an accompanying moral if this is also mentioned in the film. In contrast, implicitly derivable meanings range from additional contextualisations of the explicit meanings, providing social valuations of the explicit patterns that are not themselves thematised within the material of the film, up to more or less 'hidden' meanings—Bordwell terms them 'symptomatic'—that are compatible with the film but which also make contact with broader issues in society, reflecting the 'ideology' or concerns which the film 'unintentionally' manifests. Bordwell argues that particularly the latter processes require strict methodological principles in order to be kept within reasonable limits; a point that we will return to repeatedly below.

Discussions of where and whether exact boundaries can be drawn between these areas continue and show interesting parallels with similar discussions pursued for other communicative forms, including language. The complexity of the process of understanding often causes doubts to be raised that less abstract 'elements' can be identified before more abstract contextualising configurations have been fixed. This is a traditional philosophical concern taken up again and again and in various guises; we will return to several of the arguments as they apply specifically to film and our position with respect to them in subsequent chapters. For the present, however, we can pick out one general idea standing behind Bordwell's distinction that brings out well the direction we will take.

In order to achieve good analyses of film, we believe that it is better, before proceeding to interpretation, to make explicit just what is—in a sense that we will make precise below—'in' the filmic material under investigation. We claim that this is *the basis for any further consideration that a viewer (or analyst) can reasonably undertake*. Investigations which do not work in this way may also say interesting and useful things, but we will not consider them here as *analyses* of the films addressed: they are instead "symptomatic readings guided by a hermeneutics of suspicion" (Bordwell, 2005: 266). Our position throughout this book will be that we now know enough about film and its workings to move beyond this—not very far beyond this perhaps, but still enough to be worthwhile and necessary for advancing the state of the art.

We will accordingly be focusing on the 'comprehension' end of a viewer's engagement with films. We quite deliberately avoid any statements concerning the evaluation of aesthetic merit or the 'deeper meanings' of film in terms of cultural, historical, or social configurations—i.e., 'film interpretation' in Bordwell's sense above. Our analysis starts (and stops) at a more basic level: we will be seeking an analytic framework that allows us to bring out a particular 'bandwidth' of meanings that films 'commit to', and under what conditions, so that the foundation for further, more interpretative work can be maximally strengthened.

Despite this self-imposed limitation, there are many difficult, some would even say contentious, issues raised by choosing to approach film in this way. A further task of this introduction is therefore to ease us into the approach as a whole, motivating our particular demarcation of issues and the directions in which we will be seeking solutions. The next section starts on this directly by means of some examples. Although these examples all represent straightforward, commonplace cases of filmic comprehension, pulling them apart will reveal several lines of stress where traditional film description is in need of further support and where we can begin to look through to the foundations below.

1.1   Distinguishing the filmic contribution to meaning

As remarked above, our approach makes several basic assumptions—but perhaps the most fundamental assumptions of all are that it is possible for a sequence of moving images to signal meanings that are *not limited* to a redescription of what the images show, that are describable *independently* of any putative authorial intent, and which enter into *active negotiations* of more abstract interpretations with recipients as more than equal partners (i.e., 'pre-arrange' and 'pre-figure'). This means that we will argue that there is information that is beyond the 'referential' story events but which must nevertheless be seen as 'non-negotiable' with respect to the film. The film consequently 'commits to' more than is directly portrayed. What this entails is crucial for understanding what we will be examining in this book, what not, and why.

To see this, we must characterise more finely the meanings grouped under Bordwell's 'comprehension' area. Bordwell relates narration and its interpretation primarily to what he describes as "the experiential logic of understanding a film's narrative" (Bordwell, 2007: 98). This foregrounds a position in which "the process of understanding many things in films is likely to draw upon ordinary, informal reasoning procedures" (Bordwell, 2007: 136). This is often described employing notions such as 'scripts' or 'schemata' (cf. Bartlett, 1932), made popular in Artificial Intelligence (cf. Schank and Abelson, 1977) and since applied in a broad range of 'cognitively'-oriented disciplines, including approaches to film studies (cf. Bordwell, 1985; Branigan, 1992). While no doubt at least partially accurate—and we will see more of this in our detailed analyses in the middle chapters of this book—it also clearly locates the main guiding force of understanding in our knowledge of everyday situations and practical knowledge rather than in film.

The evidence for 'additional' information in film is considerable, however. This is commonly characterised as part of a film's *style* (e.g., Bordwell and Thompson, 2008: 7) and, particularly for film, these 'non-representational' effects are impossible to ignore; they force themselves on the viewer with an immediacy that appears far more effective and affecting than their equivalents in texts. We consider these kinds of meaning as making an essential contribution to how films work and how they can be reliably understood. Not including this kind of information within the comprehension level makes subsequent interpretation appear more difficult, and less constrained, than it actually is. We will argue throughout this book, therefore, that it is both possible and necessary to be far more systematic and detailed with respect to the fine-grained operation of this area.

We can gain useful leverage on this issue by invoking three broad types of meaning proposed within the linguistic theory that we draw on for inspiration in Chapters 2 and 3 below. These are conceived as providing general organising principles, called **metafunction**s, for all societally-anchored meaning-making.

The *ideational* metafunction is responsible for constructing worlds of activities, events, people and objects as well as their qualities and quantities (also grouped together as *experiential* meanings) and their various inter-connections (grouped together as *logical* meanings). The *interpersonal* metafunction is concerned with enacting interaction and evaluation and with appraisal, expressing emotion and emotional responses. And the *textual* metafunction is the 'second-order' phenomenon of deploying patterns from the other areas to build coherent and cohesive 'textual' wholes—i.e., of turning individual characterisations of the world or evaluative appraisals into textured unities capable of far more complexity in the 'messages' they can communicate.

The first two categories are already well explored for film. The ideational is involved in representations or mental models of the world, information generally taken to include knowledge of the form that people talking to each other are spatially and temporally co-located, as are observers and the things being observed, or that after going into a restaurant, one sits at a table, or that going up to the door of a building is followed by being inside that building, and so on. The ideational content that is portrayed corresponds to the 'world of the story' or, as it is called in film studies, the *diegesis* (cf. §5.2). The second category, the interpersonal, is centrally involved in considerations of *affect* and has been discussed for film by Smith (1995), Tan (1996), Smith (1999), Plantinga and Smith (1999) and others—particularly from the perspective of the orchestration of affect through structures of narration.

But the third area, the textual metafunction, is in need of considerably more attention. We will see that this area has a rich and complex organisation in its own right and needs to be described in its own terms. Rephrasing Bordwell from above, our focus in this book can be characterised as an investigation of 'the *textual* logic of understanding a film's narrative': this textual logic has, to date, been addressed piecemeal, if at all, even though it forms a critical part of the interpretative chain from perception to understanding. Revealing the operations of this aspect of how films make the meanings they do is therefore our principal goal.

4s   slow zoom   8s   slow zoom   16s   slow zoom

Figure 1.1   Alternating slow-zoom construction from Eyes Wide Shut *(1999, 2:00:35)*

A simple example will already clarify the kind of meaning involved here. Consider the short extract shown in Figure 1.1 taken from Stanley Kubrick's *Eyes Wide Shut* (1999); the fragment starts at around two hours and thirty-five seconds into the film (i.e., as we shall write from now on, 02:00:35). Here we see an alternation between the main character (Tom Cruise) and a newspaper article that he comes across more or less by chance and which is centrally important for the story. Significant for us here is that over the entire fragment there is a slow camera zoom—i.e., there is a continuous effect of moving gradually closer, first to Tom Cruise, then to the newspaper, then to Tom Cruise again. This is not an ideational meaning—we nor anyone in the world of the film actually move here. It certainly does, however, have some interpersonal meaning, in that it suggests an emotional state and invites the viewer to share some concern. But, more importantly for our point here, it *also* involves a clear textual meaning. The particular use of the technical feature of the zoom *necessarily* groups this collection of shots together into a larger unit: i.e., no viewer can sensibly fail to see that these shots combine and, in some sense, are making a 'single statement'. This is carried quite explicitly by the continuous zoom, over and above the particular world of the story depicted, and so is committed to by the film in the sense we are introducing.

Variants of zooms functioning textually are easy to find. Several can be seen, for example, in Alfred Hitchcock's *Vertigo* (1958), the most complex occurring around 01:53:00 involving a zoom towards the perceiving character (James Stewart), a similar zoom into the perceived object (a necklace), followed by an equally fast zoom *out* from a painting of that object (by which the perceiving character recognised the object in the first place). In many cases, such zooms can be seen more transparently, or 'iconically', as depicting some kind of focus of attention. Zooms and similar dynamic reframings have long been considered in this way: they are taken as signalling a figure's perception of some story relevant detail. In the present case, however, this transparent basis is insufficient by itself.

Here, the newspaper is bound visually and aurally into the zoom-realisation: i.e., the newspaper is subjected to the zoom just as the human character is, although clearly we would not want to say that the emotional response of the newspaper is being emphasised or that the newspaper is in anyway affected by being read. But this is what a strict iconic interpretation in terms of ideational or interpersonal meanings might require us to say: if the continuous zooming in on Tom Cruise means that Tom Cruise is centrally affected, why then should the corresponding continuous zooming in on the newspaper be any different?

Clearly, no viewer would see this as a possible option. We have instead a particular conventionalised usage involving filmic commitment both to additional information about characters' responses and to how *sequences* of shots are to be combined into larger units to carry that information. The continuation of the 'single' movement across these shots is therefore a *textual* contribution—it takes on a *structural* role, holding the elements of the scene together and distinguishing them from their environment. Considering this simply as 'audiovisual style' is then insufficient—it contributes already to filmic comprehension, guiding the viewer to particular conclusions concerning how the story is being told.

This phenomenon shows us several things. First, we cannot simply take the quality of a single shot, such as a zoom, and treat this independently of its filmic structural context. The move in on Tom Cruise is only intelligible in the context of the segment as a whole. Second, the function of a technical feature, here the zoom, can be one of creating *textual* units and is not restricted to suggesting particular 'interpretations' of shown story events. The signals involved are, what is more, directly available in the film and so we again need to see the film as 'committing to' certain aspects of its organisation. These then belong equally to a film's comprehension even though they are not directly concerned with the 'story itself' or the referential unfolding of story events.

This textual operation of building structured coherence from the local information provided in individual shots and sequences of shots will be one of our main areas of development below: it plays a foundational role in almost *all* film fragments. Our more detailed examples in this chapter accordingly begin by delineating more finely some of the filmic phenomena to be addressed within this area. This will establish the main questions that we will be addressing in the rest of the book.

1.2   Examples of filmic 'textual organisation'

To bring out some more of the variety exhibited by the 'textual logic' that organises films, we next take a sequence of images from the end of one scene and the beginning of another in *The Bourne Identity* (2002) directed by Doug Liman; we will define 'scene' more formally in subsequent chapters—for now we simply assume a more or less standard theatrical definition such as "a significant event taking place in a single location" (e.g., Kawin, 1992: 243). Equally informally for the present, we will ask just what there is to interpret in this extract and what the film's contribution to that interpretation is. This will get us directly involved in film analysis and starts introducing some of the terminology needed. The fragment to be discussed is set out in Figure 1.2.

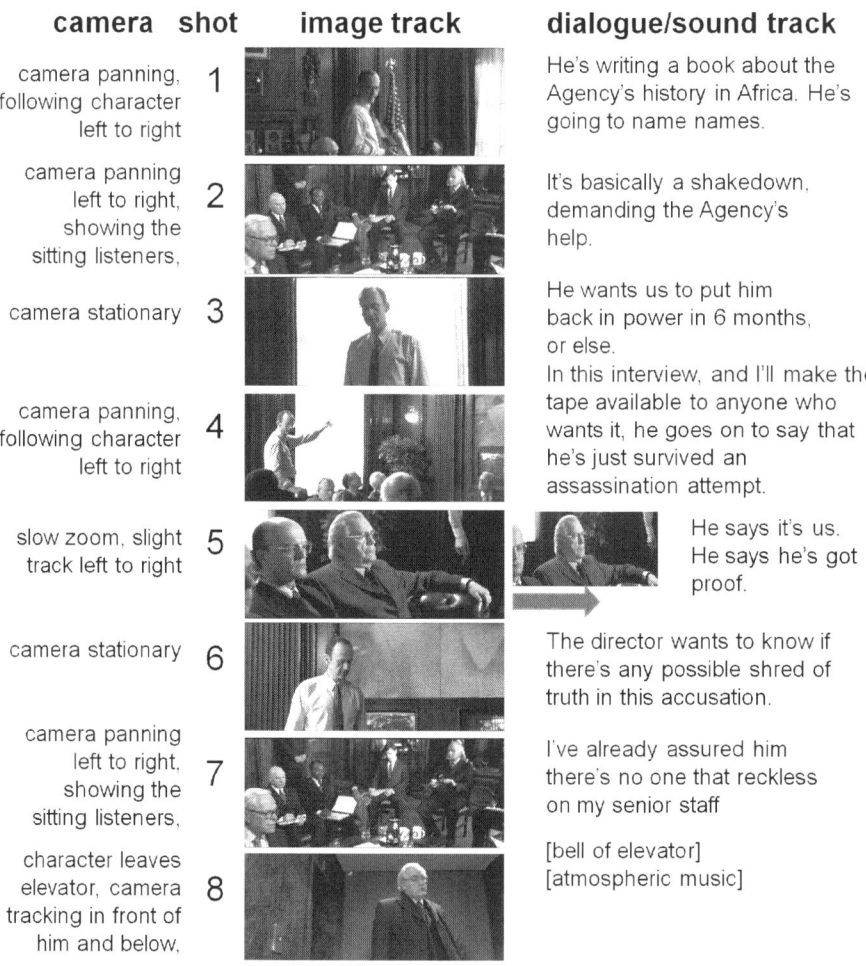

camera shot	image track	dialogue/sound track
camera panning, following character left to right	1	He's writing a book about the Agency's history in Africa. He's going to name names.
camera panning left to right, showing the sitting listeners,	2	It's basically a shakedown, demanding the Agency's help.
camera stationary	3	He wants us to put him back in power in 6 months, or else.
camera panning, following character left to right	4	In this interview, and I'll make the tape available to anyone who wants it, he goes on to say that he's just survived an assassination attempt.
slow zoom, slight track left to right	5	He says it's us. He says he's got proof.
camera stationary	6	The director wants to know if there's any possible shred of truth in this accusation.
camera panning left to right, showing the sitting listeners,	7	I've already assured him there's no one that reckless on my senior staff
character leaves elevator, camera tracking in front of him and below,	8	[bell of elevator] [atmospheric music]

Figure 1.2   Short extract from Liman's The Bourne Identity *(2002, 00:11:36–00:12:10) depicting a briefing at the U.S. Central Intelligence Agency*

The scene, already in progress as the fragment starts, is labelled as taking place in the U.S. Central Intelligence Agency building in Langley, Virginia, and begins just over 11 minutes into the film. The 'content' of the extract, i.e., what it depicts, is a briefing where a higher ranking CIA official is reporting on the contents of a video interview given by an 'exiled African leader' to a group of people listening. Prior to this extract, the film has introduced us to none of the characters present; it has, however, informed us that there was indeed an assassination or attack mission of some kind, that it had failed and that there is very probably some CIA involvement. What we then see in this extract is the filmic construction of a pointing finger—immediate suspicions are raised about one of the characters that the scene introduces. Our question now is how does the film achieve this? And, more specifically, exactly *what* is it that the film is achieving? As we shall see, these two issues are often conflated and, when this happens, an entire road of access into understanding film is closed.

In our analyses, we will generally divide film fragments into *shots*; this, as we shall see below and particularly in Chapter 5, is a standard division used within film analysis for a variety of reasons. For now we will consider a shot simply to be the result of a single continuous 'take' delimited by 'cuts' brought about by stopping and restarting the camera; between one take and the next, therefore, camera angle, distance, height, location, what is being filmed, etc. may all change. Later in the book we will move from this, 'production'-oriented view of the nature of a shot to a more 'recipient'-oriented view—but for present purposes we can overlook this distinction.

Figure 1.2 then offers us a kind of *transcription* of the film segment we are analysing—this transcription, although still very informal, contains the details *relevant for the discussion*. This is always the general task of a transcription: to focus attention on particular aspects of the film relevant for the analysis; we will explore several distinct kinds of transcription as we proceed. The transcription here is presented as a table in which each row represents a single shot. The central column of each row shows a single image selected as representative for the shot as a whole. Naturally, while the camera is running, it can also be moved about, be pointed in different directions, and employ zooms and other technical effects. To capture this, the leftmost column of the table describes any movements or other effects of the camera that occur *during* the shot.

A standard vocabulary has evolved over the years within film studies for characterising these aspects. Distinct terms are used for the various axes along and around which the camera may be rotated or moved, and for the 'distance' of the camera from what is being filmed (i.e., the *pro-filmic* material in front of the camera). 'Distance' is often translated into how much of a figure or human character can be seen in the frame: in extreme close-up a single detail, such as the eyes, hands and so on, may be visible; in close-up, just the face, and so on. These categories—variously termed shot range, shot type, camera position, lens length—are repeated in all textbooks on film and are indispensable tools of the trade. We provide our own summary in Figure 1.3 and give more pointers in the *Further Reading* section at the end of the chapter. In many respects, these categories represent physically manifested properties of the filmic image: although there is some variation in how, for example, the camera distances are described

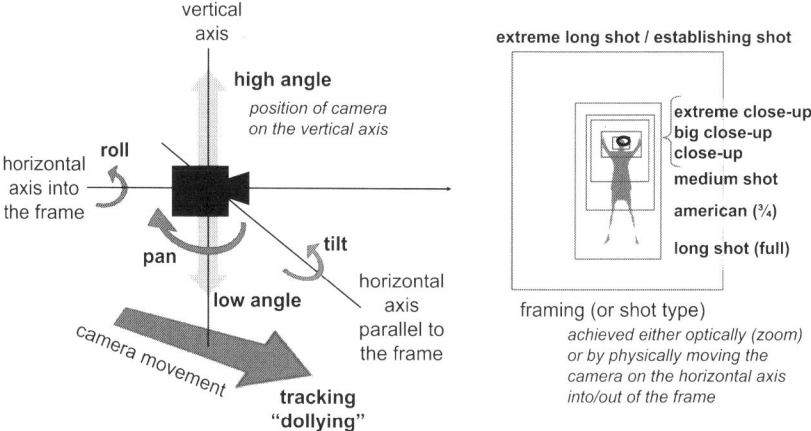

Figure 1.3   Basic vocabulary for describing camera movement and 'posture' during film shots

due to their inherent reliance on their depiction of the main characters in a shot, there should not in general be any substantial disagreement about what is being shown.

Finally, since films these days are rarely silent, our transcription also needs to provide a trace of the relevant information that is being conveyed aurally. The rightmost column of our transcription therefore describes any sounds or dialogue that occur during the shot. In this short extract there is only one person speaking—the person giving the briefing shown in the first image; we can therefore omit an explicit note of who is speaking, although this would in general be necessary. During and across shots this person moves around the conference room, occasionally pointing to images on a large video screen, while the other people shown in the fragment sit, taking notes.

We now go through the fragment in detail: ideally one would at this point want to watch the relevant parts of the film oneself so as to be assured that we are indeed describing what occurs in the film but, in place of this, we trust that the running 'gloss' of the filmic material that the transcription provides will suffice.

The first four shots are a kind of one-sided dialogue: the character speaking presents information and the listeners listen; we are shown the listeners first of all just prior to the present extract without any differentiation of individual characters—they are simply 'the listeners'. Their presentation is restricted to a controlled smooth 'pan' (cf. Figure 1.3) of the camera from left to right showing who is there and what they are doing. In contrast, the camera individuates the speaker, 'panning' with him as he moves around the room, sometimes moving to the left, sometimes to the right, sometimes staying still. In the shots of the speaker, the tops of the heads of the listeners can also often be seen, thus presenting the viewer with no grounds for doubting that a single room and the events taking place in it are being dealt with. The film, in other words, 'commits to' this presentation.

Then, in the fifth shot, something completely different occurs. Rather than showing the person speaking (who continues to speak during the shot) or the anonymous group of listeners, the camera remains stationary framing two people far more closely than the others and with one in the centre of the frame. These figures are dressed in a similar fashion to the previously shown members of the audience and this, together with the continuous audio track, leaves little doubt for the viewer that we are now focusing in on some particular members of the audience; in fact, these two are barely identifiable in the previous shot and so the present shot does not rely upon this.

During this shot, the camera further isolates the latter individual (played by Brian Cox) by slowly zooming in on him, moving the camera slightly to the right so that he remains centred and becomes the main occupant of the frame. This is shown in the second image in the row for the fifth shot in the table. In general, we may need to show more than one image within a single shot if the quality of the image changes substantially, as is the case here, and in such cases we show images representative for each 'relevant part' of the shot side-by-side. The following shot, shot 6, returns to the speaker, before the final shot of the scene presents in a somewhat faster pan the group of listeners again.

There are two completely commonplace aspects of film in operation here that we wish to emphasise. First, camera movement, position and changes in image quality are being used to *guide textual focus* and, as a consequence, also constrain the inferences that viewers are invited to make. And, second, the particular inferences followed up will usually *combine information* from the different informational sources available. We return to both of these aspects at length below as they form central components of our account: we will characterise quite precisely what it means for a film to 'guide focus', drawing on some modern linguistic notions of discourse, and also suggest how distinct kinds of information can be combined, drawing on our treatment of film as a 'multimodal' artefact.

For now, however, let us consider a 'common-sense' interpretation of what is occurring in this extract. This is, in all likelihood, as follows. We are told that there has been an assassination attempt and that there is proof that it was the CIA who was involved. Simultaneously to the statement that "it was us" the camera picks out and focuses one particular figure from the group of listeners. Picking out one particular person from a group would not be done without a reason, so it must be particularly 'relevant' for us to consider this character rather than the others. He also looks ill at ease. There is then a 'good chance' that he was involved in this shady enterprise, even though the others (including the director of the CIA apparently) are not aware of this. The final statement "I've already assured him there's no one that reckless on my senior staff" is uttered simultaneously with the final pan around the listeners, which is also itself an indication that the listeners can now be identified as being just that group of 'senior staff' mentioned. Thus we have the implication that there is one of the senior staff who was indeed 'just that reckless'. To cement the assumption, the very next scene (punctuated by the ringing of the elevator bell and underscored with quietly ominous music) shows the previously focused character, still looking worried.

This line of interpretation is completely straightforward and most viewers would, we expect, come to these, or very similar, conclusions aware neither of there being any other possibility nor of the amount of 'inferential work' they have had to perform in order to come to the conclusions they do. The interpreter is seen as a 'problem solver' working out what was intended on the basis of 'what makes sense' for the world of the story—this is the 'referential' component of comprehension in Bordwell's terms introduced above (Bordwell 1989: 8; Bordwell and Thompson 2008: 60). As we acknowledged there, this is certainly part of the complete story. One of the major advances of film theory, along with many other current approaches to the appreciation of art works, has been precisely this move to grant the spectator an active role in the appreciation and interpretation of a film, i.e., to do justice to 'the beholder's share' in interpretation (Gombrich, 1959).

But this is also where the common-sense view does less than justice to the organisation of the film: it relies on the interpreter to come up with all the leaps of deduction required and under-values just how much help the film artefact itself is providing. Where we believe we need to go further, therefore, is to consider more closely how precisely the work of reaching interpretations is shared out *between* interpreters and film. If the interpretation is left too much to the viewer, then the likelihood of a large proportion of viewers coming to the *same* interpretation is much reduced. More important is to characterise how it is that such similar interpretations are reached: what is it in the film that guides those interpretations or, in the words of the opening quotation, how does the film 'pre-arrange its reception'?

The case at hand is, of course, very simple—that is why we chose it. There are *clear signals in the film*, what Bordwell elsewhere has called *cues* (e.g., Bordwell, 1985: 31–32, 223), that there is interpretative work to be done. But, understanding how these signals contribute to an interpretation requires us to unfold several rather different levels of abstraction still often conflated or omitted within film theory. If we are to achieve a generally valid account, and not one that is restricted to a particular film sequence that we happen to be analysing, then we cannot make statements of the form 'we know this person is guilty because the camera zooms in on him', or 'having the camera linger on someone in a group means that they are guilty' and the like since, clearly, this is not what such signals mean *in general*.

This issue is quite complex and has been much discussed in the film literature: it turns out to be very difficult to say what particular filmic signals mean. Some authors have suggested, for example, that zooming-in is a sign of emotional intensity, or that it brings the viewer closer to a protagonist, and so on—but whether or not some interpretation holds remains an open issue to be resolved in *each particular case*. Nevertheless, the filmic signals appear to contribute *something* determinate, otherwise viewers' interpretations would be far more varied than they actually are.

This is also by no means to deny that there are *other* interpretations that could have been made at this point in the film—especially if the film had unfolded differently prior to the fragment shown. For example, if we knew for a fact that the person picked out knew nothing about the assassination attempt but had been seen in a previous scene interacting with someone else (call them person B) who had been acting in a suspicious manner, then the interpretation might well shift to run more along the lines of: 'now this person knows/suspects that it was B who did it'. This interpretation, which, as it turns out, is actually the case in *The Bourne Identity*, is very different to the preceding one. Nevertheless, as we will argue at length in the following, *the meaning of the particularly filmic contribution has not changed.* Shot 5 still directly informs the viewer (in a sense that we will also make explicit in subsequent chapters) that the person focused upon has a story-relevant connection within the unfolding narrative. This is a *textual* meaning and is *all* that is being told visually.

It is then from the dialogue that the viewer is given additional information forming part of the ongoing development. In this case: there has been an assassination attempt organised by the CIA and, we may assume, first by our background beliefs concerning how such organisations run and second by the explicit statement "I've assured him there's *no one* that reckless" (emphasis added), that this means that there is someone who must have ordered this to take place. The questions 'under discussion' at that point in the story are then 'is there someone who did this?' and 'if so, who?'. At the same time that these questions are raised verbally, we are informed visually that there is a story-relevant connection with a particular person. Taken together, we therefore have a range of abstract meanings being made visually in the filmic organisation, and a range of more concrete meanings being stated in the spoken dialogue component. Combined the result ends up far greater than the sum of the parts.

While a variety of diverse alternative shots might have been used instead of shot 5 in our example, it is obvious that not *any* shot would have done. If the presumably intended interpretation is to be achieved then the shot that is used has to fulfill some constraints (cf. Grodal, 2009: 46–47)—most particularly, making sure that the individual character is some how presented in a way that successfully picks him out as distinct from the others in the room. This could fail for a large number of reasons: for example, if we do not recognise that we are still in the same room as before, that the person shown is not evidently one of the listeners, etc. Many of these signals fall under what is discussed in film theory and practice as *continuity editing*—i.e., when a film is constructed in such a way that cuts and transitions within scenes go largely unnoticed during viewing (cf. Bordwell and Thompson 2008: 231–241; Prince 2007: 159–182). When, as here, the transition across shots 4 and 5 does not for a moment suggest to viewers that some different time or place is involved, then continuity has been achieved. Despite this 'perceptual' transparence, however, it should never be forgotten that creating continuity from fragmented material is a highly complex achievement requiring considerable skill to realise (cf. Prince, 2007: 159): that is, continuity needs to be created; it does not just 'happen'. There are accordingly many textbooks and works on the practice of film going to considerable lengths precisely to explain its mechanisms.

It may also be a goal for various narrative and stylistic purposes for a film *not* to suggest certain connections, or to hide them. Here the converse problem holds: how can we know that a shot does *not* open up a particular line of interpretation, or even opens up a misleading one. These can all be *intended* interpretations in the sense relevant to us here.

We do not consider it sufficient, therefore, at least for a theoretically well-founded understanding of how films work, simply to let the problem of matching particular cues to functions go unaddressed, assuming that viewers will work out what is going on in any particular case on the basis of context and thereby relieving us of the task of finding any more general meanings. It often seems relatively straightforward, after all, to say *in retrospect* that some camera angle, some particular zoom, etc. meant that some character was scared or unsettled; and, indeed, this is often the kind of 'detailed' analysis that is given: such-and-such an effect 'means' that the victim is powerless, etc. And yet, despite the extreme flexibility and malleability of technical filmic features and their containing shots, there are clearly boundaries—not just any variant will do for some particular function.

Bordwell refers to this view of functional cueing by invoking natural motivations drawn from the story telling, often characterised, as we remarked at the beginning of this chapter, in terms of 'cognitive' or 'narrative' schemata borrowed from cognitive psychology. In Bordwell's characterisation of the film-making process, then, particular decisions are made during the making of a film to solve specific problems raised by getting the narrative onto film and subsequently, because the viewer is also following the narrative arc, he or she will be able to assign an appropriate interpretation to the devices employed. The development of the narrative will as Bordwell suggests, no doubt, contribute to the interpretation given to any cue—but then the challenge is to account for how this works in detail, i.e., to uncover mechanisms by which 'micro'-organisational decisions deployed in films lead viewers to make the *situated* interpretations intended. There is much more to tease out here than is commonly assumed.

We saw in our very first simple fragment from the previous section how a technical feature, such as the zoom, can be employed to impose organisation on a film. Then, in our *The Bourne Identity* extract, we also found a strong structural commitment induced by technical features: the dialogic organisation between speaker and listeners, even though 'passive', nevertheless signals shot 5 to be showing one of the listeners. These are *in addition* to other cues presented in the shots. The kind of structural unity at work here is called *contingent*—i.e., it depends on the concrete shots that occur in order to be brought into existence but, once present, it brings determinate consequences for possible interpretations. Just how 'contingent structure' works for creating meaning will be an important topic in Chapter 2.

A considerable part of the challenge of understanding the workings of films, however, is that it is not possible to limit *a priori* just what technical features of films are going to serve which roles. We see this well in the following example.

Figure 1.4 shows four shots from the beginning of the last 10 minutes of Rainer Werner Fassbinder's *The Marriage of Maria Braun* (1979). This is in certain respects similar to the last case but is drawn from a quite different film and again serves a rather different purpose. As the form of our transcript suggests, the construction of this segment is different again to our previous examples. In particular, there is considerable camera movement within shots—in many cases the camera freely follows the two characters, Maria Braun (Hanna Schygulla) and Hermann Braun (Klaus Löwitsch), as they move around the rooms of the house—sometimes showing both characters, sometimes one, sometimes intermittently neither of them—and shot duration, as we shall see, is crucial. Throughout the scene we can also hear two independent sound 'tracks': the dialogue of the characters (including naturalistic sound) and the commentary of the final stages of the football World Cup Final in 1954 with West Germany playing, and in the end narrowly defeating, Hungary. Although significant for the interpretation of the film as a whole, we will largely omit the contribution of both sound tracks for current purposes. Finally, the dots indicate that the first and last shots are incomplete as presented in the figure.

Since there is so much happening within some of the shots making up this extract, simply showing representative images does not provide enough information. To counter this, we include in the figure a further device occasionally applied in more detailed investigations of the spatial configurations in film (cf., e.g., Branigan, 1976): a diagram of the *spatial relationships* holding between and among the characters together with approximate camera positions and angles taken up during the fragment. In our analyses below, we will draw on this representational device when spatial relationships are particularly relevant for understanding what is occurring. From the present diagram we can see that in the selected extract, Maria Braun begins by the stairs in the hall of her house (position A), then

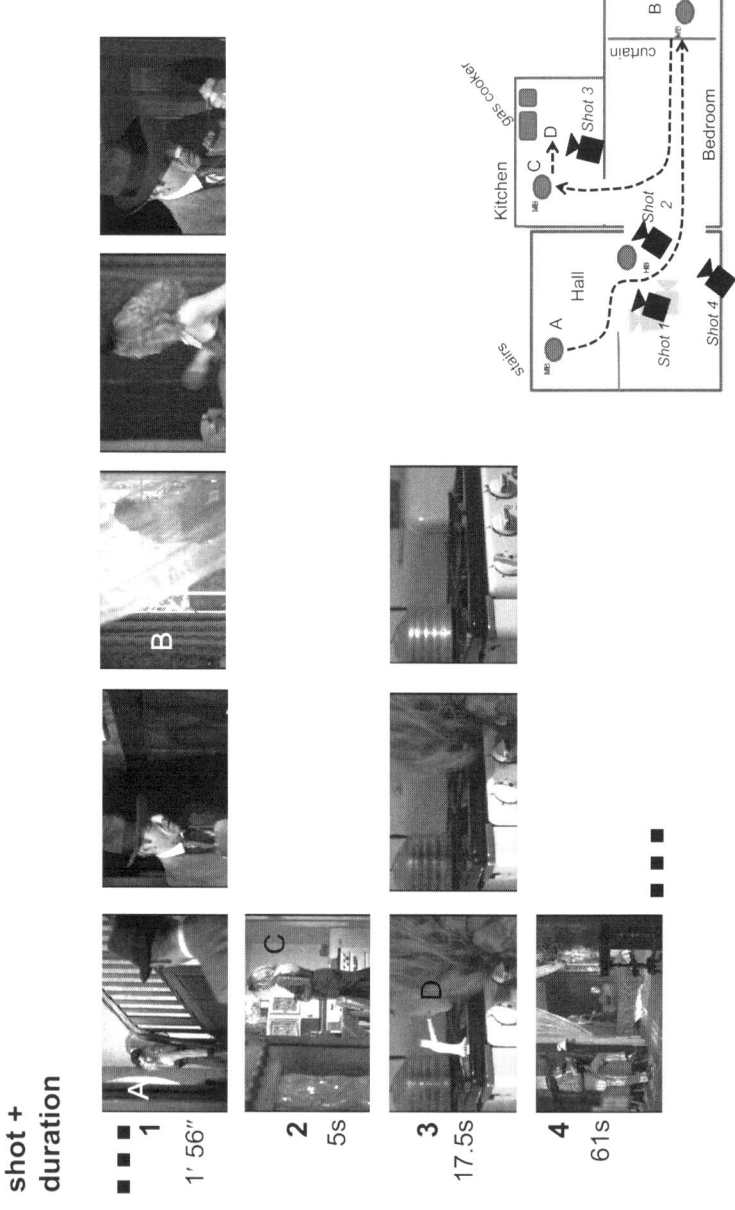

Figure 1.4   Four shots from Rainer Werner Fassbinder's The Marriage of Maria Braun
(beginning at approximately 01:51:00)

goes by Hermann Braun to the far end of the bedroom (position B), and then comes back and passes out of sight into the kitchen to the left: this is all within shot 1; we will discuss breaking up such shots into analyseable units more in Chapter 5. Shot 2 then shows Maria Braun in the kitchen (position C) and shot 3 focuses on her lighting a cigarette in the flame of a gas cooker (position D). Shot 4 finishes the example with her coming back into the bedroom.

The similarity with the first examples that we want to discuss is that, here too, there is a clear guiding of the viewers' attention and lines of inference. However, in this case this is not achieved with a zoom or with camera movement, but with a *lack* of movement or zooming. In Shot 1 we see the main characters moving around the house with the camera following as described above. This shot is already very long by today's standards (almost 2 minutes), although the movement of both characters and camera work against any impression of 'staticness'. In Shot 2, Maria Braun has moved into the kitchen; she is shown standing and getting a cigarette ready to light and the shot lasts almost 5 seconds. The next shot is the one that does the direction: Maria Braun lights the gas, turns up the flame, and lights her cigarette. She then blows out the flame. Following this, the shot continues unmoving and without any other camera effects *for another 10 seconds*, simply showing the gas cooker with the sound of gas hissing clearly audible (along with the football commentary). Then, in shot 4, the movement around the house continues with another long (60 seconds) dynamic shot. Eight minutes later, the house explodes as Maria Braun returns to the kitchen, again ostensibly to light a cigarette.

In the midst of a highly dynamic sequence of shots, then, shot 3 leaves the camera unmoving, filming the gas cooker for a total of almost 18 seconds. This demands that the viewer take note. Whereas in the previous examples, it was the relative stability and camera zooming that identified particular shots as requiring particular interpretations, here it is the lack of movement and, above all, the *length* of the shot that act as signals. One could almost say that, in the present case, what acts as a signal is the marked *lack* of signals!

Our examples so far all therefore make the same general point. It is often how an indicated shot or shot sequence *contrasts* with its environment that is significant rather than particular qualities of the shots themselves. Film theory often reminds us of this: there is no 'fixed' meaning for particular camera angles, zooms or other arrangements (cf. Sharff 1982: 32; Prince 2007: 22; Bordwell and Thompson 2008: 192)—low angles do not 'mean' power, high angles do not mean 'fate', and so on. But it is important to draw the correct conclusions from this concerning how we can further advance our understanding of how films work. After all, as we asked above, if there are no fixed meanings, how is it that films are so reliably understood? The usual response is that it is 'context dependent': but this names a problem or a question, not an answer. *How* does contextually dependent interpretation work in the case of film?

Edward Branigan has phrased both the problem and a direction for seeking solutions aptly as follows:

> "Every process of signification is a *formal play of differences*. ...An important consequence of [this belief] is that there are no inherent meanings. For example, a dissolve in film does not inherently signify a short lapse of narrative time; in a particular *system*, however, a dissolve may mean just that. ...In addition, the meaning is not unique—other physical properties may be replaced by another device ... precisely because it is system, not material form, which determines meaning." (Branigan, 1984: 29)

This fundamental aspect of the organization of film has important consequences for how film can be studied. First, it is necessary to move beyond the position that a flexibility in ascribed interpretation means that we can describe interpretations of technical devices only vaguely, describing how they appear to work only in each particular case—a criticism also raised by the film semiotician Christian Metz, from whom we will hear more below:

> "The conclusion which most authors draw from this is that the cinematic figures [...] acquire a precise meaning in each context, but that 'taken in themselves' they have no fixed value. If one considers them intrinsically, one can say nothing about their meaning; one can at the most draw up a disparate list of their particularly frequent or particularly normalized uses." (Metz, 1974*d*: 133)

Such positions reappear whenever a loose transcription in terms of technical devices is drawn upon to make some argumentative point about a film's interpretation. It is problematic, however, precisely because it fails to make explicit just how some combination of devices comes to take on particular functions within a film.

Both Metz and Branigan end up coming to similar conclusions on this point despite considerable differences in their theoretical orientations. In order to delimit the interpretations placed on technical devices within appropriate and justifiable boundaries productive for meaning making within film, the interpretation of these devices has to be made against the possibilities defined by particular *systems of meaning* constructed and activated in the course of particular films. That is:

> "...what has explanatory power is not the [...] context as 'brute' film text, but this same context to the extent that it contains within itself a textual system. In other words, certain cinematic processes acquire a fixed meaning only in relation to *filmic systems*." (Metz, 1974*d*: 134, emphasis added)

Finding these 'systems' that contribute to filmic interpretation and provide sense to the stream of technical features deployed has proved itself to be a major stumbling block for taking film analysis further. More detailed characterizations of the "formal play of differences" underlying every "process of signification" have proved particularly resistant to isolation: it is simply unclear which groupings of filmic technical features will do the job. Without systems of *contrasts*, there are no formal 'differences' out of which processes of signification can grow and the entire process does not get off the ground.

We see this as one, perhaps the, central problem of film analysis. To support more systematic interpretative analysis, and without denying that certain distinctions may appear more 'natural' than others, it is nevertheless necessary to find systems of contrasts that organise and pre-structure the filmic devices employed. If we can find ways of making the connection between technical details and sources of interpretation more explicit and reliable, we will be in a far stronger position for pursuing analysis.

Our aim in this book is therefore precisely to move us in this direction, to set out one way in which we can take systematically guided steps that increase abstraction away from the filmic material and towards interpretations, via the explicit definition of filmic systems of meaning. In order to follow this kind of meaning-making further, we will need to be able to explore such systems, finding how to recognise them and to describe them and their effects as they occur. Moreover, we will need to do this within a framework that moves beyond discussion of particular analyses of particular cases.

Our approach, to be refined as we proceed, is then essentially to divide the process of interpretation into several related layers of description as we have begun suggesting above. There we have seen at least two such levels at work: on the one hand, the contribution of the film and its organisation itself—what is shown and how—and, on the other hand, a logically separate process of relating recognised contrasts to the unfolding interpretation specific to the film under analysis. The segmented zoom of our first case above, for example, combines the story-relevant focusing of attention with a structural function, linking together sequences of shots within larger narrative 'wholes'. In contrast, the zooming-in of our second case means that the viewer is being told that there is some story-relevant connection between the unfolding story and the person being focused upon. Then, in our third case, the technical detail of shot *duration* was deployed for focusing attention. In all three cases, therefore, we have technical cues describable at one level of abstraction being used to give rise to general *textual* meanings, such as focusing attention on some figure, object or unfolding event in the film, that then needs further interpretation against the background provided by knowledge of what is happening in the film. Structuring this *interaction* between film and interpretive context is then our goal. For this, we need to provide an analytic framework that allows us to capture appropriately the fine-grained detail of the filmic contribution as well as the systems of contrasts that provide meanings to those details.

To develop this framework, we will employ two particular further sources of theory: 'multimodal semiotics' and 'multimodal documents';

these will be introduced in the next chapter. Drawing on these areas will provide us with precisely the reorientation to the 'object itself', i.e., whatever particular film is under investigation, that we need, while at the same time supporting the climb up the ladder of abstraction to reach interpretation that is our goal.

1.3   Redrawing boundaries

Our orientation here to the 'film itself' echoes in some respects Bordwell's (1985) and Thompson's (1988) call for a reorientation to the specifics of individual films and to a 'new' formalism, one capable of relating the technical details of films to the use of those details in the service of solving practical problems of filmic narration. In this *neoformalist* approach, the perceptual object of film is subjected to a range of analytic procedures so as to bring out its individual contributions to filmic signification. Our approach can best be seen as a further progression in this direction with some additions and changes suggested by our rather different starting points.

In particular, one aspect of what we are attempting here consists in the redrawing of certain entrenched boundary lines within film studies. These boundaries, due in part to the concerns of individual researchers and specific states of development reached by the contributing disciplines, need to be reconsidered at this time because of several important theoretical developments relevant for the investigation of film. Such redrawing of boundaries is not, of course, always acceptable to those concerned since boundaries are not natural categories and often have considerable (personal and institutional) work invested in them. The benefits of any changes proposed need then to be clearly demonstrated and so this must also be one of the tasks we take on with this book.

The state of film studies that we are reacting to can be characterised very broadly as building on the following grouping of contributing disciplines and orienting research issues. Which paradigm is considered 'dominant', most highly valued, etc. depends as usual on who is writing the story. But our intention here in setting out this landscape is limited—we wish to paint a picture only in the broadest possible brush strokes in order to characterise the boundary changes we will be exploring; it is not intended here to offer any deep analysis of the historical development of film studies—for this readers are referred to more exhaustive and accurate considerations of film studies as a field such as Dudley Andrew (1976) or Lapsley and Westlake (2006).

Our foreshortened version of 'history' begins in the 1960s with the proposals of a new, 'more scientific' and 'rigorous' approach to film analysis made by employing techniques and terms from the field of *semiotics*. We will say more in the next chapter about just what this is and how its interaction with film studies played out. For now, all that is required is to note that this interaction was far from smooth; there was considerable argument about the sense and use of the entire enterprise, arguments that in many respects still shape attitudes today.

One rallying point for many of these disagreements was the lack of attention that early 'structuralist semiotics' appeared to pay to the 'subject'—i.e., the individuals actually watching films. The largely linguistically-inspired semiotic accounts of the time seemed to render the subject redundant. It was the formal features of the 'text', be that filmic or belonging to some other medium, that determined the reading positions possible. This was then seen as, on the one hand, separating both subjects and films from their social and ideological contexts and, on the other, privileging one particular, 'scientific' reading of texts before all others (Lapsley and Westlake, 2006: 55–59). Political critique, particularly of 'Hollywood' films and the film industry, was becoming a dominating discourse within film research at that time and so the a-historical, a-social perspective assumed for this early semiotics simply did not fit.

Several research programmes arose in film theory in response to these concerns; for present purposes we can usefully pick out three that are of particular relevance—the *Further Reading* section at the end of this chapter points to some others.

First, one broad programme was developed within film studies that sought to combine ideological critiques of society from a primarily Marxist perspective, psychoanalytic treatments of dream, fantasy, etc. drawing primarily on Jacques Lacan and his extensions beyond Freud, and semiotic theories of signification (cf. Baudry, 1974). Variations in these themes and their further developments are widespread and have constituted important shapers of film research ever since. The combination as such was supported by according 'language' a central role throughout. For Lacan, for example, the subconscious was already structured 'like a language' and so, through the link with the previous linguistically-inflected semiotics, was presented as a logical next step (Lapsley and Westlake, 2006: Chapter 3, 67–104). This 'second semiotics' of film was then a semiotics of psychoanalysis.

The second programme, in parallel and overlapping with the first, related film studies more directly to the study of literature. Here the methods and approaches developed for studying works of literature were also considered applicable to the study of film. Such approaches have in common that they are essentially oriented to the 'text', as literary work, and avail themselves of methods drawn from narratology, post-structural, feminist, post-colonial, transcultural and other forms of literary analysis. This programme therefore itself includes a very broad range of approaches within it—overlapping in some places with the previous one. Common to all perspectives, however, was the assumption that how people respond to film is similar, and can be analysed in similar ways, to how people respond to literary texts (cf. Wilson, 1986; Paech, 1988; Currie, 1995).

The third, and for current purposes final, programme, considers film more as an object of perception. Here the basic idea is that how people respond to film builds substantially on how people respond to the world in general: i.e., perceiving what is happening in a film fragment shows many parallels with perceiving what is happening around us in any case. Perception delivers a break-down of the visual and acoustic field into objects, properties, relations, movement, etc. and interpretation of that information draws on our general understandings of what objects are, what actions are performed, what motives people might have for their actions and so on. This also informs the general area of *cognitive film theory* (cf. Bordwell, 2009).

The *methods* traditionally associated with these three programmes differ considerably, which is one of our main motivations for dividing them in the way we have. The first and second programmes are, however, more similar in that both are 'discursive' in their style of argumentation: particular sets of terms and relationships are applied to talk about film and films and the success or otherwise of the argument is generally assessed by how well the argument 'convinces', picking examples from analysed texts as required to illustrate the argument's plausibility (cf. Bordwell, 1989; Zöllner, 1989). The difference between them lies more in the weight given to specific details of the texts under analysis in the selection of examples and the extent to which a pre-structuring body of theory (e.g., to take a common example, that of psychoanalysis in various forms) is applied to organise the results.

In contrast, the third set of approaches is typically more 'empirical' in orientation, relying on detailed technical, even mechanical, analysis of the objects of study and their reception. Here we find all psychological approaches to film that consider experimental methods the soundest approach to follow as well as 'cognitive' accounts more broadly. Since cognitive film theory draws primarily on cognitive science, it is naturally open to approaches to film rooted in perceptual psychology and to cognitive approaches to knowledge representation of this kind; here models of problem-solving, both in general and for 'texts' in particular (cf. Graesser, Singer and Trabasso, 1994) are assigned an important role.[1] We will hear more of these approaches in subsequent chapters.

Figure 1.5 suggests something of the connections and boundaries that we see exhibited in the study of film over the past 50 years. Direct input of results and approaches is indicated by arrows; looser, more formative in-

---

[1] A useful informal way of characterising positions here is in terms of just how much 'help' a text/film gives the problem-solving process. The minimal approach is to assume a loosely structured collection of cues that the problem-solving process can consult at will (e.g., Bordwell, 1989, 2007); other models may posit stronger organisations of cues (cf. Wuss, 1990, 1993). This reflects the extent to which 'textuality' is seen to reside as a richly structuring resource within the artefacts analysed. The stronger this organisation, the more it can operate as *instructions* that guide interpretation. This is the essential role of the *textual* metafunction as we introduced it above.

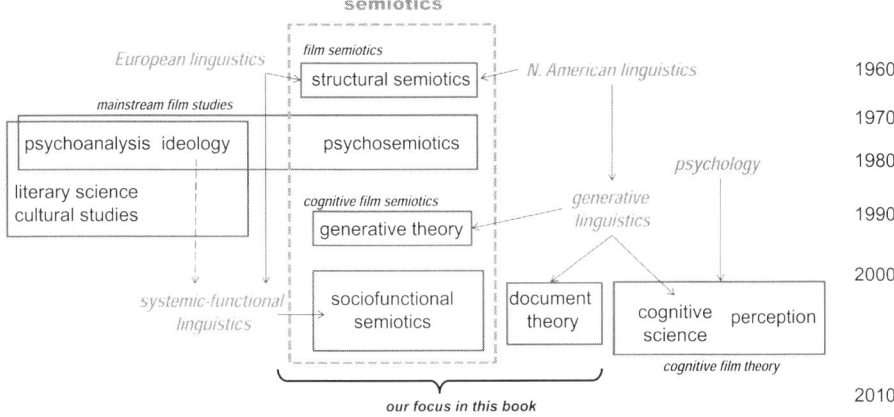

Figure 1.5   A schematic map of the major disciplines contributing to film studies and the position of our approach within this

fluences are indicated by arrows with broken lines. The central dashed box labelled 'semiotics' groups together a rather diverse range of approaches: we will see in the chapter following some of the reasons for this. The other boxes of the diagram indicate more established or reliable disciplinary and methodological groupings. Our own approach then draws on the contributions bracketed together at the bottom of the figure.

We will be attempting to redraw some of the boundaries established between research programmes in the following way. We see the assimilation of semiotic accounts within the psychoanalytic and ideological approaches of the first programme to be misleading in several important respects. The kinds of signifying processes investigated within the psychoanalytic tradition do not provide the necessary foundations for characterising signification in general—and particularly not for *externalised* representations such as film. In fact, we consider this entrenched association between a received view of 'semiotics' and 'psychoanalytic approaches' to have done considerable harm.

On the one hand, literary approaches to text successfully produce very general, abstract, socially and individually revealing interpretations of literary (which now includes filmic) works essential for understanding the value and relevance of those works. The connection of these more hermeneutic interpretations to the details of the texts giving rise to them is, however, often a matter of debate and depends to a large extent on the appositeness of the 'examples' selected.

On the other hand, 'perceptual' or cognitive approaches to film are becoming ever more successful at revealing how fine-grained filmic cues can trigger particular lines of interpretation in their viewers—this is gradually revealing convincing mechanisms for how filmic interpretation functions in specific situations of reception. But here precisely the converse problem is found: it is the construction of *broader* social and functional interpretations of films on the basis of these recognised cues that becomes difficult.

We thus find a considerable 'gap', in fact, several gaps, between the diverse levels of interpretation and analysis available. Identifiable low-level technical details of films do not of themselves give access to sensible mid-level interpretations and the path from mid-level interpretations to interpretations of an entire work still rests on anything but firm foundations. Particularly in Chapters 2 and 3, we will argue that more up to date, essentially multimodal, accounts of semiotics and of semiotic artefacts can provide exactly what is missing here. The analysis of film—both when considered as text and when seen as 'similar to reality'—demands powerful theoretical and technical tools whose principal focus is *signification* itself. Without this, there is little guidance of what lower-level patterns to focus on and why—be those patterns perceptual, textual or ideological—and accounts proposed at higher levels of abstraction remain overly subject to intuitive and impressionistic descriptions. This then imposes significant limits on the theoretical positions that can be achieved.

The effective removal of considerations of semiotics from empirical film analysis was largely the result of the emergence of the first broad programme described above, combining ideology and psychoanalysis within a kind of 'psychosemiotics'. Whereas semiotics has developed further on a variety of fronts, the view of semiotics from film studies still tends to be channelled almost exclusively through psychoanalytic accounts. With the exception of a limited attempt to extend structural semiotic and generative linguistic notions in the form of a 'cognitive semiotics' of film by Buckland (2000), the semiotic line has since been considered by many to have been closed. Another one of our general aims in this book will therefore be to 'reclaim' a place for an appropriate semiotics adequate for the task of analysing film and able to do full justice to the range of forms and meanings at issue.

This is why we position semiotics in the 'centre' of our diagram. We take a proper understanding of signification and its processes—i.e., of the functioning of *semiosis*—as precisely the missing glue that might allow the distinct analytic enterprises mentioned above to work together, alleviating the problematic division between considerations of film as 'similar to literary text' (the left-hand side of our figure) and as 'similar to reality' (the right-hand side). Using this 'semiotic glue', we will attempt to define a framework in which analyses can be pursued that, on the one hand, are anchored in the details of technical form but which, on the other hand, can nevertheless serve as a basis for broader, more abstract interpretations.

1.4   Organisation of the book

Our undertaking here is naturally a rather ambitious one and so we will only be able to start out on the path we have chosen. This will involve taking film to be a complex semiotic mode whose analysis requires consideration along several semiotic dimensions. The remaining chapters of the book perform this development, introducing the constructs necessary for this kind of analysis while discussing throughout examples that show the tools at work. Our hope is that this will place the reader in a more secure position for at least starting empirically well-founded analyses of film of the kind we suggest to be necessary.

The particular course that we follow begins in Chapter 2, therefore, with a re-evaluation of the relationship between film and semiotics. Chapter 3 then shows how complex *multimodal* semiotic systems can be characterised, focusing progressively on film. Chapter 4 then introduces the most influential, if also controversial, linguistically-inflected semiotic approach to film to date, that of Christian Metz. The core components of our framework then follow in Chapters 5, 6 and 7, presenting examples as we proceed of how the approach *guides* film analyses in order to raise the accuracy and inter-subjective viability of analysis carried out within it. Chapter 8 then brings the entire framework together and offers a walk-through analysis of a substantial portion of a single short film. Finally, in Chapter 9, we summarise the main contributions of the book and point out those areas of future development that we now consider most pressing.

Further reading

Following each chapter, we will present a short collection of further references that take up points touched on but not dealt with in the chapters themselves. For example, for good **general introductions** to the vast area of film studies, particularly focusing on the films themselves and the most widely applied approaches to their analysis and interpretation, we can particularly recommend Prince (2007), while the relevant chapters from Bordwell and Thompson's (2008) *Film Art: an Introduction* are in any case compulsory reading for anyone analysing film.

Extensive examples of **filmic techniques** are given in Reisz and Millar (Reisz and Millar, 1953, 1968) as well as in glossaries and overviews of terms available both in print (e.g., Hayward, 2006) and online—see, for example: Daniel Chandler's at http://www.aber.ac.uk/media/ Documents/short/gramtv.html or Manfred Jahn's at http://www. uni-koeln.de/~ame02/pppf.htm. More practical film production-oriented introductions are offered by Zettl (1973) and by Thompson and Bowen (2009*a,b*) for shots and editing respectively, as well as in classic texts such as Arijon (1976), Sharff (1982) and others. Monaco (2000: 195–212;

2009: 221–234) offers useful comments concerning the 'fuzzy' nature of several of the standard sets of terms employed in film analysis and how their application may depend on other features of the image, such as *aspect ratio*, i.e., the shape and proportions of the frame, as well as a broad consideration of the field as a whole.

We provide film segments as examples of our analytic methods throughout the book and employ several kinds of **transcription** drawing on such technical features. It is interesting that explicit descriptions of how to perform and use such transcriptions to construct *film protocols* are more prevalent in German introductions to film studies than they are in the English literature—Nelmes (2007*b*) offers a prime example of this tendency, although otherwise providing an accessible overview of many areas of film interpretation. In contrast, various levels of granularity are offered in Hickethier (2007: 33–36), Kuchenbuch (2005: 37–61) and Korte (2004: 26–66). Ochs (1979) offers a now classic discussion of the interplay between theory building and transcription for language and Bellour's (1975) related observations on the difficulties in 'citing' film for analysis—as well as his adopted solutions mixing images, tables and texts—have been seminal.

Although we isolated three main research programmes within film studies for discussion above, there are of course others—such as, for example, work moving more on the boundaries of **film and philosophy** (e.g., Cavell, 1980; Allen and Smith, 1997; Smith and Wartenberg, 2006; Livingston and Plantinga, 2009), on **feminist film theory** (e.g., Penley, 1988; Chaudrini, 2006; Nelmes, 2007*a*), or considering the nature of the **filmic 'experience'** as such (e.g., Deleuze, 1986; Sobchack, 1992). The reader is referred to more general introductions to film studies to get a more adequate sense of this range of approaches (e.g., Prince 2007: Chapter 12, 436–473 and Nelmes 2007*b*).

There is also a long tradition of studying film from the perspective of **mass communication and media** (cf. Thornham, Bassett and Marris, 2009). Here the focus is on the social configurations into which films fit, their general effects on audiences, and their production, political, institutional and commercial contexts–i.e., macro-phenomena—accordingly aligned methodologically more with the quantitative methods of the social sciences. Work of this kind is obviously important for an understanding of film but the textually articulated details of specific films that forms our main focus here are often in the background in such studies. This changes somewhat where **individual reception situations** are explored (cf. Suckfüll, 2000; Suckfüll and Scharkow, 2009; Wuss, 2009) and the workings of individual differences again become relevant (for example, for pedagogical or didactic purposes: Hackenberg 2004).

Finally, for details almost without end for all of the **films** mentioned in this book, '*The Internet Movie Database*' at `http://www.imdb.com/` is invaluable.

2   Semiotics and documents

"Chief among the drawbacks in the basic arguments of the semiological enterprise is that extremely far-reaching conclusions are made on the basis of a theory of structural linguistics that in certain ways formed the foundation for modern linguistics, but that is no longer taken seriously by linguists themselves as a proposal about the nature of language or, by extension, of human nature." (Cadbury and Poague, 1982: 69)

As mentioned in the previous chapter, we draw on two theoretical contributions from outside of film studies to provide the foundations of the analytic framework we develop. On the one hand, we build on a particular branch of semiotics, that of **socio-functional semiotics** and, on the other, on modern methods for the description and analysis of *documents*—particularly, as we shall see, dynamic documents that are designed and structured to play out in time. In this chapter, we present our motivations for these choices.

The interaction of film studies and semiotics has been long and complex. We noted above how the move to psychosemiotics meant for many film theorists a parting of the ways. Our adoption of certain tenets of semiotics here cannot therefore go without some explanation. It is quite ironic that many of the original grounds for not considering film as a 'language-like' system have long since also been found to apply to language itself and linguistics and semiotics have grown to meet this. This sea change has, however, had little impact on film studies. In Section 2.1, we accordingly give a brief indication of just what we take semiotics to be and how it relates to film. In particular, we will open up the key semiotic constructs of *stratification* and *discourse*. This will establish the directions from semiotics that we accept as well as delineating more clearly some versions of semiotics and its proposed relation to film that we will *not* be considering.

Even in studies of film that do draw on semiotics, misunderstandings and misapplications of basic semiotic categories are common and descriptions of previous semiotic approaches to film too often remain sketchy and/or inaccurate. We need to be aware of this and, where necessary, to make corrections. We will also need to distinguish carefully just in what sense we are using the term 'discourse', since it appears in various disciplines doing rather different work. Our usage is neither that of the large-scale social-cultural configurations discussed by Foucault nor that behind the contrast *histoire-discours* found in narratology (drawing on Benveniste, 1966; Genette, 1980); it is instead drawn directly from a socio-functional linguistic orientation as one quite specific level of semiotic patterning.

Below we will clarify this further both for language in Section 2.2 and, in the chapter following, for film.

The second area we draw on, that of modelling techniques and abstractions developed within **document theory**, is introduced in Section 2.3. This is still relatively unknown in film studies; its application to date has largely been restricted to technical issues of film representation, of standardisation for digital distribution and of automatic processing. Adopting the fine-grained frameworks for characterising filmic material and its organisation that this area provides offers a solid ground for the interpretative mechanisms that we construct in subsequent chapters.

Finally, in Section 2.4 before concluding the chapter, we bring the two perspectives of semiotics and filmic documents together in a preliminary discussion of one 'standard' film example: a particular segment drawn from Orson Welles' *The Lady from Shanghai* (1947) that highlights several of the points that we wish to make. We will argue that combining the two perspectives allows us to address a range of basic filmic organisational issues without losing sight of the more abstract functions and meanings carried by filmic artefacts. Indeed, only with this combination do we have the vocabulary necessary for describing actual filmic material in a, on the one hand, suitably concrete and, on the other, nevertheless sufficiently abstract fashion to support the close contact between empirical analysis and interpretation that is our goal.

2.1   Semiotics and its relations to film

One of the earliest definitions of semiotics is the general study of "the life of signs within society" (Saussure, 1959[1915]: 16). We consider it self-evident that film is exactly the kind of entity that a reasonable semiotics should have something to say about. Films are artefacts particularly designed to carry meanings, to have effects on their viewers, to build and combine patterns made in a variety of materials—visual, acoustic, spatial and more. In short: films are very complex 'signs' in their own right, including within them a broad range of further signs, such as spoken language, written language, visual representations of diverse kinds, spatial organisations, proxemics, codes of dress and other social conventions and so on—all orchestrated to create rich and complex webs of meaning.

Despite this surfeit of 'semiotic activity', the value, and even relevance, of semiotics for film has been contested on many grounds. It is therefore important that we briefly position ourselves, and the kind of semiotics that we will be adopting and developing further, so as to illustrate why we consider earlier criticisms of semiotic approaches not to apply. So deep now are the (often, as we shall see, quite justified) prejudices within film studies against certain styles of semiotics that, for many, combining semiotics and film is considered an inappropriate endeavour almost by definition. This obliges us to try to open up at least a small crack in this wholesale rejection since, without the theoretical framework of an appropriate semiotics, discussion of film and its nature is considerably weakened.

We can as a consequence see this section as a small contribution to the philosophy of semiotics and signs—a contribution broadly analogous to Berys Gaut's appeal for philosophy in film studies in general:

> "The contribution of philosophy to our understanding of film so far has not lain chiefly in identifying new issues or puzzles about film, which have been largely set out by film theory. Rather, philosophers have chiefly contributed by bringing greater conceptual sophistication to the debate. Notions of realism, language and interpretation are of central concern to philosophy in general, and it is unsurprising if philosophers have succeeded in identifying a great deal of confusion in how they have been handled in film theory." (Gaut, 2010: 5)

While no doubt true, it is also the case that there is similarly a 'great deal of confusion' in many philosophers' approaches to meaning whenever non-semiotically informed models of 'semiotic artefacts' are attempted. The corresponding lack of *semiotic* sophistication leads to foundational problems, particularly when considering complex, relatively 'new' multimodal artefacts such as film. We will see several such models and the problems they encounter below.

The origins of the kinds of semiotics that we will be applying follow at first the traditional path beginning from the American pragmatist philosopher Charles Sanders Peirce and the Swiss linguist Ferdinand de Saussure,. Their proposals for systematic accounts of what 'signs' are and how they function were subsequently developed further by the Danish linguist Louis Hjelmslev's 'algebraic' formulations of semiotics—algebraic understood here as an abstract focus on structures and relations independent of any particular systems of signification.

It was precisely this independence that then encouraged attempts in the 1960s and 1970s by Roland Barthes, Umberto Eco and, of particular significance for film, Christian Metz to apply lessons learnt from the semiotics of language to other semiotic modes. Good basic introductions to all of these writers can be found in the relevant chapters of Chandler (2002), while somewhat more technical detail is provided in the corresponding sections of Nöth's (1995a) *Handbook of Semiotics*. It is primarily this kind of 'structural semiotics' that has previously been applied to film (cf. Figure 1.5 of the previous chapter) and which subsequently brought considerable disagreement in its wake.

The particular style of semiotics that we draw on for our framework developed in a rather different direction. Based on the work of Gunther Kress and Theo van Leeuwen (cf., in particular, Hodge and Kress, 1988; Kress and van Leeuwen, 2001; van Leeuwen, 2005b; Kress, 2009, 2010), this account originated as a multimodal extension to *systemic-functional linguistics*, an approach to language developed by Michael A. K. Halliday and colleagues and quite directly descended from Hjelmslev, the Prague School of Linguistics, and British Contextualism (Halliday, 1978). This perspective adopts a *social* foundation and sees language, its development and use all as social phenomena anchored into the social interaction of individuals in social contexts. These functional aspects are taken to be determinative both of how language as a semiotic system 'plays out' over time and of the structural configurations that it develops internally to support its functioning.

Kress and van Leeuwen then take this further to argue that any semiotic system will be subject to societally-driven determining forces in a similar manner and, because of this, may be expected to exhibit broad similarities in their organisation (cf. Kress, 2010: 35–36). This is not then to argue that other semiotic systems will resemble (natural) language, but rather to propose that all semiotic systems, language included, are necessarily subject to some very general semiotic requirements that originate in the use of those systems by communities of users with particular concerns and requirements. Differing semiotic systems may support these concerns and requirements in different ways, but there will nevertheless remain certain kinds of abstract similarities. As we shall see, many of the traditional problems raised with applying notions of semiotics to film are placed in a very different light when we adopt this kind of starting point rather than earlier structuralist and 'generative' versions of linguistics or semiotics.

Earlier criticisms of the application of principles from semiotics to film have revolved around several issues; we pick here two that are of particular relevance for advancing the discussion: first, a, sometimes justified, charge of linguistic imperialism, i.e., the imposition of models derived from the language system on other areas of signification; and second, the problems of an overly static, a-historical and non-social view of meaning.

We address these critiques in turn, introducing our own view on the semiotic issues involved along the way. A third, from our perspective very valid source of criticism that we will not address revolves around the widespread suspicion mentioned in the previous chapter that semiotics is inseparable from psychoanalytic approaches. We do not consider this for the simple reason that this turning was never taken by the semiotic approaches with which we will be concerned—such considerations are, therefore, not relevant for us here, despite the very heated debates it has given rise to.

Criticism 1: Linguistic imperialism

Semiotics has long been closely associated with linguistics, and it is with respect to language that the most extensively articulated accounts have developed; in almost all areas of semiotics, descriptions are attempted either by taking language as a model or by drawing explicit contrasts to language. Saussure was in no two minds about this: he saw linguistics as a model, a 'master-pattern', providing a frame for investigating semiotic systems of all kinds (Saussure, 1959[1915]: 68). Beginning in the 1960s, the successes achieved with the study of linguistic signs then naturally led on to discussions of signs 'in general'—as noted above for Barthes, Eco and others.

But, the argument in film studies goes, what has this to do with *film*? Time and again it has been demonstrated that film and language—in the sense of natural human languages as spoken the world over—have 'nothing in common'. We cannot find archetypal linguistic categories such as 'parts-of-speech' (nouns, adjective, verbs, etc.) in the filmic image. We cannot even find clearly distinguishable parts analogous to language's decomposition of sentences into phrases and phrases into words. Moreover, no rearrangement of shots can ever give rise to an 'ungrammatical' sequence in the way that shuffling words in a sentence can. Nor does film (at least with current technology) enter into the 'speech circuit' considered by many to be essential for language learning: viewers are not automatically producers.

Filmic images are also typically considered to lack the indirect, *conventional* relation to their referents that language exhibits: an image of a rabbit shows a rabbit, it does not involve the arbitrariness of connection evident in the words "rabbit", "Kaninchen", "lapin", "ukulaitchiaq", etc. This property of construction by convention, fundamental to Saussure and many others, appears to be missing for film and, as a consequence, it is often argued that no process of 'film acquisition' in analogy to 'language acquisition' can exist. As the philosopher of film and literature Gregory Currie boldly declaims:

> "Films and novels are alike in that they require us to make inferences to the intentions of a maker; they are unalike in that, while literature requires also a linguistic competence on the reader's part, film requires only a naturally given competence with visual depiction." (Currie, 1997: 54)

These and similar suggestions made over the past 40 years provide strong support for believing that any talk of the 'language of film' is at best metaphorical—film is not a *language* in the same way that English, German, French or Inupiaq are.

Nevertheless, regardless of whether or not any of these arguments actually hold (since there is still debate), we are still a considerable distance from any sound conclusions whatsoever concerning the relevance of semiotics for the study of film. This is one of the (many) problems caused by treating complex semiotic entities, such as 'language' or 'film', as monolithic wholes. 'Language' is by no means a unitary, atomistic concept—its description involves many essential semiotic dimensions and, as we shall argue throughout this book, several of these *are* relevant for film.

In fact, they are more than relevant; we consider them crucial for understanding film. Without them, basic properties of complex signifying practices are left only poorly articulated and articulable. Moreover, film in particular is such a complex signifying practice that we can ill afford to approach it without the powerful analytic tools that an appropriate semiotics provides. Linguistically-inspired semiotics then has much to offer precisely because linguistics as a science has now explored many of the semiotic dimensions necessary in considerable detail. If moved to an appropriate level of theoretical abstraction, this knowledge stands us in good stead for the consideration of film.

Discussions of the relation between the study of film and linguistics rarely take such developments into account and operate as if 'structural semiotics' was still the order of the day. In the 1960s it was common to see linguistics only in terms of sounds, grammar and vocabulary. For example, Barthes proclaimed in his structural semiotic analysis of narratives, which originally appeared in 1966:

> "As we know, linguistics stops at the sentence, the last unit which it considers to fall within its scope. . . . [t]here can be no question of linguistics setting itself an object superior to the sentence, since beyond the sentence there are only more sentences—having described the flower, the botanist is not to get involved in describing the bouquet." (Barthes, 1977a: 82–83)

Dry fare for the linguist indeed. This 'received position', in part derivable from Saussure, is still with us today—although echoed primarily by those more on the edges of linguistic research, including some philosophers and film researchers.

Elsewhere in Barthes' writings 'linguistics' is used in a much broader sense, but our purpose here is not to try and pull apart the distinct meanings Barthes intended; rather we are simply drawing attention to a legacy of belief that restricts the scope of linguistics essentially to grammar and which is, with respect to the current state of the art, hugely inaccurate. This legacy continues to distort discussions in linguistics, literary studies, psychology and, of primary concern to us here, film studies to this day.

Barthes himself also saw a way to move beyond the flower to the bouquet, however. Immediately following the above quote, he continues:

> "And yet it is evident that discourse itself (as a set of sentences) is organized and that, through this organization, it can be seen as the message of another language, one operating at a higher level than the language of the linguists. Discourse has its own units, its rules, its 'grammar': beyond the sentence, and though consisting entirely of sentences, it must naturally form the object of a *second linguistics*. . . . The new linguistics of discourse has still to be developed, but at least it is being postulated, and by the linguists themselves." (Barthes, 1977a: 83, emphasis added)

At the time Barthes wrote this there was very little idea how such a 'second linguistics', that of discourse, could work. Thus, although even early on we can find work on film that emphasises film's discoursal nature, accounts of that nature were restricted—discussions either fell back on notions of grammar or looked outside of linguistics altogether, probably the most common model drawn upon being that of an increasingly extended notion of *narrative* (cf. Cohen-Séat, 1948; Mitry, 1998[1963]; Metz, 1974*a*), as we shall see more of below.

The field of linguistics has now moved well beyond this. What Barthes somewhat expansively terms 'another language' in the above quotation is, in modern terms, simply a further *stratum* of the semiotic system that is language. The linguistics of discourse, i.e., the linguistic study of the stratum of discourse, is now an established area within linguistics with its own substantial results. Some of these results concern something that could not have been foreseen at the time of Barthes' article, however. In particular, it was not yet known just how different in important respects the mechanisms of grammar and of discourse would be: this will have essential repercussions for our development of an account for film below. Early more or less loose usages of 'grammar' for film (cf. Spottiswoode, 1935) continue to this day, with talk of 'grammars' of everything from the 'shot' and the 'edit' (Thompson and Bowen, 2009*a,b*) to 'colour' (Kress and van Leeuwen, 2002), to 'television production' (Davis, 1974), and to murder (at least in film: Oeler, 2009). Given what we now know about the workings of grammar we can, and arguably should, be more discriminating in our use of terms: the grammar of verbal language has some very specific properties that cannot be assumed to hold for other levels of organisation, *even within the semiotic system of language.*

This then reveals the first of the fundamental semiotic dimensions that we will employ in our exploration of film: the dimension of **stratification**. In general, a semiotic system can be described in terms of a set of inter-related strata, each capturing properties of the system at differing levels of abstraction. We already made use of this notion in our illustrations of filmic meaning in the previous chapter when we suggested that there are various 'levels of abstraction' to be considered when analysing film. We can now characterise this notion more precisely by drawing on what we know about stratification from a semiotic perspective.

The levels of abstraction appropriate for a complete semiotic account range from high level considerations at one extreme down to the concrete materiality of expression at the other and, within the current state of the art, naturally some strata are better understood than others. A distinction is traditionally made here going back to Hjelmslev between the *content* and the *expression* planes of a semiotic system, each of which is further subdivided into *form* and *substance*. The expression plane for language is typically taken to include graphology and phonology (cf. O'Halloran, 2008: 449), while that for visual images has been suggested to include colour, shape, framing and perspective (cf. Eco, 1976; Bertin, 1983; Tufte, 1983; O'Toole, 1994; Engelhardt, 2007; O'Halloran, 2008). Although not made prominent in Hjelmslev's account, the *materiality* of expression exerts a significant influence on how a semiotic system develops—for example, even for language, whether its materiality involves visible marks (i.e., written) or sound (i.e., oral) is of considerable import (cf. Ong, 1982). In general, the semiotic function of the material is to provide a perceivable substrate in which 'traces' of semiotically charged distinctions can be left. A proper consideration of materiality and its consequences is, if anything, even more crucial for film and so we will return to this at several points below.

Semiotic systems also differ considerably with respect to how complex their non-material strata may become. Verbal language, for example, is richly stratified, while other systems may be simpler. As indicated above, the most abstract levels of abstraction proposed within systemic-functional linguistic theory for verbal language are essentially social. The role of the semiotic system is then to place text and texts in relation to communicative genres, ideologies and communities. Research in these areas is often still quite exploratory, however, and so we will not follow this further here (cf. Halliday, 1978; Martin, 1992; Martin and Rose, 2007). Nevertheless, notions of genre and possible relationships to ideology are clearly just as important when investigating film (cf., e.g., Ryan and Kellner, 1988; Altman, 1999; Keppler and Seel, 2002; Laetz and Lopes, 2009) and so cannot be omitted from any complete account. Our bracketing of these more abstract strata for the present must not, therefore, be seen as anything other than a temporary narrowing of attention.

The relationships *between* strata can also be complex: within socio-semiotic accounts strata are connected to one another by the formal relationship of *realisation* (following Hjelmslev, 1961) or *meta-redundancy* (following Lemke, 1991, 2000). A good way of seeing this is in terms of 'patterns of patterns': that is, patterns at a lower level of abstraction (e.g., sounds in a language or the notes produced on a piano) can be grouped and recoded in terms of patterns at a higher level of abstraction (e.g., morphemes and grammar in language or forms such as the sonata for music).

This sidesteps rhetorical questions sometimes brought against semiotic approaches which ask unanswerable questions concerning what the signified of a particular sonata or of a shot employing some particular editing or framing technique might be (e.g., Bordwell, 2005: 252). Associating lower-level patterns with higher-level patterns is to assign them *social value* and does not require us to answer referentially-inflected questions about possible 'representations' at the level of signification. As we shall clarify further below, this is also reminiscent in some respects of Bordwell's (1989: 203) model of critical interpretation in which filmic cues are linked to interpretative schemes; however, as noted in the previous chapter, we look to the semiotic framework to provide a stronger foundation and more structuring both for the cues and for the interpretative schemes.

An important aspect of any work investigating a semiotic system must then be to identify the system's strata. The traditional way of motivating linguistic strata, for example, relies on the notion that higher strata *abstract* across patterns of lower strata while lower strata *generalise* across the requirements of higher strata. The semantic stratum accordingly provides an abstraction over the kinds of patterns found within grammar, while the patterns of grammar generalise across the particular situations in which language is being used and the particular communicative goals being pursued. This is one of the considerations that has led to the recognition that a distinct *discourse semantics* stratum is required because any particular discourse function can generally be expressed by means of a broad range of grammatical alternatives.

Different strata may also require differing internal mechanisms. For example, for verbal language the main principles within the strata of syntax and semantics involve the *compositional* construction of meanings from parts. Human languages appear to operate within a particular range of syntactic possibilities that conspire to support this compositionality. Any particular language 'selects' from this general range of possibilities, thus determining which utterances will be considered grammatical and which not. For our present concerns, it makes no difference just how this 'selection' comes about—some schools of linguistics favour notions of innate principles triggered by input 'data' (cf. Chomsky, 1966), others favour construction according to forces of interaction within concrete situations of use (e.g., Halliday, 1975; Tomasello, 2005). Regardless of theoretical approach, 'native speakers' of a language come very quickly to have a strong sense of grammaticality: certain combinations of words just do not work.

A very different set of mechanisms is now accepted for the workings of the stratum 'above' this: the stratum of *discourse semantics*. There is, for example, no such thing as 'ungrammatical' discourse. This means that the process of meaning construction within the discourse stratum cannot rely on the compositional construction of meanings from structurally well-behaved configurations as is generally the case in syntax. Precisely how this functions we will return to in a moment when we deal with the second area of critique brought against semiotics. Here we will simply note that henceforward we will restrict our own use of the term 'grammar' to entities that exhibit those properties found within the correspondingly named stratum of the linguistic system to avoid confusion—that is, we will *not* use any such notion as 'film grammar' and so on loosely or metaphorically.

The observation that differing mechanisms may be required for different strata can also be turned back on itself in order to *motivate* the recognition of different strata. We can deduce the existence of a separate stratum of discourse precisely because it does not rely on compositionality. Moreover, and rather more controversially, we can deduce equally that the discourse stratum is *distinct from general knowledge of social situations*. This is because the general-purpose reasoning required at that level is more complex than is plausible for the real-time processing of natural discourse. This will prove to be equally relevant for film and so we return to this in more detail below.

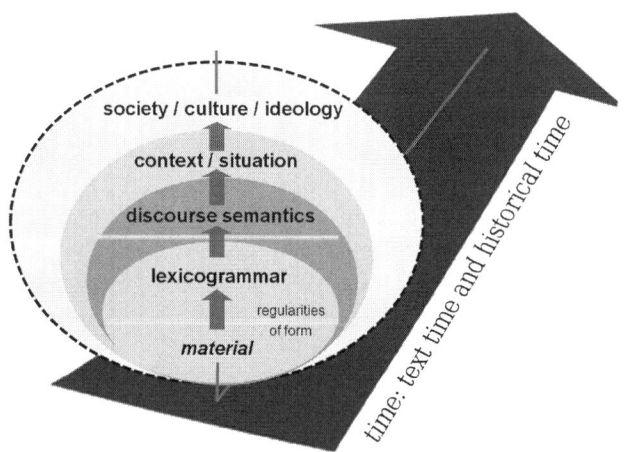

Figure 2.1   The stratified view of the language system according to the socio-semiotic functional perspective

Figure 2.1 brings all of these considerations together and depicts the natural language semiotic system as seen from the perspective of socio-semiotic theory. The strata of the semiotic system are shown as embedded circles, each more abstract stratum embedding and including those less abstract strata within. These strata do not, therefore, align straightforwardly with the well-known division into syntax, semantic and pragmatics proposed for language by Morris (1938) and sometimes also found in treatments of visual media (e.g., Sachs-Hombach, 2006)—both *below* syntax and *within* the often somewhat undifferentiated notion of pragmatics there is much more detail that must be brought out.

In addition, all the embedded circles come together at a single point or share a common tangent at the bottom: this represents the interface with the 'outside world' given by the material substrate where the contribution of all strata must be made evident to have any effect. In an important sense, and conformant with many tenets of post-structuralism, all that we actually have access to is the 'signifier' in Saussure's terms: the traces of semiotic undercurrents left in the material form. This also orients us more towards Peircian semiotics and the *processes* of semiosis than to the more static viewpoint often attributed to Saussure—a point that will gain in relevance as we proceed.

Finally, the entire system is also necessarily anchored into time: from the local time-scale of individual texts and individual interactions (*logogenesis*), through the medium time-scale of an individual child's acquisition of the system (*ontogenesis*), on to the long-term scales of historical change (*phylogenesis*), the system is in constant flux. Change and variation is considered an intrinsic property of such semiotic systems: each 'use' of the system can push its development along particular trajectories rather than others (cf. Lemke, 1991; Labov, 2001; Giddens, 1984; Thibault, 2006) so there is a constant feedback cycle between system and text, between potential and actual. It is then indicative of this approach as a whole that the notion of 'sign', traditionally prominent in semiotics, has receded into the background. We are much more concerned with the conditions under which 'signs' can come into being: and for this we require the semiotic system standing 'behind' or 'beneath' any such usages rather than some list of the signs themselves.

In summary, returning to the original point of critique with which we started, we have sought here to make it clear just how far accounts of the linguistic system, of the concerns of 'linguists', have moved over the past 30 years. Any statement from within film studies that 'language' and 'film' are incommensurable, that semiotics can have nothing to contribute to the fine-grained, empirically motivated analysis of film, needs therefore to be weighed against the state of the art we have sketched and not against the explorations of the 1960s. Even though the view of the semiotic system set out here is primarily derived from detailed explorations of the linguistic system, it will nevertheless be relevant to the concerns of film in several respects. We will, for example, take its basic dimensions of semiotic organisation as a skeleton around which a generic approach to *multimodality* can be set up—the most important aspects of the framework identified so far have been stratification, discourse and materiality and these continue to apply when we move away from language. Chapter 3 will add several more relevant for film, focusing progressively on film as we proceed.

These semiotic distinctions already provide support, however, for some of the more sophisticated considerations of film wished for by Gaut above. In particular, it should be easier to avoid misleading statements or arguments built in the form: 'Film is X' or 'Film is not X'. Many discussions of the nature of film and filmic meaning, including some which adopt a more philosophical orientation, are still prone to this form of nominalism. 'Film' as such is then assumed to have particular properties rather than localising these properties appropriately within particular strata of the semiotic artefact as a whole.

A prominent example of this that we will return to in detail in Chapter 5 below occurs in statements concerning the nature of the filmic image as 'already containing meaning' (due to its showing some pro-filmic material, i.e., the material apparently in front of the camera when filming; cf. Chapter 5) and so being 'obviously non-linguistic in its organisation' (because linguistic elements such as the units of sound do *not* already 'contain meaning'). This reduces film as a whole to certain properties of its visual track, i.e., just *one* of the strata involved in its making of meanings—which is hardly to do justice to the complexity of the semiotic system of film as a whole. Carrying this style of argumentation back to language should entail that verbal language does not have any meaning either because, considered individually, its sound-elements do not. Statements that might hold of some particular stratum of a semiotic system cannot, therefore, be simply expanded to apply to the system as a whole.

Our description of the semiotic workings of film in the chapter following will describe in more detail how multimodal semiotic systems, including film, go about their business of making meanings. For now it is sufficient simply to note that totalising statements about what film is or is not are insufficiently discriminating and often serve rhetorical purposes rather than contributing to accurate characterisations of film. Keeping the semiotic system of Figure 2.1 in mind is then one very good way of recognising and countering this argumentative strategy when it occurs.

Criticism 2: Static codes for encoding/decoding meaning

Our mention of time and change as an intrinsic component of semiotic systems above is also important for the second critique that we wish to defuse. Ranging across most of the early discussions of semiotics and its application to film was the suspicion of an outdated structuralism that abstracts away from both the historically-situated individual subject and the ideologically-loaded context of society—both now central facets of the consideration of film as well of many other areas in the humanities. And indeed, the linguistics of that time was certainly closely associated with a socially impoverished 'communication model' taken over from information theory, in which a speaker and a hearer exchange messages along a channel, relying on a shared code to encode the message at one end and decode it at the other.

This model motivated many of the counter-arguments brought against linguistically-inflected semiotics and was also a significant contributing factor leading to the move into psychoanalytic approaches. These came to propose that the cinematic **apparatus** exhibits an *intrinsic* ideological commitment in two respects: first, by virtue of the camera's enforcement of a spatial perspective aligned with the 'dominant ideology' (i.e., Renaissance perspective) and, second, by the film projection situation itself enforcing a visually dominated immobility reminiscent of Jacques Lacan's *mirror stage* (cf. Baudry, 1974).[1] The tendentious claim made within this school of psychoanalytics that the subconscious is somehow 'structured as

---

[1] Early static views of texts and early psychoanalytic descriptions were actually strikingly similar in their assumption of passive recipients being 'subjected' to external control, but further discussion of this here would take us too far afield.

a language' further helped to divert attention away from linguistics proper and the continuing developments being made there.

This view of a static, structural nonsocially-aware linguistics is no longer tenable. The 'conduit' metaphor (Reddy, 1979) by which language acts as a simple transmitter of coded messages has been rejected, even within linguistics, while the close interplay between society, culture and language has long become a commonplace of linguistic theorising. It is also necessary, therefore, to see how the model of language that we are drawing on here has moved a considerable distance beyond such earlier perspectives and, as a consequence, is now fully compatible with the more sophisticated accounts of the relations between individual, society and ideology that are necessary for treatments of semiotic artefacts such as film.

Nevertheless, it will still be beneficial to describe the origins of these earlier problematic approaches to film semiotics more closely. We mentioned above the difficulty faced by early semiotic and linguistic attempts of expanding into Barthes' 'second linguistics' of discourse and text. The film-semiotic theories of the 1970s found themselves up against the same fundamental problem: there was very little idea at that time of how to relate the rich 'work-internal' organisation apparently exhibited by texts or films to the evident 'work-external' interpretative processes of actual readers, hearers and viewers.

Traditional semiotics and early text linguistics accordingly addressed work-internal aspects by employing the notion of *semiotic code*, such as the code of theatre, the code of fashion, the code of language, the code of lighting, and so on (cf. Monaco 2000: 419–421 or Monaco 2009: 471–473)— all generally presented as static constructions along the lines of information theory's communication model. The 'classical' definition of code within semiotics is still of this kind. A code is made up of "pairs of mutually pertinent classification systems" that correlate signifiers and signifieds (cf. Krampen, 2010: 130). Opponents to this view found the lack of explicit attention to history, change and, particularly in the case of film, to ideology and the activity of the spectator, a profound lack—understandably so.

The resulting 'received position' has structured discussion of the relation between film, language and semiotics to this day. This is brought out well in the following extended quotation from Bordwell that we alluded to in part above:

> "In most semiological theories codes are systems of rules that match signifiers (a pattern realised in a physical material) to signifieds (concepts). Artistic norms are far more fluid; they are not fixed rules and often bear no conceptual meaning. What is the 'signified' of a musical piece in sonata form, or a centered compositional design? What is the 'signified' of aperture framing or a planimetric shot? These devices fulfill functions; they achieve effects in dynamic relation to other choices; but they cannot be isolated as 'signifiers'. Norms are pressures to make movies in one way or another, but they are merely regulative, not constitutive. They offer options, but the presence or absence of

any norm will not make something 'unfilmic' in the way that flouting syntax will create word salad. True, many schemas, such as shot/reverse shot, are sometimes referred to as part of 'film grammar', but cinema has nothing like the rules determining verbal expression. Filmic norms are like social norms in general—not interrupting, passing the salt, holding the door open for people who follow you. If we want a linguistic analogy for film style, the closest would be not grammar but pragmatics, the loose and tacit conventions that enable us to use language for manifold purposes." (Bordwell, 2005: 252)

Almost all of the problematic conflations of important semiotic dimensions inherent in early semiotic accounts are identified and criticised here. 'Semiological' theories (Saussure's term for semiotics) are associated with codes that are considered to be rigid 'systems of rules' and such systems of rules are assumed to operate in ways similar to 'syntax' and 'grammar'. This makes them inappropriate for film, since in film there are no such 'regulative' mechanisms. Just as with Barthes above, the connection suggested to pragmatics at the end of the quotation is on the right track in as far as it moves us out of the stratum of grammar and on towards discourse—but this is then immediately conflated with social action in general, such as passing the salt.

This assumed centrality of general notions of inferential problem-solving is also echoed in influential linguistic approaches such as Relevance Theory (Sperber and Wilson, 1995), an approach occasionally cited by film theorists purely on the basis of its inferential emphasis (cf. Currie, 2010: 110–112). In this account, semantic representations are derived largely 'mechanistically' following a semiotic code, but only in order to serve as a starting point for the real process of inferential interpretation (Sperber and Wilson, 1995: 175–176). In treatments of film, this is similar to Bordwell's 'explicit' meanings used in Chapter 1 and, among treatments of literature, to some notion of 'literal meaning' that can then be subjected to interpretation (cf. Currie, 1995).[2] Strongly pragmatic or contextual approaches to language of this kind and avowedly non-codal approaches to film thus share a position in which: (a) inference takes over the 'significant' work and (b) that inference is not influenced by the specificity of the semiotic code involved; i.e., problem-solving is problem-solving, regardless of the problem:

> "Inferential communication involves the application, not of special-purpose decoding rules, but of general-purpose inference rules, which apply to any conceptually represented information." (Sperber and Wilson, 1995: 176)

In contrast to such views, it is important to see the critical role of 'inference' for *any* account of meaning: meaning is simply not a 'static' phenomenon. However, this must also be done with an appropriate con-

---

[2]Although one distinctive difference between these positions is that, in Currie's view, film has no such 'literal' meanings upon which interpretation can be built; we return to this issue below.

sideration for the requirements of semiotic strata and the dimension of stratification. In contrast, the code-is-syntax equation is derived from, on the one hand, Saussure's deliberate methodological focus on an a-historical language system and, on the other, a communication model of the exchange of coded meanings. This fails to bring together inference and stratification, with the consequence that treatments in terms of codes are isolated from the very inferential mechanisms essential for them to function.

Many researchers have oriented towards this dichotomy over the years and have used it to motivate an explicit alignment towards a pragmatic orientation *instead of*, or *in opposition to*, notions of semantics and semiotic codes. Under this view, it becomes natural to find theoreticians both in film theory and linguistics lining up on one side of the divide rather than the other—as being 'for' one (e.g., inference) and therefore 'against' the other (e.g., semiotic codes); Noël Carroll is very clear on this:

> "I am not a code/semantic theorist. Indeed, throughout my career as a film theorist, I have always explicitly stressed the importance of inference over decoding as a model for many aspects of cinematic comprehension." (Carroll, 1996*a*: 331)

Such avowals only make sense when the notion of 'semiotic code' is that of 'syntax': 'code' is conceived as a collection of 'rules' of a rather simple kind serving to encode and decode the message that is sent. Under such accounts the viewer easily becomes a 'prisoner' of the message, following the directions set out by the intentions of the message's originator. This position fails on a number of grounds—most significantly, on the one hand, the lack of a place in the account for the social and individual positioning of the viewer and, on the other, the centrality afforded to the presumed 'intentions' of some message sender, a construct itself deeply problematic for accounts of meaning.

Whereas the role of inference in syntax and semantics is limited, it is nevertheless present. But for discourse, inference plays a fundamental role. Moreover, the *kind* of inference necessary in order to treat discourse is quite distinctive and, as we shall now see, this will prove just as essential for film as it is for verbal modes of discourse.

2.2   The nature of discourse semantics

The model of the socio-semiotic linguistic system we have now introduced allows us to develop a very different position to the code-is-syntax view revealed in the previous section. We have noted how the strata of grammar and semantics and that of discourse employ different mechanisms, including different forms of inference. Let us now set this out in more detail since we shall see that there is much here of relevance for film.

As noted in the quotation from Barthes above, linguistic theories in the 1960s and 1970s had already begun to concern themselves with *text as phenomenon*, i.e., extended stretches of language in context. But, since there was actually very little idea at that time what this entailed, explanations were sought 'outside' of the text—for example in this historical period, in common-sense reasoning and psychological processing. This orientation stretched throughout the 1970s and the early burgeoning of the field of text linguistics (cf. de Beaugrande, 1980; de Beaugrande and Dressler, 1981) and is still widespread today. However, although there can be no doubt that there are cognitive mechanisms of this kind operating, this is far from the full story.

Formal and functional work on dynamic semantics and discourse organisation (cf. Martin, 1992; Kamp and Reyle, 1993; Asher and Lascarides, 2003) has since changed the state of the art in discourse linguistics decisively. Many *text-internal* mechanisms are now known to operate in natural language texts to *precisely guide* processes of interpretation. As our examples of the previous chapter were intended to establish, it is now appropriate to consider the extent to which similar processes can usefully be posited for film.

Strong support for this line of investigation is provided by several of the properties now known to hold for discourse. To illustrate this, we will work through the principal mechanisms of the discourse stratum developed within the formal framework of Asher and Lascarides (2003) and then outline its extension to film. In Asher and Lascarides' account, incoming utterances are incorporated into an unfolding discourse by seeking out 'discourse relations' that serve to bind the new content with the 'old', already established content. Discourse relations act as mediators between the semantic commitments of linguistic form and the broader 'knowledge' of interlocutors and also include semantic commitments of their own that must be met (or assumed) in order to hold.

Meaning construction thus operates as a process of finding discourse relations to 'glue' contributions together. This is in stark contrast both to the compositionality found in syntax (the stratum below) and to the realm of common-sense reasoning, beliefs, mental states and problem solving (the stratum above). According to Asher and Lascarides, these distinct strata are best served by distinct logics with differing formal properties (cf. Asher and Lascarides, 2003: 431), thus providing again indirect evidence that these should indeed be maintained as separate strata.

The division of logics and strata allows the process of discourse interpretation to be restricted to just what is necessary to fill in certain 'gaps' created by linguistic forms and their sequential presentation in discourse. This provides a more plausible picture of how very similar interpretations of intent can be derived so quickly and so reliably by hearers during real-time discourse processing than some 'loose and tacit' body of conventions. To show the mechanism working in more detail, consider the following very simple example adapted from Asher and Lascarides (Asher and Lascarides, 2003: 90–95):

Peter fell. John pushed him.

In this 'mini-discourse', we have two semantic 'messages' that can be constructed on the basis of compositional semantics: one involving Peter falling down at some point in the past relative to the time of speaking/writing, and one involving John pushing Peter at some point in the past relative to the time of speaking/writing. To 'understand' the discourse, we have to see how these messages are related—i.e., we need to find appropriate discourse relations.

Whereas a 'common-sense' view might hypothesise that a hearer just tries to imagine the situation and see what 'makes sense', the fact that these messages are presented in sequence in a discourse *itself adds additional information*. The mechanisms of the discourse stratum provide substantially more guidance concerning just what 'possibilities' to check than those available in the common-sense view. In a narrative genre, for example, the 'default' discourse relation for combining sequences of sentences in unmarked past tense is *temporal succession*; in descriptive genres, the default is different. *Discourse* knowledge of applicable relations thus begins to organise and prioritise inferences of a very particular kind: in order to hold, the knowledge constraints of the postulated relation need to apply. In the present case, the knowledge commitments of the suggested discourse relation are straightforward: there must actually be a temporal succession of the events referred to. Thus, the first information to check in interpreting the mini-discourse is whether this plausibly or actually holds.

In the current example, it arguably does *not* hold since it is relatively common knowledge that pushing can lead to falling and not *vice versa*; falling therefore is most likely to follow pushing rather than preceding it. As a consequence, temporal succession then *fails* and the 'next on the list' of relevant discourse relations must be checked: this is, in this genre, the relation of *explanation*. The commitments of this relationship are a reversed temporal relationship: i.e., that the second, incoming message occurred *before* the first, established message. This does plausibly hold here and so we, and the hearer, can integrate the second utterance as an 'explanation' of what has just been said.

A discourse is taken to be 'coherent' when all its parts can be brought into relation to one another by means of applicable discourse relations. In the present case, finding the *explanation* relation to be applicable was then sufficient. Different approaches to discourse semantics may place additional constraints on how this binding together of messages may operate and on which particular discourse relations there are, but the general point remains: we now have a principled mechanism for the construction of meaning in discourse.

Crucially, this mechanism is, as evinced by our repeatedly writing of 'plausible' interpretations and of relations 'plausibly' holding, an essentially *defeasible* and *abductive* process of hypothesis construction (cf. Fann,

1970; Wirth, 2005). This level of interpretation then naturally intervenes between the semantic configurations delivered by compositional sentence semantics and the characterizations of general knowledge and rational action of a full contextualized interpretation, each described according to Asher and Lascarides within their own distinct kinds of logic (Asher and Lascarides, 2003: 431).

The role of discourse relations within the process of discourse interpretation is then one of guiding the construction of plausible accounts of what is meant. Unconstrained, such processes of interpretation would be in danger of resembling a free association of ideas, which is clearly a long way away from the kind of directed 'hypothesis building' that appears actually to occur. Abduction is an ideal mechanism for this. As Peirce describes it:

> "Abduction makes its start from the facts, without, at the outset, having any particular theory in view, though it is motived by the feeling that a theory is needed to explain the surprising facts. ... Abduction seeks a theory. Induction seeks for facts. In abduction the consideration of the facts suggests the hypothesis." (Peirce, *Collected Papers* §7.218)

That is, a discourse interpretation becomes a *theory* concerning the state of affairs that the discourse is constructing. Finding (at least) one theory is the condition that must hold for a discourse to be considered coherent.

Such theories may be quite complex and bring to bear a range of additional requirements and assumptions in order to be considered to hold. The details of these theories define the *minimal semantic commitments* that must be made for the discourse to be understood. We provide more detailed examples of this below.

For verbal language, there are many further arguments against the simple common-sense view of discourse interpretation as a more unguided inferential process. A particularly striking illustration is shown in the following 'mini-discourse':

Mary is annoyed. Fred ate soup last night.

Asher and Lascarides (2003: 438) point out that it is unlikely here that there is some already existing 'schema' or expectation that eating soup is particularly annoying. *But the implicit assertion of an explanation rhetorical relationship still appears to occur*. This suggests that it is the interaction of discourse relations and particular properties of the messages that are being combined that guides discourse interpretation. We do not simply have messages that need to be combined 'somehow'—the entire process is far more focused.

In the present case, there is a semantic requirement established lexically, i.e., by the meaning of 'annoy', that there can be a cause; not specifying the cause then leaves a 'gap' or 'hole' that can be filled not only syntactically (i.e., compositionally) within the same sentence, but also discoursally by an appropriate *discourse relation* via the mechanisms of discourse. This then leads directly to the 'theory' that the event of Fred's eating soup stands in some causal relationship (possibly indirect) to the event of Mary's becoming annoyed. The discourse under this interpretation is taken to *assert* the theory, even though no such assertion is explicitly present in the individual surface forms making up the discourse's sentences. That this combination is lexically constrained in the present case can be seen by the fact that many other events, although equally subject to causation, do *not* give rise so readily to this train of interpretation. The sequence:

Mary drank beer last night. Fred ate soup last night.

is far more likely to move interpretation towards an 'addition' of descriptive information than a postulation of explanation.

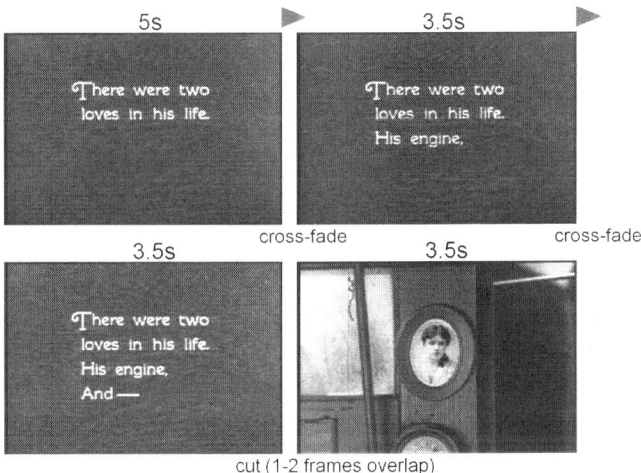

Figure 2.2   Sequence of intertitles from The General *(1926) starting at approximately 00:02:00*

Such semantic holes can be established in various ways and, central for us here, this can also operate *across modalities*. Figure 2.2 shows an early example of this that nicely combines the different aspects of concern: a series of intertitles from *The General* (1926) by Buster Keaton. The first two shots of the extract are held together by the linguistic resources of the discourse stratum. The sentence of the first shot indicates (cataphorically: i.e., looking *ahead* to what is coming: Halliday and Hasan 1976: 56) that the reader is likely to hear of "two loves". The second shot partially fills this in with the noun phrase "His engine": this is a rhetorical relationship of *elaboration*. The third shot then takes this further by adding "And". This could be analysed both syntactically and discoursally: either we have a syntactic and compositional addition to the previous noun phrase "His engine and..." or a further discourse extension; the consequences for the semantics are for current purposes equivalent. The dash following the "And" in the third shot indicates that there is a gap to be filled discoursally, this time by typographic means. And the fourth shot provides the final answer: but this time *visually*.

While what is occurring here should again, we trust, be perceived as straightforward, the mechanisms employed that *make* it straightforward need to be properly appreciated. As Asher and Lascarides show with respect to language, the combination of semantic contributions both discoursally and here across modalities is being finely guided by explicitly present cues in the artefact. There is no operation of 'common sense' necessary here. And this is crucial when the range of *potentially* relevant connections explodes—as it does with any normal discourse, both within language and within film.

When we move specifically into the visual track of film, we will see that semantic holes of this kind can be created in a variety of ways—probably the most well-known example being the *point of view* structure, in which a character's looking pointedly off-screen creates a gap for the next shot to show what was being looked at (cf. Branigan, 1984). The similarities between filling in linguistically incomplete structures and visually 'incomplete' structures have been discussed previously by van Leeuwen (1996); below we take this considerably further.

The actual discourse relations that are defined for natural language are rather more complex and numerous than we can show here. However, since our focus will be on *filmic* relations of this kind, we do not need to provide any more detail of the linguistic discourse stratum at this point. The general idea of the mechanism should now be clear. The essential advance that this view of discourse brings is that it becomes possible to explain formally within a rigorous linguistic framework how meaning can be constructed outside of the constraints of syntax.

This turns out to be critical for film. Earlier accounts often assumed that a 'syntax' was the precondition for meaning to be possible at all, since without a mechanism for *combining* meanings, any system would clearly be deficient. This assumption has subsequently surfaced in discussions of film in one of two ways: first, some authors have claimed that since film clearly does *not* have a syntax in this linguistic sense, then linguistically-inspired accounts cannot be adopted (cf. Currie 1995: 134; Currie 1997: 56); second, other authors have claimed that since film does make meanings then it must also have some kind of syntax analogous to language after all (cf. Chateau 1976, Carroll 1980, Möller-Naß 1986, Buckland 2000). The former accounts are, as we have now seen, simply outdated, while the latter accounts attribute inappropriate properties to film as such—we shall discuss this further in Chapter 3.

Modern approaches to the mechanisms developed for discourse semantics now describe in detail how meanings can be assigned to dynamically unfolding sequences of units *without* positing inherently problematic notions of 'text grammar' or syntax. Whereas there is no sense in which the kinds of meaning-making mechanisms operational in film resemble those of the compositional semantics found within sentences, they *do* resemble precisely the kinds of mechanisms that are observed in discourse. This advance, showing how meaning construction works in the face of moment-by-moment contingency, is arguably one of the most significant advances that linguistics, construed broadly, has made in recent years. The relevance of this for our current concerns is then that the architecture involved appears to reflect a property of complex semiotic systems in general.

The discussion here has been fairly condensed and technical. Let us therefore summarize once more the main points that have been made since it is these that provide the underlying foundation for the framework that the rest of the book develops. First, discourse interpretation relies centrally on a *distinct* level of discourse semantics with its own kinds of operations—operations which can only be described as a type of *inference*. We need then both the orientations of semiotic codes and of inference: they belong together. The question is not one of either/or, it is one of precisely *which kinds* of inference belong *where*. Within syntax and semantics, the inference is that of compositional semantics; within discourse, the inference is a kind of defeasible logic based on the Peircian notion of abduction (cf. Wirth, 2005). These mechanisms of discourse semantics do not reduce to general principles of intelligent behaviour or purposeful action.

Moreover, inference is involved in *all* kinds of discourse. For example, within the linguistic system, regardless of whether we are dealing with narrative, description, argument, or any other genre, the basic discourse organisational properties of the semiotic system do not change. This opens the door to a common consideration of *non*-narrative genres, a theme which is gradually receiving more attention both in the study of film (cf. Rieser, 2007) and in narratological studies more generally (cf. Wolf, 2007); many 'textual' properties attributed previously to narrative, including most famously the 'double temporal structuring' of text and story (cf. Chatman, 1978; Genette, 1980) also need to be considered across genres. In all cases, without the intervening level of a discourse stratum, discourse interpretation remains radically underconstrained and there can be little expectation that text interpreters would come to the highly focused and shared interpretations that they evidently do.

For language, the socio-semiotic and formal approaches to discourse strongly suggest the value of an additional stratum of discourse with its own resources and mechanisms, while more 'pragmatic'-oriented accounts, such as Relevance Theory (Sperber and Wilson, 1995), argue that common-sense reasoning will do the job on its own—a proposal commonly echoed for film (e.g., Bordwell, 2005; Currie, 1995, 2010). In the case of verbal language, however, we take the fact that Sperber and Wilson's account remains informal, 'philosophical' and descriptive of individual cases, whereas Asher and Lascarides' account, for example, is already supporting larger-scale automatic and semi-automatic derivation of discourse interpretations on a broader scale, to tell its own story. Indeed, whereas Relevance Theory opens up a host of open-ended interpretative problems that need to be resolved on the basis of assumed relevance, Asher and Lascarides' account "can determine exactly at what point we can stop performing inferences on the text" (Asher and Lascarides, 2003: 441); this interpretative boundary is precisely what we need to plausibly constrain 'lower-level' interpretative activity and usefully complements and constrains established notions of *narrative*, *diegetic* and *perceptual* completion (cf. Thompson, Noë and Pessoa, 1999; Bacon, 2011)

Guided discourse interpretation on the basis of discourse relations and an abductive logic of theory construction appear essential to make the entire process work—to *guide* the interpretation process appropriately. Therefore, although the lack of a discourse semantic stratum may appear simpler, it actually serves more to complicate unnecessarily our understanding of discourse interpretation.

2.3   The film as cinematographic document

Whereas in the previous section we discussed the motivation for building on a particular line of development within semiotics for addressing film, in this section we motivate the use of a body of knowledge that has not so far been widely applied to filmic analysis: that of **document**s.

This is beneficial for several reasons. As even our straightforward examples in the previous chapter have shown, we need to break down our objects of analysis quite finely, at least as far as 'shots' and, as we will see below, sometimes even further. This is, however, only half of the picture—unless we can put the parts back together again in appropriate ways, we have not really 'analysed' a film at all. Showing how films work will require us to bring mechanisms to bear that primarily have the role of *constructing* coherent structures and organisations from parts rather than segmenting.

We can consider film in general, therefore, as an artefact with articulated parts designed to be put back together in various ways by its users. This is one of the contributions that our adoption of mechanisms from document theory will provide. As we proceed through the book, we will present increasingly fine-grained definitions that constrain precisely what kinds of filmic document structures can be constructed on the basis of the filmic material at hand.

The material constituting the document parts and structures of a filmic document must then also be seen as providing access to 'information' otherwise no construction would be possible. This is typically the case for any semiotic object, of course: such objects function as complex 'signs' in the most primordial sense of pointing to 'something that is not there': they are therefore in essence *information-bearing*. Artefacts having precisely these properties have been the focus of the study of representing, constructing and providing access to documents for over thirty years. And, during this time, there has been increasing attention given particularly to *dynamic* and *time-dependent* documents. It is this area that is most specifically relevant for film and which we will build on here.

Making a connection between film and documents also has further useful consequences. The constructs that we now apply to film are drawn from a document framework that naturally includes a far broader range of artefacts than 'films' as traditionally conceived in film studies—this locates film, including both narrative and documentary films, against the broader background of video surveillance, video protocols of medical operations, visually-displayed temporally dependent information, interactive animations within hypermedia, and many more. Although we will not be addressing these kinds of documents in the present book, much of the basic framework we develop carries over to these documents and provides a strong foundation for their further study.

This also extends beyond the static-dynamic divide, drawing on commonalties in description that a modelling as documents naturally supports. For example, static visual documents employ a broad range of *spatially-*organised information, such as *page layout* (for further references, see the *Further Reading* section). This can then also be taken over for certain kinds of dynamic documents, including film. Most obviously, for example, a film may show information that is an example of a layouted page—even a shot of a newspaper or other 'printed' material, such as a graph in a news report or scientific film, requires viewers to employ their knowledge of the workings of static documents.

Alternatively, and more interestingly, individual shots in film can also employ the communicative resources of spatial 'page layout': this is typically discussed in the film literature only sporadically with respect to specific phenomena or specific films. For example, any explicit use of text incorporated within an image that is not a straightforward re-presentation of the 'story world' activates the communicative resources of layout; interpretations of such shots can sensibly call on treatments of how such spatial configurations work outside of film. Two examples of this kind of integrated usage of text are shown in Figure 2.3: the first taken from Esteban Sapir's *La antena* (2007), in which text that might 'normally' occur as intertitles often appears fully present in the diegetic world, the second from an early sequence in David Fincher's *Fight Club* (1999), which draws on intertextual and intermedial references to mail-order catalogues.

A film shot can also draw on the resources of spatial layout for its visual presentation *as a whole*—most obviously in the case of *split screen* where the screen is divided into several areas, each of which depicts its own visual material (Wulff, 1991; Garwood, 2008). This *spatial phenomenon* carries over from static documents to dynamic documents: that is, in order to

La Antena (2007, 01:19:25)

Fight Club (2007, 00:04:58)

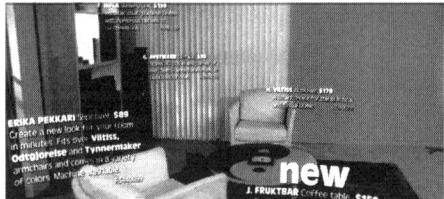

Figure 2.3   Integrated text-image scenes from Esteban Sapir's La antena *(2007) and David Fincher's* Fight Club *(1999)*

relate the various parts of the screen, viewers can draw freely on those relationships known for relating spatially distinguished elements within static documents—such as contrast, elaboration, comparison, labelling, etc.

There is much more to be studied here, particularly as technological advances have made it as straightforward to combine dynamic elements in spatial relationships on the page/screen as has now long been the case for static elements. And, as always, the addition of the temporal dimension adds considerably to the range of effects that can be pursued—effects ranging, for example, from the shot-by-shot changing sizes and arrangements of individually framed scenes that became the hallmark of the US TV series *24* (cf. Allen, 2007) to the complete dynamic interweaving of regular and irregular 'frames' in Ang Lee's *Hulk* (2003). Figure 2.4 reproduces a representative example from each; the segment from *Hulk* shows a telephone conversation between two of the main characters (played by Sam Elliott and Jennifer Connelly) in two different locations, *not* a single location occupied by two people; several further examples of this kind are discussed by Prince (2007: 142). In both the cases of *24* and *Hulk*, however, the fact that we can only show a static image on the page detracts considerably from the main innovations involved, since these are essentially dynamic.

24, Season 3, Episode 5pm-6pm: 41:20

Hulk (2003, 2:05:36)

Figure 2.4   Dynamic split screens from the US TV-series 24 *and Ang Lee's* Hulk *(2003)*

Much of the framework that we will be building on as we proceed draws on work on hypermedia presentations and standardisation attempts for describing video form and content as pursued within technical bodies such as the Motion Picture Expert Group (MPEG) and the World-Wide Web working groups on multimedia presentations. Here we find proposals for standardised specifications aimed at allowing timing, layout, animations, visual transitions, and media embedding, etc. to be captured and reproduced. In many respects these specifications can be seen as an extension of the language used for web pages, expanded so as to deal with the complexities of time-based presentations. Our account makes direct contact with these developments and so can be considered as an extension of such approaches particularly targeting the demands of film analysis. Many aspects of these schemes can, moreover, be directly imported for detailed film analysis as they offer explicit characterisations of image qualities, camera movements, audio qualities and much besides (cf. Martínez, 2002*a*). We will not, however, provide any details of these frameworks here; we will focus instead on just those aspects useful for our immediate concerns. These will be presented independently of any specific standardisation efforts.

The appeal to principles of document description also applies at an abstract level related to film's nature as a *designed* artefact. This is an interesting point of difference to considerations of film in terms of language—utterances are not designed in a similar sense. Processes of design typically work with already 'externalised' fragments and more naturally tend to 'multiple authorship': a complex designed artefact may reflect the contributions of many who, to a greater or lesser degree, exert a shaping influence on the final result. This is one of the reasons why authorship is commonly considered to be a contested notion for film; its origins in the idealised literary case, where the creative writer is alone responsible for their work, does not simply transfer to filmic production. Useful discussions of the differences are given by, for example, Livingston (1997) and Gaut (2010: Chapter 3, 99–151).

A very general characterisation of this combined collective decision-making standing behind the creation of any film is provided by the document process of *layouting*. This is an abstract mechanism that applies equally to both static and dynamic media and which offers a powerful conceptual tool for setting out quite explicitly the kind of segmentations that film, and other media, regularly employ. A detailed characterisation of the layouting process will form a major part of the model we present. This will allow us to describe the structural properties of all forms of filmic segmentation, or *montage*, within a general framework that naturally includes spatial and temporal considerations.

We return to the layouting process in a moment, since first we must introduce the basic components of a document in order to describe where and how layouting fits within this.

2.3.1   Three general perspectives on documents

For documents in general one can essentially adopt three perspectives: the **content view**, the **logical view**, and the **layout view**. These perspectives are suggested graphically in Figure 2.5. In this section, we will characterise them in general and then in Chapters 5 and 7 work with them for capturing the specifics of films.

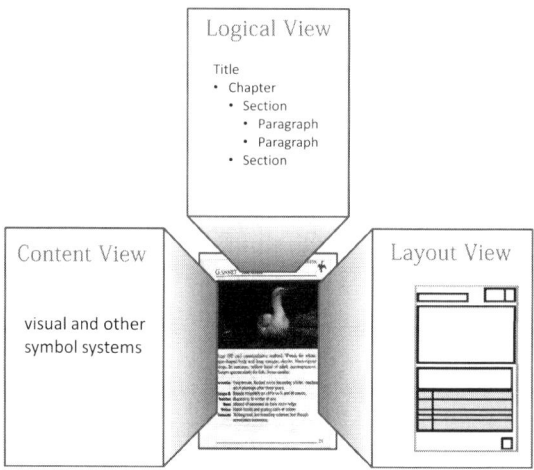

Figure 2.5   Three basic perspectives on a document

The content view perspective covers the 'typical observer' interest in a document: that is, assuming for now a range of presumedly intended 'readers', what these readers will generally orient towards will be the 'represented content' of the document. Although much can be said about such content, in this book we will only consider this view to the extent that it is relevant for building our analytic framework for the moving image. From the document perspective, the notion of content used corresponds to the body of material that has, by some means, been selected for presentation within some document; with respect to the document, therefore, it can be seen as 'pre-existing' and the main question concerns the organisation that is imposed upon it in order to construct a document.

We will impose constraints on the kind of content that is admissible as we proceed. For example, and to begin, since we will be focusing exclusively on filmic documents in this book, the content will be taken to be 'raw' recordings or creations of some pro-filmic material. This can be taken as corresponding loosely to the various 'takes' produced during filming before being edited into their appearance in the final film. For film, therefore, the 'shot' serves as a typical example of a content portion.

Such content portions may be constituted by material of different kinds. All that is required for current purposes, however, is that we can assume that these content portions 'contain' or 'point to' the desired content in some sense. We will also assume that this content can, at least in principle, be 'labelled' with respect to some place of occurrence and a time of occurrence. Such labelling may be specific (New York, Times Square, 3am-4am, 23rd January 2010) or generic ('the kitchen', sometime before lunch). The content therefore makes available particular 'space-time slices' of some real or created world. Content portions may then themselves also have internal structure; this can be pursued both formally, in that a space-time slice may be made up of 'smaller' space-time slices, or in terms of the content, i.e., there may be particular objects, events, actors, locations, etc. identifiable in the material.

For material to become useful as a document, it is necessary to provide its users (either human or machine) with a way of structuring its content. This is achieved first by imposing a *logical* organisation on that content. This logical view in essence covers part-whole relationships, groups content portions into larger structures of related content, and is typically modelled as a tree structure. In a text such as this one, for example, the logical view models such properties as a sentence considered as a part of a paragraph, the paragraph as part of a chapter, a chapter as part of the entire book, and so on. For characterising the overall structural organisation of a document, it is the logical view that is decisive and 'prior'. For film, the logical organisation might then characterise 'scenes' as grouped into 'acts' and 'acts' as making up the entire film (i.e., viewed dramaturgically, cf. Kawin, 1992: 68–69, 243). Much of the work of *basic film interpretation* will come down to reconstructing the logical organisation on the basis of the audiovisual material presented to the viewer.

Finally, to make a document 'readable' for human observers, there is the further step of selecting a particular *layout* for the logical organisation. This 'renders' the content of a document for presentation on some 'output device', or display medium, such as a sheet of paper, a display screen, etc. Thus, in our view, any document is seen as a collection of logically organised content that is rendered appropriately for display in some output medium.

The actual rendering, i.e., selecting and converting content portions, is where the *layouting process* plays its role. This process is responsible for allocating content to particular forms of presentation and allocating these to, for visual documents, geometrically describable layout objects that can then be displayed on the output medium. Typically, such presentations are also more or less richly structured; the result of the layouting process we accordingly term a **layout structure**. Any document artefact, in our case film, is therefore to be seen as the result of performing a layouting process. This determines the final form of the presentation as accessible to its recipients.

Both the logical view and the layout view allow decompositions. In both cases these are seen as hierarchical tree organisations, consisting of tree 'nodes' that may be further divided up into 'dependent nodes'. This leads for both perspectives to three distinct *types* of objects:

- a root node of a document, which we call the **document logical root** or the **document layout root** respectively depending on which perspective the tree structure is representing;

- terminal nodes, i.e., nodes at the leaves of the tree, which we term **basic logical objects** or **basic layout objects** respectively;

- all other nodes that lie between the root and the terminal nodes, which we term **composite logical objects** or **composite layout objects** as appropriate.

It is the layouting process that relates the two perspectives to one another: i.e., each layouting process produces from the logical tree a corresponding layout tree. For time-based documents such as film, it is this layouting process that is responsible for the serialisation of pieces of content that are to be represented in the output medium. Constraining these general structures will provide us with the very fine-grained characterisation of filmic organisation we need for detailed analysis.

A layouting process can in general consider several simultaneous 'streams' of output that then converge in a final artefact—in book production, for example, one stream might serve for page headers containing chapter names that reoccur on each page (as in this book), while another stream might consider the 'actual' contents. Examples from film include cases where there are one or more sets of subtitles being given, or if the screen is split functionally in some other way—as in Mike Figgis' *Timecode* (2000), which employs four continuous audiovisual streams shown within a 2×2 grid. Distinguishing output streams in this way simplifies the overall description of the layouting process considerably. For current purposes, however, we will primarily consider layouting processes that operate with respect to a *single* output stream. Since this stream can itself be multimodal—i.e., both sound and image may be combined within a single stream—the restriction will not constrain us too much concerning the kinds of 'filmic documents' that we address.

Making the particular assumption of a single stream at this point then allows us to start with an account where an observer only accesses one 'film-image'—although this 'image' may also extend over various time extents depending on the granularity that is adopted. Since below the 'observer' will play a central part in our framework, it is useful to begin our development of the framework with this constraint in place. By this means we avoid for the time being the problems introduced by non-sequential access to content—as commonly found, for example, in the layout of content on the two-dimensional page in printed or electronic documents and, in film, as soon as split screen or similar techniques are employed.

2.3.2 Time-based documents and their use as a description for films

We have so far introduced three perspectives that can be taken on documents of all kinds and discussed in general terms the individual organisations presumed within these perspectives and the relations between them. For filmic artefacts we naturally focus on documents where time plays a central role. On the one hand, the material constituting the content portions of the document generally unfolds in time and, on the other, this content is also presented on an output medium as a temporal stream. This is related to the classical distinction made in accounts of narrative concerning 'story time' and 'narrative time' (cf. Chatman, 1978; Genette, 1980); in some respects we can see the document-based distinction as a 'technical reconstruction' of this basic property of texts. Its formalisation within the document perspective will allow us to be very precise about the possibilities involved.

To begin, we can adopt definitions compatible within the MPEG-7 standard (Martínez, 2002a: §3.1.3), which is a metadata toolbox especially designed for audiovisual documents. A very general construct there is the **segment**, defined as some 'section of an audiovisual content item'. Such segments have considerable internal complexity and carry both spatial and temporal properties, as well as indications of regions, shapes, audio and so on. A segment is therefore a result of some spatial, temporal or spatio-temporal partitioning of the audiovisual content.

In the general case, such segments may include components that may be spatiotemporally connected or non-connected. Spatial connectivity is seen here in a very restricted sense in that the connectivity has to be *explicitly present in the visual image*; temporal connectivity is similarly restricted— here referring to preservation of consecutive video frames or audio samples taken from the audiovisual content; we provide more details of the use of such connectivities during analysis in Chapter 7 below.

Particular segments associated with audiovisual content may be further decomposed into subsegments. Again, in the general case, this can result in quite complex organisations. For example, this is where it is determined which pieces of content can be rendered as 'neighbours' (both spatially and temporally) on the output medium. For any filmic document it can then be asked whether a segment as a layouted temporally ordered collection of shots can also include gaps and whether segments can overlap.

Figure 2.6, adapted from the MPEG-7 standard (Martínez, 2002a: Figure 9), shows four exhaustive possibilities for the decomposition of an arbitrary time-based parent segment (including therefore entire films) into dependent segments. The principles generating the different alternatives are whether or not the child segments completely cover the time extent of the parent segment and whether or not some time segments are presented more than once, giving rise to temporal overlaps. Cases (a) and (b) show cases where there are no gaps; cases (b) and (d) show cases where there are

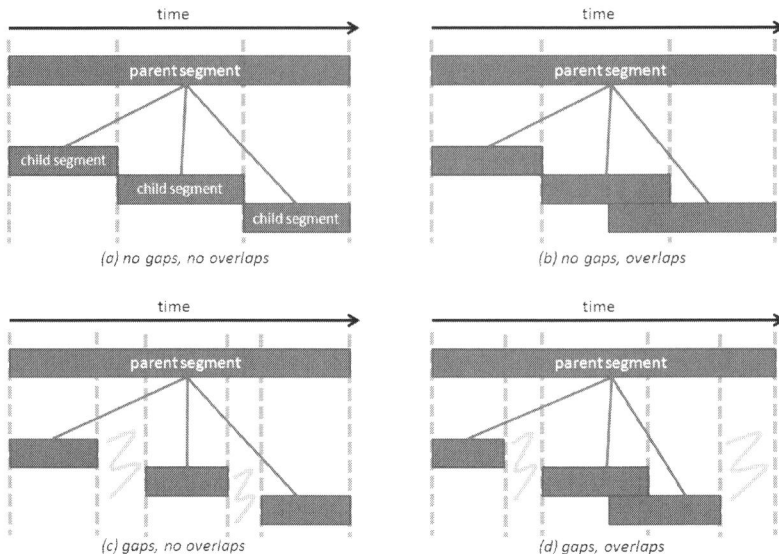

Figure 2.6   Logical possibilities for dividing a parent audiovisual content node across child nodes (adapted from Martínez, 2002a: Figure 9)

overlaps; and so on. When the child nodes in the tree completely cover the extent of the parent, they are said to *partition* the parent. In the first case, therefore, we see a straightforward decomposition where a continuous and 'gap-free' segment is broken down into three subsegments that collectively entirely cover the parent segment; in the second, the three subsegments also cover the parent segment but with overlap; in the third material is omitted from the parent; and in the fourth there is both omission of some material and other material shown twice.

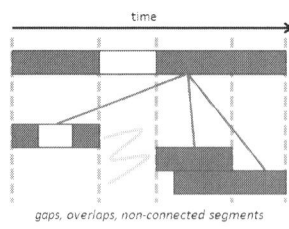

Figure 2.7

Complex segment decomposition

In addition, any individual segment can also be either *connected* or *non-connected*. This means that a single segment may contain temporal gaps. During the layouting process, therefore, a segment may be constructed as a node which introduces 'internal' gaps within itself. A complex example given by Martinez is illustrated in Figure 2.7. Both the originating parent segment and one of the child segments are non-connected. Thus the parent segment is divided into three subsegments, one of which itself contains a gap, and two others whose temporal durations overlap. The dependent subsegments do not partition the parent and so the entire configuration also exhibits a gap.

Spelling out these alternatives serves two purposes: on the one hand, it shows something of the considerable complexity inherent in the *form* of such artefacts and, on the other, it also shows that we can nevertheless characterise this complexity quite precisely. Particularly the latter property will be of considerable utility below when we characterise the alternatives taken up in film and explore their functions. The segmentation process shown here can be continued indefinitely: that is, each subsegment produced can itself be further segmented by a layouting process in the same way, potentially introducing further gaps, non-connected segments and overlaps. The final state reached represents a layout structure defining a collection of ordered, possibly overlapping basic layout objects in the sense defined above.

The alternatives discussed here have been derived from the general possibilities offered by the decomposition of a document and so can also be taken to cover the possibilities of film in general. For a specific classification of the options actually taken up in film, however, we need to provide further constraints. To get us started in formulating these constraints, we can begin with the most simple film imaginable, a recording of some continuous slice of the spatial-temporal world with a stationary camera and unchanging lens properties. Examples would include *actualités* of the Lumière brothers showing everyday events such as factory workers leaving a factory in *La sortie des usines Lumière* (1895) or a train arriving at a station in *L'arrivée d'un train à La Ciotat* (1896), as well as straightforward cases of video surveillance. A first attempt at a definition of a **cinematographic document** would then insist that the following conditions hold:

- each basic document logical object can be assigned to at least one audiovisual content portion,
- a layouting process exists which generates a basic layout object for at least one audiovisual content portion of each basic logical object of the document.

This guarantees that a 'delivery' path exists between the originating audiovisual content and a layouted document that provides access to that content. For all more complex variations introduced by editing practices of any kind, however, we will need additional constraints.

Let us then divide one of the *actualités* into *two* segments, assuming for the present that nothing is actually left out as covered by case (a) in Figure 2.6. It is then the task of the layouting process to determine precisely how these shots are included within the final document. Therefore we need to insist that the presentation of the shots is not just 'left open' but will take on a specific determinate order. Note that this is independent of any chronological ordering present in the material being presented: this is purely to do with the *presentation* time. If the layouting process does not enforce this, then we are dealing with some media *other than film*, such as, for example, a multimedia installation or perhaps some hypermedia presentation. For *cinematographic documents*, it needs to be the case that the layout enforces a strict temporal order of presentation on the set of all shots present in a document.

Combining these considerations gives us our first formal characterisation of what we will be considering to fall under cinematographic documents. Such documents must in general meet the following *definition*:

Definition 2.1   *A document is termed* **cinematographic** *if,*

1. *each basic document logical object can be assigned to at least one audiovisual content portion of the document,*
2. *a layouting process exists which, for each basic logical object, generates a basic layout object for at least one of the audiovisual content portions associated with that logical object,*
3. *the document is* linearly layoutable *with this layouting process, i.e., the set of content portions can be assigned to a set of basic layout objects that are totally ordered (spatially and/or temporally) by the layouting process.*

This is sufficiently general to apply both to all physical manifestations of films, whether on reels or as electronic documents, and to all 'kinds' of films, ranging from single-shot films up to arbitrarily complex variations introduced by more or less sophisticated segmentations. It also illustrates the method of development that we begin with in Chapter 5 and then unfold in considerable detail in Chapter 7, in which we will progressively introduce finer and finer definitions that allow us to pinpoint the particular kinds of filmic organisations employed in film. Our analyses will then draw on the application of the definitions given, which will place considerable constraint on what analyses can be offered. Accordingly, for ease of reference, we gather all the definitions developed over the course of the book together in Appendix A at the end of the book.

2.4   A combined view: filmic documents for filmic discourse

In this final section of the chapter, we provide a first example of how the various contributions introduced so far can come together to form a unified account. We began above by relating a substantial number of arguments and debates between different approaches to film in the past to a lack of appropriate differentiation in the models of semiotic systems adopted. We do not believe it possible *not* to assume a model of the semiotic system involved—the only difference is whether this is done explicitly or implicitly. Debates continue over such basic divisions as realism/formalism, interpretation/meaning, code/interpretation, sentence/text, grammar/discourse, language/film and many more—these are not only core issues for any account of film, however: they are also core *semiotic* issues. This demonstrates just how central an appropriate semiotic model is. Simplified accounts of complex semiotic systems collapse distinctions in ways that often render the remaining discussions inherently flawed.

We have suggested that the single most far-reaching simplification of this kind that has hindered progress hitherto is a lack of an appropriate consideration of the fundamentally different contributions of *grammar* and *discourse* when considered as abstract components of a semiotic system. Much of our discussion in the rest of this book is therefore tailored particularly to bringing out the role played by these semiotic levels in relation to a semiotic system as a whole and to film in particular. This means that, building on the accounts of discourse developed for the linguistic system, we can now take up again the task of investigating *filmic discourse*. For this, we need to uncover precisely the mechanisms which pick out certain technical features of film to guide particular interpretations rather than others.

We have argued that this is more than general 'problem solving', or an application of general schemata: it is in addition part of the particular way in which film *works as a mode of discourse*. This should help tell us more about how viewers can process even novel depictions in film that may not conform to ready made schemata. Just as appears to be the case with language, the deployment of discourse constructions may be seen as the guide that keeps interpretations on track. Under this view, then, only when we have added this aspect to our analytic framework will we really be in a position to say that we have understood how films are making the meanings they do.

Sometimes attempts to tie down the process of interpretation of the less abstract technical details of film in this way are argued to devalue the active role of the interpreter, the creative act of constructing meanings for the work seen, and thereby run the danger of falling back to earlier, less developed periods of film theory. But this is again to overlook the very different kinds of interpretative work going on with respect to film, collapsing together distinct layers of semiotic abstraction that need to be distinguished. We see any conclusion of the form that because texts can be interpreted differently by individual readers, then there are no statements that can be sensibly made concerning elements and relationships within texts that are largely independent of individual readers, as fundamentally flawed. Showing the relative stability of less abstract semiotic strata is, in fact, one crucial way of bringing out just how distinct 'voices', social positions, presuppositions, etc. can be orchestrated within 'single' texts.

We have already seen examples of the way in which distinct levels of interpretation are required in our discussions of film extracts in Chapter 1. In the portion of *The Marriage of Maria Braun* (1979) that we discussed, for example, there was a quite distinctive construction of interpretative *uncertainty*; it is then important to situate such uncertainty at the appropriate level. The extended unmoving shot of the gas cooker shown in the segment (cf. Figure 1.4, shot 3) made it quite clear that no secret was being made about the possibility of an impending explosion: the film *tells the viewer* that the gas is still on and that it was Maria Braun's deliberate action that caused it to be left on.

Note that this is *not* a matter of subjective interpretation; any viewers who do not draw this inference from the filmic material have not understood what they have seen. This can certainly arise: for example, the viewer may not know what a gas cooker is, or that gas is highly flammable if collected together in sufficient quantities, etc.; but the film in no way indicates that it is expecting its viewers not to be in possession of such everyday contextual knowledge. Then, in stark contrast to this, the film does *not* tell the viewer whether this was suicide or not, despite some indications in this direction, or a socially-programmed act of self-destruction, as perhaps Scharf (2008) might argue. Thus, although the filmic cue is unambiguous, this by no means implies that all interpretations following for the film are determined.

What the film does, which is even more interesting, is to open up a precise area of uncertainty: was the explosion deliberate or not? That is: the film has been structured to ask a question. This uncertainty is not the uncertainty that might arise if we just did not know what had happened in the house and there was suddenly an explosion. The filmic construction of the segment *precisely raises both the question and the uncertainty around its answer*—as Bordwell (1985: 228) observes, a typical convention of 'art cinema'.

We can now develop this further using the results of the present chapter. To show such effects at work, we can posit two levels of interpretation: the information that is communicated filmically and directly, and the subsequent interpretations that a viewer may make drawing on these (and other) sources of information. In this way, we can see that fixing the interpretative contribution of filmic constructions on the basis of fine-grained technical detail in no sense precludes subsequent, possibly divergent interpretations of knowledge, motives, and so on. Indeed, it is the fine-grained analysis that establishes the basis for such interpretations, both for the analyst and for the viewer.

It is worthwhile emphasising this point even further. Some introductions to film talk of both 'micro' and 'macro' analysis: the former requiring more or less fine-grained analyses of what appears on-screen and the latter delving more into interpretation and significance. It is stated that the macro should depend on the micro but, equally, that it is often not possible to carry out the micro without considering the general themes, narrative arcs, evaluations and genre-relations attributed to the film as a whole. The result is that there is no clear method for relating the two levels of analysis—on the one hand, high-level interpretations appear accompanied by bits and pieces taken from the micro analysis whenever they appear beneficial for supporting the interpretative claims being developed and, on the other hand, micro-level details come sprinkled with interpretative additions that can only be drawn from a prior interpretation of the entire film. This state of affairs obscures considerably the 'how' of filmic meaning-making: low-level details suddenly crop up attributed with far more meaning than can reasonably be read off what is occurring while, at the same time, the sources of these attributed meanings float under-constrained by the details on-screen.

The decoupling of the macro and the micro then too often leaves low-level descriptions as more or less complex 'recounts' of what can be seen and heard—recounts, moreover, that are readily prone to an inadvertent skewing to support the interpretations being pursued. For some film theorists, the logical conclusion here is that the lower-level details are actually so subservient to the broader goals that they cannot sensibly be isolated without the macro already in place. Although some approaches are happy to embrace a state of affairs in which we have to know what we are seeing before we can see it, we consider this to render the working of film far more mysterious than is warranted.

To show these considerations in action with a rather more complex example, we present a preliminary treatment of a case well-known in the film literature: the 'button-pressing' segment from Orson Welles' *The Lady from Shanghai* (1947). In several articles including discussion of this film segment, George Wilson uses the analysis to argue against the possibility of approaching filmic meaning in a 'bottom-up' fashion based on the technical details observable in individual shots (Wilson, 1986, 1995). As Wilson concludes:

> "As in actual perception, these judgements about the content of the film will normally not be the rule-governed upshot of features depicted within the shots. ...if these considerations are correct—if even our rock-bottom judgements about the *identity of objects and events* within a film fail to satisfy the model of units and structural laws—then it is hard to grasp how more sophisticated judgements about filmic content and signification can reasonably be expected to satisfy the model either. The example from *The Lady from Shanghai* is useful because of the intuitive simplicity of the content in question. It thereby illustrates the hopelessness of finding some more fundamental 'level' where the projective account might finally take purchase on the film." (Wilson, 1995: 63, original emphasis)

Here again we find traces of the syntactic model criticised above: the 'projective account' refers to some notion of compositional syntactic construction. Wilson's point in some respects then reduces to the observation that one cannot create high-level interpretations by syntactically composing 'objects' and 'events' found at some lower level. This, while no doubt true, does not support his other conclusions about the non-existence of levels.

The essence of the interpretations at issue is that the segment appears to be so constructed to lead to an interpretation where the main female character has consequential effects on the real world, including a car crash, simply by pressing some buttons on an intercom-like device in the drawing room of her home:

> "it appears as if the pressing of the button has mysteriously caused the accident." (Wilson, 1986: 1)

The problem then discussed is that although this interpretation cannot literally be true—there is no physical or psychic action-at-a-distance involved that could bring about such a state of affairs—there is nonetheless some level of interpretation where this supports the overall story in which this character emerges as a schemer of schemes, setting the men around her on various errands whose real purpose they remain largely oblivious of. Wilson's problem is then that it is only possible to draw on this larger-scale interpretation when the analysis takes into consideration the narrative structures and purposes of the film as a whole; otherwise we would not know that this interpretation is a relevant one for the film. Although there are many valuable points made in the rest of Wilson's analysis, this overall claim is unjustified and even obscures how analysis can sensibly proceed.

A further treatment of the segment, building in part on Wilson's, is provided by Edward Branigan, who observes that Wilson's description in terms of just three shots (truck pulling out in front of car, woman pressing button, car hitting truck) actually simplifies the segment at issue considerably (Branigan, 1992: 39). Branigan identifies 15 shots constituting the segment, which tallies with our own viewing; key frames of these shots are shown in Figure 2.8 in order to follow through our reconstruction of the analysis in detail.

Just before this segment starts, one of the male characters in the film (the private detective Broome, played by Ted de Corsia) has been shot in the garden of the house and we have seen various characters' reactions to the sound. Then, in the first shot of the fragment, we see the main female character, Elsa Bannister (Rita Hayworth), the eponymous lady from Shanghai, coming towards the camera and about to press some button on a device on a low table in the foreground; in the second shot, we see that this device is one for calling servants in various rooms around the house and Elsa presses the button for the kitchen. The third shot then cuts to the kitchen where the man who has been shot crawls through the opening door and across the floor towards the camera. In the fourth shot, Elsa looks into the middle distance and presses a button again. Shot 5 then cuts back to a view of a car driving by, a car that we had seen two of the main male characters driving off in just prior to shot 1. Shot 6 accordingly shows the two characters (Michael O'Hara, played by Orson Welles, and George Grisby, played by Glenn Anders) sitting in front seats of the car and shot 7 presents their point-of-view driving along the dark road. Shot 8 cuts to a truck pulling out of a side-turning and shot 9 shows us the truck coming into view, presumably also as a point-of-view from the car as in shot 7. In shot 10 we see again a finger pressing the button for the kitchen.

Figure 2.8 *The 15 shots constituting the 'button-pressing' segment from Orson Welles'* The
Lady from Shanghai *(1947, 00:49:20)*

Shot 11 then presents a close-up of a board of indicators, presumably showing which room is calling for the servants' attention followed by shot 12 where the man who has been shot climbs up into frame in front of the board now in the background. Shot 13 shows the two figures in the car reacting in shock to the upcoming collision, previewed in shot 14 by rapidly approaching the back of the truck, and shot 15 concludes the segment with the windscreen of the car being smashed.

There are, as Wilson and Branigan note, several distinct interpretations that one could make both of what is occurring in this segment and of its particular *style* of presentation for the narrative as a whole—indeed, one could without effort extend the range of potential interpretations significantly. However, just as was the case with our *The Marriage of Maria Braun* example discussed above, there are also commitments being made here by virtue of the fragment's *form* and these cannot be seen to be subject to the same degree of intersubjective variability. Just as a particular selection of shots made an unmistakable assertion in *The Marriage of Maria Braun*, here as well a similar uncertainty is directly *asserted* by the film.

To show this, our analysis starts with a precise characterisation of what is being depicted in the segment. We accordingly treat the fragment as an extract from a cinematographic document and consider its component segments within the distinct document views we introduced above. In terms of the logical organisation as motivated in part by their spatio-temporal contents, we distinguish four logical segments: one in the drawing room, one in the kitchen, one on the road and one in the car. These contents are, in the present case, unproblematically present in the image material itself and so are straightforward to follow.

Figure 2.9

Establishing the kitchen locale in The Lady from Shanghai *(1947)*

The two male figures are seen arriving in the car and are shown again getting into the car and driving off just prior to this segment; for this reason we will simplify the discussion a little at this point and combine the internal and external views concerning the car. The kitchen locale has been introduced before as well: one of the male characters, Michael O'Hara, sits in it until he, too, hears the shot that the other fires (cf. Figure 2.9). And the drawing room is established by having Elsa Bannister run into the darkened room to look out of the window at the sound of the shot (cf. Figure 2.10). Dramatic background music runs throughout the segment from the sound of the shot until when the two male characters get back into the car, and then picks up again with the segment shown in the main figure above.

The content portions of this part of the film are shown approximately synchronised in Figure 2.11. The three horizontal bars represent the principal settings we have identified. In the final document of the film only

Figure 2.10   Establishing the drawing room locale in The Lady from Shanghai *(1947)*

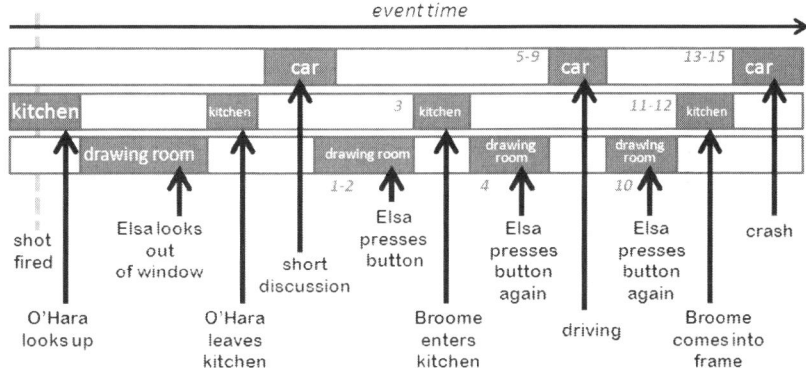

Figure 2.11   Content portions corresponding to the 'button-pushing' segment in The Lady from Shanghai *(1947)*

portions of these time-slices are actually shown; therefore, for the purposes of describing the film here, whether these portions were filmed continuously and then segmented to produce non-connected segments in a first stage of layouting or filmed in distinct takes is of no consequence; the description could naturally be refined with a detailed shooting script. The blocks filled in show the actual shots or film segments present in the final document, identified loosely by their content and labelled with the shot numbers used in Figure 2.8 above.

It can also be noted here that some of the temporal relations are not necessarily clear: for example, the short discussion in the car immediately preceding our extracted segment leaves perhaps rather more time than necessary for Elsa to get across the drawing room from the window to the button device and so there may be some temporal overlap involved. A similar uncertainty occurs immediately following the extract, a shot showing Elsa finding the mortally wounded Broome in the kitchen: the seconds shown in the track concerning the car would scarcely give her time to get from the drawing room to the kitchen. These are probably motivations for the fact that both this latter shot and shot 1 are introduced by a rapid *cross-fade* rather than appearing with sharp cuts as in the other shot transitions: they thus may also be taken as indicating slight segment boundaries.

Given these locales and their logical organisation, it is the task of the layouting process to ensure an ordered rendering of these in a viewable document, i.e., the film. This can be done in many different ways as suggested in our discussion of segmentation in the previous section. The first communicative task to be achieved is to signal their simultaneity: this can also be done in many ways although no doubt the most well established is by cross-cutting. Just like any other technical device, however, this is not an unambiguous expression of temporality: as we will set out in detail in subsequent chapters, its commitment is more 'abstract' and 'text-internal'. *Alternations* of this kind actually express a notion of 'comparison', a demand of the viewer that they compare the segments being presented in some way. If no common grounds can be found to motivate the comparison, then the alternation will not be perceived to work smoothly. This is a kind of filmic discourse relation, requiring that the viewer construct a particular kind of theory to make it hold. In this case, the theory that needs to be constructed is that some *shared* configuration of relationships can be found or hypothesised to glue the segments contributing to the alternation together. Such configurations can be temporal, but can also be based on other relations.

We can characterise, for now informally, the result of the layouting process invoked in the present case as shown graphically in Figure 2.12. The task then presented to a viewer is to recognise the systematicity of the alternation as soon as it becomes visible that there is an alternation at work. When we consider the transition from shot 2 to shot 3, it is difficult, as both Wilson and Branigan observe, to avoid at least some suspicion of causality. A clear movement in one shot is followed within a fraction of a second by an equally clear movement in another shot; this interpretation is probably even stronger nowadays than it was when the film was made since it is now far more usual to have things happen 'at the push of a button'. This notwithstanding, the transition here is extremely sudden: there is no view of the door not in movement before Broome pushes through it; it is already in movement as the shot begins. There is then almost a 'match-on-action' constructed—i.e., when an action is begun in one shot and a similar action is continued in the next—despite the actions being unrelated.

There are also further links between the two shots that increase their connectedness: the button pressed is clearly labelled 'kitchen' and we know that the room involved in shot 3 is indeed the kitchen. The filmic construction here is therefore strongly proposing to the viewer that there is some connection between events, regardless of any support this may have in the world of the story. We would predict that if the first pushing of a button were followed instead immediately by, for example, shot 5, with the car speeding by, the suggestion of causal connections would be very

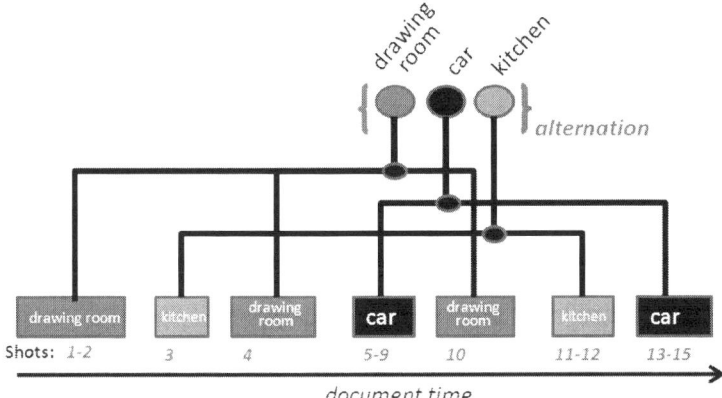

Figure 2.12   Layout structure corresponding to the 'button-pushing' segment in The Lady from Shanghai *(1947)*

much weaker if present at all, despite Wilson's discussion of his three-shot simplification in much these terms.

Our approach in contrast suggests that it is only the fact that Wilson's three-shot version is embedded within the actual alternation that our layout structure shows that his analysis becomes plausible. *Once a causal relationship has been suggested*, it is not so easy to retract. The discourse relation of alternation requires a relationship to hold over transitions, and the first transition from shot 2 to shot 3 offers us causality. The next transition from shot 4 to shot 5 must necessarily be coloured by this prioritisation of expectations. Moreover, in the third transition, from shot 10 to shot 11, the relationship *is* one of causation: the indicator on the board is presumably showing the room in which the button is being pressed. The local structure of this segment is then very much one in which causation is asked to play a significant role in the theory of events that a viewer has to construct to achieve coherence.

This is then similar to the interpretations reached by both Wilson and Branigan, but our more explicit allocation of the steps in that interpretation to distinct levels of abstraction allows us to sidestep particularly Wilson's negative conclusions concerning the viability of detailed analysis. Wilson sees the two interpretations that (1) in this segment we just have two unrelated depicted events intercut (the pressing of the button and the car) and that (2) in this segment we have the woman 'causing' bad events in some mysterious way, to be completely irreconcilable and to require a consideration of the film as a whole:

"The moral is that it is impossible to resolve a question of segmentation as elementary as the choices between (1) and (2) independently of a thorough analytical viewing of the total film. In this extreme but instructive case, we cannot even identify the *simpler fictional occurrences* in the film without an appeal to the widest framework that contains the problematic three [sic] shots. If this is so, then, it must be a mistake to believe or hope that segmentation can be treated as prior to, and foundational for, interpretation. In general, the way in which we will be inclined to divide a stretch of film into 'interacting levels and units' will rest on large problems about how narrative, narration, and associated aspects of structure are to be construed." (Wilson, 1995: 62)

This conclusion is ill-founded. Our segmentation of the film drew on notions of how a cinematographic document is constructed and the audiovisual information presented in that document. This segmentation is not dependent on our 'inclinations' to analyse the narration in one way or another.

Although this might appear at first glance to fly in the face of more hermeneutic approaches to interpretation, particularly of literary interpretation, in which "we can comprehend the details of a work only by projecting a sense of the whole" (Armstrong, 1990: 2), actually it does not. In addition, our analysis avoided being forced back to providing explanations of the course of events in terms of our common-sense understanding of what is going on, which would indeed, as Branigan notes, give us problems with causality. The film's organisation calls for the construction of a partial theory involving causality—but precisely how the female character causes what and in what way is left mysterious, presumably exactly as intended. In other words, a narrative 'gap' is constructed that will certainly require consideration of the larger-scale narrative patterns pursued in the film, but the gap is only constructed by the workings of the segmentation elucidated here.

There are, of course, many other interpretations that are compatible with this segmentation. For example, in Randy Rasmussen's account of the fragment, the cross-cutting is taken more straightforwardly as an indication that "No one character is in a position to comprehend or control everything" (Rasmussen, 2006: 122). Nevertheless, his description in general allows presumed film noir motifs, including that of the *femme fatale*, to permeate the description throughout—in sharp contrast to that of Cowie (1973: 103), who writes of "the beautiful female beyond reproach" who, only at the end of the film, is revealed as having been far more involved in events than previously portrayed. This latter view can also be applied to the segment analysed here. In almost all episodes up to this point in the film and continuing beyond, almost until the grand finale, the main female character has not been particularly active causally—quite the contrary.

Another reading of the button-pushing segment, therefore, is that while everything happens around her, the main female character is actually left in her drawing room ineffectually pushing buttons that no one answers. For this interpretation to stand, all that is required is for the common relation that holds the alternation together to be hypothesised to be one of *being ignored* or something similar rather than causality. Thus: in shot 2 she presses a button for someone in the kitchen, but in the kitchen no one answers; in shot 4 she again presses a button, but in shot 5 the two active male figures speed purposefully on their way quite independently of her; and in shot 10 she presses the button once again, and is ignored yet again because the other male character is not in a position to answer.

The narrative gap set up by this reading, one of ineffectuality, would then need to be considered against other theories set up elsewhere in the film in order for its merit or otherwise to be evaluated. This is the point made in numerous approaches where the necessity of approaching a film 'holistically' stands in the foreground—all analysis is to be undertaken on the basis of a deeper understanding of how a film is working in its entirety. Our account here in no sense stands in opposition to such interpretative styles; our point is that this stance neither warrants a lack of attention to filmic details in their own right nor precludes consideration of a positive and relatively stable meaning contribution from such details *within the relevant strata of the semiotic system*. Thus, for the current example, regardless of the fact that an 'ineffectuality' interpretation would be almost the reverse of the 'hidden shaper of events' one, the segmentation of the filmic material and its commitment to an abstract constellation of inter-relationships *does not change*. At this level of description, we indeed have a more foundational 'level' of filmic organisation—one that we consider necessary for all motivated interpretations of broader narrative significance that may follow.

Critiques of assuming particular units for analysis that draw positively on the flexibility of interpretation offered by the hermeneutic cycle, such as Wilson's, themselves commonly discard the necessary 'wider frameworks' within which such interpretative practices must be placed. That is: the interpretations pursued *only make sense with the assumption of particular semiotic modes*. There is no way of providing an interpretation of the segment we have just considered from *The Lady from Shanghai* without the prior adoption of a particular collection of semiotic modes to give meaning to the exercise.

We will need to return to several aspects of this critical point in subsequent chapters. In the next chapter, for example, we take up the requirement that semiotic modes must be assumed in order to impose order on materiality at all, while in Chapter 5 we describe how the assumption that we are analysing the semiotic mode(s) of *film* itself already brings with it certain commitments of interpretation. This is the status of the units of analysis that we have drawn upon here—units that are sufficiently abstract that they are not contingent on the specifics of the plot at hand, but which *are* contingent on the assumption that the material is to be considered as part of the signifying practice of film.

Of course, no analysts would, we take it, argue that filmic details are to be ignored. The issue here is more the weight that is given to a first round of interpretation that does more than simply make technical details available for subsequent consumption in the justification of top-down interpretation. This overlaps partly with Bordwell's critique of 'meaning-making' within critical institutions (Bordwell, 1989). It goes further than this, however, in restricting the very broad constructivist notion that Bordwell adopts of having meanings essentially made by interpreters. Whereas meanings ontologically only arise in the heads of interpreters—that is, following Peirce, without an interpreter there can be no meaning—just which meanings are to be constructed and which not is by no means a free choice of the individual. And this brings us back into the realm of Saussure's observations about verbal language as a *social fact*.

This has been described and argued by Berys Gaut in terms of an 'ought' of interpretation: that is, the interpretation of given artefacts is usually not free in the sense of being left up to the individual interpreter; the artefacts themselves have been produced in such a way as to have a generically intended 'correct' manner of interpretation. This correct manner is not determined by the individual interpreter, but by the norms and conventions within which the artefact appears as a potential object of interpretation. Thus, although interpreters have to do the actual work of interpretation, and in this sense 'construct meanings', they do not themselves determine how they *ought* to go about this work (Gaut, 2010: 173).

This kind of 'guided construction' is not yet sufficient, however, to distinguish between several distinct theoretical and philosophical positions on meaning:

> "Different theorists have different views about how what we ought to imagine is determined. Intentionalists hold that what ought to be imagined is determined by the filmmakers' intentions. In general, communication-theorists believe that what the audience ought to imagine is determined by the 'sender' of the message, whilst semioticians maintain that it is determined by the 'code' of the film." (Gaut, 2010: 174)

Bordwell, Thompson, and many others, argue that what most usefully should be taken as determining the 'ought' of interpretation are the norms of film-making provided by the historical and cultural context within which any film is made and the solutions employed in a film for the practical problems of achieving narration. Gaut, Walton Kendall, and others add to this aspects of the creator's intentions, accepting that an artefact is intendedly designed and not solely a product of its socio-historical environment.

Many sources of difficulty come from using terms that hide immense semiotic complexity as if they could be considered without a semiotic foundation: a, if not the, prime case in point being, of course, the term 'meaning' itself; discussions of the term abound and this is not the place even to offer a sketch of the literature on the subject. Nevertheless, in contrasting, for example, 'constructivism', which has viewers and hearers constructing meanings, 'formalism', which has meanings arising on the basis of the formal, intrinsic features of an artefact, and 'intentionalism', which has meaning safely in the hands of the author, one is already on very thin semiotic ice—amply demonstrated by the long history of debate concerning whether the meaning of a work is 'in' the work, in the 'head' of the author, or in the head of the receiver. Within each of these perspectives, the term 'meaning' is used in distinct and, very often, semiotically confused ways. Even the appearance of a phrase such as 'the meaning of the text' is most commonly an indication of confusion rather than a usable framework.

More nuanced discussions in the area therefore typically face the problem of differentiating types and subtypes of the notions addressed, such as Bordwell's (1989) distinct types of meaning introduced at the outset of Chapter 1, or the 'patchwork' theory proposed by Gaut (2010: 180), in which a large (and relatively disorganised) collection of meanings, intentions, constructs and phenomena circulate in the process of meaning construction/discovery. Gaut's conclusions are, however, in one respect very similar to those reached here:

> "The general mechanism for discretionary construction, then, is the determining of indeterminates left open by the work. This kind of construction is restricted, since the determinate boundaries are fixed by the work. ... There are thus 'gaps' in the work, in the sense that certain features of the fictional world are not explicitly specified in the work." (Gaut, 2010: 190)

Unfortunately, how this might work in detail is left unspecified.

Similar notions have a long history in work on literary interpretation of course; in one of the earliest proposals developing this idea, Iser (1978) suggests a detailed account of the role of gaps in driving reader response. However, although there are certain overlaps with the kind of view that is now emerging in linguistic work on discourse, there is also an important difference concerning just how gaps arise and their nature and precisely the same consideration arises with film, echoing some of our opening statements in Chapter 1.

Whereas much work on literature and film assumes the gaps that drive readers to be *referential*, i.e., related to the information (or lack of it) that a text/film makes available about its portrayed world—its *diegesis*—those gaps of primary concern to us here are anchored formally within the *linguistic and filmic forms* themselves: that is, to take the simplest example, we consider a point-of-view sequence not to operate by introducing a referential gap of the kind: 'oh, I wonder what s/he is looking at', but rather by virtue of a *textual* gap that is intrinsic to how discourse operates. The former option lets in common-sense and problem-solving; the latter 'shortcuts' such considerations by means of the mechanisms of conventionalised (albeit in this case also quite naturally motivated: cf. Chapter 5) discourse interpretation.[3]

We can bring all of these considerations together as follows. The position we adopt is also committed to there being an 'ought' of interpretation as Gaut proposes: semiotic artefacts are not produced free of intended usage—this would contradict their status as artefacts. Moreover, in terms of the ways listed by Gaut above in which this 'ought' of interpretation is to be fixed, our position is clearly most closely aligned with the last alternative: the semiotic. We too see the 'semiotic code' of a film as offering the means by which 'gaps' can be created for guided, discretionary interpretative work. But, as we have argued at length, the view of 'semiotic code' we adopt differs substantially to those typically found in film studies. And this is crucial because it turns the loose patchwork of contributions described by Gaut into something much more organised and productive.

Without a sufficiently strong semiotic framework, attempts to articulate definitions of words, such as "meaning", are made considerably more difficult and fragile than is necessary, easily falling back to a problematic assumption that the word is 'automatically' picking out some single coherent domain of reference. To go further, therefore, we believe that the level of abstraction of the discussion needs to be raised in order to bring the (semiotic) processes involved within semiotic systems into clearer view.

Our position, analogous in its starting orientation to that of Iser, will be that a work establishes a potential for interaction between the artefact constituting the work and its receivers and that that potential is *intended* by its creators. Intending effects is only possible, however, against a background of shared expectations, and this is a large part of the work provided by a semiotic system. Thus creators do, certainly, put something into an artefact that is intended to be seen and reacted to, i.e., they leave material traces of semiotic 'decisions'. Interpreters can find these cues or miss them, but the cues are nevertheless intendedly 'immanent' to the work. Meaning, in this sense, is not then solely the preserve of the recipient, even though the work of *following* the traces, and filling out the potential they open up, can only be undertaken by some concrete observer. Taken together, this shows that meaning is equally not solely the preserve of an artefact's creators, nor of the artefact—precisely what is done where then becomes far clearer when placed against the background of a stratified semiotic system.

2.5   Summary and Conclusions

In this chapter, we have motivated our adoption of socio-semiotics and some modern accounts of 'documents' as semiotic artefacts. Although

---

[3]Useful discussions of distinct kinds of gaps at work in film and other visual media can also be found in the German *Bildwissenschaft* tradition, see Liptay (2006).

semiotics in particular has received considerable criticism over the years in its relation to film, we see many of the problems that have arisen to be quite natural considering the complexity of the endeavour. Any 'general study of signs', i.e., of all entities that can be given some interpretation, is going to be tremendously broad in scope and so it should not be that surprising that absolute clarity concerning just what a semiotic system might be was not achieved overnight; in fact, there is still substantial foundational work to be done.

Much early work in the field was therefore grappling with new phenomena, developing both the theory and its application as it went. It is then natural that some earlier accounts of semiotic systems were stretched to, and beyond, breaking point—especially when faced with the complexity of film. Thus, while the importance of earlier explorations into the uncharted territory of the semiotic treatments of film should not be undervalued, their relevance for current research also needs to be relativised. Many of the problems and conceptual difficulties faced at that time still influence commentators and critics of semiotics written today. Readers of such critiques need therefore to be very careful concerning just what position on semiotics is being assumed; to the extent that the position attacked is outdated, the critiques may well be as well.

On the basis of newer results concerning meaning-making within discourse, we have suggested that this may also be useful for film. And, indeed, suggestions that film should be considered a form of discourse go back a long way (e.g., Cohen-Séat 1948, Metz 1974*a*, Colin 1985, Colin 1989*a*: 166, Palmer 1989: 306). Just how this was to be achieved, however, was originally as unclear for film as it was for texts. We have now outlined a generic view of discourse that may be equally applicable to both text and film. Nevertheless, whether there is actually a level of discourse semiotics of this kind at work for film can still be considered as a very real *empirical* question. The extent to which we can really follow this direction for film is therefore the basic organising question that this book raises. The remaining chapters constitute our tentative, but nevertheless affirmative, answer.

Further Reading

Good overviews of the **interactions of semiotics and film studies** can be found in Stam, Burgoyne and Fliterman-Lewis (1992), slightly modified extracts of which also appear in Stam (2000). Chandler (2002: 83 and 213–219) offers more detail concerning the received view of Saussure as neglecting discourse and discusses subsequent moves away from semiotics as well as work in socially-oriented semiotics and poststructuralist semiotics.

Further discussion of the definition and further development of Hjelmslev's notion of **stratification** can be found in Taverniers (2008, 2011). Introductions and overviews of the various positions taken within linguistics on **discourse relations**, ranging from the semiotic to the psychological, can be found in Knott, Sanders and Oberlander (2001) and Bateman and Rondhuis (1997). For an extensive discussion and references concerning early considerations of **film as discourse**, see Siegrist (1986). And for more on the **problem solving** paradigm in film studies, see Burnett (2008).

The meaning communicated by combining textual and visual information by virtue of **page layout** mentioned in this chapter is a subject of considerable research in its own right, beginning in the seminal explorations of Barthes (1977*a*) and continued further to this day (Martinec and Salway, 2005; Stöckl, 2004; Bateman, 2008). The **communicative function of page layout** as a whole—i.e., text, images, typography and their spatial distribution on the page—is now studied extensively both within **document design** (cf. Schriver, 1997) and within socio-functional and other approaches to semiotics (cf. Kress and van Leeuwen, 2006).

For specifications for **non-static multimedia documents**, the situation is more complex. Proposals such as SMIL (the Synchronized Multimedia Integration Language), a W3C recommended XML markup language for describing multimedia presentations (http://www.w3.org/TR/SMIL/; cf. Bulterman and Rutledge 2008), and international standards such as MPEG-7 (ISO/IEC JTC1/SC29/WG11), intended primarily for storage, searching and retrieval of multimedia content (Martínez, Koenen and Pereira, 2002; Martínez, 2002*b,a*), offer substantial tools for describing such documents, their parts, subparts and spatiotemporal behaviours.

Finally, for detailed descriptions and discussions of the plot line, background and filmic techniques employed in *The Lady from Shanghai* (1947), see Rasmussen (2006: Chapter 3 '*The Lady from Shanghai*: Lethal Habits', 104–135), Naremore (1978: 151–163) and Cowie (1973: 96–107); further detailed film interpretations from a variety of perspectives can be found in Graham (1981), West (1982), Telotte (1984), Radell (1992), Pippin (2011) and the references given there.

3 Constructing the semiotic mode of film

"The problem for us is not ... to complete semiotics, but to transform it." (Colin, 1985: 15, translation from Buckland, 2000:141)

Descriptions and theories of film commonly distinguish 'tracks', 'channels' or 'codes' that need to be considered alongside one another when describing and analysing film. This can be done with respect to the more or less independently variable 'information channels' distinguishable within films—such as sound, lighting, dialogue, music and mise-en-scène, i.e., everything that is put 'into' a shot to be filmed. We made similar separations on a rather opportunistic basis in our transcriptions of filmic extracts in previous chapters. However, as with most pre-theoretical considerations, there is actually much more to be said. Although useful as a descriptive step, defining tracks informally in this fashion postpones much for the next stage of work: showing how information in different tracks may be usefully combined to form a far richer resource for making meanings than any of the tracks considered in isolation. This moves us on into the realm of **multimodality**.

We have already at several points made passing reference to the obvious multimodality of film. However, to do justice to this, we believe that we also need our accounts of semiotics to be multimodally 'aware'—even treatments of what traditionally have been considered 'single modes', such as language, go astray when multimodality is not considered as an intrinsic component of how semiotic systems are defined (cf. Norris, 2004).

Most existing treatments of multimodality are, unfortunately, less helpful here than might have been hoped. In work performing concrete analyses of multimodal artefacts, the 'modes' of multimodality are more often presumed than defined. The precise nature of 'mode' in multimodality remains, therefore, unclear and a variety of descriptions circulate in the literature. For some, modes are "the 'stuff' which a culture uses as the means for the expression of [its] meanings" (Kress, 2000: 185) and form 'a regularized organized set of resources for meaning-making' (Jewitt and Kress, 2003: 1); for others, a mode is 'never a bounded or static unit, but always and only a *heuristic* unit' (Norris, 2004: 12). Some writers even suggest that it is not possible to define or list semiotic modes at all (e.g., Forceville, 2006: 382).

'Mode' also often occurs alongside, in contrast with, or as a synonym for a collection of similar terms, with usages and meanings overlapping to varying degrees in different communities. For example, from the perspective of mass communication, the term 'media' might refer to particular distribution channels (TV, print-newspaper, Web, etc.); in linguistic communication models the medium might be more the *physical* medium carrying the language; and, when considering art, one commonly encounters usages such as the 'medium of film', of literature, etc. Particularly in this latter context, we can find striking similarities between the usage of the term *medium* and the understanding of semiotic mode that we will build on below.

We can see this well in the following positions. Jerrold Levinson writes as part of his discussion of art and art works, to which we return later in this chapter, that:

> "... for *medium* in the present context is *not* equivalent to *material* or *physical dimension*. Rather, by a *medium* I mean a developed way of using given materials or dimensions, with certain entrenched properties, practices, and possibilities. 'Medium' in this sense is closer to 'art form' than to 'kind of stuff'." (Levinson, 1990: 29, original emphasis)

While, in a very different tradition, Stanley Cavell proposes:

> "The first successful movies—i.e., the first moving pictures accepted as motion pictures—were not applications of a medium that was defined by given possibilities, but the *creation of a medium* by their giving significance to specific possibilities. Only the art itself can discover its possibilities, and the discovery of a new possibility is the discovery of a new medium. A medium is something through which or by means of which something specific gets done or said in particular ways." (Cavell, 1980: 32, original emphasis)

Both of these positions pick out an area of reference analogous in many ways to that we would assign to 'mode'—in particular, mode/medium is seen as an active shaper of expression possibilities rather than a passive transmission carrier. This is very much the direction we follow here.

Broad characterisations of this kind do not yet tell us much about how modes may be identified or combined in the service of making meaning, however. To bring us further, our task in this chapter will consequently be to reconstruct the relationships involved *semiotically*. For this we take as starting point the account of semiotic systems described in the previous chapter—particularly that illustrated in Figure 2.1—abstracting away from the language bias of that system and adding in the phenomenon of multimodality as an essential property. Following this consideration of semiotic modes and multimodality in general, we will have all the necessary machinery in place to make our move into film. We will then treat the *specifics* of filmic meaning-making as an instantiation of the broader conception of semiotic systems achieved.

3.1 Semiotic multimodality

There are several sources of difficulty in providing definitions capable of serving as the foundation for further, more precise investigations into multimodal artefacts and how such artefacts manifest and manipulate the modes they deploy. One that is particularly tenacious has been the common linking of 'mode' with *sensory* modalities (for further discussion, an overview and references, see Nöth, 1995*b*: 175). When this is done, it may be assumed that the modalities under investigation are actually rather unproblematic and self-evident since visual, auditory, tactile, etc. information is evidently distinct. Under this view, 'language', 'graphics', 'music' are so obviously different that there is little need to labour the division further. This tendency is common in both technological approaches and non-technological (i.e., linguistic, cognitive, semiotic, etc.) approaches to multimodal analysis—two areas where multimodality and its treatment have received considerable attention (see *Further Reading*).

The focus on sensory modality has made it difficult to achieve workable definitions of 'semiotic mode'. Too often it is presumed that one knows which particular modes are operative in an artefact even prior to investigation. This is one reason why many multimodal 'analyses' still go little further than detailed 're-description' and anecdotal discussion.

To move forward, we return to the following, for us crucial, observation by Kress and colleagues. We take this as a fundamental starting point for any approach to multimodality:

> "…the question of whether X is a mode or not is a question specific to a particular community. As laypersons we may regard visual image to be a mode, while a professional photographer will say that photography has rules and practices, elements and materiality quite different from that of painting and that the two are distinct modes." (Kress, Jewitt, Ogborn and Tsatsarelis, 2000: 43)

This observation, echoing the concerns of Levinson and Cavell above, makes it clear that a semiotic mode is developed by virtue of the work that a group of users puts into employing some material substrate as a tool for constructing meaning and is neither a 'pre-given' fact to be taken for granted nor a simple product of sensory capabilities. Whereas both Levinson's and Cavell's arguments centered around artworks, we generalise this here to apply to *all* kinds of meaning-making: i.e., modes are ways "through which or by means of which something specific gets done or said" (Cavell, 1980: 32) employing specific materialities as material substrates.

Many distinct kinds of material substrates have been adopted throughout history for building semiotic modes of varying degrees of complexity. In general, it is important to realise that *any* material substrate can be made to serve this function: all that is required is that the material is sufficiently 'controllable' as to admit of *purposeful articulations*—i.e., that members of the societal group investing effort in the development of the semiotic mode can manipulate the material sufficiently well as to leave traces recognisable as such by other members of that group.

This necessary pre-condition of controllability is intentionally very broad and does not predispose us in advance to consider any particular class of semiotic modes rather than another. We consider it useful to return to this foundation whenever multimodal analysis is to be undertaken. It allows the researcher to approach the question of just which semiotic modes are being deployed in an unbiased fashion that is open to empirical investigation. Thus, whereas in this book we will be considering it self-evident that film *is* at least one and possibly several semiotic modes, i.e., some combination of ways of making and communicating meanings, we will *not* be assuming that we already know exactly which modes are involved. As mentioned above, the commonly assumed tracks of filmic artefacts represent a useful starting point, but no more than this.

Our account of semiotic modes begins then by taking up the model that we derived from both functional linguistics and formal approaches to discourse in the previous chapter. In fact, our depiction of the linguistic semiotic system given in Figure 2.1 of that chapter was already far broader than strictly required for a treatment of language. We did not specify there, for example, the precise materialities employed. We now quite deliberately de-commit from any particular materiality in order to develop a proposal for semiotic modes in general that will also provide a foundation for our return to film in particular.

Letting our model apply across all semiotic modes collects together a useful bundle of organisational dimensions as well as important semiotic relations holding between those dimensions. The dimensions that we have identified so far are the *strata* of the semiotic system, with their varying degrees of abstraction and internal mechanisms, and the *realisational* relationships holding between these. As we shall see, the ways in which particular modes may fill this generic pattern with life may differ, but we take the distinctions themselves to be constitutive for semiotic modes. This is, therefore, a statement concerning the *ontology* of semiotic modes, a statement set out independently of film in somewhat more detail in Bateman (2011), where the general model is applied to several kinds of phenomena currently studied in multimodality research.

A distinctive feature of this view is the place granted to the stratum of discourse semantics. Indeed, we propose that the presence of a discourse stratum should be adopted as a defining property of semiotic modes as such. Without a discourse semantics, a semiotic mode can only be effective within very particular contexts of use with little possibility of extension— something perhaps most similar to the traditional account of 'semiotic codes' from structural semiotics and its discussions of traffic lights, traffic signs and other intrinsically restricted sign systems (cf. the discussion in the previous chapter).

It is important here to note that the restricted nature of such systems is not due to their limited, 'digital' nature. This can be seen from the example of the *thaumatrope*, a toy popular in the nineteenth century that combines two images to form a third in the manner suggested in Figure 3.1. When the cord to which the central disk is attached is twisted, persistence of vision makes the images on the front and back sides of the disk appear to merge into one. This 'system' only requires two signs: the images provided on each side of the disk. Nevertheless, for each minimal observable change made to these drawings, we have a difference in the observed result

Figure 3.1   A thaumatrope

when the disk is spun. The system as a whole thereby functions in a continuous, non-digital fashion. This composition of images can be seen as a kind of 'syntagmatic' operation, i.e., a method for bringing distinct components together (cf. §3.2 below). Nevertheless, the meanings that can be made with the system are still extremely restricted. What is missing in this case, just as with the traffic lights, is a stratum of discourse semantics.

Discourse semantics in general provide the resources by which less abstract 'utterances' (construed very broadly, i.e., as the 'result' or 'product' of meaning-making acts) can be related to concrete situations of use. The additional stratification of a discourse semantics enables semiotic systems to generalise across different contexts by providing schemes that guide contextual interpretation. This is clearly missing from the thaumatrope—after the component signs have been merged, there is no further systematic contextualisation that will lead to the image being 'read' differently.

In contrast, evidence of a discourse semantic stratum at work can be found whenever the interpretation of a particular configuration of lower-level articulations depends on context. In our linguistic examples in the previous chapter, we saw that the discourse relations potentially applicable were sensitive to the presumed genre: this information cannot be derived 'compositionally' from the forms themselves. Such 'defeasible' inference is the hallmark of discourse interpretation: the lower strata have provided particular information, e.g., division into units with particular properties, and the discourse semantics then provides the candidate interpretations possible for that information. This applies to most of the meanings assigned to complex semiotic organisations—i.e., they are *situated discourse interpretations*.

Film provides many examples of this and so there is little reason to suspect *a priori* that we are not dealing with a semiotic mode as defined here. If, for example, we consider the distinct interpretations that are possible for a sequence of shots punctuated by a black screen, we are

Figure 3.2   *Example of apparently clear filmic punctuation (fade-to-black) being used for distinct aesthetic and narrative effects in Kieślowski's* Three colours: blue *(1993) with Juliette Binoche*

already at the heart of discourse interpretation. The most common reading of such a visual event is that a boundary in the unfolding story has been reached—a change of scene, time or place. But this is an interpretation that can also turn out to be false as repeatedly illustrated in, for example, Kieślowski's *Three colours: Blue* (1993); a typical case is shown in Figure 3.2. We know, therefore, that the interpretation is a *discourse* interpretation and not a property of some filmic 'grammar' working in terms of compositional semantics and a syntax.

Many of the 'rules' of film design and interpretation (e.g., camera angle reflects power, maintenance of the 180° rule, and other often stated contributions to the 'grammar' of shots, etc.: Thompson and Bowen 2009*a,b*) are of this kind; further examples and early theoretical discussions of this issue can be found in Möller (1978), Bordwell (1982), Branigan (1984: 29), Palmer (1989) and Stam (1989) among others. This, as we illustrated in our final example in the previous chapter and in contrast to the position of, for example, Bordwell, is strongly suggestive of the need for a proper discourse semantics within accounts of filmic semiotic modes. The leap to assuming ready equivalence with social conventions and general problem-solving by means of cognitive schemata is too hasty.

Our approach can therefore be seen as refining the following recent description of communication offered by Gunther Kress:

> "three assumptions are fundamental: *communication happens as a response to a prompt; communication has happened when there has been an interpretation; communication is always multimodal.* Because *interpretation* is central, so therefore is the *interpreter; without interpretation there is no communication;* yet it is the *characteristics,* the shape, of the *prompt* which constitute the ground on which the *interpretation* happens." (Kress, 2010: 36, original emphasis)

This functional position presupposes both the work of a 'designer', in constructing an artefact that will be supportive of interpretation, and the actual work of interpretation that needs to be brought to the artefact by its 'audience'. The account does not, however, provide us with any detail concerning just how such interpretation might work, nor does it tell us how interpretation and the 'shape' of the artefact interact. For some artefacts (such as our thaumatrope example above), there is little to say: the interpretation foreseen does not go beyond the picture displayed. But for other artefacts, films among them, there is both considerably more flexibility and more structured *guidance* of the interpretations appropriate. This is then what our account is aiming to reveal and articulate for the particular case of filmic artefacts, relying throughout on a suitably developed stratum of discourse semantics.

For the purposes of our framework here, we adopt the 'tri-stratal' organisation for semiotic modes, as introduced in the previous chapter, for semiotic modes in general. The discourse semantics of this system provides defeasible rules of interpretation that are typically applied to show how interpretations can be uncovered dynamically while at the same time sensibly constraining the range of interpretations that are relevant. Discourse semantic rules therefore control when and how 'world knowledge' is considered in the interpretation process—something that will come to be crucial below when we need to provide just such an access for guiding film interpretation.

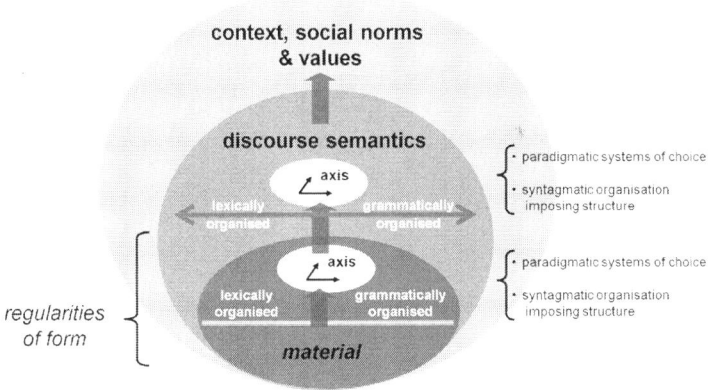

Figure 3.3   Graphical depiction of the semiotic system constituting an arbitrary semiotic mode

For ease of reference we show in Figure 3.3 a slightly extended version of our general characterisation of a semiotic mode. This is taken to apply for semiotic modes developing with respect to any materiality. The extent to which the structure as a whole is 'filled out' depends, as described above, on the work a community of users puts into its use. The innermost oval includes the organisations most immediately imposed on the material substrate up to some kind of 'grammar' in the strict linguistic sense of compositionally constructed units of analysis. These strata are relatively underdeveloped for film and, as we describe in detail in Chapter 5, their work is mostly taken over by the human perceptual system—that is, they are closely related to 'natural signs', signs that function without the establishment of convention. The middle oval is, in contrast, where we see a considerable development for film. We return to this in Chapter 4 below.

Before proceeding further to see how film works with and within these semiotic principles, we need first to introduce two further aspects of semiotic systems of importance for considering film. The first is the nature of the *internal organisation* within semiotic strata—i.e., the kind of units and relations applying within semiotic strata. The second is *mode composition*— i.e., how distinct semiotic modes relate and combine their meaning-making potential, an area obviously crucial for film.

3.2   The internal organisation of semiotic strata

One important way in which characterisations of semiotic systems within the linguistic tradition have gone beyond more generic accounts of signs developed within traditional semiotics is in their treatment of the *internal organisation of sign systems*. Distinctions usually drawn in semiotics among signs generally focus on the relationship between signs and their referents.

Thus, we have the two-way distinction of signifier and signified from Saussure, and the three-way distinctions of representamen (sign vehicle), interpretant (sense) and object (referent) from Peirce (e.g., Peirce, *Collected Papers* §2.228): each taking up slightly differently the relation of sign to referent and how and where this connection is made. Even the probably better known distinction between signs drawn by Peirce in terms of icon (sign by resemblance), index (sign by causal relationship) and symbol (sign by convention) maintains a focus on signs as individual entities.

What is left unaddressed in these considerations is the way in which collections of signs are organised *together* within any stratum of a semiotic system. This is vital, however, since it is in the nature of semiotic systems to be constituted by entire collections of signs standing in more or less complex inter-relationships. This is as important, if not more so, than any relationships assumed between signs and referents and is succinctly captured in the structuralist dictum, attributed variously to Antoine Meillet, Saussure and others, that language is a system *où tout se tient*—i.e., a system in which 'everything holds itself together':

> "everywhere and always there is the same complex equilibrium of terms that mutually condition each other. Putting it another way, *language is a form and not a substance*." (Saussure, 1959[1915]: 122, original emphasis)

Thus, individual signs by themselves, to the extent that this is still a meaningful description, only receive significance by virtue of the relationships of *difference* they stand in with respect to other signs.

Saussure (1959[1915]) then identified two fundamental ways in which signs could be in relation. These were relationships along the axes of

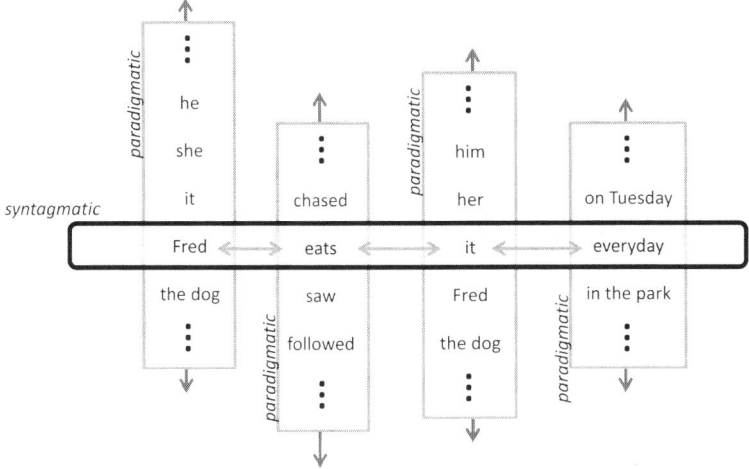

Figure 3.4   Simple linguistic example of the paradigmatic and syntagmatic axes of organisation

paradigmatic organisation (or 'association' as Saussure termed it at that time) and of **syntagmatic** organisation. This fundamental distinction has received considerable development in the tradition of Hjelmslev and Halliday and now offers a backbone for any linguistically-inflected semiotic account. We propose that all non-material semiotic contributions must be characterised in terms of these axes of organisation. Even though this is also commonly found in discussions of film, we will see below that the filmic application of these constructs leaves much to be desired and has led to considerable confusion in the development of usable accounts. It is therefore a further aim of this book to clarify this situation substantially.

The purpose of the paradigmatic axis of organisation is to relate items as *alternatives* to one another; in contrast, the purpose of the syntagmatic axis is to link items together in structural configurations. The original formulation of these theoretical constructs was primarily shaped by traditional discussions of grammar and, particularly at that time, 'paradigms' of morphological conjugations. A common conceptualisation of the two axes of organisation is consequently as shown in Figure 3.4, in which the horizontal axis suggests the syntagmatic organisation and the vertical the paradigmatic organisation. This makes it clear that behind the structural configuration manifested in the sentence "Fred eats it everyday" stands an entire range of 'choices' that a speaker brings both to the selection of each item and to the *structuring* of those items. Although critical, this latter aspect is often neglected in non-linguistic accounts.

This is often the kind of example with which paradigmatic and syntagmatic organisation is introduced in discussions of film (cf. Kawin 1992: 57), but it is also misleading in at least two respects. First, it suggests a comparison between *grammar* and film which we have already argued at length to be inappropriate. Second, and rather more subtle, it suggests an *identification* of the terms that may appear along the syntagmatic and paradigmatic axes: that is, this kind of example makes it appear that the *word* 'eats' is simultaneously syntagmatic and paradigmatic. Although this is still also found in some linguistic descriptions, our treatment differs from this in that we follow more closely the descriptive apparatus developed in systemic-functional linguistics that we set out below. Considering terms to be both syntagmatic and paradigmatic easily leads to confusion—particularly when dealing with more abstract and complex systems such as film. Below we will draw the two axes apart more succinctly, while nevertheless formally defining the ways in which they are linked.

Given these problems with simple linguistic examples, James Monaco's introduction to the paradigmatic/syntagmatic distinction in film is in many respects more appropriate (Monaco, 2000: 418; 2009: 470). Instead of falling back on linguistic syntax, Monaco takes an example explored by Barthes (1964) concerning the more semiotically neutral case of clothing. He suggests, for example, that the collections of items of clothing that one may actually be wearing together—e.g., shoes, socks, trousers, sweater, hat—correspond to the syntagmatic organisation, whereas the distinct *kinds* of clothing that one may choose for different parts of the body make up the paradigmatic organisation—e.g., around the waist and below: skirt, shorts, kilt, trousers, etc. In the 1960s and 1970s, this less linguistically-biased usage also found its way into a broad range of 'linguistically'-inspired approaches to the semiotics of a variety of cultural domains.

The loosening of the example is not without its own corresponding dangers, however. The clothing semiotic system has only a weak structuring imposed by the conventions of what is worn where: that is, if one really wanted to, it would be perfectly possible to wear, for example, a skirt, shorts and trousers all at the same time—even though they might 'more normally' be considered alternatives; the *interpretation* of these unusual combinations would then fall to a discourse semantics.

This is completely different for the syntagmatic structuring within linguistic syntax—a stratum characterised by structures that are highly recursive. Each of the elements that we find on the paradigmatic axis depicted in Figure 3.4 may *itself* be broken up into an internal set of paradigmatic/syntagmatic distinctions. For the noun phrase 'the dog', for example, we have the paradigms of determiners—'the', 'a', 'some', 'any', etc.—and of head nouns—'dog', 'cat', 'elephant', etc.—which then have to be combined in syntagmatic organisations typical of noun phrase structure, such as 'determiner' followed by 'head noun'. Discovering the precise properties of this level of organisation is a central concern of linguistics and, for some linguists, almost defines the field. It is not the case then that elements from the paradigmatic dimension within linguistic syntax can be freely 'chained' together and an interpretable structure (or even, possibly, a structure at all) will result. The distinct semiotic systems of language and clothing impose very different degrees of constraint on what is possible within them and, in particular, within their respective strata. The precise placement of film between these extremes is still largely a matter of empirical investigation.

We argued in the previous chapter that, in general, the distinct strata of a semiotic system may employ quite distinct mechanisms. Despite this, it is advantageous to take the paradigmatic/syntagmatic semiotic distinction as a basic organisational principle reoccurring across all strata and all semiotic modes. When considered at a suitably abstract level, the distinction offers strong methodological and descriptive guidance concerning how any semiotic stratum is to be explored. To be successful, however, this must be seen not only in far broader terms than is the case with linguistic syntax but also as maintaining more complex structuring mechanisms than suggested by less strongly organised semiotic systems such as clothing. We now set out this abstract view in more detail so that our foundation for film is securely in place.

3.2.1   Representing the paradigmatic axis of semiotic description

The paradigmatic organisation of a semiotic system is most appropriately construed as providing abstract 'systems of choice' that capture the *abstract alternatives* available for particular elements of structure. The syntagmatic axis of a semiotic system then provides an organisation for re-expressing, or 're-coding', those paradigmatic choices in structural configurations sufficient to allow interpreters to recover them. This means that we can never 'see' the paradigmatic organisation directly. The paradigm is essentially an abstraction: a collection of possibilities that a semiotic system treats as qualitatively different. It is only the structural configurations of the syntagmatic axis that leave observable traces in distinctions drawn in some material form. The paradigmatic description in contrast provides a rich organisation for the 'space' of semiotic decisions available within any semiotic system.

To avoid confused descriptions it is essential to make clear just what the 'scope' of any semiotic choice is. We can only contrast features that genuinely stand as alternatives. Linguistically, for example, we cannot usefully include 'the' and 'dog' as *alternatives* within any system of choice because there is no linguistic element, no item of the syntagmatic organisation, where this would be a meaningful opposition. The choice between 'the' and 'a' might form a paradigm, as would that between 'dog' and 'cat', but at no point in structure is a speaker faced with a dilemma of the form: 'for the meaning I currently want to express, is this best captured by *a* or *dog*?'— these alternatives are too disparate to sensibly compare, as indicated by the fact that they necessarily take up very different positions within linguistic structures. This fine-weaving of paradigmatic considerations and syntagmatic organisation is one of the strongest features of the socio-semiotic view developed within the Hallidayan linguistic tradition (Halliday and Matthiessen, 2004). It provides crucial theoretical and methodological constraints that prevent the construction of 'pseudo-paradigms' of nonsensical choices.

Powerful descriptive mechanisms for representing paradigms of choice are now well developed. For this we adopt the so-called **system network** used extensively within systemic-functional linguistics for capturing linguistic paradigmatic generalisations. A system network sets out both the alternatives that a semiotic system may make available at some 'point' and the *dependencies between* such choices. Thus, it is not only the case that a semiotic system offers a choice; the results of making some choice rather than another may lead on to other, dependent choices that would not otherwise have been available. Moreover, in order to become available, some choices may require entire collections of other choices also to have been made. And, finally, some choices may themselves lead on not to single further choices, but to entire sets of choices. The resulting web of dependencies is the reason for terming the description a *network*; the organisation of choices can itself become extremely complex.

We can also distinguish paradigmatic organisations according to their internal complexity of organisation. The more complex organisations, where the inter-connectivity and inter-dependencies present in the network are extensively developed, can be described as exhibiting a 'grammatical' organisation; more straightforward organisations, where there is simply a choice among collections of equally ranked alternatives, are described as exhibiting a 'lexical' organisation. This is by analogy to the organisation of the linguistic stratum of lexicogrammar, where rich inter-connections are representative of grammatical organisation and simple sets of unstructured alternatives correspond more to 'open-class' lexical items, such as, for example, the nouns or verbs of a language. The open-class choices tend to be very specific—in the case of lexicogrammar, leading to particular words, whereas grammatical alternations govern entire constellations of syntactic structures.

We can posit a similar range of internal organisation for semiotic modes in general; Figure 3.3 above accordingly described within its strata both 'grammatically organised' and 'lexically organised' resources. The degree of complexity is one indication of the amount of work that a community of users has invested in the mode. Thus, for example, where for a non-expert film viewer there may simply be a choice between black-and-white and colour, for the expert there would be considerably more internal organisation, ranging across different film stocks and types of recording (analogue, digital, etc.), lighting and so on. Very detailed paradigmatic descriptions are now available for the strata of the linguistic system; here, however, we naturally focus on film.

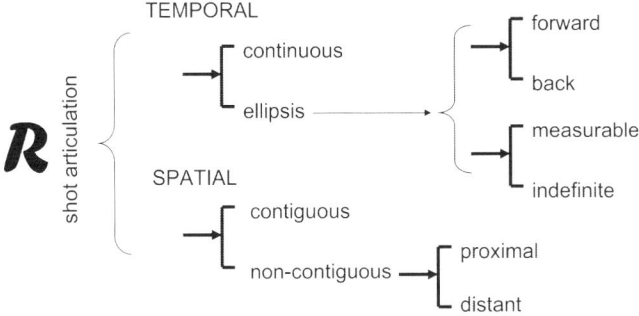

Figure 3.5 Paradigmatic overview of the possible relations between shots (R) articulated by Burch (1973)

Descriptions that can be considered paradigmatic treatments of film have most commonly been developed when addressing the question of the relations that might hold between shots in a film. There has been considerable interest in this issue throughout film's history and these relationships, i.e., the workings of **montage**, form central components of many accounts, including our own. Early attempts to systematise montage include Pudovkin (1926), Arnheim (1957: 94–98), Burch (1973: 3-16) as well as that of Christian Metz to which we will return at greater length in Chapter 4. Here we will use the proposal of Noël Burch to illustrate how system networks directly capture abstract paradigmatic choice.

Burch succinctly sets out a range of relationships for combining consecutive film shots by working purely deductively from the assumption that both temporal and spatial relationships must hold. That is, most generally, when one shot follows another, it is possible to classify the relationship between those shots both in terms of the temporal relationship obtaining and the spatial relationship obtaining. The starting point of the paradigmatic description is then the syntagmatic configuration of the 'shot-shot relationship'. Then, given this analytic unit, the network of choices offers two sets of possibilities, one for time and one for space. For time, the relationship might either be one of continuity, where the second shot immediately follows the first, or there may be some discontinuity, where some kind of gap occurs. A similar distinction can be made for space: either the second shot continues in the same space or there is a spatial gap of some kind. In both areas, there are also further choices available. In total, Burch suggests that there are "15 basic ways of articulating two shots" (Burch, 1973: 11)

We can succinctly capture all of the possibilities Burch sets out by forming a system network as shown in Figure 3.5. Here classification is expressed in terms of 'systems' of alternatives (e.g., either 'continuous' or 'ellipsis') arranged in order to capture their inter-dependencies. Cross classifications, or *simultaneous choices* such as those at the beginning of the network on the left of the figure, are indicated by rightward facing braces. The left-most cross-classification therefore defines a parallel classification along the paradigmatically independent dimensions of space and time, thereby capturing Burch's assumption that each inter-shot relationship must always be seen from both of these perspectives.

The figure also shows the further choices that Burch discusses; in the terms of system networks, these further choices are referred to as being more *delicate*. Choices thus become more delicate as we move from left to right in the graphical representation. Here we can see, for example, that there is no further temporal choice following on a *continuous* relationship between shots; such sequences then cover simple cuts that continue some action, shot/reverse-shot sequences in conversations, and so on. For *ellipsis*, however, we again have two parallel options: there is a choice of (a) whether we have jumped forward or backward in time with the ellipsis and (b) whether we can tell how far we have jumped or not.

A 'measurable' jump might be when we start with one shot showing someone beginning to walk across a large enclosed space, such as a train station or a restaurant, and the next shot shows that person reaching the other side of the station or their table. This means that we are invited to presume that the time taken was the 'normal' amount of time it might take to cross the space indicated at the speed the person was moving. An 'indefinite' time relationship might be required if the second shot instead shows the person sitting on a train or even getting off a train—we know that some time has elapsed but have no direct indication of how long that might have been.

A similar, more delicate distinction is offered along the spatial path: if the relationship is 'non-contiguous' in space, then either the next shot may indicate that there is a close spatial relationship—for example, by showing a different part of the same space as might occur in match cuts of various kinds, such as eyeline matches, match-on-action and so on—or distant, by showing no familiar details that would allow the spatial relationship to be derived.

The network also shows how Burch's '15 basic articulations' comes together. The simultaneous sets of choices indicated by the curly braces require us to *cross-classify* the features involved; this gives us a total of 5 temporal options multiplied by 3 spatial options. Two shots might then, for example, be related as {continuous, proximal}, meaning that time has continued running and we have not moved far in space, or as {forward, indefinite, contiguous}, meaning that the second shot is in the same space as the first but an indefinite amount of time appears to have passed—and so on, up to the 15 distinct relations covered.

Cross-classification is a very powerful representational mechanism and we will use it later on when we develop our own account of inter-shot relationships. If independent dimensions of description can be isolated, as time and space are in Burch's proposal, then the overall description in the form of a system network remains relatively straightforward, even though the number of distinguishable relationships can become very large very quickly. As we shall see below, this is one way in which we can counter early doubts about the possibility of capturing the very diverse relationships that appear to be observable in film.

A further essential component of this kind of description is an explicit statement of the relations that hold between the paradigmatic choices and their *syntagmatic* consequences; this was mentioned above with respect to the necessity of deciding on which units one is dealing with and in controlling the interweaving of paradigmatic choice and syntagmatic structures. Each major class of syntagmatic unit is the site of operation for its own network of paradigmatic options. The paradigmatic options taken up determine the internal structure of that unit by associating with each choice collections of *syntagmatic* realisational constraints.

The syntagmatic and paradigmatic components are therefore seen as an inseparable whole: paradigmatic choices without statements of their syntagmatic effects are, in essence, empty promises; they classify but do not say what consequences the classifications bring with them. They therefore remain unverifiable and untestable. Only when we also state structural consequences can we examine whether a proposed classification is sufficient for some body of data or not.

In the case of our example from Burch, the structure assumed was very simple: one shot related to another. Nevertheless, Burch himself saw this as an essential foundation for further work:

> "I feel that the shot transition will remain the basic element in the infinitely more complex structures of the future." (Burch, 1973: 12)

Although there have been several acknowledgements of the necessity of admitting 'larger' structures within film, just how this might be achieved has remained an open and hotly contested issue. How we can move on to more complex structures will consequently be one of our major concerns in subsequent chapters.

3.2.2   Representing the syntagmatic axis of semiotic description

We still need to characterise the notions of filmic structure that are required in more detail. However, at this preliminary stage, we can say rather less about the *general* representation of syntagmatic organisations across semiotic systems. This is partly due to their necessarily closer link to the particularities of the material substances in which they must be inscribed. It is also strongly dependent on the degree of internal stratification exhibited in a semiotic mode. As suggested above, there is little need for us to consider the highly complex accounts concerning syntactic syntagmatic organisation developed within linguistics since there is very little evidence that these are relevant for film.

Most generally, we can only expect that a syntagmatic description will include statements concerning the kinds of units that are motivated within a stratum (which we show at length for film in Chapter 5) and how these units may relate to one another. Such relations are commonly characterised in terms of syntagmatic *constituency*, as in syntax, where one unit may be a part of another, or in terms of *dependency*, where one unit depends on another but is not part of that other. A proper specification of the syntagmatic axis of a stratum then describes as many properties that hold over such structural configurations as are necessary and motivated to capture the properties of the stratum in question.

Returning again to our thaumatrope example (Figure 3.1) for an illustration, we can readily see that the syntagmatic organisation of the system is particularly simple: there are just two 'units', made up by the images on each side of the disk. These are 'composed' when the cord to which the disk is attached is spun. This axis of rotation then also yields particular syntagmatic constraints that must hold across the units: unless the images 'match', spinning the cord will not result in perceptible results. The matching of the images corresponds to a notion of dependence between syntagmatic units. Moreover, although the material substrate of these syntagmatic units was traditionally paper, there are now also computer simulations of thaumatropes which, as a consequence of their very different physical realisation, can exhibit quite different properties. We have here, therefore, an extremely simple syntagmatic system nevertheless dependent for some of its properties on its material substrate.

At the present point in our discussion, even though there is considerable evidence that the discourse strata of language and of film may show useful similarities, whether or not, or to what extent, this might extend to their respective *syntagmatic* organisations remains uncertain. We will therefore proceed very cautiously: our approach will be to remain focused on film rather than linguistic discourse, only adopting mechanisms and techniques for description that are clearly motivated empirically by the needs of providing an account of film.

3.3   Composing and combining semiotic modes

One of the primary motivations for adopting our rather foundational approach to multimodality is that it allows us to explore more effectively the way in which modes can be *combined*. This is perhaps the key issue for the analysis of multimodality as such: the challenge is to develop accounts which can shed light on just what the *benefits* of combining modes are. This is commonly seen informally as some kind of 'added value': but it needs to be spelled out in considerably more detail how that adding of value comes about. We will not be able to provide any exhaustive account here, but we do need nevertheless to position ourselves with respect to this issue since the combination of modal contributions is an essential feature of filmic meaning making.

Before proceeding, it is important to note that simply having information in various modalities or sensory channels in close proximity is by no means sufficient to talk of 'multimodality'. Accordingly, several authors working within different traditions have attempted to characterise how information comes together more precisely. Levinson, in his discussion of artworks mentioned above, for example, describes artworks appearing to combine a variety of 'modal' contributions at some length. As he points out:

> "Most (though not all) artistic entities described as multi- or mixed-media phenomena would be what I am labeling juxtapositional hybrids..." (Levinson, 1990: 31)

That is, they "form a whole by summation and not by merging or dissolution of individual boundaries" (p31). This is the central issue for a theory of multimodality in a nutshell: just what *are* the ways in which semiotic modes can be brought together and what does the combination achieve?

Working towards answers to these questions, Levinson proposes three distinct *kinds* of hybrids: hybridisation by **juxtaposition**, **transformation** (or alteration), and **synthesis** (Levinson, 1990: 30). Similar considerations are voiced by W.J.T. Mitchell in terms of **nesting**, in which "one medium appears inside another as its content" and **braiding** "when one sensory channel or semiotic function is woven together with another more or less seamlessly" (Mitchell 2007: 401 or Mitchell 2005).

Among these distinctions and connections, the weakest is clearly juxtaposition or nesting: summation without merging or dissolution. Then come transformational hybrids, where a particular art form is modified in the direction of another by the addition of certain properties of that form. Levinson offers kinetic sculpture as an example: here sculpture is the starting point and to this are added some limited aspects of dance. The result is unlikely to be called a kind of dance, it is more a variation of sculpture (Levinson, 1990: 33). Thus, in some sense, sculpture has been 'transformed' by addition. The final and most complex case, hybridisation by synthesis (Levinson) or braiding (Mitchell), is where:

> "the objects or products of two (or more) arts are brought together in such a way that the individual components to some extent lose their original identities and are present in the hybrid in a form significantly different from that assumed in the pure state." (Levinson, 1990: 31)

Levinson considers Wagnerian opera as clearly being a fused hybrid, vacillates a little on the case of silent film—whether this is a transformation of photography towards theatre or vice versa—before tentatively accepting synthesis status. There is probably little doubt that post-silent films need to be considered as a case of synthesis and, accordingly, Mitchell proposes them as a clear example of braiding.

Although these accounts are attempting to draw out the conditions under which the deployment of multimodal resources makes *extensions* in meaning possible, there is still a considerable way to go (see *Further Reading*). Moreover, in the case of film, we find meaning-making practices ranging across the full continuum of separate and combined semiotic modes, with many transitional cases corresponding to transformations apparently still ongoing.

The modes contributing to these combinations can themselves most straightforwardly be considered in terms of the standard divisions suggested by Metz (1972*a*). Metz sees five different but co-present material 'signifying substances' in film: the moving photographic image, the recorded musical sound, recorded phonetic sounds, recorded noises, and graphical material—i.e., "the graphic outline of written items (credits, various inscriptions incorporated into the image, intertitles in the silent film, etc.)" (Metz, 1973: 90). Multimodal extensions then build on both the individual and the combined structuring possibilities that these components provide.

Metz considers what happens when the 'signifying substances' of noise, musical sound and phonetic sound are 'recruited' by film as follows:

> "when these three signifying substances are used *in a film*—i.e., in a new and radically different context where each is 'caught' with the two others and with the moving image in an original network of interactions which are moreover tighter and more organised than in any other case—it is questionable how far these are still the *same* substances." (Metz, 1973: 94, original emphasis)

But it is rare that the semiotic properties carried by the originating contributes are completely replaced.[1] For example, speech in film will still be subject to all we know about dialogue and performance and linguistics, but it may *also* take up structural roles in integrating series of shots, in allowing narrative development across scenes to be maintained, adding inflections to the images shown and so on.

Therefore, *in addition* to the information provided in each of the sources of information individually, i.e., the visual and the sound track, modes frequently work together in order to provide cues concerning the 'structure' that a viewer is being invited to attribute to a film as it unfolds. Thus, continuous music with no overt change in general qualities will contribute to a perception of shown images as some ongoing dramaturgical event, whereas breaks in musical style may well indicate event boundaries (cf. Holman, 1997; Cohen, 2004). Some then go so far as to consider film as already essentially a kind of 'intermodal' meeting house of semiotic

---

[1] There is a suggestive parallel to be drawn here with Bakhtin's (1986: 62) definitions of primary and secondary speech genres and the use that the latter make of the former—in a sense, 'recruiting' them. Space precludes further discussion here, however.

contributions, an idea also underlying notions of *filmic cohesion* (Tseng, 2008).

We have seen several illustrations of this particular aspect of multimodality at work above. In our first film extracts discussed in Chapter 1 we were already combining information from the visual and sound tracks to support our segmentation. In our analysis of the extract from *The Bourne Identity* shown in Figure 1.2, for example, we drew a sharp scene boundary between shots 1–7 and shot 8; this was supported not only visually but also by the very different sound quality—punctuated by the elevator bell, shot 8 continues with atmospheric music that was not present in the previous briefing shots. A similar structuring function was performed by the accompanying, non-diegetic music in the button-pushing segment from *The Lady from Shanghai* discussed towards the end of Chapter 2. In our account below, therefore, we will always be drawing on combinations of materials; this will lead us to a rather more complex view of filmic structural organisation and its capability to guide interpretations.

3.4   Materiality and 'epistemological commitment'

Having discussed something of the general notion of semiotic modes and their combination, we now need to bring the materiality of multimodality back into the picture. It is now by and large accepted that different materialities bring with them different constraints on how a semiotic mode might work. Kress (2010: Chapter 5, 79–102) discusses this in terms of mode *affordances*, a notion drawn from the ecopsychological approach of James J. Gibson (e.g., Gibson, 1977).

According to Gibson, we can characterise many aspects of perception in terms of the interaction between entities and their perceivers. That is, a chair is directly perceived as something for sitting in, a door handle as something that a hand interacts with to open or close a door, and so on. The door handle is then said to 'afford' door-opening, the chair 'affords' sitting, etc. Transferred to the area of multimodality, the idea is that distinct materialities may be interacted with in different ways, thereby bringing about distinct tendencies for the development of semiotic modes.

Kress gives the following example taken from his studies of multimodality in schools:

> "in a science classroom the issue of plant cells has been discussed. The teacher might ask: 'OK, who can tell me something about a plant cell?' or she might say: 'OK, who can draw a plant cell with its nucleus?'. The response to the first request might be: 'Miss, the cell has a nucleus.' The response to the second has to be a drawing—very likely with the nucleus placed—as a dot or smaller circle—somewhere in the larger circle." (Kress, 2010: 16)

Kress's point is that the choice of representation, the choice of semiotic mode—here either language or a drawing, has a decisive effect on just what information is given. This is taken not only as a choice of what to express, but as a *commitment* following from the selection of mode. Whereas the linguistic variant has the student focus on issues of classification and part-whole relationships, the drawing as shown to the left of Figure 3.6, for example, requires that the drawer commits to just where the nucleus is positioned within the cell, how large it is, what shape it has, etc. Kress terms this the *epistemological commitment* of the semiotic mode.

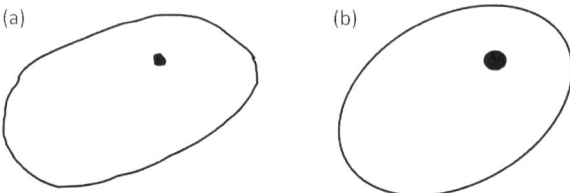

Figure 3.6   *A drawing of a cell with a nucleus similar to that discussed by Kress (2010) and a geometrically regular variant*

Such epistemological commitments generally arise from the properties of the materialities deployed. Clearly, drawing something on a two-dimensional surface cannot be done without simultaneously positioning what is drawn somewhere. This then forces attention to certain relationships and information rather than others. Kress's concern is with the consequences of such choices for literacy and the necessity of being explicitly aware of the differences that mode choices entail.

Our focus here will be slightly different. The tight connection that we have now formulated between materiality and the other strata of the semiotic system requires us to be more detailed about just what commitments a materiality brings with it and which not. We do not see this as exclusively the consequence of a materiality, however; clearly any particular materiality affords certain kinds of abstract distinctions and commitments that may differ from the distinctions and commitments of others, but precisely which commitments are being made can still *only be described* when we have fixed the semiotic mode being deployed. Elsewhere we have also drawn attention to the problems that this raises for multimodal literacy (cf. Bateman, 2011); for film the issue takes on a rather different significance, one crucial for the definition of units of analysis as we shall see in Chapter 5.

Consider again the cell drawn in Figure 3.6(a). Although the positioning and shape of the elements of the drawing are fixed and determinate, this is in itself *not sufficient* to say that these are 'committed to' by the drawing. The materiality alone cannot commit us to a reading of the drawing in which the nucleus is precisely the shape that it is and positioned precisely where drawn. The drawing is equally consistent with an interpretation that states that the nucleus is 'somewhere' inside the cell and probably not precisely in the middle or right at the edge. That is, certain determinate properties expressed through the material are interpreted in this semiotic mode—a mode that we could perhaps name 'approximate illustrative sketch'—as inherently vague qualitative assertions about the entities depicted. Other features equally inherent in the material representation are 'filtered out': for example, we probably do not assume that the cell wall and the nucleus are coloured black (although this may turn out to be the case). In general, just what the assertions being made are, and how tightly circumscribed by the measurable properties of their material rendition they are, depends on the conventions established in the semiotic mode.

This issue has been discussed at some length for representations by Nelson Goodman. In his attempt to provide a general view of symbol systems and their workings in art, he proposes a framework within which it is possible to distinguish more clearly between different kinds of representations. One illustration he offers begins as follows:

> "Compare a momentary electrocardiogram with a Hokusai drawing of Mt. Fujiyama. The black wiggly lines on white backgrounds may be exactly the same in the two cases. Yet the one is a diagram and the other a picture. What makes the difference?" (Goodman, 1969: 229)

The difficulty here is again precisely that of knowing what semiotic mode is to be assumed in the interpretation of the material traces lying before a prospective interpreter. It is by no means the case that this is always obvious. The geometrically regular diagram shown in Figure 3.6(b), for example, might suggest the application of a quite distinct semiotic mode to that shown in Figure 3.6(a), even though it is obviously showing information by and large equivalent to that on the left of the figure. Its very geometric precision suggests that whatever is shown is not by chance, that this is in some respects a 'tighter' rendition of properties of the cell and its nucleus.

The semiotic mode at issue here might then be something like 'scientific technical drawing'. Nevertheless, just how much tighter, and precisely which features may be committed to (e.g., is the nucleus black?), is again only to be determined absolutely when we know the semiotic mode(s) intended by the designer/drawer. In the rather more usual case that we do not know, or have access to, this information, then the properties of the artefact must be used to defeasibly *assume* which semiotic modes are to be taken as applying.

Goodman's classification pulls apart representations that can be seen as 'diagrams' and representations that can be seen as 'pictures' by placing them along a scale of commitment: at the picture end of the scale, there are no material features of the representation that can be safely said to be irrelevant for its interpretation; at the diagram end of the scale, the material features that are relevant are significantly restricted. Thus, in an artwork such as a painting, even the precise brush strokes and the apparent force with which they were applied may well be considered significant—absolutely any change in the representation results in a different artwork (or *could* do: for further refinement on this notion with respect to some borderline cases, see: Levinson 1990: 126); in a graph, in contrast, the only relevant features might be the positions picked out on indicated X and Y axes: the thickness of the line showing the graph, just like the thickness of our cell wall above, might be irrelevant—i.e., "some features that are constitutive in the pictorial scheme are dismissed as contingent in the diagrammatic scheme" (Goodman, 1969: 229). The elements of the pictorial scheme are then said to be relatively **replete**.

Goodman points out that this characterisation distances the discussion from problematic considerations of 'resemblance' and instead allows

> "for full relativity of representation and for representation by things other than pictures. Object and events, visual and nonvisual, can be represented by either visual or non-visual symbols. Pictures may function as representations within systems very different from the one we happen to consider normal; colours may stand for their complementaries or for sizes, perspective may be reversed, or otherwise transformed, and so on." (Goodman, 1969: 229)

This turns out to be important for film also. It is by no means obvious just what 'features' of the filmic material substrate are carrying what kinds of meanings. Any notion of 'natural' representation is by itself far too weak to build an appropriate theory of filmic meaning.

Combining strata with multimodality provides a more appropriate framework for viewing many of the problematic cases and distinctions Goodman illustrates and prepares us well for the treatment of film. The diagram and the picture, for example, correspond to distinct semiotic modes and therefore naturally bring differing kinds of commitment to their interpretation of the material traces of their semiotic 'choices'. Moreover, we can dig deeper in order to draw out another critical consequence of anchoring our semiotic modes with respect to their materiality. Since any semiotic mode is responsible for determining just which range of physical properties in the material substrate are to be 'claimed', it can readily be the case that distinct semiotic modes can operate simultaneously with respect to the *same* physical substrate. That is: the materiality may be articulated simultaneously in a variety of ways independently of one another.

In discussions of film, this is most commonly recognised in terms of the distinct 'codes' that are taken to apply simultaneously and with which we began chapter: a particular film segment will make choices concerning lighting, framing, clothing, acting styles, and so on—all carried at the same time by the audiovisual material. Even within the purely visual track, there are a broad range of articulations layered one on top of the other or, perhaps better, 'side by side' or superimposed. The complex audiovisual material substrate of film thus includes many kinds of articulations that have already been considered from semiotic perspectives in other domains.

As a consequence, determining which kinds of distinctions carry which kinds of semiotic modes constitutes a long running theoretical debate in film theory concerning just what the 'necessary' properties of films are, which particular semiotic codes are specific to film and so on. This addresses questions concerning the *ontology* of film (cf. Metz, 1974*d*; Carroll, 1996*c*).

Our semiotic re-construction of multimodality as such provides a solid approach for re-thinking many of these discussions and we build on this further in Chapter 5. For the present, however, we can note that it is natural within our extended view of semiotic systems that multiple modes can develop on the basis of single physical substrates by selecting to manipulate only a subset of the physically variable dimensions on offer; further examples of this are discussed in Bateman (2011). In Chapter 5 this will be of particular importance to us when we make extensive use of this semiotic property in order to define the particular kinds of analytic units adopted for our framework.

This also reemphasises the point made above concerning the inappropriateness of adopting a sensory-channel based view of mode. Since material substrates are typically extremely rich in the sense that they exhibit many kinds of physical qualities that can be varied independently of one another, they offer a correspondingly rich potential for carrying simultaneous patterning. Each sensory channel may therefore be carrying a host of distinct semiotic modes. Sound can be made to carry a variety of frequencies at a variety of volumes and, if we add in both ears, in a variety of locations. Similarly, a visual image can be made to carry distinct shapes, colours, textures, brightness, and so on. All are available for the development of semiotic modes and film makes extensive use of this possibility.

3.5   Summary and Conclusions

In this chapter, we have set out a general model for semiotic modes, building on the preliminary model developed with respect to the language system as suggested in Figure 2.1 of the previous chapter. This may be applied for discussing and analysing complex multimodal artefacts of all kinds. Here we have considered this model particularly for the case of film, suggesting how it may offer a semiotically more appropriate foundation for taking up discussions of film and filmic meaning-making. The analysis and interpretation of film is then seen to be constrained by the historically-situated and variegated states of the semiotic systems that constitute the medium.

One of the primary benefits of adopting such a foundation is that it provides a model that spans fine technical detail within its lower levels of abstraction and stretches to highly abstract notions of filmic genre and tradition within its 'higher' strata. This view of semiotic systems leads automatically to the kind of guided, discretionary constructivism delineated by Berys Gaut in the discussions of the previous chapter but, at the same time, provides considerably more detail concerning the kinds of mechanisms and phenomena that will need to be taken into account. These mechanisms are themselves broken down along the particular semiotic dimensions defined within the framework, including stratification and the paradigmatic/syntagmatic axes.

To provide the strongest possible foundation for this approach to film, however, we need to fill in more of the semiotic detail of the 'lower' strata of the filmic semiotic system. This will be our task throughout the rest of the book.

Further Reading

Work in **multimodality** is currently booming. Relevant notions are explored in many areas, including the 'image sciences' (German: **Bild-wissenschaft**, Sachs-Hombach 2006) and **socio-functional multimodal semiotics** (e.g., Lemke, 1998; O'Halloran, 1999; Liu and O'Halloran, 2009). **Intersemiotic cohesion** (Royce, 2007) is an important construct here, as are **semiotic metaphor** (e.g., Forceville, 2006) and **semiotic blending** (cf. Goguen, 1999; Fauconnier and Turner, 2003). For overviews of current issues in socio-functional multimodal semiotics in general, see van Leeuwen (2005a) and Martin (2011).

For technological approaches to multimodality, such as that found particularly in **human-machine interaction research** and **multimedia**, see, for example, Bordegoni, Faconti, Maybury, Rist, Ruggieri, Trahanias and Wilson (1997), Oviatt (1999) and Wahlster (2006).

For the definition of **semiotic mode** underlying the approach taken in this book, see Bateman (2011). A useful attempt to pull apart and define the often confused constructs of **mode and medium** and **modality and mediality** is presented by Elleström (2010) starting from the perspective of *medium*, rather than that of semiotic *mode* as done here.

The consequences of overly weak semiotic foundations for considerations of the relation between film and discourse can be found in many places. Even the often cited conclusion reached by Christian Metz that film is a **language without a *langue***, i.e., "language without a language system" (Metz, 1974a: 59–65), has its origins here. Metz quite correctly relates film to discourse, but then had nowhere to anchor this theoretically. Discourse is then reduced to *parole*, i.e., language-in-use, which confuses a stratificational relationship with a realisational/actualisational relationship. Discussion in, for example, Heath (1973) identifies some of the problems here very well.

4 Christian Metz and the *grande syntagmatique* of the image track

> *"Much has been written about the* **grande syntagmatique**: *for it, against it, based on it. The work for it has perhaps been excessively subservient. That against it has recently lacked intellectual generosity and imagination." (Bellour, 2000d: 193, originally published 1976)*

> *"Who is Christian Metz and why is everybody saying these awful things about him?" (Callenbach, 1975: 19)*

With the semiotic foundations introduced in the previous chapter, we can now turn to film in close-up. We have characterised up to this point just what goes into the definition of a semiotic mode and how this brings together a physical substrate and non-material strata of discourse semantics and context. It is therefore also appropriate at this point to relate this development to what is still generally considered the high point (some have said 'low point'!) of the linguistically-inspired semiotic analysis of film: the *grande syntagmatique* of the visual track developed by the film semiotician Christian Metz in the 1960s (cf. Metz, 1966; 1974a: 119–133).

The *grande syntagmatique* proposed an abstract classification of the meaningful possibilities available to a film-maker when conjoining shots in narrative film. This is the level of film *montage* that we introduced in the previous chapter to illustrate the paradigmatic axis of semiotic representation. Montage was first given central pride of place in film theorising by Pudovkin (1926) and Eisenstein (1963), and has remained a defining aspect of what constitutes film ever since, including both the more 'symbolic' uses of Eisenstein and the narrative constructions of, for example, D.W. Griffith (cf. Wees, 1973).

The Metzian *grande syntagmatique* received immense criticism in its time but we will see that only some of that criticism was valid—and, even when valid, most often for the wrong reasons. The lack of a detailed semiotic framework capable of addressing issues of multimodality and discourse effectively blocked off further development. This made it difficult to learn from the critiques and to improve the model. Moreover, discussion of both the original scheme and proposed revisions has in the vast majority of cases continued to draw on a view of linguistics that has scarcely changed since the time of Metz and which has little to do with the current state of the art. These problems notwithstanding, the *grande syntagmatique* still structures discussions of the relations between film and semiotics today and so no account in this area can omit positioning itself with respect to both Metz's approach and the critiques brought against it. Placing this discussion against the background now provided by our extended view of semiotic systems and semiotic modes will bring out both where weaknesses became an inherent part of the model and places where we can now move forward.

The task of this chapter will therefore be to briefly introduce the *grande syntagmatique* so that its approach and terminology is clear. We will then discuss some of the common critiques made of the framework and run through some of the revisions that attempted to improve on it, showing how these also suffered from a lack of appropriate semiotic foundation. This will position us for the development in the next two chapters, where we take up a radical reconstruction of the task that the *grande syntagmatique* was originally intended to perform.

4.1   The original model

One of Metz's goals in the work within which the development of the *grande syntagmatique* took place was to consider very critically the question of whether film could be considered in any sense to be a 'language'. To the extent that similarities could be found, this would naturally offer explanations for how film could work as a carrier of meaning. We have listed some of the more straightforward problems with assuming film to be a language in previous chapters; many of these points were also articulated clearly by Metz over the course of his deliberations.

The fundamental problem facing semiotic approaches to meaning-making in non-linguistic semiotic modes such as film is to find opportunities for enforcing the basic Saussurean semiotic position we introduced in Chapter 2 and built on further as part of the paradigmatic dimension in Chapter 3—i.e., meaning is established only through differential *systems of contrast*. It is these contrasts that provide the 'limitations' against which a given semiotic artefact can situate itself with respect to options *not* taken up. Only then can it become meaningful because, amongst infinite variation, it is not possible for an interpreter to know when something *meaningfully* 'different' or 'similar' to something else has been articulated. The question that faced film semioticians at the beginning of the 1960s was then precisely that of discovering systems of contrast. As discussed in Section 1.1 of the introduction of this book, if there is infinite variation we have no *formal play of differences* (Branigan, 1984: 29) with which to 'get meaning-making off the ground'.

Unfortunately, since film images appeared to be 'pictures' and were therefore, in Goodman's terms (cf. §3.4), *replete*, absolutely any change in their composition results in a different image and so infinite variation appears an intrinsic property of the medium . This made it seem unlikely that it would be possible to isolate systems of contrasts and, from a Saussurean perspective, the entire enterprise of film interpretation was rendered curiously inscrutable. We can also see this in terms of the view of semiotic systems and semiotic modes we have developed here. The need for systems of contrasts is a direct consequence of the requirement that a semiotic mode has access to a 'controllable substance' within which it can draw its recognisable distinctions. Articulating these distinctions within substance is a prerequisite for leaving semiotic traces for interpreters to interpret—a point made by Hjelmslev and drawn on further by Metz (1974d): messages are only messages with respect to codes and so, if there is no code (because there is infinite variation and thus no distinctive differences), there can be no message.

This apparent *lack* of distinctive traces is a reoccurring problem with all 'natural signs'—i.e., signs that are taken to function by virtue of what they show rather than by convention. Such signs are also sometimes referred to as 'short-circuit' signs since they go straight from signifier (if it can still be called signifier) to signified, short-cutting the intervention of convention. Although there have been proposals (e.g., Wollen, 1998) to pay more semiotic attention in the analysis of film both to 'iconic' signs, i.e., signs that signify by resemblance, and to 'indexical' signs, i.e., signs that signify by causal traces as in (traditional) photography, this is not straightforward within the Saussurean tradition. Saussurean semiotics is instead firmly centred on arbitrariness and on the 'negative' definition of meaning by means of contrasting distinctions—i.e.: language is a form and not a substance (cf. §3.2). Thus, given the importance of convention in establishing meanings within such sign systems, signs without these properties are effectively marginalised. We return to this aspect of film from our more refined semiotic position in Chapter 5.

For current purposes, we can note that there are several lines of development that can be taken with respect to this problem and the apparent inapplicability of the notion of 'semiotic code' for film—most of these have already been indicated generally within the survey map of the field of film studies that we offered in Figure 1.5 in the introduction, but it is useful to highlight them again here to place our discussion of Metz's account within a broader context.

One direction, as visible particularly in the post-Metzian development of film semiotics drawing on the psychoanalytic work of Jacques Lacan (for the individual subject) and Louis Althusser (for the embedding within ideology), is to deny the lack of arbitrariness and insist that the interpretation of even apparently natural signs is intrinsically intertwined with convention and social context after all—particularly since these signs are created and shown by devices (an *apparatus*) which are considered anything but devoid of ideological import (Baudry, 1974). Within this perspective, attempts to remove codes are seen as a naive 'realism' that is ideologically pernicious by virtue of its rendering the workings of ideology and power invisible. Discussions here include debate concerning the arbitrariness of conventions of visual perspective when considered cross-culturally, since not all cultures have adopted this in their artistic traditions. Work in this direction therefore sees the rejection of the notion of semiotic codes as simply misguided.

The most directly contrasting position to this instead pays increasing attention to the perceptual and cognitive basis of film reception. From this viewpoint, we understand what we see or hear in a film because our perceptual system directly delivers the required access—that is what the perceptual system is for. This is to argue that quite different interpretative principles apply when we are dealing with natural signs than with conventionalised signs such as language and so other methods are called for (cf. Prince, 1993).

Both of these directions have positive aspects. For example, it should in many respects be self-evident that audiovisual perception plays a critical role in supporting film reception. There are numerous psychological experiments carried out with 'naive' film recipients, e.g., young children or, when available, communities that have not been exposed to the moving image through television or film, that show that a broad intelligibility is available from a very young age independently of the degree of prior exposure (Hochberg and Brooks, 1978; Smith, Anderson and Fischer, 1985; Hobbs, Frost, Davis and Stauffer, 1988; Hochberg and Brooks, 1996). However, on the other side, the naturalistic realism this seems to suggest is at odds with the equally evidently constructed, often narratival, nature of film, which can by no means make claims of unmediated access to some 'objective reality'.

We will return to this apparent dichotomy in the next chapter when we introduce and motivate our approach to basic filmic units for analysis in detail; as a precursor to our own approach, however, we consider first a third path that was taken by Metz. Metz explored a position by which he could *both* accept film as being, in many respects, made up of natural signs with their accompanying infinite degrees of variation—and thereby quite distinct to, for example, the words of a verbal language— *and* seek a semiotic characterisation in terms of differences. The manifest intelligibility of film, not only at the level of the individual images but also at the more seemingly conventionalised levels of narration and story-telling, led Metz to consider the basic assumption that film is made up *exclusively* of infinitely varying natural signs untenable. He concluded that there then had to be some *other* level(s) of characterisation that would provide the formal distinctions necessary to build a code. This would then cover the meaningful options for creating filmic meaning that appear to be regularly employed by both film viewers and film-makers.

Metz's breakthrough was to consider the 'large' units of film, rather than individual images, in order to generalise over infinite variability—i.e., to consider *collections* of consecutive shots within the image track (Metz, 1974*a*: 120). Metz argued that it is precisely here that we find the possibility of substitution, commutation and other semiotic/linguistic operations that would support the construction of recognisable structural configurations as required. Whereas individual images might then vary indefinitely, *combinations* of images appeared much more tightly constrained in terms of the meanings that could be made. In fact:

> "Although each image is a free creation, the arrangement of these images into an intelligible sequence—cutting and montage—brings us to the heart of the semiological dimension of film. It is a rather paradoxical situation: Those proliferating (and not very discrete!) units—the *images*—when it is a matter of composing a film, suddenly accept with reasonably good grace the constraint of a few large syntagmatic structures." (Metz, 1974a: 101, original emphasis)

Thus, while no image ever entirely resembles another image, the great majority of narrative films resemble each other in their principal syntagmatic figures.

Metz's starting point was then to consider the alternative options that a film-maker might take up when producing a structurally 'autonomous' segment within a film. How precisely such autonomy was to be defined subsequently became a point of debate and criticism, but the general idea is that we have some kind of narrative unit such as an episode or 'scene' in a dramaturgical sense (Kawin, 1992: 243) that needs to be 'expressed as film'. The resulting system of options Metz termed the *grande syntagmatique* of the 'larger units' (i.e., combinations of shots) of the visual track. The *grande syntagmatique* was to provide a generic classification that captures within a single systematic description all the possible ways in which filmic segments can be meaningfully constructed, ranging from their smallest elements, the infinitely varying shots, up to 'autonomous' units.

Metz's classification of alternatives accordingly begins with the *autonomous segment*. This is the *filmic realisation* of what, on some higher, more abstract level could be described as a unit of narrative, a single 'episode' with some 'unity of "action"' (Metz, 1974a: 124). Such an autonomous segment might then appear in film as a single continuous unit or, alternatively, could be broken into combinations of smaller-scale units—cf. also on this point: Monaco (2000: 220; 2009: 244). The *grande syntagmatique* termed these combinations filmic *syntagmas*. Each individual type of syntagma calls for particular distinctive patterns of relationships holding over its elements which add specifically filmic meanings.

The classification went through several versions, beginning with the account set out in Metz (1966). Subsequently, particularly in the discussion presented in Metz (1974a: 103–104, 122n), Metz critiqued and improved the framework in response to the requirements of carrying out particular film analyses. Some of the problems that were encountered and how they were addressed are interesting in their own right since they bring out quite general problems that any account needs to consider; we will return to some of these in our discussions in subsequent chapters—particular those that revolve around the question of how units can be defined and related to one another. This is an area for which our account provides very detailed proposals.

Our introduction of the *grande syntagmatique* will draw for the present, however, exclusively on the version given in Metz (1974*a*: 119–146); this is the version that is generally presented in overviews of Metz's work. Its distinguishing feature is a strongly hierarchical organisation—as Metz observed:

> "It appears that the different types and subtypes ... can be redistributed into a system of successive dichotomies, according to a procedure commonly used in linguistics. This scheme gives us a better outline of the *deep structure* of the choices that confront the film-maker for each one of the 'sequences' of his [sic] film." (Metz, 1974*a*: 123, original emphasis)

The *grande syntagmatique* is then the classificatory structure that results from the successive dichotomies that organise the syntagmas. We set this out graphically in Figure 4.1 following Metz's numbering of the individual types for ease of reference below.

It is telling that the quotation given here already shows several problems directly due to the lack of more developed semiotic models at that time. The general linguistic frame Metz assumes refers to notions taken from Chomskyan Generative Grammar—e.g., 'deep structure', which was construed purely in syntagmatic terms. The reference to 'choice' is, in contrast, purely paradigmatic and so this fits uncomfortably alongside an essentially syntagmatic modelling style. We will need to return to this conflation of semiotic dimensions at many points as we proceed.

The classification begins with the straightforward question as to whether an autonomous segment is divided into sub-units or not—i.e., whether it is a shot by itself or a combination of shots. A shot by itself can already serve several distinct functions: Metz distinguishes here between shots that themselves carry the narrative forward (*sequence shots*) and *inserts*.

The sequence shot is a collection of actions that appear to have been taken within a single take; the internal organisation of such shots may be complex but was not considered to fall within the kind of distinctions that Metz was pursuing with his syntagmatic articulation according to shots. Metz did note, however, that many of the kinds of meanings that can be expressed with sequences of shots can also be achieved with particular filmic configurations *within* single shots. We will return to our treatment of this phenomenon in Chapter 5. This situation was a disruptive gap in Metz's account since, when considered from a narrative perspective, it readily gives rise to rather counter-intuitive segmentations.

A standard example of this problem was presented by Colin (1995*b*) in his treatment of the opening scenes of Orson Welles' *Touch of Evil* (1958). The film begins with a long single take followed by equally related further

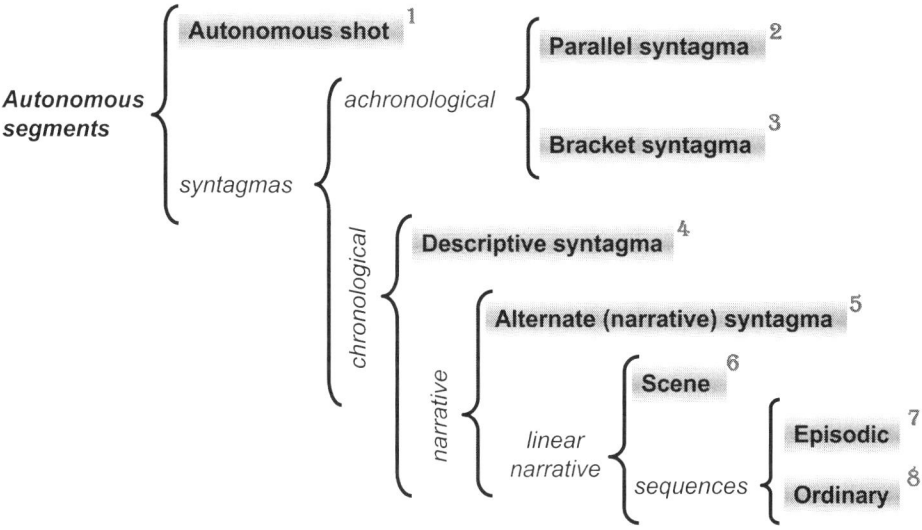

Figure 4.1 *Metz's* grande syntagmatique *of the image track of narrative film; adapted from* *Metz (1974a: 146)*

action in a separate shot. Within the *grande syntagmatique*, however, the analyst is forced to divide the continuous narrative action at this point because two very different kinds of syntagmas are involved. Similar points are made in Elisabeth Ezra's recent investigations of early single shot films (Ezra, 2000: 35), in which many of the possibilities that Metz attributed to complex syntagmas can already be observed within single shots. There have long been grounds, therefore, for a critical re-consideration of this particular area of Metz's framework. A rather more fine characterisation of the particular roles played by inserts was offered in this spirit very early on in a study by Fledelius (1978), for example.

This area of discussion can also be seen more generally as offering a further example of the problem and importance of specifying within any semiotic stratum precisely which units of analysis are being addressed. We return to this in more detail in subsequent chapters; here it will suffice to note that although many of the filmic alternatives that Metz describes are genuine semiotic alternatives (i.e., part of the paradigmatic description), the precise filmic *unit* they apply to (i.e., the syntagmatic description) is still in need of a more general characterisation.

The other subtype of autonomous segment, the insert, provides further individual aspects of filmic development, related or not to the unfolding narrative in several distinct ways. Metz identifies four kinds of such inserts, described as follows (Metz, 1974a: 125):

  i. nondiegetic insert: an interpolated shot showing something unre-
      lated to the ongoing narrative,
  ii. subjective insert: an interpolated shot showing the impressions or
      perceptions of a character,
  iii. displaced diegetic insert: an interpolated shot taken from some other
      time or place in the narrative,
  iv. explanatory insert: an interpolated shot showing some extra detail
      of information from the narrative at that point.

The notion of 'autonomy' appealed to here is evidently of a very particular kind. Metz is referring to 'local' autonomy with respect to internal
composition and integrity of the segment as a unit; he is not referring to
the relationship between such autonomous units and the place they take
up within the unfolding film as a whole. This lack of description of how
autonomous segments relate to other autonomous segments remained
an unsolved issue for Metz and, indeed, requires a far more developed
notion of discourse semantics and organisation in order to be addressed.
We return to this and provide our solution to the problem in Chapter 7.
For now we can note that there is considerable complexity hidden even
in the only 'non-syntagma' of the *grande syntagmatique*; a point sometimes
brought as criticism against the framework as a whole, clearly picking out
a place where further refinement is necessary.

The filmic renditions that then stand as *alternatives* to these autonomous
segments within the *grande syntagmatique* are organised primarily around
time, space and topic. This follows from the orientation adopted to issues
of plot and narrative development. Their organisation follows from Metz's
assumptions drawn from linguistics at that time that a branching structure
of this kind would be well suited to explaining the choices available to
film-makers and interpreters.

The first major discrimination among the syntagmas is between those
whose elements are related by time (chronological: subtypes 4–8) and those
whose elements are not so related (achronological: 2–3).

The chronological subtypes include pure description, where there is
generally spatial continuity but not necessarily forward progression in
time, and narrative, where time moves forward across the elements of the
syntagma. For the latter there are further discriminations made between
syntagmas where time moves continuously and without breaks across the
shots of the syntagma (subtype: 6), syntagmas where time can jump forward between consecutive shots, for example cutting 'dead time' because
nothing of interest to the film is happening or to speed the progression
of the narrative (subtype: 8), and syntagmas where there is an alternation between ongoing actions, as typically occurs in the filming of chases
when first one proponent and then the other are repeatedly shown in rapid
succession (subtype: 5).

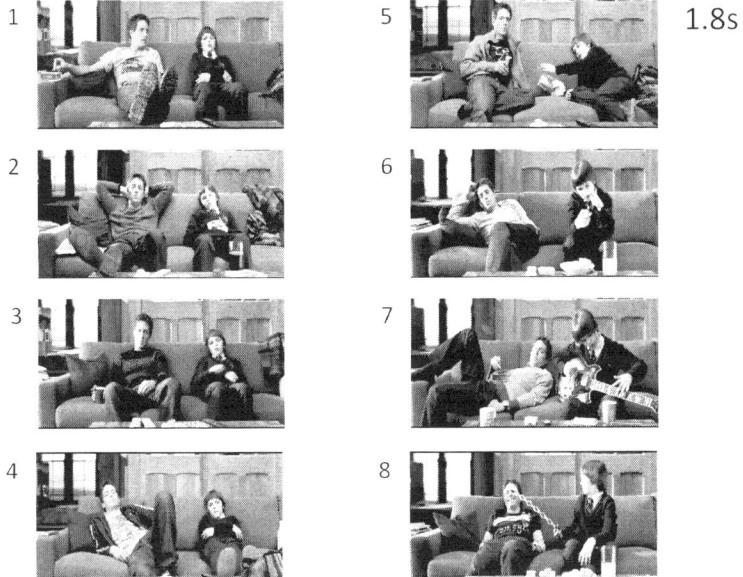

1.8s

Figure 4.2   An example of a Metzian episodic sequence from Paul and Chris Weitz's About a boy *(2002: 0:38:49–0:39:07)*

There is also a rather more complex syntagmatic type in which there is a general forward progression in time but the elements are selected according to some particular organizational feature or property important for the film (subtype: 7). The standard example given for subtype 7 is the indication of the progressive deterioration of Kane's marriage in Orson Welles' *Citizen Kane* (1941) by presenting in sequence selected scenes at the breakfast table spanning what must be several years: the elements are necessarily temporally ordered (otherwise a deterioration would not be recognisable) but they are selected according to this overarching topic rather than narrative consecutivity. This construction is so distinctive that it seems a fairly evident quotation whenever it occurs; a variation on the theme is shown in the extract from *About a boy* (2002) in Figure 4.2, in which we see the core episodes from a slightly longer and more complex sequence spanning just over two weeks.

The eight shots in the figure show eight different days over which the relationship between the two main characters (Hugh Grant and Nicholas Hoult) develops from strained indulgence to a more friendly, relaxed acceptance. Each day is shown in a single shot lasting around 1.8 seconds; the fragment as a whole is framed within a larger segment that uses the device of a daily television show to make clear that no doubt can be entertained that we are in fact dealing with separate days, as is further supported by the changing clothes of one of the characters (the other is in school uniform and so does not vary) and their respective changing postures and activities.

The achronological subtypes in contrast consist of elements related by *topicality* where the members of the syntagma show some kind of connection in terms of the themes or values relevant for the film: such as, for example, presenting shots indicating wealth, or poverty, or authority, or injustice, etc.; the crucial defining characteristic is consequently a lack of intended temporal commitment. The two subtypes, the *parallel* syntagma (2) and the *bracket* syntagma (3) are themselves distinguished in terms of more complex properties. Metz describes the parallel syntagma as bringing together 'two or more alternating "motifs"' (Metz, 1974*a*: 126) but without temporal or spatial relationships; whereas the bracket syntagma provides brief scenes selected as 'typical examples of the same order of reality' (Metz, 1974*a*: 126) to illustrate some point made by the series rather than in the individual shots. Classic examples of the bracket syntagma are segments made up of views of country life, which thereby come to represent 'country life' as such rather than the specific houses, fields, or animals that may be picked out.

Although Metz's account is often described in terms of 'shots' and we have used this perspective ourselves in our examples here, it is important to keep hold of the semiotic principle mentioned above at the outset that Metz was actually dealing with the filmic *realisation* of more abstract narrative concerns. It is these narrative unities, therefore, that actually drive segmentation, even though Metz's own descriptions were not always consistent with this. Heath (1975*a*), for example, notes the uneasy combination of shots and units defined dramaturgically in Metz's description.

The completely different ontological statuses of Metz's autonomous segment and the remaining syntagmas is also indicative of the strain placed on the account by its lack of explicit semiotic stratification. Although the autonomous shot and the other syntagmas appear side-by-side in the classification, the former is defined according to the *signifier*, i.e., it is demarcated only within the form, whereas the latter are defined according to the *signifieds*, i.e., Metz's assumed dramaturgical unities of action, location and time. This point was also made by Metz but was not followed through with respect to its consequences for theorising the *grande syntagmatique* as a whole.

The difference between autonomous shots and syntagmas was nevertheless fundamental: in contrast to the perception of a picture, or continuous image, it is only at the level of montage that film becomes for an observer recognisably 'digital'. On this level the sense of a syntagma can only be discerned by an act of cognition which 'knows' how two or more shots are to be combined.

4.2   Two examples of analysis with the *grande syntagmatique*

We now present two brief analyses following Metz's account in order to illustrate the approach in action. The first is from Metz's own most detailed attempt to apply the framework, a complete analysis of Jacques Rozier's *Adieu Philippine* (1962); the analysis is presented in Metz (1974*a*: Chapter 6, 149–176). We recommend that readers also make themselves familiar with this analysis and, if possible, viewing the film itself would also be helpful (see *Further Reading*).

The film is set primarily in Paris and Corsica and is concerned with a young man working in a relatively lowly position in a television studio (Michel, played by Jean-Claude Aimini) and his meeting with two young women, Liliane (Yveline Céry) and Juliette (Stefania Sabatini), just prior to being sent off to the French-Algerian war. For each proposed autonomous segment, Metz sets out the form of transition with the segment preceding ('filmic punctuation') and its classification according to the *grande syntagmatique*. The characterisation of the transitions is an additional piece of information sometimes helpful for the classification offered but not systematically related.

We focus here on Segments 2 and 3 of Metz's analysis. Segment 2 consists of 34 individual shots spread over four minutes, while Segment 3 consists of 39 shots over two and a quarter minutes. Several of these shots last less than a second and there is a considerable number of camera movements, 'jump cuts' and other transitory phenomena. The first of the segments is located mostly in a television studio where a music performance is being recorded; the second segment is in a café. The granularity of these analyses is therefore quite different to that we have used so far, since it is primarily autonomous segments as a whole that the *grande syntagmatique* asks us to look at rather than shots. Naturally, we must also examine the shots constituting such segments for the analysis to proceed, but the analysis result is nevertheless for the segment as a whole. The move to consider segments is clearly a potentially useful reduction in granularity that helps us towards narrative and discourse concerns.

Segment 2 is classified by Metz as an 'ordinary sequence' (syntagma type 8 in the diagram above). Metz's motivation for this classification is that "a single action is presented in its chronological order though certain moments of it are skipped" (Metz, 1974*a*: 151). In particular:

> "We see Michel leaving the studio to fetch an earphone. He encounters two young girls in the entrance hall, climbs into the television mobile unit where the director is working, returns, and, on his way back, talks to the girls, whom he then brings into the studio. After the broadcasting of the show is over, he goes up to them and makes a date to meet them in a café." (Metz, 1974*a*: 151)

 Michel goes to the mobile van to get some headphones and meets Liliane and Juliette standing outside

 the musicians play

 in the van, the preparations are heating up and recording starts

 Liliane and Juliette watch

 Michel invites Liliane and Juliette inside

 the musicians play, Michel stands around and helps to move cameras

 Michel suggests that they all go for a drink

Figure 4.3　Selected frames from Segment 2 of Jacques Rozier's Adieu Philippine *(1962) according to Metz's numbering scheme*

We show some selected key frames of this segment in Figure 4.3. Metz actually considers the beginning of this segment to *overlap* with the end of the previous segment. This naturally suggests that there may be some loose ends concerning the definitions of units since if segments may overlap we need to be clear about just how extensive such overlapping can be and under what conditions it can occur. Metz claims that this is quite common and is analogous to similar constructions in music—we return to this issue in detail in Chapters 5 and 7 below.

The next segment follows with a specific and pronounced 'montage with effect': we are suddenly shown a close-up of a jukebox with no clear reference to what has been seen so far. The next shot, however, reveals that we are in a café and Michel is sitting together with Liliane and Juliette. Metz classifies this segment as a 'scene' (syntagma type 6) with the uninterrupted action 'conversation in a café'. Metz emphasises that the frequent changing of angles with shot/reverse-shot alternations as speakers change during the dialogue mostly constituting this segment is not a reason to change the classification to a formal 'alternation' (syntagmatic type 5) because the discontinuities are *camera breaks* and not *diegetic breaks*—only in the latter case, Metz argues, would any classification other than 'scene' be required:

> "The alternation, a simple switching back and forth of the camera, has no *distinctive* function in this instance." (Metz, 1974a: 152, original emphasis)

This can be shown, Metz says, by imagining a 'commutation test' whereby the shots in the scene are replaced by ('commuted with') a single take with a stationery camera; since this would be perfectly possible here, we are dealing with a 'scene' rather than something more complex.

This is an important aspect of the classification, since the structure of the segment consists almost exclusively of the A-B-A-B pattern of dialogic interaction and this is clearly an 'alternation' of *some* kind—this structure is not therefore considered by the *grande syntagmatique*. Again, the reduction in granularity to group these alternations together as a scene is potentially useful. But, in both cases, Metz's reliance on an interpretation that demanded segments to make up dramaturgically individuated scenes led many critics to argue that the *grande syntagmatique* was not itself adding anything new. As Noël Carroll bitingly phrased it:

> "Restating obvious facts does not constitute a scientific break-through. Of course, one might argue that Metz's is the first formulation of a theory that will become very informative. To this, I can only reply that Metz's taxonomy is one of the unlikeliest promissory notes in the history of science." (Carroll, 1974: 61)

The grounds for the severity of this evaluation are, however, not entirely clear. There are further distinctions made within the *grande syntagmatique* that do suggest additional criteria for segmentation and this is where an original contribution was clearly already being made.

For example, the very first segment of *Adieu Philippine* receives a very different classification to those examples just presented. The film starts by presenting a collection of shots that together give an impression of a hive of activity as the television studio gets ready to record the music performance. There are (at least at first viewing: we will have more to say about this in Chapter 7 below) no particular individuals picked out in this segment and it stands as a story-motivated background for the film credits. Since this is not chronological according to Metz, i.e., the shots could have been presented in almost any order and would have still evoked the same busy impression, the *grande syntagmatique* classification is as a 'bracket syntagma' (syntagma type 3). This changes as the film transitions into Segment 2, which is clearly concerned with Michel and unfolds strongly chronologically as we have seen.

The change in classification then *requires*, according to the logic of the *grande syntagmatique*, that a new autonomous segment be started: that is, there are explicit grounds provided for one segmentation rather than another. This is the work that the *grande syntagmatique* begins to try to address: providing objective criteria for particular segmentations rather than others. Although we may still disagree concerning the correctness of some of those segmentations, as well as on just where the segment boundaries are, this is nevertheless a useful goal for an empirically pursuable film analysis. A similar line of argumentation holds for the transition into Segment 3. Segment 2 has temporal gaps and so is an ordinary sequence (type 8); the segment in the café has no gaps and so again belongs to a *different* category, that of a scene (type 6). It must, therefore, be segmented separately following the logic of the *grande syntagmatique*.

This shows clearly the intended role of the *grande syntagmatique* classification scheme: the explicit constraints offered by its taxonomy restrict the analyses that can be made so that a higher degree of intersubjective agreement might be pursued, thereby raising the likelihood of empirically verifiable analyses. When we return to the syntagmatic axis of film in Chapter 7, we will see that it is possible to develop this kind of description in considerably more detail and that this brings further significant restrictions to bear on just what analyses can be constructed. As first steps in this direction, however, the *grande syntagmatique* was without doubt invaluable.

As a second example, we consider just one segment from Roth's (1983) syntagma-by-syntagma analysis of Sergio Leone's trilogy *A Fistful of dollars* (1964), *For a few dollars more* (1965) and *The Good, the Bad and the Ugly* (1966)—in particular, segment 32 from *A Fistful of dollars* (Roth, 1983: 86–87), which begins around 0:59:44. The events in this segment essentially concern the main character's (Clint Eastwood) rescue of the female character Marisol (Marianne Koch) by disposing of the 'bandits' guarding her. Meanwhile, the main group of bandits hears the shots that Clint Eastwood's character lets off and they all set off on horseback at high speed from their ranch to the outhouse where the rescue action is taking place. Marisol is then reunited with her husband and son and after a brief dialogue with the Clint Eastwood character, they leave the area. The main group of bandits then arrives on the scene. The putative autonomous segment here also consists of a considerable number of shots (43 shots running over approximately 200s) and so in Figure 4.4 we again show only a representative selection of key frames.

Roth classifies this segment as an 'alternate syntagma' (syntagma type 5) on the basis that there are two locales with two action tracks running in a way that is intended to be interpreted as simultaneous. Thus, while the rescue and reunion is taking place at the outhouse, the bandits are on their way to the scene. As Roth notes here, it is clear that the main action is the rescue, with the approach of the bandits serving to add urgency to the scene. The segment is distinguished both from the segment preceding and that following, both classified by Roth as ordinary scenes. This Roth also relates to distinct stages in the narrative development: the former is preliminary to the rescue, the latter provides Clint Eastwood's character with more information concerning the bandits' plans. The rescue action

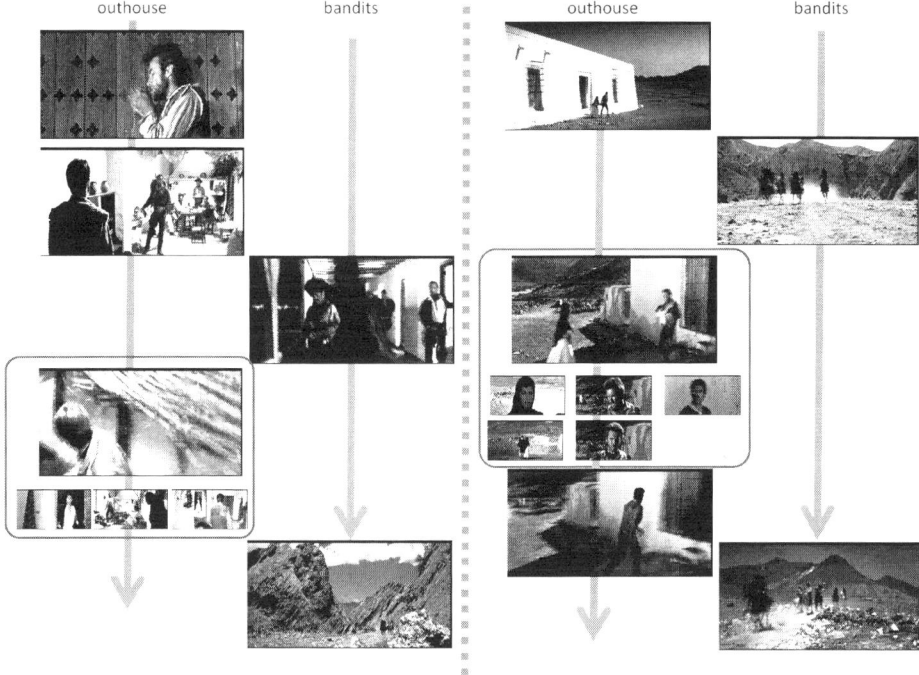

Figure 4.4   Segment 32 from Sergio Leone's A fistful of dollars *according to Roth's numbering scheme*

track contains considerable additional organisation in its own right: first there is the exchange of shots filmed with a dialogic ABAB structure (consisting of around 20 shots), then there is an actual dialogue between Clint Eastwood's character and Marisol (consisting of 14 shots). The number of shots carrying the *alternation* is actually minimal. In both cases, then, we see a significant increase in the level of structural abstraction that can be imposed on the film during analysis as well as criteria for motivating the particular segmentations adopted.

Despite these potential benefits, the level of detail required in a Metzian-style analysis was still considered by most analysts of the time to be too high for the rewards gained. Analyses of complete films have accordingly been very rare. Of these attempts, and in addition to those just mentioned, the most accessible is probably that of Vincente Minnelli's *Gigi* (1958) as presented by Bellour (2000d); for others see the *Further Reading*. Critics of the approach generally found such analyses unrevealing, however. After spending considerable energy segmenting a film, it was unclear to many just what had been gained. It seemed that much of the main work of analysis still needed to be done (cf. Cegarra, 1973; Carroll, 1974; Nichols, 1975; Henderson, 1977). In many respects this was true: it was left unspecified just how autonomous segments, once identified, could be related *to one another* and to their functions within the overall structure of the film: that is, there was no indication of how the syntagmas identified combined to yield narrative, or other, interpretations.

This was certainly an unsatisfactory position. It is evident that even among those segments we have used as illustrations here, there are many more relations that need to be brought out. Metz may have taken this task to belong exclusively to the area of *connotation* and so excluded any characterisation of this. Metz states throughout his argument that he wished to focus on the denotational in order to provide a basis for subsequent connotational interpretations. But then it is less convincing why precisely the segmentation level picked out by the *grande syntagmatique* and no other was to be considered denotational.

As we shall develop in considerable detail below, the main problem is that, despite its name, the *grande syntagmatique* in fact has a very weak notion of syntagmatic organisation—i.e., there is no structure. Without a stronger specification of syntagmatic organisation, there is no way of constructing both smaller units (in order to bring out the considerable internal detail of the segments that was passed over in the above descriptions) and *larger* units, which can help move us towards more adequate interpretations of filmic interpretation as a whole.

While Metz had already drawn attention to structural configurations that appear to go beyond the scale of his own 'large' structures and his typology, a simple statement that there are film segments of various scales does not take us very far in creating a more comprehensive account. In contrast to this, the detailed analysis offered by Fledelius (1978) states not only that there may be larger syntagmatic organisations, a position that Metz was quite willing to countenance, but, more usefully, that these larger syntagmatic structures may *also* be subject to the *grande syntagmatique*, thereby bringing the smaller and larger scales into relation:

> "A further development of Metz's system consists in the perception of the film in its entirety not as a single string of paratactic syntagmas, but as a pyramid-like hierarchy of superior and subordinate syntagmas. ... [Our] analysis led not only to the identification of units larger than the syntagmas, but also to the conclusion that these units can be classified according to the same categories as the syntagmas, only with the difference that they are syntagmas of syntagmas, not syntagmas of shots." (Fledelius, 1978: 48)

This observation gets at the heart of syntagmatic structure in a way that provides a strong foundation for turning the *grande syntagmatique* into a powerful framework for the analysis of entire films. We return to this line of development in the chapters following.

4.3   Revisions and rebuttals

When the *grande syntagmatique* was originally introduced, it raised a considerable furore. Some, more semiotically-inclined film researchers took it as heralding a new era of scientific film analysis, providing a level of detail and objectivity lacking in previous accounts. Others took its precision and rather limited interpretative statements as being absurdly reductive, doing a considerable violence to the subtlety and range of filmic meaning. Film theory was at that time beginning to turn to postmodern, poststructuralist theories (cf. Figure 1.5 above) and many accordingly saw Metz's proposal as the hopeless relapse to an outdated 'master code', willfully ignorant of the importance of embedding interpretations in societal (i.e., ideological) debates and the psychoanalytic details of the subjects performing such interpretations.

The criticisms and reviews offered then ranged from short dismissals to lengthy, almost line-by-line exegeses of variable quality. While some points were well made, there was also the general difficulty discussed in previous chapters of dealing with phenomena on the 'bleeding' edge of the state of the art in semiotics. Moreover, despite these debates, the Metzian system is still the one standard semiotic approach described in textbooks. James Monaco, in the third edition of his introductory film textbook from 2000, was still writing:

> "...despite its idiosyncrasies and occasional confusions, it remains the only recent attempt to comprehend the complex system of montage." (Monaco, 2000: 220)

Several factors contribute to this kind of evaluation both of Metz and of work that continued in the tradition he started. One of these is the sense that, although a brave attempt, the Metzian style of filmic analysis is itself inherently flawed. Thus many writers who have since proposed analyses reminiscent of that proposed by Metz show few qualms in taking the Metzian categories and redefining them to their own needs without too much further motivation (e.g., Bellour, 2000*b*; Kuchenbuch, 2005); closer analyses, corrections and refinements of Metz's account have mostly been passed over with little (if any) comment.

It is now no longer necessary to engage with the considerable body of Metzian criticism in detail; instead, we can usefully classify the problems and critiques raised against the *grande syntagmatique* according to the following three points:

- robustness,
- exhaustiveness,
- usefulness.

'Robustness' refers to how well the definitions apply to data—if it is clear which cases fall under which classifications, then we can call the account robust. Independent 'coders' using the classification are then likely to come to the same conclusions about segmentation and the classification of the units so segmented. When the definitions of classifications are weak and difficult to apply to actual cases, however, this leads more often to arbitrary decisions and two independent analysts are unlikely to come up with the same analysis: this is also known as the problem of inter-coder reliability. Many critiques of Metz have pointed to this difficulty, arguing that even his own offered analysis of *Adieu Philippine* contains classifications that do not fit his definitions.

The second difficulty, exhaustiveness, can also reduce reliability. An account is exhaustive when we can find an appropriate classification for any film segment encountered: that is, it has a claim to dealing with the full range of phenomena that actually occur. Naturally, this is typically a goal rather than a state reached in practice; the question reduces to how often a problematic new case is encountered. When this occurs with almost every segment analysed, then there is much to do; if such occurrences are rare, however, then there is a better chance that the account is approaching a reasonable coverage of the domain.

And finally, there is the problem of usefulness: what one can do with an analysis in the terms of the *grande syntagmatique* once performed. Answers to this latter question are mixed: Roth (1983) suggests how classifications for entire films can be used to suggest genre and even director groupings; but this hypothesis has not been subjected to any detailed testing. Another hypothesis might be that the syntagmas show some principles or mechanisms of actual filmic interpretation by recipients at work: this is precisely what a construal of the *grande syntagmatique* as a discourse semantics would lead to—but here again there has been little exploration. The references to narrative and its 'logic' inherent in the definitions that Metz offers have remained more suggestive than demonstrated and leave certain segmentation decisions less well motivated than ideally the case.

As we develop our framework further in the following chapters, we will be seeking a reworking of some of the properties and specification of the *grande syntagmatique* drawing on the more developed view of multimodal semiotic systems that we now have available. The result will extend significantly beyond Metz's account along both the paradigmatic and syntagmatic axis and will make claims, at the level of description we are addressing, of both robustness and usefulness. In addition, with respect to exhaustiveness we will be able to identify quite precisely some areas that are not yet fully included, although our account opens up a precise place for that further development within the broader framework as a whole.

To begin illustrating how this development can proceed, we set out in the rest of this section some of the particular points of critique brought against Metz and their suggested extensions to the model, interpreting these in each case against our definition of semiotic modes. This will show quite precisely where further steps need to be taken and how.

4.3.1   Three common points of critique

It is also necessary before proceeding to the proposed extensions of the model to briefly consider some of the more 'philosophical' or ideological positions taken against the *grande syntagmatique*. These are often employed rhetorically to undermine the relevance of Metz's treatment and so must be moved 'out of the way' to avoid cutting off the discussion before it starts. The individual critiques offered are far too numerous to consider individually but three areas of critique commonly reoccur: first, that Metz reduces all film to narrative; second, that Metz reduces filmic organisation to linguistic syntax; and third, that Metz commits to an inappropriate acceptance of realism and the 'naturalness' of the image. We shall see that all three arguments fail to engage when we consider extensions of Metz's framework against the backdrop of a more appropriate semiotic foundation.

Metz reduces film to narrative.   One area of critique was based on Metz's focus on film as a vehicle for narrative. Metz argued that film had become the sophisticated means of signification that it is primarily by virtue of adapting itself to the requirements of effective story-telling. This was seen by some to constitute an ideologically inappropriate marginalisation of all more experimental and non-Hollywood dominated usages of the medium of film. In relation to our introduction of the discourse semantic stratum in Chapter 2, we can note that 'narrative' was not presumed or given any particularly central status there. Narrative, seen linguistically, is just another genre of language use, alongside others such as 'explanation', 'description' and so on. All of these are equally reliant on discourse semantics and, in fact, can only be defined by drawing also on the distinct use they make of discourse semantic resources. Thus, as far as the mechanisms of discourse construction within a semiotic mode are concerned, our approach will be neutral with respect to whether a semiotic artefact is narrating, describing, explaining, etc.

Although difficult to make explicit at the time that Metz was writing, there are also traces of this independence even in the *grande syntagmatique* and its definition. This is shown, for example, in the study of Fledelius (1978), which applied Metz's taxonomy to *documentary films*. The result is striking: the taxonomy remains virtually unchanged; this is one indication that the distinctions Metz was drawing can be semiotically relevant even without the restriction to narrative film. Thus, even though narrative is clearly drawn as a kind of 'guide' for the discussion, this can in no sense be seen as limiting the account *a priori*. Narrative is useful for this purpose mostly because it is a genre that has received considerable attention and so much is known about its functioning. But many of the mechanisms proposed are not, in fact, limited to narrative. This can also be seen in several more recent approaches in narratology (see *Further Reading*) and is unsurprising linguistically since narrative is in any case just one kind of discourse.

Thus, although many of the criteria that Metz proposes for distinguishing categories have their roots in the narrational and dramaturgical concerns of the film-maker and the intended uptake of those concerns by a viewer, we can nevertheless draw apart this binding with narrative as follows. Seymour Chatman proposed early on in his study of film and narrative that 'narrative itself is a deep structure quite independent of its medium' (Chatman, 1992: 403). The mention of 'deep structure', here and as we noted for Metz's description above, is unfortunate in that it draws on an inappropriate import from the linguistic approaches of the 1960s. The notions of stratification and 'abstract choice' inherent in the view of paradigmatic organisation we gave in the previous chapter provide a far more appropriate construal of the phenomena to be captured. In our terms, some abstract organization is 'actualized' or 'realized' in an expressive medium, and that medium can be language, drawing, dance or, most relevant here, film; here, therefore, we already see traces of a family of semiotic modes at work, with many similarities to be drawn out in their discourse semantics and contextualised uses.

Film segments thus characterised then stand in a *realisational* relationship to the events of the narrative: i.e., starting from a given 'event', the film-maker can decide to decompose this event into a variety of kinds of syntagmas. Most writers on film, and particularly on narrative film, have adopted some version of this dual characterization: Bordwell (1985), for example, adopts the terms *fabula* for the 'underlying' events and *syuzhet* for the filmic articulation of those events—terms drawn from the Russian formalism of the early 20th century, while Metz and his successors commonly make reference to issues of plot and its events and characters as a distinct level of description to their descriptions of montage: all such units are placed '*in* the film but in *relation* to the plot' (Metz, 1974a: 143).

Crucial, then, is the following:

> 'A salient property of narrative is double time structuring. That is, all narratives in whatever medium, combine the time of sequence of plot events, the time of the *histoire* ('story-time') with the time of presentation of those events in the text, which we call 'discourse-time'. What is fundamental to narrative, regardless of medium, is that these two time orders are independent.' (Chatman, 1992: 404)

From the broader perspective of semiotic modes, we consider this structuring as *intrinsic to discourse semantics* and so the same characterisation applies regardless of the 'genre' being expressed. Any semiotic mode provides resources for managing the textual development or 'unfolding' of its 'texts': this is the precisely the function of a discourse semantics.

Distinguishing the narrative-as-such and the filmic construal of narrative to occupy distinct semiotic strata, each with its own possible unfolding development, opens up the door to an approach to filmic meaning that goes far beyond narrative. As we shall see, as a consequence most of the distinctions drawn by Metz can readily be pursued beyond their apparent origins in considerations of narrative.

Metz reduces film to syntax.   We have seen at many places in the discussion so far that it is common practice to talk of the 'grammar' or 'syntax' of film. We have already, particularly in Chapter 2, argued that this informal usage can be misleading. Prior to the 1970s, talk of the grammar of film was generally meant in a more or less metaphorical or imprecise way—necessarily so, because the properties of 'grammar' and 'syntax' that we now know from linguistics had not yet been worked out. Then, largely due to the rise of Chomskyan Transformational Generative Grammar, comparisons and analyses of film began to draw increasingly on this new paradigm. Among some theoreticians, therefore, the 'grammar of film' was then not taken metaphorically at all, but instead as the claim that filmic messages exhibit structural properties genuinely 'grammatical' or 'syntactic' as defined linguistically.

Several researchers attempted this quite explicitly. Carroll (1980), for example, follows up the 'film-as-language' metaphor by employing an explicit combination of linguistic syntagmatic mechanisms (such as, e.g., phrase structure rules and early Chomskyan notions of 'transformations') to describe films; we see similar strategies even quite recently, as in for example the approach taken by Buckland (2000). However, complex combinations of semiotic modes such as film presented challenges that the linguistics of the late 1960s and the work building on it was simply unable to meet. Rather than providing a basis for insightful descriptions across a range of semiotic modes as then hoped (cf., e.g., Carroll, 1977), the construction of phrase structure grammars, transformations and the modules of the language system postulated within the Chomskyan paradigm instead tied linguistics, and linguistically-inspired moves into other semiotic modes, to an overly narrow *syntactically*-based view of language impossible to profitably re-use across semiotic modes. As a consequence, to this day there has been no successful application of constructs from the Chomskyan linguistic paradigm to multimodal artefacts such as film. We showed the reasons for this at some length in Chapter 2: film relies on the kind of meaning construction found in verbal language syntax very rarely, if at all. We see this direction, therefore, as a development understandable for the time, but one which, in the end, is inappropriate and misleading concerning the properties of the semiotic modes of film.

Here, quite crucially however, it must be noted that Metz's *grande syntagmatique* was *not* an approach to film of this kind—even though, as we shall see below, some further developments of the account tried explicitly to place it more within the generative grammar framework. What is required instead, and this is the direction we follow, is to relate the kind of organisation isolated by Metz to the properties of the *discourse semantics* of film, not its syntax. This distinction could only be touched upon within Metz's account itself (cf., e.g., Metz, 1974b), although interpreting his discussion in terms of discourse offers a more natural resolution of many of the problems delineated. At that time, however, there was simply no framework available for taking this line of thought further.

Metz reduces film to realism.   Finally, one last common critique that we will mention concerns the relationship between film and 'realism'. Metz, particularly in the earlier stages of his work, drew considerably on positions developed by André Bazin in which realism was film's true and proper state. For Bazin, as soon as film began 'tampering' with its ideal and mode-specific role inherited from photography of presenting reality, it was no longer to be considered acceptable (cf. Bazin, 1967; Dudley Andrew, 1976). While Metz certainly did not subscribe to this essentialist mix of aesthetic evaluations and characterisation of the medium, he did inherit a view of film as essentially 'representational'. This was also seen by some critics as an unconsidered ideological weakness in that representation was suggested to be neutral and thereby insensitive to important ideological differences in the construction of the real.

We will return to this issue in more detail in the chapter following because, in important senses that need to be clarified, we will also take film to commit to a kind of 'realism'—that is, when a film segment runs it will *of necessity* act upon viewers as if it is presenting some pro-filmic reality, some real state of affairs that was to be found 'in front of the camera'. We take this to hold across the full range of artefacts constructible and interpretable as 'film', from abstract formal experimental work to the most banal blockbuster. The nature of film as portraying something pro-filmic is therefore, for us, an *ontological* property of film: it is necessarily the case as soon as we are dealing with film and we will make extensive use of this in our formalisations of the semiotic mode of film below.

What is critical here, however, is that the pro-filmic portrayed does *not* have any claim to being real, of actually existing. Neither it, nor the camera apparently recording it, nor the film-maker apparently operating the camera, have any ontological status as belonging to reality. This can most appropriately be dealt with in terms of *representation* and its nature; the kind of reality involved in the pro-filmic is then best described in terms of Prince's (1996) notion of *perceptual realism*. As we shall see in Chapter 5, we can recast Metz's approach entirely within this framework—thereby showing the role of assumptions of the real in filmic interpretation while also disavowing realism in its older 'Bazanian' (and other) forms.

4.3.2   Refining the Metzian system

In this final subsection, we discuss some of the developments that were made subsequently to Metz's proposals. These developments were intended to deal with specific problems that had arisen with the initial application of the *grande syntagmatique* and focused on the kinds of difficulties raised in passing above. We will see again that these proposals generally suffered from the lack of precision with which the necessary semiotic categories were understood at that time. On the one hand, this commonly led to only superficial analyses, which were then interpreted as demonstrating the failure or inappropriateness of linguistic categories when applied beyond the linguistic domain; and, on the other hand, the proposals for extensions naturally suffered similar problems to the original model they were trying to rescue.

As we shall now progressively demonstrate and as suggested above, one of the fundamental problems exhibited by Metz's formulation in its original form was precisely the lack of clean definitions and descriptions of mechanisms for the paradigmatic and syntagmatic axes of organisation. Although these axes are in principle relatively straightforward, their accurate application and use had not at the time of Metz's writing had much opportunity for development. Even in linguistic descriptions there were few accounts that had really brought out the different mechanisms and principles required. Some confusion was then inevitable.

Metz himself, for example wrote in his definition of the *grande syntagmatique* the following, very symptomatic but problematic account:

> "The large syntagmatique category outlined above also constitutes a *paradigmatic category*—since, at any moment in the making of his [sic] film, the film-maker must choose from a limited series of types of syntagmatic ordering."(Metz, 1974a: 137, original emphasis)

Metz's formulation here suggests a degree of 'overlap' or mixing of syntagmatic and paradigmatic description; this occurs in several places in Metz's writings, for example elsewhere we also find the even more direct statement:

> "Thus, the terms of the syntagms (A-B) are at the same time members of the paradigm (A/B)" (Metz, 1974d: 171)

Such statements link the paradigmatic and the syntagmatic axes closely, as is necessary, but far too strongly in that the elements involved are assumed to be the same. It is clear loosely what is meant but in fact this provides a poor basis for effective formalisation and further development. We have already commented above on this tendency, sometimes even evident within linguistic accounts. For example, the potential for confusion was equally present in our first example of the paradigmatic/syntagmatic distinction in Figure 3.4 in Section 3.2. There we found syntagmatic chains apparently consisting of terms such as *the–dog–ran* intersecting graphically with paradigmatic sets such as {*the, a, this*}, {*dog, cat, man*}, {*ran, sat, ate*}, etc.

We need to look rather closely to see that this does not actually fit with how Metz is describing the relation between syntagms and paradigms above: the paradigm sets in the linguistic case do *not* overlap with syntagm 'sets'—i.e., the terms *the* and *dog* are not found in any paradigm set {*the, dog*} since, as we explained above, these terms are never in meaningful opposition. This rather implicit property is sometimes obscured by the graphic representation of the paradigmatic and syntagmatic axes as two dimensions on the page but is in fact essential: we need to pull the criteria for grouping and combining elements apart along the syntagmatic and paradigmatic axes far more clearly in order to show the central contributions made by each. This is the important function of adopting quite distinct descriptive mechanisms for the paradigmatic and syntagmatic axes as begun in the previous chapter.

Thus, although Metz was aiming at a closer connection between the paradigmatic and syntagmatic, between potential and actual, he lacked the theoretical mechanisms for making this work. Similar deep foundational problems then reoccurred in most of the attempts made subsequently to refine Metz's formalisation. These approaches commonly took their lead, as did Metz, from formalisations proposed within linguistics but, at that time, there was either a foregrounding of syntagm, making the paradigmatic a loose derivative or, less often, a foregrounding of paradigm at the expense of syntagm. We can show this here by drawing on two brief examples of subsequent attempts made to develop Metz's account further. Both examples reveal a clear awareness of the need to capture syntagmatic and paradigmatic relationships, but lack the technical resources necessary for achieving this; they are also discussed at greater length in Bateman (2007).

The first revision we discuss was developed by Michel Colin (Colin, 1995*b*: originally published 1989). Colin tried to redefine the *grande syntagmatique* by making direct use of several representational devices developed within Chomskyan linguistics. His starting point was standard phrase structure rules as used for describing regularities of syntactic structure. Such rules are expressed as 're-write' rules, in which some syntactic category is 're-written' as the categories that constitute it. Thus, for example, the syntactic regularity that a Sentence (as a syntactic category) is made up of a noun phrase (e.g., 'the dog') followed by a verb phrase (e.g., 'runs') is captured by the rule:

$$S \rightarrow NP\ VP$$

Colin adapted this for the requirements of the *grande syntagmatique* by re-interpreting the relation between elements on the right-hand side of these rules as *disjunction* rather than the usual concatenation (which he described not entirely appropriately as conjunction). In this reconstruction a rule such as

$$A \rightarrow B\ C$$

was taken to mean 'if A, then B *or* C'. The *grande syntagmatique* could then be written straightforwardly as a set of 'rules' of the form:

syntagma	→	diegetic	2-parallel
diegetic	→	specific	3-bracket
specific	→	narrative	4-bracket
etc.			

This brings out particularly clearly that Colin was attempting to get at a paradigmatic description—i.e., a description of *choices*—but did not have an appropriate descriptive apparatus for the job. Using phrase structure rules for paradigmatic description is formally confused since it mixes properties of the syntagmatic axis and properties of the paradigmatic axis. Carrying out the 're-writes' of these revised phrase structure rules then produces a 'structure', as is the case with their traditional use in syntax, but a structure that is quite non-standard and with uncertain formal properties and consequences. Colin calls this structure, summarized by Colin (1995*b*: 67) in the tree structure shown in Figure 4.5, the *selection-tree* available to the film-maker. The terminal nodes (i.e., leaf nodes—nodes without further substructure) identify the syntagmatic types.

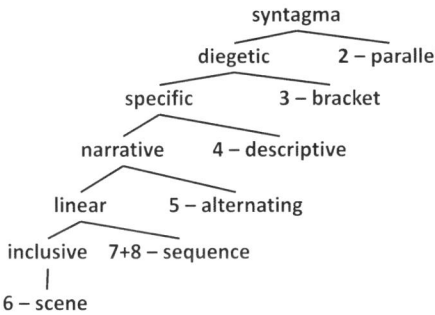

Figure 4.5   Michel Colin's reworking of the *grande syntagmatique as a 'selection-tree' (with Metz's numbering of the syntagmatic types maintained to ease comparison)*

This, as even the most superficial consideration of the contrast between this 'structure' and a syntactic structure shows, moves us into rather strange territory. A linguistic syntactic structure is never an account of selections 'available to a speaker'—it is a representation of the *results* of such selections, not the selections themselves. Nevertheless, despite this 'detour' via phrase structure rules, the formalisation did enable Colin to start attempting more rigorous and discriminating definitions of the categories involved.

This is shown in the use that Colin makes of the *non-terminal* nodes of the selection-tree. These are now taken as providing *definitional attributes* of the nodes below them. Thus, moving through the tree from top to bottom, he first distinguishes between the parallel and bracket syntagmas by proposing that the former do not play a role in advancing the narrative (i.e., *diegetic vs.* non-diegetic or 'parallel'). Second, when there are consequences for the narrative, these can either be *specific*, i.e., relating particular events of the narrative, or non-specific (or 'bracket'), i.e., concerned with general facts or states of affairs involved in or important for the narrative. Third, specific *narrative* syntagmas either concern some 'hero' or main protagonist(s) or describe particular states of affairs supporting the narrative—this distinguishes descriptive syntagmas from narrative syntagmas proper. And within the narrative syntagmas proper, there can be either *linear* or alternating syntagmas.

This reorientation to the definitional attributes is an important step towards bringing out the paradigmatic organisation inherent in the *grande syntagmatique*. It invites explicit consideration of the extent to which the classification is complete and internally consistent. It was then natural for Colin to start proposing further attributes in order to better distinguish the syntagmas being described. For example, the feature 'inclusive' is newly added by Colin in order to indicate a relationship between the spaces involved in juxtaposed shots, a move also argued for by Burch as we saw in the previous chapter. The space of some second shot may on occasions be *included* within a common spatial framework provided by the first. This allows the account to distinguish more rigorously a sequence from a scene.

A sequence is some 'itinerary' that a main protagonist follows; this can range over a variety of distinct locations and so receives the spatial feature of not being 'inclusive' (Colin, 1995*b*: 74). Segment 2 taken from *Adieu Philippine* above when Michel leaves the television studio to fetch some headphones from the mobile van outside, meets Liliane and Juliette on the way, and then brings them both back inside the studio to watch the recording, is a clear example of this.

Once the paradigmatic distinctions are recognised, they can begin to exert their own independent influence on the description. One problem often noted in critiques of the original *grande syntagmatique* was how certain choices seemed to be ruled out arbitrarily. For example, when a segment is classified to be presenting cases of a more general order, as in a 'bracket' syntagma, then no temporal organisation may be considered within the segment as these lie on mutually exclusive branches of the selection-tree. However it is certainly not uncommon to find film segments which appear to include elements of both, i.e., presenting cases but with temporality nevertheless providing a component of their organisation—in Chapter 7 below we will discuss the opening segment of *Adieu Philippine* in precisely these terms. Colin therefore tried to provide a more flexible scheme for the selection of syntagmas by focusing on the definitional attributes rather than the selection-tree.

For this he also drew on descriptive resources adopted from linguistics, this time recasting the account in terms of 'lexical subcategorization' rules.

Such rules allow each particular syntagmatic type (in Colin's case then the Metzian syntagmas) to be associated with a *set* of discriminating features rather than simply being fixed by their position in a tree structure. This migrates the definitional nodes of the selection-tree to features that may hold or not in order to describe particular syntagmas independently of any hierarchical organisation amongst those syntagmas. For example, it was then possible with the following rule (cf. Colin 1995*b*: 73 and the original version in Colin 1989*b*) to state that a descriptive syntagma (type 4) was, on the one hand, non-narratival but, on the other hand, nevertheless linear:

> descriptive syntagma → < +diegetic, +specific, −narrative, +linear >

This therefore permitted a more effective description of the *co-occurrence possibilities* of features since it avoided the requirement of the tree representation that certain features be automatically excluded at one branch even though they appear to be potentially relevant along some other branch.

The final move taken by Colin was then to improve the account still further by attempting to capture *dependencies* between the applicability of the defining features. This pulls apart once and for all the taxonomic structure of the *grande syntagmatique* and the internal organisation of its defining features. The mechanism employed for this was that of 'lexical redundancy' rules whereby syntagmas are characterised by feature *combinations* and *dependencies* as follows:

> syntagma   → < ±syntagma, ±diegetic >
> <+syntagma>   → < ±linear >
> <+diegetic>   → < ±specific, ±narrative, ±inclusive >

This opens up the 'generative potential' of the framework in that many more syntagmas are posited than those of the original *grande syntagmatique*. This was argued to offer a more empirically adequate characterisation of the possibilities actually taken up in film.

Although it is rarely presented in these terms, what Colin in fact achieved with this was one of the first clear separations of the paradigmatic and syntagmatic information inherent in the *grande syntagmatique*. Unfortunately this result was largely hidden by the more problematic artefacts introduced by the intrinsic syntagmatic orientation of the Chomksyan framework. Nevertheless, the distinguishing features that Colin identified belong to the *paradigmatic* description, while the syntagmas they give rise to are formally separated as part of the *syntagmatic* description. As a consequence, Colin's proposed lexical redundancy rules then translate straightforwardly to the paradigmatic system network shown in Figure 4.6, using the conventions for system networks introduced in the previous chapter. Here we can see, for example, how Colin's second 'lexical redundancy' rule above that the feature '+syntagma' leads directly to a choice between '+linear' and '-linear' corresponds exactly with the uppermost branch of the network in Figure 4.6.

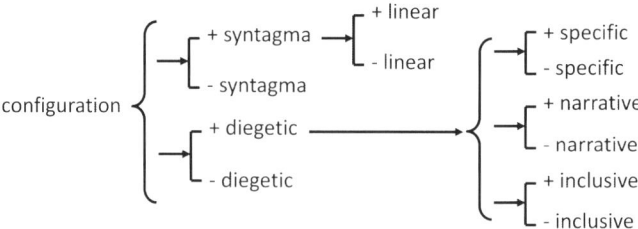

Figure 4.6   Reworking of Michel Colin's revised grande syntagmatique *represented as a paradigmatic system network*

The difficulty in reducing the constraints to a strict hierarchy promoted within the Chomskyan-derived approach then disappears—indeed, the kind of inter-dependencies revealed here is completely typically of more complex semiotic strata and their paradigmatic organisations. This transfer of the original Metzian account into a broader, more empirically-motivated paradigmatic description of film is then precisely the direction that we continue below.

A similar set of problems arose in the experiment undertaken by Möller-Naß (1986) as part of his particular critique of Metz's approach. A substantial component of this criticism centred on the assumed nonsensicality, again inherited from Chomskyan syntax, of 'meaning' without 'grammaticality'; we explained in Chapter 2 how, prior to the more recent developments in discourse semantics and its mechanisms, it was completely unclear how meaning could be constructed without syntactic constraints to support compositionality. The advances now available in discourse semantics have rendered this particular issue obsolete. However, still apposite today is Möller-Naß's discussion of Metz's formalization from the perspective of the more formal foundation for linguistic structural representations then emerging. In particular, Möller-Naß criticises the 'tree' organisation employed by Metz, correctly observing that there is an equivocation concerning the features that are used to classify syntagmatic types and the types themselves—precisely as we saw in Colin's 'selection-tree' in Figure 4.5 above.

Möller-Naß's approach to improving on this is to reorganize the hierarchy so that it properly reflects features and to explain that each syntagmatic type should be characterised by a unique feature combination, similar again to how we have now seen Colin's approach to work. Möller-Naß suggests, however, that there are two distinct kinds of features, those concerning segmentation and those concerning temporal relations. He captures each of these in the form of a structural dependency tree and states that, to do proper justice to the independence of the two dimensions represented, the tree concerning segmentation should be repeated as a sub-tree of *all the nodes of the other tree* (Möller-Naß, 1986: 338). Möller-Naß then goes so far as to suggest that the need for this degree of complexity shows that there is *no* overall system that can be sensibly described (Möller-Naß, 1986: 349).

What we actually have here, however, is the direct 'multiplication' of options that we illustrated in the previous chapter with respect to the alternatives described by Burch. There we noted that although simultaneous systems of choice commonly give rise to many distinct alternatives, their representation as paradigmatic networks provides precisely the theoretical and descriptive apparatus necessary to keep that complexity under control. This option was not available to Möller-Naß making the problem he had uncovered seem insurmountable. In Chapter 6 we will see that a subnetwork capturing segmentation can be included in parallel to other networks of choice within a single description as long as (i) we properly separate the paradigmatic and syntagmatic contributions and (ii) employ a resource such as that of the system network for capturing the necessary paradigmatic interdependencies.

In summary, both Colin's proposals for employing lexical redundancy rules and Möller-Naß's reorganization of the Metzian hierarchy show the original paradigmatic nature of the *grande syntagmatique* attempting to express itself—the descriptions developed could in some sense be called 'proto-paradigmatic' in that they strain to capture paradigmatic options within the mechanisms of syntagmatic representations. Both Colin and Möller-Naß drew attention to what they saw as the explosive complexity involved in combining features running along different dimensions. However, as observed above, cross-classification is actually a common property of properly paradigmatic descriptions of complex semiotic systems, such as verbal languages, and is a consequence of the fact that the features proposed are independent of one another: i.e., they can be 'chosen' independently in the description of a single unit.

Modern paradigmatically organised grammars, such as those commonplace in systemic-functional linguistics (cf. Halliday and Matthiessen, 2004), have hundreds of such combinations of features and remain useful and powerful representations of the grammatical systems of natural languages. This therefore provides us with a far more adequate foundation for the development we undertake below.

4.4   Summary and Conclusions

In this chapter, we have seen how the most influential linguistically-inspired semiotic account of film, the *grande syntagmatique* of Christian Metz, fell foul of a range of problems caused by the lack of a developed semiotic view at that time. Although the Metzian efforts may appear relatively modest today, the *grande syntagmatique* was for many years unusually successful in driving scientific discourse concerning film because it suggested for the first time both how film constructions, or syntagmas, could be captured in the form of an, at least in principle, complete and conceptually clean taxonomy and, moreover, how a method of successive refinement in the form of a 'if not this, then that'-progression could be applied to suggest a more effective analytic access to film structures. As we have seen, however, arguments concerning the inherent limitations and problems of the *grande syntagmatique* came subsequently to dominate. The discussion showed that the concepts developed from the linguistics of the time could not hold their own against the demands of film.

Now, with the more powerful semiotic foundation we have motivated in previous chapters, we can take up the task of Metz's account again, relying on a thorough and precisely defined set of definitions in order to remove the analytic uncertainties that Metz's original description left open.

Further Reading

Good introductions and discussions of the ***grande syntagmatique*** are given in Stam et al. (1992), while Dudley Andrew (1976: Chapter 8, 212–241) also offers a very readable placement of Metz's work within film theory generally. Somewhat more demanding, but still very useful in terms of its explicit discussion of Metz's approach with respect to the basic semiotic dimensions of *langage/langue/parole*, form/content/substance, paradigmatic/syntagmatic, etc. is Heath (1973). Further discussion of subsequent attempts to draw out the paradigmatic and syntagmatic components of the original Metzian scheme can be found in Bateman (2007).

At the time of publication of this book, **Rozier's** *Adieu Philippine* **(1962)** is available on registration free of charge from the MUBI website at `http://mubi.com/films/adieu-philippine`. **Other examples** of analysis using the *grande syntagmatique* include Koch's (1970) contrastive analysis of Ingmar Bergman's *Persona* (1966) and Alan J. Pakula's *Sterile Cuckoo* (1969). Also relevant, is Porter's (1982) application of the *grande syntagmatique* to the analysis of **television narratives**.

For further work within **narratology** applying its constructs to genres other than narrative (such as *description*), see Wolf and Bernhart (2007). For introductions to narratology as such, see the general introductions from, for example, Bal (1985), Rimmon-Kenan (2002) or Fludernik (2009) in English or Martinez and Scheffel (1999) in German. There are also now several accounts attempting to apply **narratological principles to film** (Lacey, 2000; Verstraten, 2009); several of these suffer, however, from a still rather too literal acceptance of a traditional 'communication model' inherited from work on verbal texts. The most detailed development of narratology for film where medium-specificity is thoroughly considered is Kuhn (2011).

5 Foundations for analysis: filmic units

> *"In film studies as in other disciplines, old problems tend to reappear under new names. What are the basic units of film? How are they (or how should they be) combined in the filmic composition? These are the oldest, most frequently asked questions in film theory." (Henderson, 1977: 57)*

With this chapter we come to a turning point in the book: after having argued in Chapter 1 for the necessity of fine-grained analysis that is not restricted to working out 'what is going on' and tracking chains of cause and effect, and then in Chapters 2, 3 and 4 articulating a more contemporary view of semiotics, documents and multimodality as these notions apply to film, it is now time to start building the analytic framework itself.

We have suggested that certain aspects of the approach of Christian Metz and, in particular, that of the *grande syntagmatique* offer a suitable point of departure. This apparatus is, however, considerably altered by the requirements of achieving a semiotically-appropriate formalisation. The result will be a framework that is more robust in the face of data, i.e., concrete films that are being analysed, and which can enter more effectively into the overall task of supporting film analyses and interpretations at all levels of detail, spanning from individual segments up to entire films and collections of films—although for the sake of concreteness our focus in this book will remain at the smaller end of this scale.

The details of the framework are set out in this and the following two chapters. In the present chapter we address two major preparatory tasks. First, as demanded by the semiotic representational requirements for syntagmatic descriptions introduced in Section 3.2 above, we need to consider the vexed question of filmic *units*, i.e., how do we segment what we are analysing. Second, and based on the first, we will need to be quite specific concerning just which filmic phenomena we are providing a framework for. As repeatedly emphasised, considerable problems are raised by approaches talking of 'film' as such rather than making explicit precisely which aspects of the complex artefact of film they address. Any statement of the form 'film is not like language' is then virtually meaningless (or simply wrong) because it fails to reflect the internal complexity of *both* 'film' *and* 'language' as bundles of richly articulated semiotic modes; as we argued in Chapter 2, in many respects film is not like language but, in many others, it is.

The simultaneous relevance of distinct perspectives on film makes the question of units substantially more challenging. Units, in the syntagmatic sense being pursued here, are only defined with respect to particular paradigmatic systems. In short, there may be many semiotics 'piggyback-ing' on the 'replete' (in the sense of Goodman 1969; cf. §3.4 above) nature of the filmic material substrate and the very rich range of technical features available for manipulation there. This means that distinct kinds of units may co-operate within a film extract, each responding to different systems of alternations.

Although important in their own right, many of these will now be de-liberately excluded from our account. Our goal in the present chapter is to select from this range of possibilities criteria that we consider *essentially* filmic, since it is these that offer the most detailed answers to the fundamental orienting question of this book: how do *films* mean? The two chapters following then build on this foundation to provide accounts of the corresponding paradigmatic and syntagmatic organisations respectively as motivated by and for film analysis.

5.1 The basic units of film: preliminaries

To entitle a section the 'basic' units of film verges on provocation. The question of units has been discussed with considerable heat in studies of film and the consensus achieved is limited. Doubt is commonly raised as to whether it is possible or useful to find 'units' in film at all—a view that can be traced back to discussions of a similar nature with respect to non-moving images. The continuous and replete nature of such images has led many to conclude that it is not possible to find units within images in any (non-syntactic) general way (cf. Currie 1995: 130 and critical discussion in Machin 2009: 186). Film inherits many of the same problems and adds a few more of its own.

Even to look for units may come to be criticised as falling foul of linguistic imperialism, i.e., of assuming that film is like language and possesses distinguishable units along the lines of syntactic units, which can therefore be arranged and re-arranged for expressing meanings according to some kind of 'visual grammar' or 'visual syntax'. And, indeed, there are some particular dangers to be faced in this area. Many analyses end up offering more or less exhaustive re-descriptions of everything that happens to be noticed within an image, ranging at the lowest levels of abstraction from colour, shape and texture, up to higher levels of abstraction dealing with the major themes and motifs of the image. Re-description is not analysis, however, as the valuable critique brought by Forceville (2007) makes very clear. Unless the *realisational* relationship between levels of abstraction is made explicit, little contribution to explaining interpretation and meaning-making is achieved.

The counter-belief that there can be no 'essential' units of film and that the imposition of rigid segmentation schemes is in any case unsatisfactory for insightful analysis is widespread (cf. Henderson 1977; Wilson 1995;

and our discussion in §2.4 above). But the question of units is not one that we can sidestep. To carry out an analysis demands that we make it very clear just what kinds of entities our analysis is intended to apply to.

At the same time, we will need to heed Metz's (1974*d*: 184) warnings against placing an extremely difficult problem—that of units—as a stumbling block right at the outset of investigation. The definition of semiotic modes needs to proceed in a *dialogue* between the paradigmatic and the syntagmatic: that is, we do not wait until the question of units has been 'answered' before proceeding. Any such separation of concerns would make little sense methodologically since the two axes of description can only be pursued in close connection—a semiotic interdependence characterised by Metz as follows:

> "The problem of minimal units is not an autonomous theoretical point which could be settled independently of a more general investigation of 'cinematic grammar', and *before* undertaking such a study. The minimal unit does not exist outside of the conception which one may have of the grammar, and it already engages them in their most general outline; it does not constitute a preface to it. To the multiplicity of codes there corresponds the multiplicity of minimal units. The minimal unit is not a given in the text; it is a tool of analysis. There are as many types of minimal units as there are types of analysis!" (Metz, 1974*d*: 194)

With the single exception that we no longer talk of 'grammar' as far as film is concerned and must replace this throughout by 'discourse', the position Metz formulates holds equally for us today. We need to characterise just what manner of units are going to be of relevance *with respect to the type of analysis we propose*. For this we will draw on the framework that we now have available.

The discussion of units in film can also be approached in relation to considerations of the 'essence' of film as an 'object' or artefact. Here we find attempts to delineate the properties that a film necessarily has in order to be accepted as a 'film' at all. Below we will push this further so as to motivate a particular consideration of the internal structures of films and, consequently, of their relevant units. It is essential, however, that this be pursued on the basis of an appropriate semiotic foundation—otherwise such accounts necessarily fall short of their target, despite the fact that explorations of this kind have a long history. Many early discussions, for example, were concerned with identifying specific properties of film to motivate its acceptance as an art form (for further discussion, see Sweeney, 2009), while more recent discussions range from consideration of the technical features of film (cf., e.g., Zettl, 1973; Thompson and Bowen, 2009*a,b*) to broader philosophical discussions of representation (e.g., Walton, 1984; Currie, 1995; Wilson, 1997).

Since these approaches typically provide little space for the, from our perspective, crucial role of discourse, a more useful starting point is offered by Noël Carroll (Carroll, 1996*b*). Even though Carroll does not himself make statements about discourse and its mechanisms, the account does provide a useful framework within which we can take this line of inquiry further. Carroll, as many before him, explores the extent to which conditions can be formulated that differentiate film, or the *moving image* as he characterises his domain of concern, from other, closely neighbouring artefacts or activities such as photography, theatre, painting and so on.

Towards this, he proposes the following five conditions as definitional, i.e., as contributing *ontological conditions*, for any artefact that is to be accepted as a 'moving image':

- a moving image is necessarily a 'detached display'—i.e., a representation that allows visual access to some material (in a sense that we return to in more detail below) but which does not allow observers to make any conclusions concerning orientation or placement with respect to their own bodies: the "virtual space" depicted in the moving image is not the space of the observer,
- a moving image must belong to the class of things from which "the impression of movement is technically possible",
- a moving image has 'performance tokens' that are generated from a template that is itself a token—i.e., what an observer actually sees is generated on the basis of a further artefact (the physical film strip, video, data file, etc.) which may itself be one of several instances of same,
- a moving image's performance tokens cannot be considered artworks in their own right—i.e., the way in which the film is individually projected on the screen during any particular performance is not itself evaluable as a component of the artwork,
- a moving image is spatially two-dimensional.

Figure 5.1   The Zoetrope

This definition succeeds in covering a broad range of artefacts, all of which we can readily accept as offering sites for the operation of essentially filmic mechanisms. This is also by no means restricted to particular technologies or viewing situations. The zoetrope shown in Figure 5.1,[1] for example, meets all of Carroll's conditions. This can be seen as an extension of the thaumatrope that we used as an example in Chapter 3 (cf. Figure 3.1), which typically does not satisfy those conditions because the impression of movement is not supported. In the zoetrope case, however, due to the nature of the images being combined, the resulting perception is indeed of a 'moving image' in

---

[1]Source: http://www.zeno.org/Brockhaus-1911/A/Zootrop (Zenodot Verlagsgesellschaft mbH, public domain)

the sense intended. This then corresponds to a film consisting of a single shot of indefinite length—i.e., a shot that lasts as long as the disk continues to be rotated.

Carroll's conditions succeed in going a considerable way towards discriminating between film and its close neighbours as he intended. But, despite this, Carroll concludes:

> "although I have pointed out what I think are five necessary features of moving pictures, I do not think that they are particularly central to our understanding of how moving images function. For example, we don't—at least as far as I can see at present—derive any deep insights into the effects of movies or into film style by contemplating these five conditions." (Carroll, 1996b: 71–72)

This, however, is precisely the connection that we need to make: we need to be able to find features of moving images that *do* contribute to our understanding of how they function and by means of which we can begin identifying units of analysis.

The key to taking this further is, as suggested above, to reinstate film as an *essentially* semiotic entity. Carroll comes very close to this in his discussions of 'borderline cases'. For example, considering 'movement' as an essential feature of the moving image might at first glance seem self evident, but even here there are difficulties. Chris Marker's film *La Jetée* (1962) consists almost entirely of stills edited together to tell the story and, as Carroll notes, it is straightforward to imagine a film just like *La Jetée* but with its single movement removed—there could still be little serious doubt that this is still a film. Nevertheless:

> "there is an important difference between a film image of a character, say from our imagined version of *La Jetée*, and a slide taken of that character from *La Jetée*. For as long as you know that what you are watching is a film, even a film of what appears to be a photograph, it is always justifiable to entertain the possibility that the image *might* move. On the other hand, if you know that you are looking at a slide, then it is categorically impossible that the image might move. ...Movement in a slide would require a miracle; movement in a film image is an artistic choice which is always technically available." (Carroll, 1996b: 64, original emphasis)

This quality of the moving image is picked out by Carroll's second definitional feature above.

The technical availability of movement, at least in principle, is "something whose significance the audience contemplates when trying to make sense of a film" (Carroll, 1996b: 65). This attribution of significance on the part of an observer therefore demands the *prior commitment* to some range of semiotic modes as relevant rather than another—i.e., attributing significance is a *semiotic decision* rather than something pre-given by an artefact or a question of aesthetic choice. Even though an observer can be mistaken in his or her selection of relevant semiotic modes (which is an important aspect of *multimodal literacy*: cf. Bateman 2011), once the commitment is made, the corresponding expectations necessarily follow. A film might then be best characterised as any document that affords the application of the semiotic modes of film. And, the more a document does this, the 'better', or more 'prototypically central', an example of film that document will be—although it is crucial here to emphasise that this makes *absolutely no claims whatsoever* concerning such documents' aesthetic value.

An approach of this kind was also taken up by Metz (cf. 1974*d*: 227–232), where film is considered as a combination of distinct semiotic modes just as we have argued above.[2] Metz ordered these modes along a scale of 'specificity' in order to triangulate the essence of film with respect to its closest 'neighbours' analogously to Carroll's discussion above. Some semiotic resources span a broad range of artefacts, including many artefacts other than film; others are more specific, in that they apply to a narrower range of artefacts. Film 'as such' was then defined in terms of a particular combination of semiotic contributions rather than a unique code in its own right, an approach reminiscent of several positions taken in the arts and media (cf. Mitchell 1994: 95 or 2005: 257–260).

For the visual track, Metz isolated five distinct classes of semiotic arte-facts. The most general (group 1 in the numbering scheme employed by Metz) is one which includes all artefacts that rely on *visual iconicity*; this involves depictions that are intended to bear some relationship of 'resem-blance' to what is being portrayed. Two more specific restrictions of this are group (2) *mechanical duplication* and group (3) *multiplicity*. The former was intended to include all artefacts that use photographic technologies for the creation of their images—we can now extend this to take in any process by which a 'representation' is formed by some kind of sensor imag-ing providing measurement data with respect to the external world. The latter include artefacts that rely on the possibilities offered by employing *sequences* of images rather than single images. Within this latter group, Metz proposes a further subtype: *movement* (group 4), where the image it-self is dynamic. This then distinguishes between, for example, comics and films—both include multiple images, but only the latter involve images that move (see *Further Reading*).

We now combine this with Carroll's definitional features above in order to build a more refined characterisation of the contributing properties for making filmic meanings. First, we can note that the strict set inclusion of movement within multiplicity that Metz proposes is actually too strong. Metz considered multiplicity and movement to go together "at least in the most frequent cases" (Metz, 1974*d*: 231) but the restriction is unnecessary. Movement and multiplicity are in fact in free variation: we can find exam-

---

[2]Metz's discussion was actually in terms of *semiotic codes* of course, since this was the state of semiotic theory at the time; we adapt this to our consideration of semiotic modes here without further comment.

Figure 5.2   Early investigations of movement carried out by Étienne-Jules Marey (chronophotography, 1882 and 1885): static multiplicity

ples of static multiplicity just as well as we can find examples of moving non-multiplicity——see Figure 5.2.[3]

Under the latter we include (for the present: this position will be refined somewhat below) all 'single take' films, regardless of whether these are genuinely single take in terms of production, such as Aleksander Sokurov's *Russian Ark* (2002) or the four tracks in Mike Figgis' *Timecode* (2000), or constructed so as to appear as a single take to the viewer, as in Alfred Hitchcock's *Rope* (1948) or Michael Snow's *Wavelength* (1967). These all belong to group (4) and *not* to group (3). We therefore consider it more accurate to represent groups (2), (3) and (4) as overlapping without entering into any relationships of proper inclusion.

In this we also do not follow Warren Buckland's rationalisation for including one within the other on the grounds that 'movement depends on a multiplicity of images' (Buckland, 2004: 97). This conflates the technological means by which film creates movement perceptually with the semiotically significant possibility of allowing quite different images (regardless of whether those images themselves move or not) to follow one another in succession. The former Metz (1974d: 191) places under the *technological codes* involved in "the functioning of the cinematic equipment", which is generally phenomenologically inaccessible as consisting of 'multiple' images at all. We do not, therefore, accept this as a subcase of group (3). Similarly, artefacts such as recorded audiovisual data from surveillance cameras and the like are cases of artefacts involving movement but not multiplicity. Below we will refine this further *semiotically* since the allocation here is still too centred on how the artefact is produced rather than on the semiotic distinctions mobilised by the artefact—this latter is what in the end will prove crucial.

This gives us our first foothold for a characterisation of the conditions under which various kinds of filmic meaning can emerge. Beginning with Carroll's useful criteria, we build in Metz's semiotic considerations, refined to include both a broader range of artefacts and to more accurately

---

[3]Sources: http://cs.wikipedia.org/wiki/Soubor:Thomas_Eakins_Man_Pole-Vaulting.jpg   and   http://en.wikipedia.org/wiki/File:Marey_-_birds.jpg (both public domain)

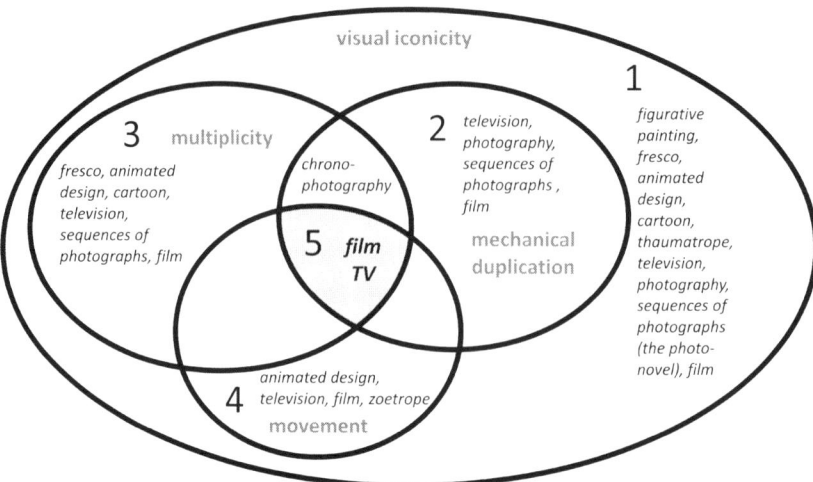

Figure 5.3   *Metz's overview of visual iconic codes relevant for the filmic image track revised with respect to multiplicity and movement*

depict the kinds of combinations of properties possible. To summarise this position, we show these inter-relationships graphically in Figure 5.3 in a style similar to that proposed by Buckland (2004: 96) and James Monaco (Monaco, 2000: 419; 2009: 471), but incorporating our changed relations between group (3) and group (4). Here we can readily see that in Metz's account it is the intersection of groups (2), (3) and (4) that narrows the field to artefacts that we would most readily include as film.

The particular significance of this formulation for us here then lies in the support it gives for linking artefacts with their possibilities for meaning-making: each identified set of artefacts provides support for mobilising particular families of semiotic modes, just as we sketched in Chapter 3. Each semiotic mode brings with it certain patterns of signification that have been developed over time by its communities of users.

Iconic depictions as a whole, for example, involve what Metz describes as the 'plastics' of the picture:

> "spatial disposition of iconic elements, the role of the frame (i.e., of the finitude proper to iconic representations) in the ordering of visual elements, distributions of masses and lines of force (thus the 'golden mean', which we know preoccupies, after painters, certain cineasts), the play of figures and grounds (principal 'motifs' and backgrounds), etc." (Metz, 1974*d*: 228)

while for mechanical duplication, *photographic codifications* come into play; these include "angular incidence (shooting angles), scale of shots, depth of field, etc." (Metz, 1974*d*: 229).

Under multiplicity we then find everything to do with sequencing, namely:

> "logical relations perceived by the spectator (like the causal relation, the adversative relation, the simple juxtaposition, etc.) between successive and contiguous images ..., diverse means of expressing temporal relations, such as simultaneity, close consecution, remote consecution, between actions represented by the different images of the sequence ('flashback', so-called ordinary chronological order, etc.), more properly aesthetic codifications: echoes of motifs or graphic contours from one image to another (with the problem of 'transition'), violent contrasts between contiguous images, etc." (Metz, 1974*d*: 230–231)

It is to this group that Metz attributes the meaning-making possibilities of the *grande syntagmatique* and this is crucial. On the one hand, the *grande syntagmatique* clearly belongs here since its foundation lies precisely in the articulation of distinct sequencings of elements provided by multiplicity; however, on the other hand, it is striking that the number of possibilities set out here by Metz under 'logical relations'—the same term that is used for such relations in current linguistic discourse semantics incidentally (cf. Halliday and Matthiessen, 2004; Martin, 1992)—is only very partially covered by his formulation of the *grande syntagmatique*.

The reason for this goes deeper than simply the fact that the *grande syntagmatique* was an earlier development. The lack of differentiation between the syntagmatic and paradigmatic axes that we illustrated in the previous chapter has significant consequences here. We have seen that some accounts have already suggested paradigmatic characterisations—those we illustrated from Noël Burch in Figure 3.5 provide a good example. But the structural configurations of the *grande syntagmatique* are, in contrast, strictly syntagmatic. Since in Metz's account the relations between these two modes of description were not satisfactorily addressed, the syntagmatic organisation was implicitly given the leading role.

This restricted the *grande syntagmatique* to only a small subset of the range of meanings that the semiotic mode of multiplicity actually provides—the paradigmatic has, in effect, been 'filtered through' the options provided by the syntagmatic. Below, and particularly in the next chapter, we will pursue this further and provide a more comprehensive account of filmic multiplicity and its meaning-making possibilities.

5.2   Audiovisual iconic representations

The fact that we are dealing here with specific *kinds* of meaning in film and not with *the* meaning of film is clearly emphasised by Metz's hierarchy of specificity of semiotic modes. This also shows us, however, that many of the articulations carrying 'meaning' within film are not specific to film at all. Thus, in line with investigations of 'transmediality' and 'intermediality' more generally (cf. Wolf, 2005), we consider it important to locate *common-alities* between film and its neighbours because, first, these relationships are also sources of meanings taken up in film and so need to be identified as such and, second, this delineates aspects of filmic meaning which we do *not* need to develop anew here—accounts can most usefully be drawn from elsewhere.

To show this, we will now briefly proceed 'downwards' through the distinct groups that Metz's characterisation has provided, relating these to the semiotic resources that they contribute. This will allow us to pinpoint the filmic phenomena that our framework aims to address and, accordingly, the particular kinds of units that we will need to consider relevant.

From group (1), Metz's iconic visual representation, we have the facts that a film will be strongly *framed*—most pictorial media currently adopt a particular fixed size and shape of image, film naturally included—and, within this frame, rich traditions of aesthetic composition operate—i.e., considerations of where the objects shown should be placed around the frame to achieve balance, in what kinds of relationships, etc. Such meanings are potentially available whenever semiotic modes associated with group (1) are mobilised (cf., e.g., Arnheim, 1982; Panofsky, 1967; Müller, 2007). We also now extend this group to include *audiovisual* iconicity, since for current purposes these sensory channels will generally need to be considered in combination.

When we go beyond group (1) to group (4), i.e., adding movement, the possibilities for meaning from group (1) remain. But we also add the possibility of synchronised (or not) sound, of following gestures, trajectories, events and processes, music and rhythm. This strengthens 'affective' considerations still further—indeed, affect is, if anything, more strongly present in film than any other iconic representation currently developed (cf. Smith, 1995; Tan, 1996; Grodal, 2009).

All of these considerations for artefacts falling within Metz's group (1) of iconic artefacts, group (2) of mechanical production, and group (4) of movement add meanings to the representation and are therefore part of the meanings made by film. But they are not as yet specifically *filmic*. Sources of meaning of this kind are made accessible by *natural perception*: we do not need to learn to see or hear the images we are being shown precisely because they are audiovisually iconic. If we can see or hear at all, then we will also be able to see and hear the content of these representations, although how much we *understand* of this content will naturally depend on the experience and knowledge of the individual observer.

Depicted activities and environment in a film will then be grasped by a viewer largely to the extent that they are perceived and understood by that viewer at all. Figures, characters, locales will be recognised—at least in general terms, if not specifically: e.g., 'some person', 'some plane', 'some cornfield', etc. The spatial relationships and motivations of entities in the audiovisual field will also be grasped relying on very much the same kind of evidence. In this sense, we fully accept that 'natural signs', which include naturalistic moving images in film, come with a significant amount of information *already present*.

Such signs are sometimes termed 'short-circuit' signs (cf. §4.1 above) by virtue of their presumed 'direct access' to what they depict. This has been a source of considerable confusion in discussions of film. Many of the pitfalls can readily be seen in pronouncements such as the following, from James Monaco's well known introduction to the study of film:

> "A shot contains as much information as we want to read in it, and whatever units we define within the shot are arbitrary. Therefore, film ... consists of short-circuit signs in which the signifier nearly equals the signified; and depends on a continuous, nondiscrete system in which we can't identify a basic unit and which therefore we can't describe quantitatively." (Monaco, 2000: 160; 2009: 178)

First, it is suggested that although there may be some small residue of meaning in the filmic sign, mostly what it means (the signified) is what it shows (the signifier); second, as already mentioned above, certain properties of the visual image (e.g., continuity) are taken to apply across the board to all considerations of film as a 'system'.

In many respects, this is simply the frequently voiced position in film that 'the medium of the movies is physical reality as such ... no matter whether it be the original or a Hollywood facsimile indistinguishable therefrom for all aesthetic intents and purposes" (Panofsky 1995: 122 and Panofsky 2004: 302); 'truth at twenty-four frames a second' in Jean-Luc Godard's old adage. But, taken at face value, this would leave film studies, as well as semiotic discussions, in a rather curious position: if film 'speaks' reality already, then the role of further *film* interpretation is marginalised. Instead what would be required is research on human perception on the one hand and social and ideological investigations of the depicted 'reality slices' on the other. And indeed, this is a position that often reoccurs in one form or another in discussion of film.

We consider such a position, in which it seems that we understand films because we understand what we 'see', as intrinsically limited. We shall argue that it redirects attention away from film and towards processes of perception and of general understanding. These processes clearly also need to be investigated and included as part of viewers' responses to film but do not cover all that needs to be said. Moreover, the position also correlates with a general tendency to move straight from perception to representations of knowledge of the world—a situation that we criticised at length in connection to earlier approaches to semiotic systems in Chapter 2 above. We can also see our position on this issue as reminiscent of Shlomith Rimmon-Kenan's statement concerning narrative that "'Models of coherence' can derive either from 'reality' or from literature" (Rimmon-Kenan, 2002: 125). The view from literature is essentially that of work-oriented *mo-*

tivations for constructing a text in one way rather than another—to this we add the mechanisms of discourse, seen generally across semiotic systems and restricted neither to verbal language nor to literature.

The view from 'reality', which is only achieved indirectly for verbal narrative, is in the case of film naturally far more strongly in evidence—precisely by virtue of the perceptual force of natural signs. The vast majority of work focusing on natural signs in cinema has therefore come to prioritise what is shown over and above its filmic discoursal organisation. This tendency runs through the entire history of approaches to film and across very different theoretical orientations. Although we will also consider the raw material of film to include, in a sense to be made clear below, 'slices' of reality, we need to do this within the context of a semiotically more effectively organised view of 'short-circuit' signs in order to get a tighter hold on the workings of filmic signification.

Within more traditional semiotics, meanings are added into images primarily in terms of interpretations, or 'connotative meanings'. These take the bare content as starting point and add further significance. Thus: some depicted events and situations forming the 'denotation' come to be imbued with extra significance by virtue of recognising social, individual or ideological import. Examples here include early work on narrative and fictional worlds, incorporating notions of events, agents and causality into 'grammar'-like structural configurations (cf. Burke 1945; Bremont 1973; Prince 1973 and many more), or notions overlapping with psychological work on schemas, frames or possible worlds (cf., e.g., Ryan, 1992). Specifically for film, several authors have proposed similar layers of interpretation for the filmic 'represented world' within which stories play out (cf. Branigan, 1986a; Wulff, 2007; Hartmann, 2007), generally extending the notion of *diégèse* introduced to film by Etienne Souriau in the 1950s (Souriau, 1951: 240); we will return to the status of *diegesis* in our account again in a moment.

Common to these approaches is the assumption that access to the worlds constructed can be usefully related to the way in which humans process natural scenes and events. It is therefore understandable that considerations of the connection between film and regular processes of visual perception go back a long way (cf. Münsterberg, 2001[1916]). Work in this tradition has come to include approaches both from a philosophical perspective, including writers such as Kendall Walton (Walton, 1984, 1997), Gregory Currie (Currie, 1996) and, again, Carroll (Carroll, 1995, 1996b) and, increasingly, from theoretical positions either oriented towards, or actually from within, psychology (cf. Prince, 1993; Wuss, 1993, 2009; Anderson, 1996; Bordwell, 2009).

Among these latter, one of the most developed and sophisticated accounts to date is that of Per Persson (Persson, 2003). Interpretation and understanding are seen here from the perspective of several levels, beginning with almost uninterpreted sense data and ending with *situation models* very similar to the non-psychological accounts mentioned above and within which general and specific cultural knowledge come together and capture the content and purpose of any film. Interestingly, even though Persson acknowledges at many points that a film as a 'discourse' will bring cues to bear concerning just which kinds of interpretations may be relevant, the treatment of these cues remains untheorised and unsystematic. Interpretation-building is driven by the *dispositions* of the viewer and the possibility is granted that some of these dispositions may be 'discourse-specific' (Persson, 2003: 22, 39); but little more is offered.

Instead the focus remains centrally on how 'non-media'-related dispositions, such as knowledge of events, causality, the mental life of agents, ideology, etc., lead to comprehension. We can see a similar emphasis in recent approaches that bring the *embodied* nature of perception and comprehension to the fore, such as that of Torban Grodal (cf. Grodal, 2009: 204). Here again, there is an acceptance that perception and its invited 'simulation' of an unfolding story world may be narratively structured in ways that are more or less effective but, apart from some suggestions concerning affective responses of suspense and surprise, that structuring receives little systematic treatment in its own right.

In contrast to this, the position we take here is again to prioritise the role of discourse as our starting point. We argued in Chapters 2 and 3 above just why we consider this necessary and the changes that have occurred in our understanding of semiotics and discourse that make it possible. This is, however, by no means seen as *opposing* the perceptual account—we consider it essential that the mechanisms we explore are seen in a *complementary* fashion to more perceptually-oriented approaches. It is in fact of considerable importance to stop the pendulum swinging back too far: we are not concerned here with reasserting the centrality of language-based models of film to the exclusion of all else. Quite the contrary: we consider models of perception and social reality to be absolutely crucial to the investigation of film. Our position is simply that they are not sufficient on their own.

Thus, although quite understandable as a justified reaction against previous static 'meaning-in-the-text' accounts, current views that seek instead to relocate 'meaning-in-the-head' (or, more accurately: 'meaning-in-the-head/body') often overshoot their target. We see this even in the following quotation from one of the classic texts heralding 'recipient-based' approaches:

> "Of course the text is a 'structured prefigurement', but that which is given has to be received, and the way in which it is received depends as much on the reader as on the text. Reading is not a direct 'internalisation', because it is not a one-way process, and our concern will be to find means of describing the reading process as a dynamic *interaction* between text and reader." (Iser, 1978: 107)

In its rejection of static models of meaning and its emphasis on interaction, Iser's account can only be welcomed. But the reliance on the reader now has to be expressed in a more differentiated manner: although solely a mental construct (and so *wholly* dependent on the reader ontologically), the way in which a text is received is not so open. In fact, and as explained at length in Chapter 2, the 'lower' levels of abstraction of discourse interpretation are very much more fixed than many non-discourse-oriented accounts assume. In the case of verbal language, the 'text cues' constituted by the resources and mechanisms of the discourse stratum are tightly constraining and it is only on the basis of representations at this level that access is provided to the knowledge required for subsequent interpretation to flower. The situation for film appears remarkably similar.

In order then to provide appropriate access to the phenomena we are addressing in this book, it is necessary in addition to open up the possibility of meanings that are *not* best anchored within details of the diegesis: i.e., we need to allow a place within any complete model for film interpretation for both 'reality' and 'discourse' as sources of constraint. For this, we return to one of the general properties of semiotic systems that we discussed in previous chapters: we know that very different semiotic organisations can be built on any individual audiovisual material substrate. This offers us precisely the space necessary to draw the two sources of constraint together.

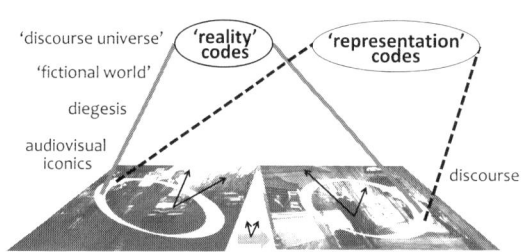

Figure 5.4   Double-coding of the moving image

We suggest this position graphically in Figure 5.4. The unfolding moving image of the film depicted at the bottom of the figure is *simultaneously* related to schemes of interpretation derived from our understanding of the real, social and physical world, which in the figure we label 're-ality' codes—"a set of perceptive, iconographic and symbolic structures that preexist the intervention of the camera" (Bellour and Metz 1971: 8 in the translation from Freadman 1986: 112)—and *also* to schemes of interpretation that derive from the nature of the unfolding audiovisual material as discourse, labelled here as 'representation' codes.[4]

---

[4]Our naming of these kinds of codes of interpretation is suggestive rather than definitive: all aspects of the filmic base are 'representational' and none gives direct access to 'reality'. However, as we have suggested, the kinds of information employed in the two schemes are quite different and this is what motivates our distinguishing them in this way. A similar distinction is drawn in Metz (1973: 92) and also by Peters (1981: 54) in terms of *mimetic codes* and *expression codes*, while there are also connections to be drawn with Thompson's (1988: 21)

Approaches developed on the basis of perception, such as Wuss (1993), Anderson (1996), Persson (2003) and Grodal (2009) as mentioned above, provide detailed accounts of diverse aspects of the reality codes—all of the levels of interpretation described in these accounts, from uninterpreted sense data to attributions of emotions, motives and ideological positionings, are seen to work on the basis of a deep analogy drawn between iconic audiovisual representations and natural perception, comprehension and embodied behaviour in the real world—"piggybacking on our nonfilmic experiences of the visible world and the social action taking place in it" as Bordwell (2005: 259) phrases it. In this book, however, our concerns follow the other path: i.e., the representation codes and, amongst these, those of discourse organisation in particular.

The representation codes of film, particularly at the lower levels of abstraction that make closest contact with the technical details of film, have to date received scant attention due to the lack of appropriate semiotic foundations. In fact, Metz's adopted motivation for the *grande syntagmatique* was one of the few serious attempts so far to uncover a representation code in our sense. As we described in Chapter 4, Metz considered the filmic images themselves, as iconically signifying, to be infinitely variable and so difficult to reconcile with semiotic approaches to meaning: he therefore sought instead to consider their functioning within a 'higher order' system of oppositions where that inherent variability was neutralised—that is, he explored a representation code distinct from the individuated details of content accessed via reality codes. While problematic in several respects, we consider this general methodology as essentially sound and, indeed, necessary. We also therefore follow this methodology.

In particular, we will articulate in detail the workings of the most prominent representation codes active in film and omit further discussion of the interpretative schemes that operate within the reality codes; we do not therefore for current purposes consider them to be distinctively filmic.[5] They are also in any case already receiving close attention within accounts such as Persson's and Grodal's and there is no need to repeat this here. Complementary to these developments, we take the representation codes as providing the essential mechanisms of *filmic* discourse construction. These, in turn, play an important role in guiding the viewer on particular paths of interpretation within the reality codes when understanding, constructing or even 'simulating' the diegesis.

---

division of 'backgrounds' for interpretation according to real-world, aesthetic and practical concerns. There are even further distinctions to be drawn out *within* the distinct types of codes. Among the representation codes, for example, we find the rich aesthetic traditions of art history and the *Bildwissenschaften* developed for non-moving images. There is, therefore, very much more to be said here.

[5] Although here, as elsewhere, there is a need for substantially more investigation. The situation when watching a film is very different to that when perceiving an actual scene and the full implications of this, even for perception, are still unclear.

The information employed in the operation of these two types of codes clearly interact and exploring their connection further is an exciting challenge for future research. It is already well documented that many of the apparently 'natural' properties observable on the basis of perception within the reality codes are substantially changed by virtue of their deployment within film and other media. The specific properties of *performance* provide many examples of this: the language used in theatre, film and TV shows variations and patterns that are different to those of non-performed language (cf. Rauh, 1987; Kozloff, 2000; Bednarek, 2010), various specific gestural codes have been studied, and even normally involuntary actions such as the distance taken up between figures (cf. *proxemics*: Hall, 1968; Harrigan, 2008) and eye contact and blinking (cf. Bordwell, 2007: Chapter 11) are modified when contributing to discourse (cf. §3.3 and the discussion of mode 'recruiting'). The potential for more or less extreme 'deviations' from any claim to naturalness for actors and actions as textually constructed entities can also be seen in this way—that is, there is no *requirement* that a filmic discourse respect reality codes.

The complexity of interaction possible between the two types of codes is, however, no reason for conflating them—quite the contrary: it is only by separating them and identifying their individual contributions and mechanisms that we can begin to understand the evident *meaning multiplication* that is at work. There is very much to do here, with ramifications well beyond what we can sensibly discuss in the present work. The goal of this book therefore remains more modest: we aim to provide a sufficiently tight theoretical and descriptive hold of the basic filmic representation codes in order to enable any future research involving the discoursal properties of film to proceed on a safer footing.

5.3   Perception, perceptual realism and reliable measurement

We can see from the above discussion that the connection between film and perception is justifiably a deep-rooted one. We have suggested, however, that it is then particularly important to bring the areas involved together in the right way. Since both reality codes and representation codes rely equally on *perceiving* the audiovisual substrate, we also need to consider the role that perception will play for our account. To a certain extent, this is the exact dual of the way in which textual cues are treated in psychological approaches to film; although not central for our concerns, perception cannot be ignored. The task is then to pick out precisely those properties of perception that are essential for furthering our account of discourse.

Film, as an application of photography, was traditionally considered to be anchored to the real scenes that were positioned in front of the camera during filming—photographic images in general were seen as "produced under such circumstances that they [are] physically forced to correspond point by point to nature" (Peirce, 1931-1958: §2.281). This mode of representation accordingly falls under the Peircian category of indexicality (cf. Peirce, 1931-1958: §2.248): the image is a 'trace' of what is depicted. This is the original sense in which Metz's group (2), mechanical duplication, is meant and forms the basis of his commitment to 'realism' as discussed in the previous chapter. It also came to support notions that photography comes with implicit claims of 'this is how it was' and 'having-been-there' and was the basis of the much discussed realist prescriptivism of film theorists such as Siegfried Kracauer, André Bazin and others (cf. Kracauer 1993[1927]: 425, Bazin 1960, Barthes 1977c: 44–45 and others). Thus, although scenes may have been acted—i.e., actors are playing parts rather than possible intended 'original' people, etc.—the scenes themselves were by and large existent and prior: i.e., pro-filmic (Souriau, 1951: 240).

The digital 'revolution' has, of course, rendered much of this line of discussion obsolete. Any assumption of pro-filmic 'reality' actually says nothing about that reality's supposed objectivity or independent existence. This makes the account of **perceptual realism** proposed by Stephen Prince (Prince, 1996) one that is particularly valuable for our approach. Prince draws on numerous examples from manipulated or artificially created images in film to show that the old connection of film (and particularly photography) with the Peircian category of indexicality had long been overdue for replacement. This situation notwithstanding, perception of what is shown in film still appears to function very much *as if* what is shown is 'real'. We can therefore stay with Metz's assessment precisely because this 'real or created' world in front of the camera must be *treated* as real for the purposes of subsequent discourse interpretation regardless of its actual ontological status as existing or not.

Moreover, since the perceptual system has evolved to be robust, even considerable transformations of natural cues will still be effectively interpreted. This means that we can adopt exactly the same position when visual depictions are far from naturalistic. Our 'abstract sense' of placing something before the camera can readily be stretched to include animations and other obviously non-realistic presentations that may obey their own physical laws. The precise style of interpretation brought to bear will depend on the semiotic mode being performed, but this does not alter any of the basic points just made. We may still flinch as the cartoon character hits the ground after falling apparently endlessly after running off a canyon wall or is hit with an oversized mallet, just as a shot of some cartoon characters engaged in various actions trigger 'natural' hypotheses concerning the unfolding of 'normal' world-time. Robust perception then supports considerable variation in just how closely what is presented needs to correspond with the pro-filmic and, even, as to whether there are any pro-filmic events at all.

Figure 5.5   *Non-naturalistic imaging from the beginning of Bryan Barber's* Idlewild *(2006): the figure on the left of the frame grows larger while the rest of the shot continues unaffected*

Basic properties of the perceptual system will then always hold. For example, the 'assumption' of object conservation is a fundamental one built into the perceptual system and readily accommodates changes that, strictly speaking, are not found in nature. Similarity with other changes that *are* found will generally suffice. One case of this is shown in Figure 5.5 in which we see three frames taken from a single shot near the beginning of Bryan Barber's *Idlewild* (2006). These are clearly not 'realistic' representations but nevertheless allow the viewer to anchor what they are seeing with respect to re-constructed pro-filmic 'content'—even though the final effect in this case can, as we describe below, only be considered a *discourse* one.

The perception of artificially created images therefore 'piggybacks', on the perceptual cues familiar from natural scenes, augmented by graphic conventions established by traditions of painting, drawing and cartoons as necessary. The former require no special learning, whereas the latter of course do. The robustness of perception allows us to maintain the important notion of **reliable measurement** in film, a concept that we will make considerable use of below (cf. §5.3), even in the face of manifestly non-naturalistic visual effects—effects ranging across speed of presentation (time lapse, slow motion), image quality, and particular processing tricks such as changing the size of individual elements within an image as we have just seen.

For the present, then, this means that we no longer need to commit to Metz's group (2), mechanical duplication, as a necessary contributing factor for film. Although Metz's concern was explicitly *not* with cartoons and other animations, there is now little to be gained with such a separation—particularly so, since more recent computer image creation techniques for photo-realistic depictions are fast dissolving the boundaries between cartoon and filmed action. Thus, the functioning of perceptual realism in no way requires totally accurate or complete representations. We accordingly modify group (2) along the following lines: artefacts falling under this group 'employ cues to appear perceptually real', regardless of whether this is done by mechanical duplication or some other means.

The information provided in such 'reliable' recordings can also be usefully related to Bordwell's (1985: 113-119) account of the *scenographic space* of film, the "imaginary space of fiction, the 'world' in which the narration suggests that fabula [i.e., story] events occur." This space is built on the basis of audiovisual cues—and Bordwell provides an extensive list—just in the way that perceptual realism would suggest. Now, although for the reasons mentioned above we will not consider the various multiple levels of the diegesis presented within the world of the fiction, there are further manipulations of this material that we do need to consider—precisely because this process *is* specifically filmic.

These diverse techniques then *rely* on perception and, in particular, on natural processes of guiding or directing *attention*, but film actively intervenes and manipulates this possibility for its own purposes of discourse development. Seen semiotically, we have here abstract *textual functions* of picking out entities relevant for the exposition that is realised in material form by shaping the audiovisual material so as to bring about attention shifts. We consider higher-order meanings of this kind essentially 'filmic' because they demand just the controlled articulation of audiovisual content that film provides. The form of the perceived audiovisual information is manipulated in order to create a higher-level set of meanings oriented towards the construction of the discourse and not just to 'show what's happening'. Without access to a reproducible controllable substrate of film, such meanings and their respective semiotic modes would not have had the environment they require in order to develop.

With perceptual realism in place, we now build on it further to specify more formally the kind of artefacts to be found under Metz's groups (1), (2) and (4). For this, we also start making more extensive use of our characterisation of film as a type of document from Chapter 2.

In Section 2.3 in particular, we identified three distinct kinds of objects making up document structures: root nodes, basic objects (i.e., terminal nodes), and composite objects (i.e., nodes lying between the root and the leaves of some tree). A cinematographic document was then defined to exist when the following three conditions are met: first, each basic document logical object can be assigned to at least one audiovisual content portion; second, there is a layout process that generates a basic layout object for each content portion of each basic logical object; and third, the resulting layout imposes a strict linear order on those layout objects (cf. Definition 2.1). The second and third conditions will play more of a role below when we define the syntagmatic organisation of film. Here we focus on the first condition and characterise 'content portions' so as to bring out some of the necessary features that we will be relying on as we proceed.

We proposed before that the 'content portions' of cinematographic documents can be seen as 'space-time slices' of some real or created world. Now we can be more precise about what this means. This real or created world only needs to be made accessible by the workings of perceptual realism rather than by having actually to exist. This also sets some limits on the required properties of document content portions: they need to provide sufficient information to support the assumption of perceptual realism. Thus, even though it is possible to subject such representations to substantial distortion, the effects achieved can nevertheless all be seen as expressive variants on the *recording and presentation* of a pro-filmic space-time slice.

This allows us much of the benefit of assuming a variant of realism without realism's inherent philosophical awkwardness when dealing with representations. For current purposes and the growth of many of the semiotic modes of film, we can henceforth ignore the difference between real and non-real audiovisual material substrates and draw on basic properties of the real when defining our filmic units. Such properties range from physical features to more interpretative and evaluative levels of signification as mentioned above with respect to diegesis and the reality codes (cf. Figure 5.4).

Building and refining on this, we now impose the additional condition that the audiovisual content portions of film can be *considered* to be **reliable space-time measurements** of perceptually real pro-filmic events. This is to make explicit and emphasise within our account a property only mentioned intermittently in discussion of film previously. Gaudreault, for example, in a consideration of early film, draws attention to the fact that the possibility of 'narrative manipulations' was much restricted in early, single-shot films because of

> "the isomorphism existing between the film's time-space and the time-space reality it documents. In other words, the simplicity of the film comes from the camera's isolating such a singular, continuous moment for its privileged audience. ... Within such a one-shot system, there is no danger of unmatched shots or temporal overlap, that is, the repetition of part of an action that concluded the previous shot. A condition for discontinuity is shot *multiplicity* ..." (Gaudreault, 1983: 314; emphasis added)

Enforcing this isomorphism allows us initially to see a document as only requiring of a viewer that he or she follow what is being shown within the bounds of perceptual realism. This limits the complexity of content that can be expressed but, at the same time, already applies to the overwhelming majority of shots found in actual films. Within and across such content portions, it is then possible for distinct semiotic modes to develop, each picking out entities and qualities in order to carry their respective systems of contrasts.

We shall see below that it *is* possible to create continuous filmic fragments that do *not* represent reliable space-time measurements. However, for the present, we will exclude these from the discussion—below we will argue that such constructions are only motivated by a further, intermediate step of discourse organisation that we have to pass through first. This seems to have been the case in the history of film development—supported by a variety of production and other related practical reasons as Bordwell

(1982) suggests—although other developmental paths may perhaps have been conceivable.

Within a stratified semiotic framework of the kind we propose, we therefore see perception—visual, aural and their combination—as a complex process, but not a *filmically* complex process. This is precisely mirrored in our document view.

For non-multiple artefacts, we have a situation in which the entire audiovisual content of the film is allocated to a single document element. That is: we have only one basic logical object that is an immediate child of a single composite logical object. In the terms of Figure 2.6 above, there is simply no decomposition. We term documents of this kind *non-structured* and show this graphically in Figure 5.6; in such document structure diagrams, we will depict logical document objects as small grey circles or dots, the structural relationships they enter into by connecting lines, and the content portions associated with any logical objects with crossed circles.

Figure 5.6
Simple path

Because perception does so much of the work here, such documents generally function transparently as long as we are still dealing with reliable audiovisual measurements. Naturally, this is only true to the extent that the measurements are sufficiently clear: out of focus blurs of colour may not be readily decodable but, here again, the problem is not filmic. Specifically filmic meanings only enter the picture with second-order patterns: such as, for example, a blurred image that *gradually resolves itself* into something intelligible. This delayed revelation of what is shown is clearly a contribution to the discourse development and can accordingly serve a variety of narrative (and other) functions.

More generally, such considerations are an aspect of the fact that the *interpretation* made of the measurements provided by the audiovisual material must always depend on the particular observers involved and their own respective bodies of knowledge, especially as more abstract levels of diegetic interpretation are taken up. For these reasons, we will always refer to interpretations, allocations of structure, units and paradigmatic relations as being relative to specific *sets of observers* rather than as properties of the artefacts analysed. Often, to emphasise this and to remind the reader, we explicitly include the phrase 'for some set of observers' in our definitions. Our model does *not*, therefore, make any assumptions concerning some 'ideal observer' or 'ideal viewer' beyond those warranted by a functioning audiovisual perceptual system.

5.4   Multiplicity: from perception to discourse

The kind of meanings delivered by natural perception for artefacts within Metz's groups (2) and (4), and by implication group (1)—i.e.,

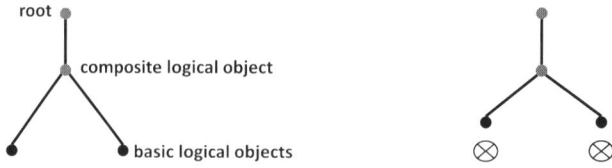

Figure 5.7   A structured logical document tree without and with associated content portions

non-structured documents—are quite limited. To take us further, it is necessary to consider the semiotic effects of moving into Metz's group (3), multiplicity. With the addition of the potential of multiplicity, the properties of the corresponding filmic documents change fundamentally, just as Gaudreault above noted. Here, basic perceptual access and assumed reliable measurement are *not* sufficient. This conclusion is important because some approaches to film interpretation now argue that perception can carry the major load in explaining how film works (cf. Anderson, 1996). But perception alone only takes us so far. We need to consider how locally coherent perceptual inputs—for example, that occurring with minimal perceptual changes within shots—can be 'glued' together to form more global coherence. This is precisely the role of discourse.

The central property of artefacts that fall under multiplicity is that they fragment the audiovisual stream. We can see this clearly in terms of our cinematographic document model. A simplest such structure, extending beyond the non-structured document illustrated above, is shown in Figure 5.7. On the left of the figure, we see the document logical structure consisting of a composite logical object segmented into two basic logical objects; the right of the figure shows the same document structure but using our notation for indicating associated content portions. Content portions are characterised abstractly drawing on perceptual realism as described above: this enables us to see such portions primarily in terms of slices of (perceptually real) space-time rather than requiring any more specific details of what is being depicted. And, indeed, this means that the content portrayed can itself become quite abstract as we mentioned above.

Documents of this kind we term *structured documents*, in contrast to the non-structured single segment organisation shown above. Expressed somewhat more formally:

Definition 5.1 *A document is termed **structured** when its logical structure contains at least two descendents (not necessarily immediate) of the document logical root.*

The document structure in Figure 5.7 is structured according to our definition because an intermediate composite logical object intervenes between its terminal nodes and the root.

The interpretative problem facing us, and also any viewer of a film, when encountering such documents is central. When there is structure of this kind, it is left to the observer to carry out a chronological and spatial aggregation of the document parts—this is generally done on the basis of the set of observations supported by the content portions. The observer must allocate (absolute or relative) diegetic times and places to single content portions (as assumed reliable measurements) and may thereby be able to establish the relations holding between them. For the present, we can assume that 'normal' spatio-temporal relations continue to hold in the worlds represented in such content portions—this is part of the benefit of importing components of a 'naive' realism.

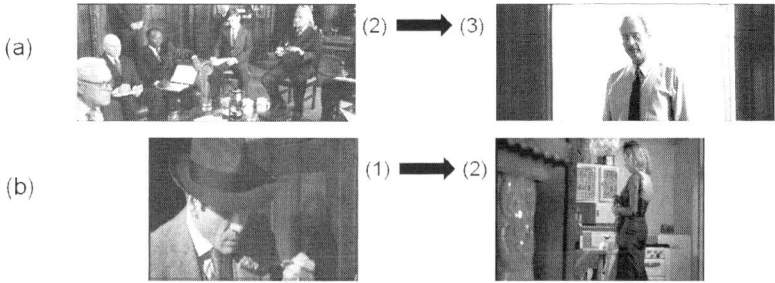

Figure 5.8   Two contrasting sets of shot transitions from (a) The Bourne Identity *and (b)* The Marriage of Maria Braun *as discussed in Chapter 1*

The situation for film interpretation is considerably more challenging when the connection between successive shots is more complex and co-herence of space and time may be difficult to ascertain and perhaps even non-existent. Consider, for example, the cases of immediately consecutive shots shown in Figure 5.8, shots taken from the film segments that we used as examples in Chapter 1. If we look at the visual information in the image track, then there is actually already a considerable 'problem' of interpreta-tion. The images share almost *nothing in common* and yet viewers will, in general, be in little doubt concerning how these shots should be related to one another. Again we have an everyday commonplace of film, there is nothing unusual going on here, but the question remains: on what basis does the viewer succeed in combining (or in not combining) shots where there may be considerable divergence in the visual (and other) information available?

This is then precisely the problem that our analytic framework drawing on notions of structured documents can provide solutions for, systemat-ically and for arbitrarily deeply embedded document structures. Let us set out the possibilities involved. In some cases, viewers may still be able to follow what is happening just as well as they could in an unstructured (i.e., uncut) version. This can happen in three ways.

First, viewers will follow what is occurring by virtual of natural mechanisms of perception as discussed for previous cases: this largely corresponds to maintaining visual perceptual cues that fall within the parameters generally known as Hollywood 'invisible editing' or continuity editing as described by Anderson (1996) . We discussed this in Section 1.1 above; continuity editing leads viewers *necessarily* (i.e., perceptually) to come to particular interpretations of the identity or non-identity of objects portrayed, of the spatial relationships between objects, and so on, even when this is not actually given in the audiovisual material. The fact that viewers stitch together disparate shots into spatially coherent locales regardless of where the shots were actually taken has long been known, going back at least to Lev Kuleshov's experiments in 'creative geography' in the 1920s (cf. Joyce, 2007: 373) and has long been considered a basic component of film interpretation (cf. Colin, 1995*a*). When shots are placed together, viewers will read 'spatial and temporal sense' into the layouted sequence if supported by the cues available. Thus, although this is a marked extension of the situation discussed in previous sections, certain cases may still fall within basic perceptual processing mechanisms. Recent work has begun to provide considerable insight into just which conditions need to be met for such 'invisibility' to be maintained and also to uncover different kinds and degrees of 'invisibility' (cf. Smith and Henderson 2008 and the notion of *edit blindness*).

Second, viewers may follow what is occurring due to their *background knowledge* concerning the types of events, entities, properties and their interrelationships that are being depicted. As long as the 'narrative situation' is straightforward in these terms—i.e., sequences of more or less familiar actions are performed—then viewers will also be able to 'make sense' of what is occurring, even across cuts. Recent work by Schwan and Ildirar (2010), for example, shows results of experiments where adults who had not previously been exposed to film or television were shown a variety of filmic constructions and constructions concerning familiar activities were nevertheless well understood. Assumptions of 'temporal' and 'spatial' continuity may in such cases then also be incorporated, thereby extending the range of cases where continuity may be effectively maintained. Within the Metzian *grande syntagmatique* (cf. Figure 4.1), we find ourselves here in the area of linear narrative syntagmas and, in particular, among 'scenes' (with temporal continuity) and 'ordinary sequences' (with possible temporal gaps omitting unnecessary detail).

And third, we have those situations where the material substrate incorporating multiplicity does *not* correspond in straightforward ways to coherent spatio-temporal 'slices' depicting familiar events. The results of Schwan and Ildirar (2010) just mentioned also show that some staples of film, such as establishing shots and subjective, 'point-of-view' shots were *not* understood by viewers unfamiliar with the medium. The kinds of 'logical connections' employed in such cases are quite distinct. This shows once again the danger of adopting a monolithic view of just what 'film' is: explanations for its functioning need to be drawn from diverse levels of interpretation. Relating what is shown to the story that is being told often undervalues the particularly *filmic* contribution made to guiding expectations—particularly in cases where what is being shown is not straightforwardly explained by common sense.

The extension into multiplicity therefore opens the door to considerably more complexity than we have seen with our previous scenarios. This also moves us into other areas of the *grande syntagmatique* and, indeed, beyond the meanings covered there to take in more of the broader range of possibilities of logical connection given by Metz for multiplicity that we cited at the end of Section 5.1 above (Metz, 1974*d*: 230–231). This has then finally brought us into the realm of filmic discourse proper—an area of meaning making that is *specifically* filmic. We will be concerned now, therefore, with just those places and moments in film when multiple images open up a gap between the operations of naturalistic and naive perception and the additional work that a viewer-observer has to put into understanding a film to see how that film is making meaning.

This situation is quite different from the case holding for non-structured documents because there an observer does not have to achieve any aggregation of individual basic logical objects beyond that already entailed by the single composite logical object identified by the logical document as a whole. The breaks introduced by segmentation in structured documents, on the other hand, open up the possibility of distinct relationships holding between segments and it is this, as we shall see, that enables narrative depth.

There has also been discussion of this point of breakage from the perspective of the historical development from single-shot to multiple-shot films. Although early multiple-shot films at first preserved the temporal and spatial succession exhibited within single-shot films, the potential of the medium to support more possibilities quickly took the upper hand (see *Further Reading*). Mary Ann Doane describes the particular case of 'parallel editing', which we will handle extensively in Chapter 7, in the following terms:

> "The yoking together of noncontiguous spaces through parallel editing forced a certain denaturalisation of the filmic discourse. It required the spectator to accept enormous leaps in space and to allow the disfiguration of continuous time, its expansion or contraction." (Doane, 2002: 194)

For us, this 'denaturalisation' of discourse is what precisely marks the birth of discourse proper, for it is only with this development that the resources of the discourse stratum are freed from the spatiotemporal contingencies of an iconic audiovisual representation and are able to begin developing their own potential for meaning.

At this point also, for the process of aggregation required in structured documents, it is essential to build on the actions of particular observers rather than assuming some 'ideal' response; this follows immediately from our locating of these distinctions within a *discourse* stratum. As mentioned above, a break between shots may be so 'minimal' and appropriately framed as to escape conscious notice by an observer at all. For such observers, the shot boundary *may simply not be there*, despite its possible 'objective' existence in the material of the film.[6] Our working assumption will remain therefore as follows: we will require that our theory and description of film is able to *accommodate differences between observers* in a smooth and robust fashion. That is: our account must allow a stretch of film that actually, i.e., physically and measurably, consists of more than one shot to be analysed in a way that accurately corresponds both to the viewer that 'sees' a cut and to the viewer that does not. Inherent observer contingency is then an absolutely basic property of all the mechanisms we propose. Given that an observer has seen/perceived 'X', then some set of specifiable consequences necessarily follow; if the observer makes different observations, then different consequences may follow. This flexibility will allow us to run the gamut of filmic interpretation, from the viewer who is almost asleep to the one who hyper-actively records every cut, every camera movement, every item of clothing and colour choice. In a certain sense, such different viewers experience 'different' films and our account of interpretation will reflect this.

5.5   Filmic units revisited: discourse-motivated definitions

After this extensive reconstruction of the semiotic modes that can be mobilised given particular technical possibilities and options within film, we can at last define the units that we need for subsequent analysis. The units we assume essential for film are those syntagmatic units that realise paradigmatic oppositions present in the discourse strata of the semiotic modes of film. The principal domain for bringing such units into being that we have been concerned with in this chapter is that supporting the interpretative work demanded of viewers when integrating separate elements into a single structured document.

Given our generalised 'textual' orientation, it is then no surprise that the criteria we adopt for recognising these units resemble in several respects those of the Russian formalists—especially as extended and adapted for visual analysis by Roland Barthes and the Neoformalism of David Bordwell

---

[6]Of course, not being aware of some detail or property of the perceptual input is by no means the same as that detail or property not having some effect on processing; it is perfectly possible for some qualities of the perceptual input to have processing effects without the perceiver being able to report just what those qualities might have been or even whether they were present. We will not, however, pursue such fine-grained distinctions further here.

and Kristin Thompson (cf. Chapter 1). Barthes describes the essence of this view thus:

> "Since the Russian Formalists, a unit has been taken as any segment of the story which can be seen as the term of a correlation." (Barthes, 1977b: 89)

Such a definition is by itself open to developments that are less helpful, however: what precisely is meant, for example, by the phrase 'term of a correlation'? Our final consideration here in this chapter will therefore be to embed this viewpoint within the more developed semiotic view we now have available so to provide a suitable interpretation for taking analysis further.

First, we make explicit how 'correlation' is to be interpreted. The semiotic construction of this style of definition goes back to Saussure's distinction between the syntagmatic and, as Saussure termed it, the 'associative' (cf. Saussure 1959[1915]: 122–127 and Section 3.2). As we have described in previous chapters, although we also draw on this tradition, our framework relies throughout on particular developments of the syntagmatic/paradigmatic distinction pursued within socio-semiotic linguistics. In contrast to this, many researchers have continued to take 'association' in a looser sense analogous to 'connotation'. Clearly, however, something can be associated with almost anything and, without further theoretical constraint, it remains unclear what might be intended. Much of this flavour of loose association is retained in the wording of the quotation above. We therefore rephrase the critical point here to bring out that a unit has to be a term in a *paradigmatic system of contrast*—this means that we define **term** as a feature, or abstract choice, drawn by a system network as described above (cf. §3.2.1).

Second, we refine this further so that the potential conflation of syntagmatic and paradigmatic concerns inherent in the formulation is removed. As we mentioned in relation to our discussions of Metz above, a unit cannot itself be a term in a paradigmatic opposition, since units belong to the syntagmatic axis. Therefore, we need to see a unit not as a term in an opposition, but as the *realisation* of such a term. That is, a term is an abstract choice, or *feature, in networks*, made available in a network of options (cf. the examples given in previous chapters in Figures 3.5 and 4.6), while the realisation of a term is the *structural consequences* that that choice leaves in form.

As a simple illustration, consider the contrasting structures of the two sentences 'he did go' *vs.* 'did he go?'. These structures can be seen as realisations (i.e., structural consequences) of the choice between the two terms 'assertion' and 'question' respectively. The terms of the 'correlation' are then simply 'assertion' and 'question'; the structures of units that result are their realisations. These distinct 'levels' need to be distinguished because they enter into quite different kinds of relationships and rely on distinct kinds of mechanisms; this was explained in detail in Chapter 3 above.

In semiotically and structurally-inflected approaches, one principal criterion for determining potential syntagmatic units is then that of 'commutability', i.e., the possibility of changing the order of elements in order to produce distinctive variations in significance. While variations in significance are captured in terms of the networks of choices relating distinct features (or terms), distinct orderings of units are the structural consequences of those different choices being made. The commutability of units is therefore one of the standard ways in which paradigmatic distinctions can leave the material traces necessary for their recognition. Using our linguistic example again, we can see the different orders of units in the sentences 'he did go' *vs.* 'did he go?' as directly showing material traces of the paradigmatic opposition assertion/question. By virtue of the commutability, we have good evidence that there *is* a correlating variation in significance to be considered.

Applying this to film, our characterisation of filmic artefacts in terms of document structure is then most obviously compatible with a treatment of document units in terms of (perceived) shots. In fact, film 'shots' offer a straightforward unit of this kind almost by definition since it is precisely their function to be placed in alternative orderings during editing to achieve distinct effects. This has made the shot the most commonly adopted unit across all styles and periods of film analysis. At the same time, however, the shot has also been one of the most contested units of analysis, with numerous commentators seeing it as a sometimes convenient, but in general purely formal artefact of filmic construction. It is now, for example, extremely difficult to find cases of meanings constructed across sequences of shots that could not *also* be constructed within shots.

Even constructions which would appear at first glance to be totally incompatible with a single shot can generally be built by an appropriate selection of technical features. Consider, as one case in point, the Metzian bracket syntagma, i.e., a syntagma bringing together 'typical examples of the same order of reality'. In Figure 5.9 we can see a segment best described as a bracket syntagma *even though it unfolds as a single unbroken shot.* This extract, taken from Paul Weitz's *In Good Company* (2004), shows three interactions between the 'ruthless new employer' (Topher Grace) and individual employees losing their jobs, thus conforming well to Metz's definition for bracket sequences despite the fact that we have an autonomous segment without internal syntagmatic structure on the shot level.[7] Also according to our document model, this fragment can only appear as a simple non-structured document fragment.

---

[7]We will refine Metz's analysis in subsequent chapters to provide a more appropriate classification of bracket syntagmas in general: note here, for example, that this fragment is also no doubt intended to function diegetically (cf., e.g., Table 6.1). This does not effect the current point of discussion, however.

Figure 5.9   An example of a probable Metzian bracket syntagma within a single shot from Paul Weitz's In Good Company *(2004)*

We characterise this situation as one in which the audiovisual content may involve gaps of various kinds which are not recoverable *audiovisually* from what is actually shown; Bordwell (2005) discusses several challenging examples of this phenomenon. Such cases go beyond the kind of filmic examples discussed so far precisely because they violate our condition of 'reliable measurement'.

Similar examples of 'single shot' syntagmas can be found for all of the Metzian categories—a point made by Metz himself in his often cited footnote concerning how the internal organisation of extended autonomous shots seems to parallel that observed across shots: i.e., "the autonomous shot is somehow apt to 'contain' all the other varieties of shot" (Metz, 1974*a*: 133n). As a consequence, Metz himself was well prepared to countenance more flexibility than a strict adherence to 'shots' would have allowed. As discussed in Chapter 4, he proposed that segments may also be treated as autonomous shots if they 'are not interrupted by a major change in the course of the plot, by punctuation or by the abandonment of one syntagmatic type for another' (Metz 1972*b*: 72 as translated in Bellour 2000*d*: 195).

This 'montage *within* shots' (cf. Eisenstein 1963; Mitry 1998[1963]: 127; Fledelius 1978: 42 and others), and the corresponding ambivalence it appears to establish concerning shots and their neither sufficient nor necessary role in constructing filmic meaning, has complicated discussions of units in film theory considerably. In many cases it has led practical film analysis to a more opportunistic adoption of units according to whatever appears to be useful for the analysis at hand (cf., e.g., Bellour, 2000*d*: 203). This leads to several problems, including most particularly the non-reproducibility of analyses when carried out by different analysts. Without clear criteria, the units that might be distinguished are far too weakly constrained. We will return to this issue explicitly in Chapter 8 below when we contrast directly our style of analysis with some of these earlier alternatives.

In Chapter 4 (§4.1) we also saw that, for Metz, the primary unit of filmic analysis was considered in terms of dramaturgical 'unities of action' rather than some purely formal breakdown into shots. Now we can incorporate this properly into the framework. The units of analysis that we rely on have now been characterised semiotically in terms of *realisation*: i.e., the more abstract semiotic units functioning within the semiotic modes of film can be seen as materially realised as shots. However, and quite crucially, shots are *just one kind of filmic segment* that may function as realisations. Metz was moving in this direction in his consideration of montage to be just one 'elementary form' where the relations between visual elements from which syntagmas are constructed *coincide* with the relations between shots (Metz, 1974*a*: 134). We now push this further and consider shots to be just one possible realisation of the 'terms' (i.e., features) of the structural discourse mode of film.

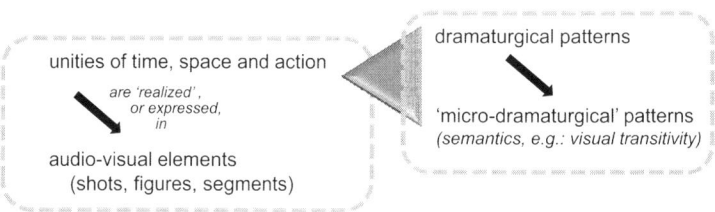

Figure 5.10   The realisational relationship between dramaturgically-relevant unities of time, space and action and visual elements expressed in the technical features of film

This rather more complex constellation of relationships is suggested graphically in Figure 5.10. On the left-hand side we show the realisational relationship holding between configurations such as those underlying Metz's *grande syntagmatique*; on the right-hand side we see some of the 'connotative' semiotics (cf. Hjelmslev, 1961; Heath, 1973; Barthes, 1977*a*) building on these unities. These latter range over the fine-grained information offered in audiovisual elements—i.e., the bare 'semantics' of what is depicted, who does what to whom, where and when—up until broader narrative arcs and motifs that may play roles in structuring entire films or collections of films according to the instantiated 'reality codes'. We thus build into our model and further articulate formal distinctions between such traditional concerns as, in the terms set out by Bellour (1974: 7), that "elusive but powerful sense of dramatic or fictional unity" on the one hand and "the more rigorous notion of identity of setting and characters in the narrative" on the other. Throughout we see the realisational relationships between such levels as central.

In the case of straightforward structured documents in which the condition of reliable measurement holds for content portions, the realisation of the discourse stratum of the structural semiotic mode can be taken simply to be shots. For more complex intra-shot organisations such as that illustrated in Figure 5.9 above, the space-time measurement offered by the segment becomes *unreliable*: that is, time and space do not unfold as portrayed. Here there *is no pro-filmic space-time slice* that could be recorded in the way that is visually depicted.[8] In such cases, the units realising terms of the discourse semantics are no longer shots but identifiable elements *within* shots. The interpretation of such segments is accordingly quite sophisticated, making demands of their viewers well beyond simple perception. Indeed, there are many theoretical possibilities here still waiting to be tapped (Wolf, 2006), but the success of such manipulations is far more closely related to discourse interpretation than it is to basic perception and so has already moved into areas specifically concerned with film.

We suggest the contrast between a traditional multi-shot syntagma and a variant expressed using inner montage graphically in Figure 5.11. This takes the *In Good Company* example again, showing how unreliable measurement is itself signalled in several ways, including the slow pans back and forth across the room passing the 'landmark' given by the fish tank on the one hand and the marked change in figures on the left of the room on the other. Configurations of this kind are also found in the more straightforward case of shots that depict several events unfolding in time without any temporal manipulation: i.e., the traditional *long take* or *sequence shot* (cf. Prince 2007: 180–181 and our reworking of this in terms of the *scene shot* in the next chapter). It has been found that viewers can often segment such shots into 'events' rather reliably (cf. Zacks and Tversky, 2001; Zacks, Speer and Reynolds, 2009) and this can be taken as additional evidence for maintaining the kind of 'stratification' that our figure suggests.

---

[8]This is not to say that filming this scene could not have been done quite simply by having the actors playing the employees quickly duck out of the picture when their turn was done. The pro-filmic world generated by the film is, however, quite different: this world is one in which characters would spontaneously change into other characters. Since this violates assumptions of physical reality, it needs to be rejected as an interpretation and so the 'reliable measurement' assumption is withdrawn. We specify this more formally in Chapter 7.

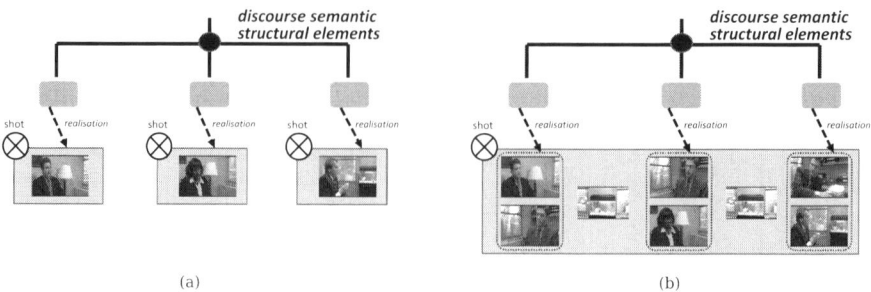

Figure 5.11   Contrasting realisational relationships between discourse semantics and shots for (a) segmented and (b) 'inner montage' variants

Realisations that explore the opposite logical alternative are equally possible—i.e., having a single discourse semantic unit that is realised in multiple shots. Such cases are occasionally considered in the film literature. Bordwell (1985: 85–88), for example, examines this in terms of 'time dilation', of which one of the most famous cases is the 'plate smashing' scene of Eisenstein's *Battleship Potemkin* (1925). The effect of this very rapid sequence of shots is difficult to characterise; it certainly adds to the intensity of the scene. The operation of the effect may well be attributed partly to the fact that there is *no single pro-filmic event* of plate smashing captured in the film. As Bordwell notes, there seem to be at least two combined events of plate smashing edited together; thus, here once again, the condition of reliable audiovisual measurement has been violated.

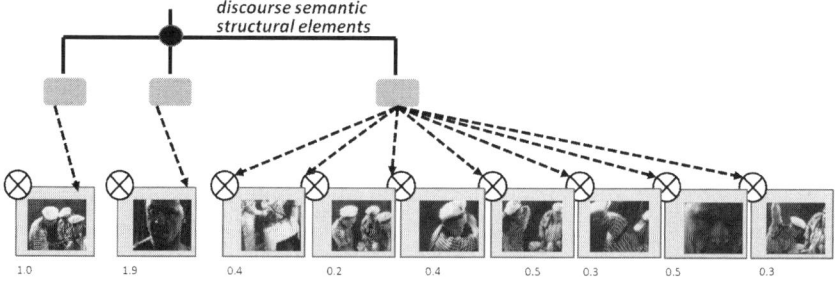

Figure 5.12   Realisation of discourse semantic units in the plate-smashing scene from Eisenstein's Battleship Potemkin *(1925)*

We show the corresponding 5.5 second segment in Figure 5.12 using the same graphical notation as above: the reader is referred either to the film itself or to Bordwell's account for the individual frames depicted: each shot in the rightmost series shows a sailor in various stages of raising a plate over his head and bringing it down to smash against a table or washing board.

Whereas the first two shots of the segment are still traditional and can be seen as realising two units in the discourse structure, the final discourse unit is expressed through no less than seven very brief shots ranging from 0.2 to 0.5 seconds in duration; the entire plate-smashing episode thus takes up just over 2.5 seconds and may well not even be perceived as seven distinct units. Although this kind of very fast cutting is now much more common than previously, its psychological and affective consequences remain open research questions.

These examples show that there are several structurally complex possibilities available when selection and organising content for expression. Nevertheless, the stratification intrinsic to our model means that for present purposes we can focus on the more straightforward case of 'congruent' realisations between discourse units, content portions and shots without significant loss of generality. The details of the individual layers remain largely the same and so must be described in detail first.

5.6   Summary and Conclusions

The analytic position towards filmic units that we have developed in this chapter is in many respects a traditional one. Several accounts have been produced across the history of film studies and film theory that begin by setting out distinctions between film and other modes of expression in this way, seeking to find what makes film undeniably film. We have mentioned some of these approaches in passing above and have followed particularly the path of writers such as Christian Metz, who have adopted and developed methods from semiotics; further approaches are listed in the *Further Reading* below. Also reminiscent of many other accounts is our singling out of 'editing', *montage, mise-en-chaîne* (Gaudreault, 1988: 119), etc. as pointing the way towards the essence of particularly filmic manipulation and meaning-making.

Where we go a step further than previous accounts, however, is in the role we have given to the neglected stratum of discourse organisation within the semiotic modes of film. This moves the discussion beyond the level of abstraction of form, by which film is characterised predominantly by a catalogue of effects and technical resources, including shots arranged in sequence. Instead we come to focus not on the existence and segmentation of shots *per se*, but on their role as one of several ways of filmically realising elements of discourse organisation. Thus it is the *discourse-stratum correlate* of montage that is essential rather than physical montage on its own. This is then the reason why there has always been debate concerning marked similarities between descriptions of montage and notions of 'inner montage' within shots: we can now see both to be clarified in terms of their similar function as realising discourse elements and relations. The use of film for creating discourse has therefore remained central throughout our discussion.

These considerations combine to provide a modification and more precise specification of just what we should take the material substrate of film to be. In essence we no longer have some continuous pro-filmic perceptual 'reality' somehow captured unaltered on film. Instead we see a multiply articulated and articulable audiovisual stream allowing the carving out of several distinct kinds of units. The basic features of this view of the material substrate relevant for us here can be set out as follows.

First, the material substrate of film is essentially and only an *interpreted* material including both 'story'-related elements and technical figurae such as lighting, camera angle, camera movement, lens length, framing, colour, etc. The perceptual realism of film ensures that filmic portrayals are already in the vast majority of cases intelligible at the basic level of what is being shown and so come already imbued with considerable significance.

Second, this means that the audiovisual material substrate can be made to carry substantial sources of signification in addition to more or less straightforward 'recording', including modifications by marked camera angles, lighting, music and sound accompaniment, and so on. These are general properties that are invoked whenever we move from real scenes to represented scenes (cf. Pudovkin 1926: 58; Mitry 1998[1963]: 74 and others).

And third, the addition of multiplicity allows the medium to straightforwardly break the link between spatiotemporally continuous pro-filmic events and how those events are portrayed filmically. This is the most direct equivalent to the well-known 'double' temporal structure of narratives (cf. Genette 1980; Chatman 1992: 404): i.e., there is the time of the story, the diegesis, and there is the time of the text, how events are told or shown. When there is a perceived (by some observer) break between shots, then the viewer has the task of establishing the relationships between the units so created. For structured documents, when the conditions of transparent continuity editing are met, the perceptual system may be able to make the jump, but *because of the additional structuring of the document*, there is always the possibility here of reaching conclusions that might not hold even in the world of the film: for example, what might appear at first as a simple continuation might turn out on the basis of further information to be a flashback or an imagined or dreamt event.

In other words, the structuring gives rise to places where *discourse interpretation* is necessary in the sense elaborated in previous chapters. It is then the task of discourse semantics to provide potentially relevant relationships. This is an 'essential' property of the filmic audiovisual substrate that moves it beyond and distinguishes it from other semiotic artefacts. Although films do not have to rely exclusively on the semiotic possibilities of multiplicity, those not making use of these possibilities are severely restricted with respect to the meanings that can be made. Characterising just how an observer moves from the stream of multiple images to larger-scale structures of interpretation is then what we consider to be one, if not the, principle question to be answered concerning how films mean and the kinds of units required to support multiplicity accordingly form the 'basic' units we adopt in this book for filmic meaning.

We have seen that many aspects of film now fall outside of the range of phenomena we are immediately addressing. We do not consider, for example, individual visual components of films that are no doubt necessary for low-level perception to do its job (such as corners, changes in brightness, texture, etc.), since we do not have unmediated access to this level of perception; we see what is shown, not uninterpreted moving patches of shade and light but houses, dogs, cars, people, dinosaurs and three meter tall blue aliens and the activities any of these may participate in. Similarly, individual film frames are not perceptible and so we do not consider them relevant for the evolution of the semiotic modes of film, despite much being made in some more philosophical and historical discussions of the role of the single film-frame and its fragmentation of time (cf. Doane, 2002).

In short, our discussion of the role of perception leads us to take the workings of perception as a 'semiotic given' relative to our treatment of film. Our *phenomenological* access to film starts at this level. Precisely because our perceptual system is set up to work without our noticing it, and to work by and large to produce appropriate, 'veridical' interpretations of what is being perceived, viewers are delivered 'direct' perceptual access to the material that appears to have been filmed—i.e., as Zacks and Magliano (2011) make the point: "films do not simply present audiovisual signals. Rather, in most cases films are vicariously experienced events." This complex perceptual process is present for all films and so there are certain properties that all films will share. This then also activates diverse semiotic potentials such as dress codes, gesture codes, language codes and so on (cf. Monaco, 2000: 419–421; 2009: 471–473); these are, to use again Metz's (1973: 92) formulation, *recruited* by film (cf. §3.3).

Specifically *filmic* manipulation begins where this ends, i.e., in manipulations of the material substrate that require filmic interpretations going beyond issues of natural perception. This is not because we believe, as some earlier writers on film theory have argued, that 'simple' reproduction of reality cannot be art or is not cinematic, etc.—instead our concern has been to find those aspects of meaning making that are contributed *by film as such* rather than by other kinds of meaning-attribution, natural perception included. And, for this, we have argued that we must orient our account quite explicitly to the workings of filmic discourse.

Further reading

Sandro (1985), although now somewhat old, still gives a good overview of some of the intricacies of Metz's position with respect to **semiotic codes**, their combinations and their relationship to defining the specifics of film. For more current discussions of **medium specificity** in general and with respect to film, see Krauss (1999) and Kim (2009).

The nature of **visual and filmic units** are explored further in Barthes (1977b: 93), Peters (1981: Chapter 3) and, again, Christian Metz, who also following linguistic practice defines two abstract kinds of units present in various codes: segmental units, occupying some continuous portion of space-time, and suprasegmental units that are distributed across a film as a whole, such as colour ranges and other tonal qualities, particular kinds of camera movements or reoccurring montage strategies, and so on (Metz, 1974d). Throughout this book we focus almost exclusively on *structural* properties of filmic discourse organisation; there are also *non-structural properties* that can be treated in terms of the important analytic concept of **multimodal cohesion**. Pointers to this literature are given in the *Further Reading* section of Chapter 6.

A useful overview concerning approaches to **visual semiotics** developed by Umberto Eco (cf. Eco 1972: p236 or Eco 1976, originally presented in 1967) and Groupe μ (cf. Groupe μ, 1992)—each bringing out further perspectives within which to see the moving image—is offered by De Grauwe (2003). And Joost (2008) presents several new treatments of the **'rhetoric' of film** and its description. For more considerations of the **ontological status of film** from rather different perspectives, see, for example, Cavell (1980); Deleuze (1986); Ingarden (1989).

For further information about the current state of **perception** and **attention studies** with respect to film, see Cutting (2005); Smith (2010); Cutting, DeLong and Nothelfer (2010) and the many references contained there. Important work on the relation between **event perception** and filmic units includes that by Magliano, Dijkstra and Zwaann (1996), Zacks, Tversky and Iyer (2001), and Zacks et al. (2009). There is also traditional semiotic work on events, narrative activities and their organisation in discourse— including, for example, Bremont (1973), Greimas (1972), Greimas (1983).

There is also considerably more to say concerning both the historical development of the possibilities falling under Metz's notion of 'multiplicity' (cf., e.g., Bordwell, 1982; Doane, 2002) and the discourse possibilities that multiplicity supports across different media—such as, for example, across **film and comics** (cf. Baetens, 1993; Gaudreault and Marion, 1994; McCloud, 1994); multiplicity as such corresponds to the particular family of semiotic modes termed *image flow* in Bateman (2008).

6 The paradigmatic organisation of film

> *"...it is not sufficient to have the whole world at one's disposal—the very infinitude of possibilities cancels out possibilities, as it were, until limitations are discovered." (Sessions 1960: 169 cited by Goodman 1969: 127)*

In this chapter, we set out the paradigmatic component of the 'basic' semiotic mode that we have argued in previous chapters to operate in film. We have suggested that this semiotic mode is of particular importance for filmic interpretation because it is responsible for providing the essential properties of *dynamic image flow* (Bateman, 2008, 2011)—this is the semiotic mode that provides for the shot-by-shot construction of intelligibility in a sequence of filmic units. Without this semiotic mode in operation, therefore, understanding filmic meanings would be seriously compromised.

We have already sketched the general role that we expect a paradigmatic description to play in the kind of semiotic treatment we are developing. The paradigmatic axis at issue here needs to define the abstract possibilities for meaning-making available within the discourse stratum of film. This serves as a means of imposing order on the material of the film as it unfolds in time for a viewer. Precise requirements are made concerning the background information that must be considered in order to contextualise what is being seen and heard. Thus, while perceptual realism provides a wealth of potential information within the audiovisual stream, the paradigmatic options defined in the discourse stratum focus attention on just what is essential for making that information cohere for discourse interpretations.

Metz's *grande syntagmatique* was picked out in Chapter 4 for precisely this reason: Metz saw the orderings imposed by the *grande syntagmatique* as one way of reducing the infinite variability of 'the image track' to a relatively small collection of distinctions significant and necessary for building up an interpretation of film (cf. Metz 1974*a*: 101 and §4.1 above). Thus, despite the objections raised against many of the concrete details of Metz's proposal, we still consider the general approach to represent an important foundation for further development. This further development is taken up in this chapter.

6.1 Beyond Metz: towards a *grande paradigmatique*

Our description of Christian Metz's *grande syntagmatique* above demonstrated that both the original framework and approaches building on it have tended not to distinguish the syntagmatic and paradigmatic axes of semiotic organisation appropriately. Early proposals faced the problem that the descriptive frameworks inherited from the linguistics of the time were overwhelmingly syntagmatic in orientation. Applying this to the *grande syntagmatique* therefore tended to raise difficulties that blocked progress. Although some accounts, including the relatively recent proposal of Warren Buckland (Buckland, 2000), have suggested that the adoption of syntagmatically-oriented linguistic techniques from the Chomskyan paradigm is beneficial for film, we believe that this in fact distorts the phenomena at issue by imposing a grammatically-founded set of semiotic distinctions on what is crucially a discourse stratum. In Chapter 3, we argued independently of any particular semiotic mode that these semiotic strata need to be distinguished because they operate making use of quite distinct mechanisms.

There are, then, important grounds for taking up the paradigmatic description of film in its own right. Applied to Metz's framework, this means that we are working within the general area of filmic *montage*, i.e., the possibilities provided by film for ordering sequences of elements in various ways, placing elements in particular orders for particular effects—appropriately labelled *mise-en-chaîne* in Gaudreault (1988: 119) (i.e., 'putting in sequence': Gaudreault 2009: 91). Our paradigmatic description will, in particular, classify the kinds of *relationships* that hold between elements within particular montage configurations.

There have already been a few attempts building on Metz's framework that have tried to bring out its paradigmatic aspects more effectively. Van Leeuwen (1991), for example, provides an early purely paradigmatic account of the possibilities of montage, including Metz's proposals, explicitly drawing on the resources of systemic-functional linguistics and system networks as we illustrated in Chapter 3 with respect to Noël Burch's work.

To provide organisation to the paradigmatic description without falling back on syntagmatic notions, which is what occurs in Metz's description, van Leeuwen applied to filmic montage the approach of *conjunctive relations*—originally developed by Jim Martin as part of the discourse semantics of verbal language (cf. Martin, 1983, 1992; Martin and Rose, 2003). Conjunctive relations describe how the distinct messages constituting a text may be related to one another along a restricted number of dimensions—dimensions very similar to those listed previously by Metz (1974*d*: 230–231) and which we cited in Section 5.1 above concerning the meaning possibilities available to semiotic artefacts falling under Metz's group (3) *multiplicity*.

Just as language provides means for expressing a relatively restricted range of connections between messages, typically divided into addition, comparison, time and consequence subclasses, film and other multiple semiotic modes appear to support similar options. Naturally, however, whereas linguistically these typically occur as discourse connectives or conjunctions (e.g., the words "after", "before", "then", "because", etc.), in film the realisations are quite different and must be pursued in their

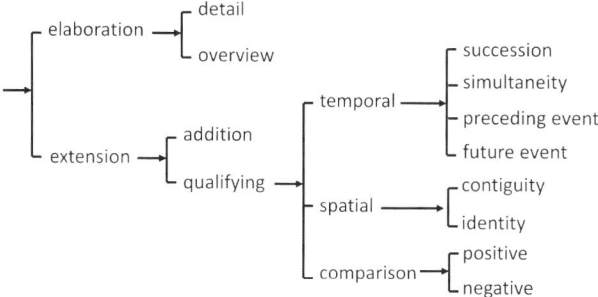

*Figure 6.1   Van Leeuwen's characterization of the possible conjunctive relation articulations
in film (adapted from: van Leeuwen, 1991: 111)*

own terms: this is the role of a more explicitly worked out syntagmatic
description. It is also the case that not all semiotic modes making use of
multiplicity appear to employ identical kinds of 'conjunctive' or 'logical'
relations. Although there may turn out to be some basic, psychologically
or cognitively motivated set of primitive relations that reoccurs across
semiotic modes, at present it is too early to reach general conclusions.
Here, therefore, we will focus exclusively on film.

Van Leeuwen describes theories of montage proposed previously precisely in terms of the conjunctive relation options that they have taken up.
This provides a useful contrast and critique of existing theories in its own
right. Pudovkin, for example, is taken by van Leeuwen to have conflated
a 'principle of non-narrative conjunction and the principle of non-linear
narration' (van Leeuwen, 1991: 85), and both Timoshenko and Metz are
shown to confuse, or conflate, 'the relations between shots or sequences
of shots, and a typology of sequences' (van Leeuwen, 1991: 86). This is
again the confusion of syntagmatic and paradigmatic organisation we
have emphasised previously but seen here from the vantage point of the
paradigmatic axis. The result of van Leeuwen's discussion was a further
proposal for the relations possible between shots; this is shown, again as a
system network, in Figure 6.1, where we see several distinctions similar to
those identified by Burch as well as further categories motivated by the
conjunctive relation analysis of verbal texts.

This network differs from the one we gave earlier to describe Burch's
account in several ways. The options under 'elaboration' capture some
of the functions of insertions into autonomous segments (cf. §4.1 above),
whereas those under 'comparison' capture some of the symbolic meaning
attributed to bracket and parallel syntagmas: positive comparison covers
similarity, for example, and negative comparison corresponds to contrast.
The network was also proposed as a tool for combining within a single
coherent system not only a classification of relations between film shots

but also a similar classification for relations *across* semiotic modes, such as, traditionally, text and image.

One difference that has less positive consequences, however, is that van Leeuwen makes no use of cross-classification—that is, the network is actually a simple taxonomy and does not bring out how distinct dimensions of classification, such as time and space in our network for Burch, may be deployed simultaneously. This may be a consequence of following the description derived for verbal language too closely. Within the linguistic system of conjunctions, for example, the corresponding classification network describes the possibilities for a *single* conjunctive relation holding between 'conjunctively relatable units' (CRU: Martin, 1983). There it is possible to state that a relation is either temporal (e.g., 'A *after* B') or spatial (e.g., 'A *where* B'). This exclusive either-or choice does not hold for film because film's much richer material substrate can readily realise multiple relations at the same time. In fact, as follows from our discussion in the previous chapter, information concerning spatial and temporal continuity is almost *obligatorily* present in single and successive shots for film; this degree of simultaneity is simply not available for language, although similar inferences can often be drawn indirectly.

When we add cross-classification to our descriptive tools, it becomes possible to start combining proposals made formerly in the literature on film in a way that integrates the positive aspects of each, avoids duplication, and invites systematic empirical investigation of their accuracy and coverage. The resulting system network we term a **grande paradigmatique**, both to bring out its obvious debt to Metz and to make explicit its exclusive focus on the paradigmatic options available within its semiotic mode.

We will now motivate the various sources of information to be adopted for inclusion in this network in detail. For example, although to begin we might have simply adopted the relationships posited to hold between two shots by Burch or van Leeuwen, this can readily be seen to be insufficient. There are further shot-shot relations already discussed in the literature that would not have been included. We should at least, therefore, also include the paradigmatic contribution of Michel Colin's account discussed in Section 4.3.2. We already re-represented there his dependencies between features expressed as lexical feature redundancy rules in the form of a system network (cf. Figure 4.5 above) and so now we can consider how to 'merge' this network into one derived from Burch and van Leeuwen.

Cross-classification again plays a crucial enabling role here. We can use it to maintain *in parallel* both our account so far and Colin's proposal that there are two primary dimensional distinctions in segment classifications to be made: syntagma or not (i.e., segmentation into sub-units) *vs.* diegetic or not. Using cross-classification, these alternatives can be added straightforwardly into the network alongside those from Burch and van Leeuwen.

A further range of options, not considered explicitly in any of the accounts described so far, is that falling broadly under the well-known 'point-of-view' construction, most extensively discussed by Edward Branigan (Branigan, 1975, 1984, 1986*b*). We do not need to repeat Branigan's account in detail here; instead we simply draw attention to the very different kind of shot-shot relation that it defines. This involves not a temporal or spatial relationship but rather one of a distinct 'level' of perception or cognition—a point also already made in the account of filmic units proposed by Peters (1981: 60–62).

We have already seen many examples where point-of-view shots play a role: typically a shot of some figure recognisably looking out of the frame in one shot is followed by another shot that appears to show the object of attention of that figure. These shots can be played out in various orders without changing the basic relationship that needs to be assumed for the sequence to be intelligible. Moreover, as described in Bateman (2009), the attribution of such a relationship is always essentially *defeasible*, that is, it might turn out to have been a wrong assumption on the part of the viewer—and, as we discussed in Chapter 2, this is a clear indication that a discourse relationship is involved.

For current purposes, we generalise beyond the point-of-view shot in particular and consider any difference in level of 'reality' indicated within a film. For example, the second shot in such a sequence may be cued not to be an object directly perceived but instead an object wished-for or dreamt or remembered. This kind of relationship is described equally abstractly in systemic-functional linguistic accounts in terms of **projection**. Projection is when moving from one unit to another, we also move from a participant in the film, text, comic, etc. to the 'mental world' of that participant. We see this in language in clauses such as 'She saw *the dog*' or 'She saw *that it was raining*' and in comics in the form of speech and thought bubbles. Although this relationship is constructed within the *grammar* in natural language, within film it is necessarily part of the *discourse* organisation. This turns out to be quite a frequent property of filmic semiotic modes—information that might be grammaticised in verbal language is instead taken up and constructed discoursally within film.

Projection has often been addressed in considerations of the relations between text and static images (cf., e.g., Kress and van Leeuwen 1996: 67 and Martinec and Salway, 2005: 340, 358) but has not so far been incorporated adequately within accounts of filmic montage. Peters (1981), van Leeuwen (1996) and Baldry and Thibault (2006: 237) all mention projecting filmic sequences, but do integrate them into a systematic account of paradigmatic sequence alternatives in general such as we are constructing here.

6.2   Capturing discourse dependency structures in film

In order to describe paradigmatic relations between elements more exactly, it is also necessary to provide more detail about the elements themselves. We saw in the previous chapter some of the basic properties of the 'stuff' out of which films are made: that is, we described how film is articulated into various units, each subject to perceptual realism concerning what is depicted. We now characterise these elements more closely in terms of the *dependencies* that may hold between them. Dependency structure is a particular kind of syntagmatic organisation and stands as a necessary correlate of paradigmatic organisation within the discourse stratum. Here, we provide a rough functional classification of the distinct kinds of dependency structures commonly occurring in film.

   We will term the unit described by our evolving description a *segment*; this will be defined more formally in the next chapter. Then, following the *grande syntagmatique*, a segment may also exhibit internal structure. We term the individual parts of such structures *elements*. A segment is therefore made up of some combination of elements: this is the *syntagmatic* organisation of the discourse stratum of film. Moreover, following Fledelius (1978: 48 and cf. §4.2 above), segments are taken to be recursive. One of the possible kinds of *fillers* for an element is therefore, again, a *segment*: i.e., segments may contain other segments as subconstituents. Each segment, regardless of where it is in a hierarchical decomposition of a film, must be characterised paradigmatically as being of a particular type. The types that are possible are provided, as we shall see, by the features defined in our *grande paradigmatique*.

   The smallest scale parts of a film's structure from the perspective of the current chapter are those units which do not divide further and which do not themselves then have a paradigmatic classification. We consider these elements to be directly subject to the principle of perceptual realism and so, in effect, pass a semiotic boundary. Here, we are dealing less with 'larger or smaller' structural segments and more with a *realisation* of a segment into a 'physically' constituted piece of film, or audiovisual *content*. Elements of this kind provide us with those 'basic units' within which the assumption of accurate space-time measurement can be taken to hold. They, and any of their subparts, thereby inherit this property and are seen as well defined proper parts (temporally and spatially) of the world slice given by the whole.

   Such subparts are not generally to be considered in terms of the distinctions drawn by the *grande paradigmatique*, although they may well be open to other semiotic mechanisms, such as that of filmic cohesion that we have mentioned in passing in earlier chapters. This means, following the argument of the previous chapter, that we can for present purposes safely adopt the shot as a basic unit that we will not, in general, need to subdivide further.

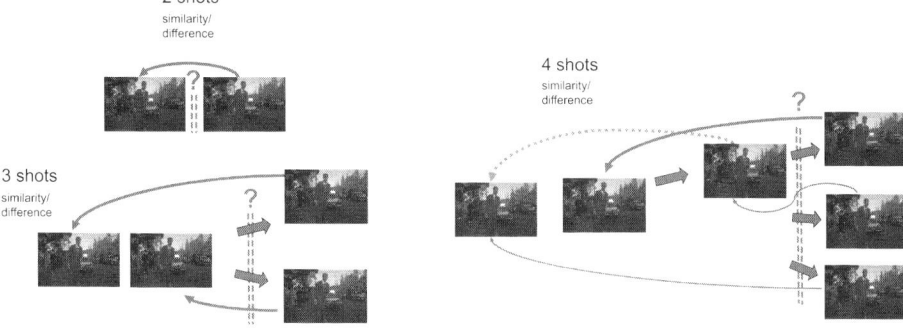

Figure 6.2   Possible relations of interconnections of similarity and difference over two, three and four shots

The essential metaphor that we employ for understanding the operation of the discourse stratum is to consider the task faced by any viewer when confronted with an unfolding film. For each new element perceived, the viewer must decide how that element is related to what has been shown before. We can generalise this further by asking the question in terms of whether the new element is 'different' or 'similar' to what has been seen and heard so far. This continual assessment of incoming material proceeds throughout the film, resulting in groups of more or less closely connected bundles of elements. The operation of this process is suggested graphically in Figure 6.2.

It turns out that there are relatively few possibilities to be considered. We characterise these in terms of **broad syntagmatic dependency types** (BST) independently of any functional classification that might be imposed by a scheme such as that of Metz. In essence, we can see this as a consideration of syntagmatic possibilities that is free of paradigmatic constraints. This will move us beyond the limited structural conception of the *grande syntagmatique* and prepare us for the further articulation of *both* the paradigmatic and the syntagmatic axes of the discourse stratum as required.

Starting with some arbitrary shot, then, the first question is to assess whether the shot following is a continuation of the same locale and time or a break to a different locale and time (upper left in the figure). This gives two qualitatively different situations and, accordingly, our first two broad syntagmatic dependency types: (1) simple elaboration, whereby each element builds on the previous ones and adds new information, and (2) simple sequences of segments, without an apparent elaborative element.

With a third shot, there are then three further assessments possible: the third shot may be an extension of the first shot, of the second shot, or be unrelated. If it is unrelated or related to the second shot, then the 'travelling window' of shots we are regarding moves on and we repeat the exercise

Figure 6.3   A diegetic insert example from Howard Hawks' The Big Sleep (1946) in which Humphrey Bogart reads some notes given to him by Charles Waldron

for the next upcoming shot. However, if the third shot is an extension of the first shot, then we may be dealing with an *insert* since some material has intervened between two similar shots. A classic example of such a (in Metzian terms) diegetic insert is shown in Figure 6.3.

This is a qualitatively different situation to the preceding cases and so we again consider this a distinct broad syntagmatic dependency type of its own: (3) insertion, whereby a new element intervenes suddenly into a segment followed by a return to that segment. The third segment in the series thus serves to 'close off' the development begun by the second, rather than allowing it to continue as would be the case with syntagmatic dependency type (1).

These first three broad syntagmatic dependency types are quite straight-forward; we show them graphically in Figure 6.4. Capital letters such as W, X, Y, Z represent some series of film segments; their alphabetic or numerical ordering denotes order of appearance in the film. An arc between elements depicts a dependency relationship.

In addition, we label the elements adopting terminology established in grammatical treatments of functional syntagmatic dependency structures (cf. Halliday and Matthiessen, 2004), within which participating elements are standardly characterized along two dimensions: the dependency relation itself and the *type* of interdependence, i.e., whether one element is reliant on another (hypotaxis) or both elements play an equal role (parataxis). Greek letters are used to indicate dependence (hypotaxis) and numbers independence (parataxis). Hypotactic structures are then structures where the relatively dependent segment β requires and builds on the relatively

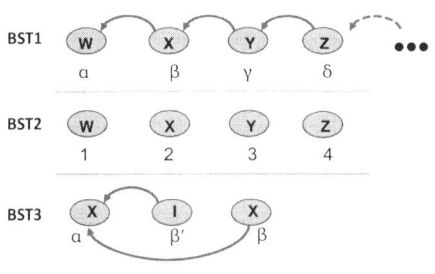

Figure 6.4   Three basic syntagmatic dependency types describing possible relations of interconnections among sequences of segments

independent segment α: this can be seen as a kind of 'addition' of information. Naturally, if one does not know what has gone before, then it is difficult to see what is being built on; this is a clear symptom of hypotactic organisation. Paratactic structures, on the other hand, are where the contributions are not mutually dependent but simply follow one another.

We will also employ a more algebraic notation to save space in descriptions as we proceed. This is entirely equivalent to the graphical form and can also be seen as offering a slight extension of the notation often adopted in descriptions of film structure in film studies. The first three syntagmatic types then appear thus:

1. **[taxis:hypotactic, open-ended]**

$$\begin{array}{cccc} W & X & Y & Z & \dots \\ \alpha & \beta & \gamma & \delta & \dots \end{array}$$

2. **[taxis:paratactic]**

$$\begin{array}{cccc} W & X & Y & Z & \dots \\ 1 & 2 & 3 & 4 & \dots \end{array}$$

3. **[taxis:hypotactic, closed-off]**

$$\begin{array}{ccc} X & I & X \\ \alpha & \ll \beta' \gg & \beta \end{array}$$

Finally, with the addition of a fourth shot, there are then three possible previous shots with which the latest shot may stand in relation; this is suggested on the right-hand side of Figure 6.2 above. Most cases here are variants of what we have seen before. However, in the particular case that shot 4 extends shot 2 and shot 3 extends shot 1, we have grounds for an *alternating segment.* This gives us our final broad syntagmatic dependency type: (4) multitracking, whereby two or more sequences of elements are woven together so that their individually contributing sub-elements are no longer consecutive. After four shots, the task repeats—no qualitatively new situations can arise. Even when there are more than two series of shots intertwined, we still have the qualitatively distinguished situation of alternation rather than a completely new kind of configuration.

This fourth dependency type is more complicated than the previous three in that it combines aspects of parataxis and hypotaxis and, as we shall see in detail in Chapter 7, actually requires a more complex document structure to be described appropriately. Here, the individual tracks are identified as being independent (at this level of description—we will see later that there are usually dependencies to be considered at higher narrative levels), whereas the elements

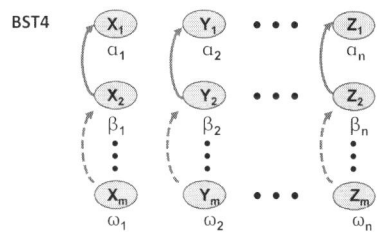

Figure 6.5

The multitracking basic syntagmatic type

within tracks must naturally exhibit dependencies in order to be successfully identified as belonging to their respective tracks in the first place.

We show this again first graphically in Figure 6.5. Here X_i, Y_i, etc. pick out single elements within dependency chains. The elements within any letter (i.e., X_1, X_2, X_3, etc.) are identified in virtue of some kind of similarity as described under dependency type (1). The elements across letters (i.e., X, Y, Z, etc.) are paratactically related tracks. Thus the vertical dimension represents how individual chains of dependency extend as the film unfolds and the horizontal dimension represents how these elements are ordered during the film: i.e., first X_1 is shown, then Y_1, then Z_1, and then X_2, then Y_2, then Z_2, and so on.

This is shown more directly in the equivalent algebraic formulation for this dependency type, which is as follows:

4. **[taxis: multitracking]**

$$\begin{array}{ccccccccccccc} X_1 & Y_1 & \ldots & Z_1 & X_2 & Y_2 & \ldots & Z_2 & \ldots & X_m & Y_m & \ldots & Z_m \\ \alpha_1 & \alpha_2 & \ldots & \alpha_n & \beta_1 & \beta_2 & \ldots & \beta_n & \ldots & \omega_1 & \omega_2 & \ldots & \omega_n \end{array}$$

Here the left-to-right sequence of the labels corresponds straightforwardly to the playing out of the elements in time as the film is shown. In the algebraic notation, however, the hypotactic and paratactic information involved is in fact depicted redundantly: the distinct paratactic chains are described both in the paratactic line by different letters, e.g., by X_1 and Y_1, and implicitly in the hypotactic line by different subscripts on the respective heads (i.e., the first, or least dependent elements) of the dependency structures, e.g., α_1 and α_2. We will therefore generally omit the paratactic line in the descriptions of alternations below to save space.

The four broad syntagmatic dependency types now provide us with a repertoire of recognizable structures independently of any particular content that any of the related shots may have. All that is required is the ability to recognize difference and similarity supporting judgements of continuity, discontinuity and temporary suspension.

Several kinds of constraints then naturally arise from these sequences' internal organisation. It is not possible, for example, to definitively recognise an insertion (type 2) in less than 3 shots. It is also not possible to definitively recognize an alternating multitrack in less than 4 shots, since *two* returns are required. Then again, since the system only permits paratactic multitracking—otherwise the contributing sequences would not be sufficiently independent to constitute separate tracks—if a third shot returns to a first shot with an *unrelated* shot intervening, this may also already suggest the possibility of a multitracking sequence; we will see an example of this below. All of the constraints suggested here will be made progressively tighter as we proceed.

We can also postulate that this characterisation of possible structures holds at each level of structure that is obtained. For example, a multitrack segment requires at least two 'tracks' to be intermixed within it but then *each* of those tracks may itself need to be classified further in terms of the structural possibilities set out here, and so on. This assumption is made on the basis of how structure works within the linguistic semiotic modes and may turn out to be too strong for film; more empirical work may well uncover constraints in this general recursivity, just as is the case with verbal language, and this is then to be captured in the same way as with verbal language—by restricting the options taken up in the accompanying *paradigmatic* description which we shall see in a moment.

Further properties of this level of organisation are revealed in the following thought experiment. Consider again the insertion sequence illustrated in Figure 6.3 above. If instead of the single insert of the cheques, we were to include several such inserts with intervening shots of the two characters then, according to our dependency schemas, this would raise the likelihood of an interpretation of multitracking. As a consequence of this, however, we would at the same time be led away from the 'simple' hypotactic dependency relation between the shots and towards a quite different interpretation in which, for some narrative or other filmic purpose, the cheques are being given their own, separate significance. This is captured in our schemas, and in the definition of dependency type (4) for multitracking in particular, by virtue of the fact that multitracking organisation requires a *paratactic* interpretation. This means that the filmic organisation is no longer expressing a dependency relationship between the figures and the cheques but instead more a relationship of equality (for the text). This is again a common property of *discourse* organisation: the classification offered is more sensitive to non-local concerns than that found within 'syntax' or 'grammar' in the linguistic sense.

Indeed, taking the experiment further, our statement above that four shots are necessary to recognise a multitrack is actually too strong, again precisely because we are dealing here with *discourse* structures. This is quite different to the situation within syntax where it might be the case that a unit requires four sub-units to be complete and otherwise is simply ungrammatical. This kind of structural constraint does not operate within the discourse stratum. With discourse configurations, therefore, it might well be possible to try and suggest a multitrack with less than the nominally required four elements. The result is not then an ungrammatical segment but one which is *less likely to be interpreted as intended* by viewers.

It is, in the last resort, up to the discourse organisation to reveal itself to viewers—the more clearly that organisation is signalled, the broader the range of viewers that will pick up on it. Any particular film cannot be *required*, however, to follow this strategy. It may be that the contrast is signalled sufficiently by other means and so the full use of four elements becomes redundant; or it may be that the film-makers do not wish to commit so straightforwardly to a single discourse interpretation. In any event, all of these are possibilities naturally suggested by discourse organisation.

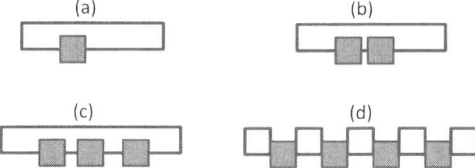

Figure 6.6   Deformable sequences showing fluid transitions between syntagmatic types

This leads to one final point of difference between the syntactic structure of verbal language and the more fluid organisation of discourse that we can only note here in passing, but which is quite important for more detailed accounts. This is the phenomenon that Metz describes in terms of the *transformation of syntagmas*. In particular, Metz notes that it appears possible to continuously transform one kind of syntagma into another—the example he offers inspired our thought experiment above: an insert can be progressively varied from a single insert, to an autonomous segment with multiple inserts, and into an alternating syntagma proper (Metz, 1974*a*: 164n); a similar point is pursued by Bellour (2000*d*: 195; originally published 1976). We suggest this path of transformation graphically in Figure 6.6.

This shows the crucial role that time plays in the unfolding of discourse structure and is also indicative of the potential influence of the very different expression-substance that film makes available for making meanings compared to that of language. This is a good example of how the 'analogue', continuous and replete nature of the image can be made to serve discourse purposes very different to those available for language. The ability, particularly but not only of images, to provide strong perceptually-anchored links between distinct sequences as they unfold provides a robust foundation for continuous variation of this kind. Adding rhythm to the mixture strengthens the foundation still further. As a consequence, treatments must always remain open to this particular quality of the medium and the potential for discourse organisation that it creates.

6.3   The paradigmatic dimensions of PROJECTION, TAXIS and PLANE

Combining all of these considerations concerning both the kinds of paradigmatic information to be included and our characterisation of broad syntagmatic dependency types active in film now leads directly to the definition of our *grande paradigmatique* as set out in Figure 6.7. The figure also indicates the sources used to motivate the component parts of the network—although for ease of reference while following through the paradigmatic analyses in this and subsequent chapters, we repeat the network without these sources at the end of the book.

The network begins with a top-level three-way cross-classification along the dimensions of PROJECTION, TAXIS and PLANE. The main contribution to syntagmatic possibilities is covered by the TAXIS subnetwork in the central band of the figure and so we will describe this first. This relates directly to the preliminary syntagmatic organisation for film developed in terms of our broad syntagmatic dependency types as well as to the discussions of filmic 'structure' already presented in previous chapters.

Each option in the TAXIS subnetwork calls for a differently structured syntagmatic dependency sequence. This is captured by giving the *realisational consequences* for each choice in the network as shown in the boxes associated with each feature. These realisations clearly differ from those traditionally used for verbal language. In particular, and as argued in the previous section, for film we explicitly make provision for *insertion* substructures (under 'hypotactic: embedding') and provide a *multitracking* facility (under 'paratactic: contrast'). Both of these can be constructed in language by explicit discourse marking but do not appear (depending slightly on linguistic framework) to require mentioning as major structuring devices in their own right. This is quite different for film where they are so frequent and so established that we need them firmly anchored in our descriptive possibilities from the outset.

The options in the network under 'hypotactic' are relatively straightforward. The kind of dependence required here is exhibited particularly clearly when there is a spatiotemporal development such that the location and/or time of a subsequent element can be related directly to the element preceding. This is our broad syntagmatic dependency type (1).

The options under 'paratactic' then correspond to dependency type (2). Paratactic relations are realised by a sequence of segments that do not stand in any dependency relationship to one another. Following this, i.e., becoming more specific in the paradigmatic description by moving from left-to-right in the network, we have a cross-classification along two dimensions. This makes use of the paradigmatic organization's independence from the syntagmatic to cover both Metz's achronological parallel syntagma and the chronological alternate syntagma (cf. Figure 4.1). Both cases establish a 'comparison' of kinds: one of topics, one of events. Precisely which of these applies is then given by the 'internal'/'external' distinction. Our application of this distinction to film draws on van Leeuwen's (1991) discussion and reflects in more general terms the division well established in narratology between *histoire* and discourse-time (e.g., Genette, 1980) that we have mentioned before.

Our naming of this distinction here consequently adopts the perspective of discourse semantics where we always start from the 'text'—thus, *internal* distinctions are internal to the text, indicating how the text itself organises its message 'rhetorically'; *external* distinctions are in contrast 'outside' of

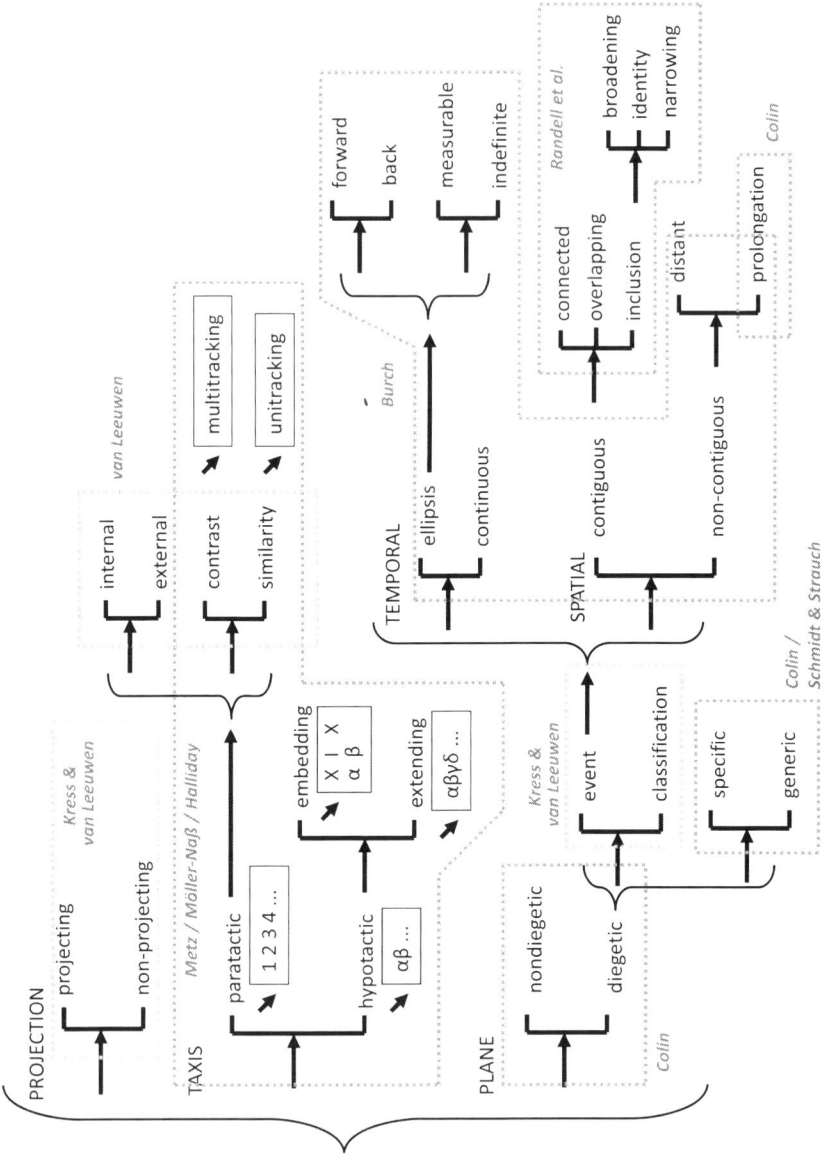

Figure 6.7   *An extension of the* grande paradigmatique *for film originally motivated in Bate-*
            man (2007)

the text and are what a text is representing or showing (cf. Martin, 1992: 178–184). External relations thus construct relations between the 'world of events' depicted in the story; internal relations construct relations in the *telling* of the story.

In addition to the internal/external distinction, paratactic is also differentiated as indicating a relation of either 'contrast' or of 'similarity' for the elements being considered. This cross-classification provides for a variety of alternations that together cover all of Metz's alternating syntagmas as well as opening up some space for some further options not systematically treated by Metz. Thus, an internal comparison is a comparison of topics and so corresponds to Metz's achronological bracket syntagma (3): 'typical examples of the same order of reality'. An external comparison, on the other hand, is a comparison between events and describes a visual rendition of events which *themselves* exhibit some kind of alternation. Metz at one point terms examples of this kind *pseudo alternation* in order to differentiate them from alternation proper as a discourse strategy (Metz, 1974a: 164n); we saw an example of this from *Adieu Philippine* in the segment in the café that we discussed when introducing Metz's analysis in Section 4.2 above. Although Metz sought to exclude such pseudo alternations, we can now naturally include them in the account as a whole. In summary, a comparison of topics (internal) typically does not advance the story-line; a 'comparison' of events, in contrast, may well advance the story-line as, for example, in a chase.

The structural consequences of the cross-classification are also useful for our account. In the case of similarity, a single relationship needs to hold repeatedly across the elements: recognising this relationship is how a viewer can 'see' the segment so classified as indicating similarity at all; without the shared relationship, there would be no similarity. Syntagmatically, this can be carried adequately by a single paratactically related segment, i.e., dependency type (2). For the case of contrast, however, successive elements are placed in opposition to one another and it is this *contrastive* relation that is repeated across the segment: a standard realisation is that each pair of successive elements must stand in contrast. Syntagmatically, in order to realise a constantly repeated relationship that is itself already intrinsically contrastive in nature, we require (at least) *pairs* of elements that can be related. The realisation of 'contrast' is then naturally the broad syntagmatic dependency type of multitracking, dependency type (4).

A further way of relating units within film is then offered by the branches under PROJECTION. Instances of filmic projection can either constitute a straightforward process of 'sensing' some phenomena or objects of perception that are contiguous and continuous in time and space with the participant, in which case we have the filmic structure called a *point of view* shot (cf. Branigan, 1984), or the phenomena can be remote in time or space, as in the case of memories, premonitions, dreams and so on (cf. Kawin, 1978). In contrast, a *non-projective* displacement in time and/or space supports standard flashbacks, flashforwards and the like (cf. Turim, 1989) that may be inserts, etc. but are not explicitly attributed to any participant in the film.

Finally, the lower subnetwork, PLANE, consists of a combination of the temporal/spatial area from Burch (1973) as described above, a proposal from Michel Colin concerning recognising 'trajectories' followed by film figures or characters (Colin, 1995a: 103), and a general characterisation of spatial relationships taken from qualitative spatial reasoning (Randell, Cui and Cohn, 1992). Here it is also useful to distinguish several kinds of spatial contiguity: in particular, between contiguity that either broadens or narrows the spatial focus, corresponding to Randell *et al.*'s spatial 'proper-part' and 'equal'. With these finer distinctions in place we can characterize the spatial contribution of 'detail' inserts as well as the use of pull-backs from particular details often used as part of establishing shots.

These characterisations are all placed together under a distinction between 'event' and 'classification', drawn from Kress and van Leeuwen's (1996) extensively motivated discussion of the various types of 'visual processes' possible in static images. Classification images typically depict objects that are not acting upon one another but which are simply placed together in the image in order to indicate relative class membership or similar non-narrative relationships (Kress and van Leeuwen, 1996: 79–89). And, parallel to this branch in the network, diegetic options are also co-classified by a simultaneous choice between 'specific' and 'generic'.

This latter distinction is proposed by Schmidt (2008) in order to fill a particular gap observed in Metz's original account. As we have seen, Metz's *grande syntagmatique* places considerable weight on the notion of 'chronology'—the 'chronological' *vs.* 'achronological' division is fundamental and is built into the definition of all Metz's syntagmas. There are, however, other alternatives for interrelationships that need to be included and which Metz did not focus sufficiently upon. In particular, the style of reference among shots may also be characterised along the dimension of 'denotative' *vs.* 'exemplificatory' introduced by Nelson Goodman (cf. Goodman, 1969: 50–51). Whereas denotation is quite familiar, relating "a symbol to things it applies to" (Goodman, 1969: 92), exemplification is less often considered, relating as it does some symbol (construed broadly) and members of a *set* of referents that share some selected properties with the symbol itself. Examples therefore 'display rather than depict or describe' (Goodman, 1969: 93).

Both of these apply to visual material. Thus, even though we assume a certain 'accuracy' or 'truth' in the filmic depiction in the sense defined by perceptual realism in Chapter 5, it still does not follow that what the shot is 'about' is then simply what is shown. Even though an observer may in general be in no doubt about what is being shown in the space-time region that a shot records, that observer still has to interpret as a

Temporality	Reference style	
	denotative	exemplificatory
chronological	Metzian narrative syntagmas, i.e., scene, ordinary sequence and episodic sequence, and the descriptive syntagma	*not foreseen in the Metzian account*
achronological	Metzian parallel syntagma	Metzian bracket syntagma

Table 6.1   Cross-classification of Metzian syntagmas according to the dimensions of style of reference and temporality

matter of discourse interpretation whether what is shown is *functioning* denotationally or as an exemplification.

Certain filmic constructions, most particularly the bracket and descriptive syntagmas, can indicate which interpretation is most likely. This was also recognised by Metz—but cases of exemplification were subsequently excluded from the chronological syntagmas as a matter of course. In fact, the two schemes of relationships—chronological/achronological and denotative/exemplificatory—are better considered as independent from one another as far as the definition of syntagmas is concerned. This then gives us a total of four possibilities following from the cross-classification of the two axes. We show this in Table 6.1, also situating the Metzian syntagmas within these as shown. We can see from this that, in principle, segments must can be analysed both denotatively *and* exemplificatorily to see which applies. This motivates their position as a *parallel* system of choice in the PLANE component of the network in Figure 6.7.

This possibility easily confuses interpretations. Pictorial representations are commonly claimed to be inherently more 'concrete' than, for example, linguistic representations. Discussions of the relations between text and image are then led to misclassify what is occurring because they assume the image *has* to be the more concrete. As we illustrated in Chapter 3, however, whether or not an image is concrete actually depends on the semiotic mode that is using the image: in certain cases it will be intended as concrete and specific, in others not. This very general ambiguity applies equally to film. In general there is always the question as to whether a given image is being used to denote what is being shown specifically or, as can equally be the case, is being shown instead in order to suggest parallelism or general classes.

Both this distinction and the previously introduced event/classification distinction from Kress and van Leeuwen we now place under the *diegetic* branch of the 'diegetic'/'nondiegetic' alternation that we included drawing on Colin's treatment. This is motivated by the fact that only diegetic segments have the opportunity of expressing topic events, classifications, spatiotemporal relations, etc. as required for both exemplification and denotation to be available as options.[1]

Moreover, considered more generally, we also need to allow that diegesis be understood as a *relative* construct: that is, non-diegetic is always seen as relative to the 'current' story track. There is nothing to prevent film-makers presenting arbitrarily many levels of apparently non-diegetic material—something used extensively to comic effect in, for example, the sketches and films of *Monty Python's Flying Circus* (1969–1974) or, in a somewhat more restrained fashion, in Woody Allen's *Purple Rose of Cairo* (1985), John McTiernan's *Last action hero* (1993) and many more, where the distinct levels may interact and even become confused; this device has also long been known in work on narratology, where it is termed *metalepsis* (see *Further Reading*).

With these final options, we have now completed our present description of the paradigmatic possibilities of the central semiotic mode of film. It now remains to show it in operation.

6.4   Two examples of paradigmatic analysis

With the framework offered so far, we can already analyse a considerable range of filmic materials with regard to their paradigmatic organisation. In all cases, the methodology for building an analysis remains the same. For each successive pair of shots, we check which possible combination of paradigmatic features drawn from our *grande paradigmatique* network can apply. This then leads to hypothesised structural configurations which successively build up layers of filmically relevant discourse organisation.

The decisions as to which features from the paradigmatic network are to be taken to apply should be made as far as possible on the basis of the audiovisual material presented, drawing on the criteria for recognising the basic syntagmatic dependency types described above. Focusing attention in this way allows us to be quite specific about the uncertainties and interpretative possibilities that a film sequence opens up for its viewers.

To illustrate how this kind of analysis works, we present two examples. The first example will show how basic step-by-step interpretation according to the options in the network proceeds, together with the link this provides to unfolding syntagmatic organisation. Our second example is then rather more complex and shows the process of mutual constraint between paradigmatic and syntagmatic axes of description operating in order to bring about higher-level narrative organisations.

---

[1] It is worth noting that this then also stands in a cross-classification relationship with the features that we have introduced above, for example, with the internal/external distinction, thereby providing still further alternation possibilities. For the 'internal, similarity' case, the comparison relationship can hold over elements either drawn from the narrative line of the film ('diegetic') or from elsewhere ('nondiegetic), leading to metaphorical comparisons, and so on.

6.4.1 Basic paradigmatic development

The first example provides an analysis of the sequence from Hitchcock's *North by Northwest* (1959) shown in Figure 6.8. This is deliberately chosen to be extremely simple in order to make the step-by-step progression clear.

Figure 6.8   Simple extract from the beginning of Hitchcock's North by Northwest *(1959)*

Here we have just four shots, the main character, Roger O. Thornhill (Cary Grant) has just got out of a taxi and is looking at it driving off; he then turns and runs up the entrance stairs of a hotel. In shot 2 we switch to a view inside the hotel lobby as Thornhill comes through the door. He walks into the lobby and past the front desk, which occupies one corner of the lobby, on his right. The camera is generally stationary apart from a smooth pan in the middle of the shot as Thornhill makes a 90° turn and continues past the front desk to a corridor leading further into the hotel. Shot 3 then shows him coming round a corner into the corridor and walking towards the camera to a door on the right; the camera is again stationary. Shot 4 then shows him being welcomed by a waiter at the door, which turns out to be the door of the hotel restaurant. Both shots 1 and 2 therefore have a cohesive camera pan to the left, following Thornhill as he moves into the hotel.

The analysis is similarly straightforward. The paradigmatic features we are concerned with have the task of classifying the transitions between shots. Thus, in the transition between shot 1 and shot 2, we have to select features from the network that describe as accurately as possible the relation that holds.

Crucially, this is done on *the basis of the images* and the *soundtrack*. We are not licensed at this point to employ unrestricted background or common sense knowledge about what is going on. This is one of the restrictions that we rely upon to move our entire account in the direction of supporting empirical analysis more effectively. In shots 1, 2 and 3, therefore, there is a match-on-action, continuous diegetic sound, and a continued cohesive 'reference' to Thornhill as he walks out of and into frame at each transition.

His continued trajectory and the matching colour and other audiovisual qualities do not suggest anything apart from a continuously unfolding event.

The match-on-action together with the explicitly cohesive devices of the hotel door, the matching decor, a sign presumably giving the restaurant's specials of the day, and Thornhill himself indicate that we are dealing with a sequence of 'dependent', i.e., *hypotactic* shots: the interpretation and placement of each shot builds on material given in the previous shot. We show this using the notation introduced for broad syntagmatic dependency organisation above thus:

shots:	*S1*	*S2*
hypotactic organisation:	α	β

i.e., S2 is related to S1 as hypotactically dependent as required. This then gives us the first feature selection we require from the system TAXIS: i.e., 'hypotactic'.

Two points must be emphasised here: first, this classification is a *defeasible* hypothesis, i.e., because we are dealing with discourse each selection of a feature is only a 'best approximation' given the evidence available at that point and may need to be revised when further information becomes available; and second, this hypothesis is clearly an interpretative 'leap' performed by the viewer: there is no necessary connection visually between the shot outside in the street and the one in the lobby—the *viewer* has done the work of putting these together (and, for this very reason, the assumption may turn out to have been wrong, i.e., it is defeasible).

Because of the defeasible nature of the mechanisms of the discourse stratum, any significance initially assumed for configurations by a viewer within the observed material may in general be overridden and changed by interpretations found for higher-order structures within the film and by subsequent information becoming available as the film progresses: we return to this process of abduction-driven revision in our detailed example in Chapter 8 below. This possibility is often used for narrative purposes within film; for example, a viewer might come to conclusions which subsequently turn out to have been wrong, even concerning basic temporal relationships between units or within units that were not previously distinguished. One good illustration of this is provided by Neil Jordan's *The End of the Affair* (1999), in which a sequence of shots appears on first viewing to represent an uninterrupted flow of time whereas in fact there are temporal ellipses where other events critical to the story have occurred. Again, we see exactly the same phenomena regularly occurring in linguistic discourse interpretation.

In the present example, then, the link between shots 1 and 2 is a clear example of Lev Kuleshov's 'creative geography' that we mentioned in the previous chapter. The viewer's work is not arbitrary, however: on the one hand, the film has explicitly selected cues to make the interpretation unavoidable—this is the evidence on which the paradigmatic classification usually draws—and, on the other hand, there are only very few possibilities available: i.e., the features of the *grande paradigmatique*.

We then need to consider the other features from the network that apply in order to reach a full classification. Continuing with the options under TAXIS, therefore, we can note that in moving from shot 1 to shot 2 that there is insufficient evidence for any possible embedding structure (i.e., [X I X]) and so the most appropriate further choice at this point is simply 'extending'. The structural consequences of this choice are shown in the box in the network and can be seen to correspond directly to the dependency structure given above.

In terms of PLANE, there is no evidence that anything but a single diegetic level of a specific event is at hand. Moreover both spatial and temporal continuity is strongly indicated (e.g., by the match-on-action). The choices from the network in this area are therefore the features: event, non-contiguous, prolongation, and continuous. There is similarly no indication that there is any change of 'mental' or perceptual level, and so the choice in PROJECTION is 'non-projecting'. Thus, for these two shots, we have the basic structural configuration of hypotactic dependency *plus* the specific set of paradigmatic features indicating the kind of inter-shot relation holding over that configuration.

When we move on to shot 3, an identical set of features would be selected for the transition between shots 2 and 3. This also now rules out the possibility of an 'embedding' structure because shot 3 does not pick up any features of shot 1. In the transition to shot 4, however, there is a slight difference in that now the focus on the entrance to the restaurant indicates that the spatial relationship may be better described as contiguous and narrowing rather than the previous non-contiguity, although the cut does not show the exact match of content and angles that would be desirable for this classification. The selection of features then continues to be compatible with the sequence of structurally dependent shots begun in shots 1 and 2.

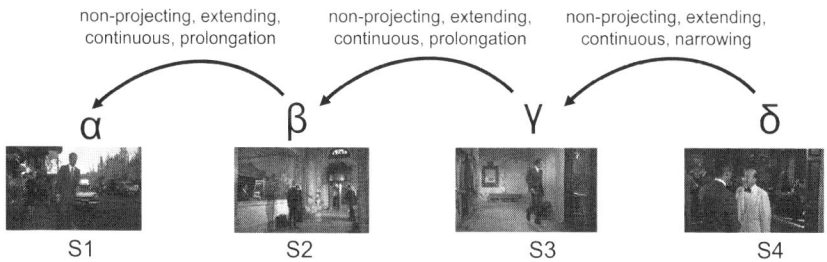

Figure 6.9   Paradigmatic analysis of the extract from Hitchcock's North by Northwest

The complete paradigmatically-motivated structure is shown graphically in Figure 6.9, which combines syntagmatic dependency and appropriate paradigmatic inter-shot relations. The organisation therefore exactly follows, and follows from, the possibilities defined in the *grande paradigmatique* network.

This style of discourse analysis can be seen as providing a kind of 'reading path' for the viewer: i.e., given the shots presented in the order given in the film, the paradigmatic relations that we assign suggest how those shots can be aggregated into a particular structural organisation that is 'meaningful' in the way the features describe. This level of description then captures which shots relate to one another and how they relate. A different ordering of the shots is quite possible filmically but would then have called for different paradigmatic relationships to be assigned—for example, since any change in order here would have interfered with both the temporal and spatial flow, different selections of features would have been necessary from the TEMPORAL and SPATIAL areas of the network.

Syntagmatically, then, we see the film document 'as a whole'—i.e., as a collection of shots that may be layouted in various ways; paradigmatically, we provide an account of the path required for any particular layout of those shots. This will be taken up further from the syntagmatic perspective in the chapter following and illustrated in detail with respect to an extended example in Chapter 8.

6.4.2   Paradigmatically-motivated discourse structure

Our second example considers a segment depicting three connected episodes taken from the made-for-TV cold war film *The Day After* (1983) directed by Nicolas Meyer; the corresponding transcript is shown in Figure 6.10, already overlayed with some of the structural information that we will derive more technically as we proceed.

The film concerns the events immediately leading up to and following a nuclear strike on and around Kansas City, focusing on the consequences of the strike for several small groups of individuals that survive the initial bomb bursts. It begins with various views around Eastern Kansas, often taken from the air, while the credits are running. From around 4'45" into the film, these views become more focused on people and activities and the main characters of the film are gradually introduced. From the first of these scenes onwards, there is often a radio or television running in the background, where news reports are giving information about increasing East-West tensions. Sometimes the camera moves during scenes so that a television screen is made clearly visible, although not obviously central; what is being discussed in the news reports is always, however, clearly audible. This news is therefore placed within the unfolding story as a backgrounded, but persistent item to consider.

The individual groups of people and their locations are identified by superimposed captions. The film runs through several of these before reaching the segments that will concern us. Immediately before our seg-

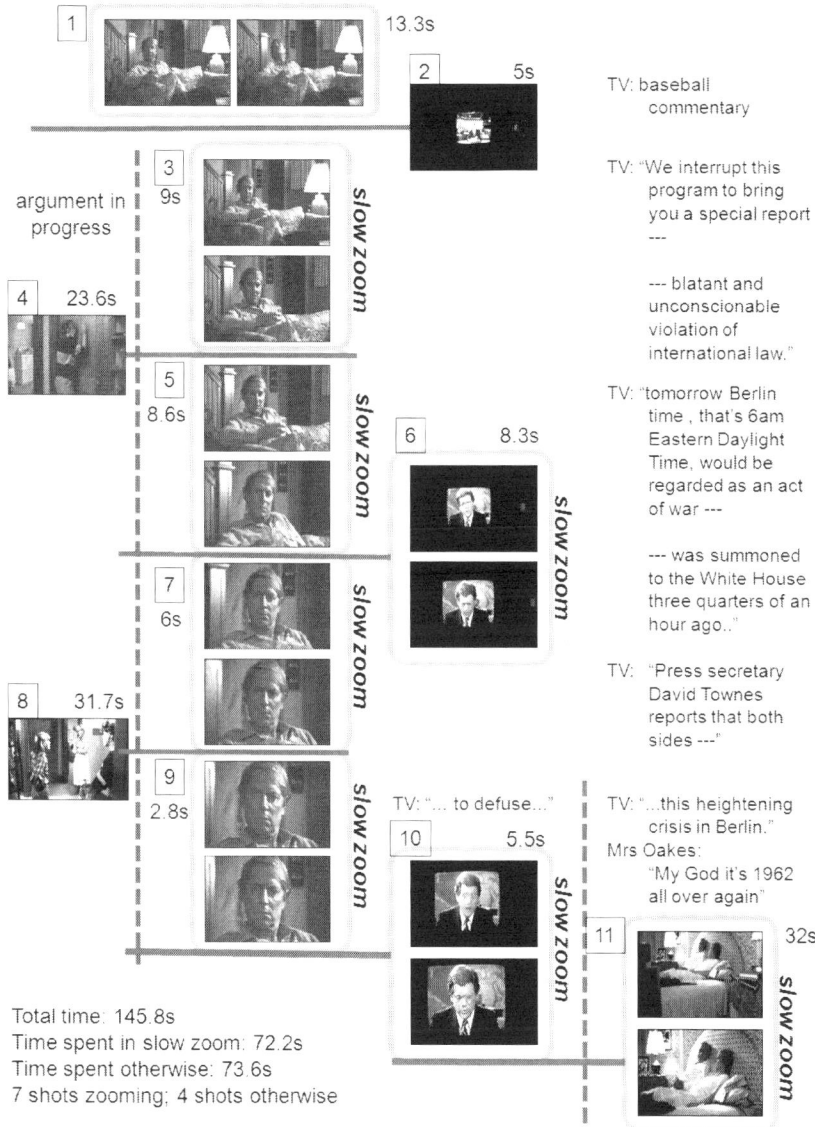

Figure 6.10 Two (or three) connecting scenes from Nicolas Meyer's made-for-TV film The Day After *(1983, 00:20:00)*

ments we see Dr. Oakes (Jason Robards) driving up to his house in Kansas City. The next shot is a close-up of a television, this time showing a Western, and introduces a scene inside the Oakes' kitchen where Dr. Oakes and his wife are preparing a meal. After some familial small talk, the scene cuts to a close-up of the TV screen showing "Special Report" in large letters. They then listen to the latest reports of a blockade of West Berlin; the film again shows here close-ups of the TV.

The film then switches back to a location that the film's introductory sequence has labelled as the "Dahlberg Farm" and the extract in Figure 6.10 that we will now analyse. The first part of the extract involves the father, Jim Dahlberg (John Cullum), watching a baseball game on TV downstairs. In parallel to this, a noisy argument breaks out upstairs between the two Dahlberg daughters. In shot 1 of our figure we accordingly see Jim Dahlberg sitting on a sofa, occasionally looking upwards, and we hear the TV commentary of the baseball game. The first three columns of the transcription in the figure thus represent 'upstairs', where the argument unfolds, and 'downstairs', where the father is watching TV. At 00:20:15, we hear from the TV "We interrupt this programme" followed by news of the crisis.

The scene is then played out cutting between Jim Dahlberg sitting on the sofa and a straight-on view of the TV screen from what could be Dahlberg's position. This entire sequence of shots of Dahlberg and shots of the TV is subjected to a continuous slow zoom. As we can see from the figure, each time we cut back to either the TV or Dahlberg we have moved closer, as if the zoom had continued across the time we were looking at the other figure. This structural unity is maintained despite the fact that, during what perceptually works as a 'single zoom', there are two quite lengthy shifts to the argument upstairs—in shot 4 lasting 23.6s and shot 8 lasting 31.7s.

The effect of this zoom is a stronger variant of that seen in our simple zooming examples in Chapter 1. Here we also see the segment's highlighting of an emotional state: the fact that Jim Dahlberg is taking in the news and is being emotionally affected by it, presumably realising some of the potential consequences for himself and his family. There is also an obvious structural role being played by the zoom: just as was the case with Tom Cruise's newspaper (cf. Figure 1.1), here the television report is similarly bound structurally into the segment since it is also subjected to the zoom.

The zoom therefore holds some collection of elements of the segment together and distinguishes them from others. There are, for example, no such zooms with a static camera in the two interspersed shots 4 and 8 of our extract, nor in the shots preceding and following the segment. The film thus *commits* to this structural binding: the length of the individual shots renders the viewer's perception of the commonality in the zoom effects to all intents and purposes unavoidable. This is, of course, strengthened still further by the continuous soundtrack of the TV commentary. We will see the syntagmatic dependency effects of this constellation of technical features in a moment.

In shots 9–11, however, the complexity is built upon still further. Shot 10 is the final one of the sequence of views of the TV shown in the Dahlberg Farm downstairs scene. Shot 11 then switches to the bedroom in the Oakes' house, depicting Dr. Oakes and his wife in bed *watching the same TV news report*; just visible in the lower left of the frame at the beginning of shot 11 is the side of the TV that they are apparently looking towards. And, throughout shot 11, the same slow zoom begun in shot 3 at the Dahlberg Farm continues, lasting a full 32s. We do not cut back and forth between the Oakes and the TV as before, but the film nevertheless commits to similarities drawn between the previous situation at the Dahlberg Farm and the situation at the Oakes house by means of the continuation of an identical technical effect.

The eleven shots making up the extract are all naturalistic and so there is no problem in taking them as reliable 'cinematographic measurements' of the material portrayed. The breaks between shots are also therefore all perceptually prominent with high contrast of visual features; we can assume that any reasonably attentive viewer will perceive these transitions and so has the interpretative task of relating the contributing elements discoursally. The fact that there are perceptible cuts means that we have a structured filmic document in the sense of Definitions 2.1 and 5.1 above. It is therefore appropriate to apply the interpretative schemes supplied by our paradigmatic and syntagmatic axes of description. As before, we will show how the interaction of the syntagmatic and paradigmatic axes guides us to an analysis.

The first two shots show Jim Dahlberg and a TV set respectively. The second shot is clearly distinct from the first shot and so we are faced with a decision as to whether this is some independent shot (paratactic) or a dependent one (hypotactic). Several filmic features suggest that there is some relation between the two shots—for example, there is both the formal organisation of a point-of-view structure as described by Branigan (1986*b*) and a continuous sound track. Nevertheless, since the shot itself has *no formal similarity* with the preceding one, an interpretation of parataxis (independence) is to be preferred.[2] The TAXIS feature selected from the network is therefore taken to be 'paratactic' with a corresponding structural realisation of [1 2] as given in the paradigmatic network as before. The syntagmatic dependency state reached with a viewer's perception of the second shot is then simply:

shots:	*S*1	*S*2
paratactic organisation:	1	2

[2] We will see in a moment that even had we selected a hypotactic relation, the continuing dependency organisation would soon require a revision to a paratactic structure and so we can safely omit this complication here.

We then fill in the remaining features to be selected from the network as required.

For the PROJECTION subnetwork, there is indeed clear evidence that the second shot depicts what the character in the first shot is paying attention to; this leads to selection of the feature 'projecting'. There is no evidence against considering the shots to be diegetic and continuous in time and space and so appropriate features from the PLANE subnetwork are continuous, contiguous, and connected—i.e., the region of watching the TV is connected to the region of the TV itself and the scenes play out in real-time. This then augments the bare syntagmatic dependency with further (defeasible) interpretations as before.

Moving on, the third shot then brings a visual variation of the first shot; this means that there is clearly a dependence relation between shots 1 and 3 and we need to start considering the hypotactic perspective also. If the second shot had *also* been dependent—for example, showing a close-up of some item in the first shot, as in the classical case illustrated in Figure 6.3 above, then we would have a 'closed-off' insert at this point. But this is not the case here and so there is already a strong indication that we may be dealing with the beginnings of a multitrack alternation. The syntactic dependency state reached is then:

shots:	$S1$	$S2$	$S3$
paratactic organisation:	1	2	3
hypotactic organisation:	α_1	α_2	β_1

Here we can see that dependencies have begun to develop that span across shots that are not immediate neighbours. This means that a hypotactic perspective should be taken into account in revealing the unfolding discourse organisation at this point.

For example, although there is no dependency relationship between shots S2 and S3, giving us a simple continuing paratactic relationship in the second line, we see in the third, hypotactic line that this is in fact dependent on something we have seen before, i.e., S1, by virtue of the hypotactic relationship: $\alpha_1 \rightarrow \beta_1$. Since, as we proceed, we will be concerned primarily with dependencies *within* the distinct chains begun as '1', '2', etc. in the paratactic description, we will from now on omit this line and rely on the subscripts within the hypotactic classification as we suggested above to avoid redundancy.

Shot 4 then takes us to a different location, which due to the recognisable character we would presume to be upstairs in the same house (since we saw this character go upstairs in shot 1 of the fragment). However, this is not indicated directly in the shot itself and so we have again an independent shot—this one independent of *both* the preceding tracks. This gives us:

$S1$	$S2$	$S3$	$S4$
α_1	α_2	β_1	α_3

We use the vertical bar to denote the 'most recently added' shots as we proceed.

The other paradigmatic features follow again straightforwardly: the paratactic relation is more specifically a non-projecting transition with continuous time and contiguous, connected location—connected again because of the character we saw previously going upstairs and the fact that the main character has also clearly indicated that he can hear what is going on there.

Shot 5 then returns us to the segment formed from S1 and S3, again setting up shot 4 as a possible insert. In shots 6 and 7, however, there is a return to the TV and so the conditions for a syntagmatic multitrack clearly hold: S6 continues S2 and S5 continues S3. This then defeasibly revises the previous assumptions made so far—the TV as an insert is finally ruled out and the features paratactic internal contrast come to the fore. The relation between shot 5 and 6 is, again, projecting.

Shots 6 and 7 then continue the multitrack and so the three shots 5, 6 and 7 together continue the alternation between the main character and the television screen thus:

$$\begin{array}{cccc|ccc} S1 & S2 & S3 & S4 & S5 & S6 & S7 \\ \alpha_1 & \alpha_2 & \beta_1 & \alpha_3 & \gamma_1 & \beta_2 & \delta_1 \end{array}$$

Shot 8 then establishes the upstairs track as its own strand in what now becomes a three-way multitrack; and shots 9 and 10 complete the scene, with shot 10 again in a projecting relationship with shot 9. Shot 8, by picking up the upstairs scene again, shows an explicit dependency back to shot 4 $\{\alpha_3 \ \beta_3\}$. Shots 9 and 10 then add in the final two alternations of the 'man watching news report'-multitrack giving the dependency state:

$$\begin{array}{ccccccc|ccc} S1 & S2 & S3 & S4 & S5 & S6 & S7 & S8 & S9 & S10 \\ \alpha_1 & \alpha_2 & \beta_1 & \alpha_3 & \gamma_1 & \beta_2 & \delta_1 & \beta_3 & \epsilon_1 & \gamma_2 \end{array}$$

before the final shot 11 presents a completely different locale: the Oakes' bedroom. Shot 11 therefore stands in no dependency relationship with the previous shots and is simply a paratactic continuation of the segment not yet classifiable more finely than having a different time, a different location, being diegetic and not a projection.

For comparison, the final dependency structure is also shown in graphical notation in Figure 6.11, which directly corresponds to the final form of the algebraic representation. This shows well how the regular grid-like structure of the 'ideal' multitrack illustrated in Figure 6.5 above can be modified substantially in actual films. The regular $n \times m$ organisation of the ideal case is here much more sparsely filled. This does not alter the account in any way however and, in Chapter 7 below, we will see how this graphical representation can be directly transformed into an explicit representation of syntagmatic alternation in film in general.

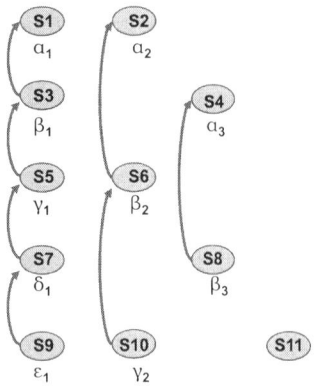

Figure 6.11

Graphical representation of the multitrack
syntagmatic organisation of the
The Day After *segment*

We have seen here so far how the syntagmatic dependency structure is deduced on the basis of the audio-visual material—given this material there is actually very little leeway for alternatives. If an observer has perceived this information then this is the dependency structure that will result. This is naturally a question that is quite different to whether some film-makers intended this to be the result or not, or whether this is the most appropriate narrative organisation that would apply. With these filmic technical features as deployed, the resulting structure provides a solid starting point for further rounds of more abstract interpretation. This is the task of the syntagmatic description.

The task of the paradigmatic description is then to reveal the meaningful relations that most likely (i.e., defeasibly) stand behind this broad syntagmatic dependency organisation. In the present case, the paradigmatic descriptions can be seen as providing a detailed record of the kinds of relationships stitching the structural tracks together. In the relatively sparsely filled multitracking array revealed in the syntagmatic analysis (Figure 6.11), we have one relatively full column—the sequence $\alpha_1, \beta_1, \ldots$ depicting Jim Dahlberg sitting on the sofa—and three further columns containing three (the TV screen), two (the argument upstairs) and one (the lead in to the next episode) elements respectively. Syntagmatically, these stand as separate but, with the paradigmatic relations identified, we can also specify the relationships holding *between* these columns.

In particular, as we have seen, there is a repeated projection relationship between the Jim Dahlberg shots and the TV screen shots. This allows us to structurally connect the two corresponding columns in a single coherent structure: the first column *collectively* projects the second column. This is also realised technically by the extended zoom. Second, we have a repeated non-projecting but spatially connected relationship between the shots of the first column and the two shots of the third, the upstairs argument. Thus, we also can relate the first column and the third column *collectively* as being in a particular spatial relationship. Finally, the single shot of the fourth column stands in a converse relationship to Shots 1 and 2: i.e., Shot 11 projects shot 10: the Oakes are also watching the same TV show/screen. This nicely connects the two episodes with a syntagmatic device that we describe more fully in the next chapter: that of *fusion*. Shot 10 then plays a role in two discourse structures simultaneously, looking both backwards and forwards in the discourse at once.

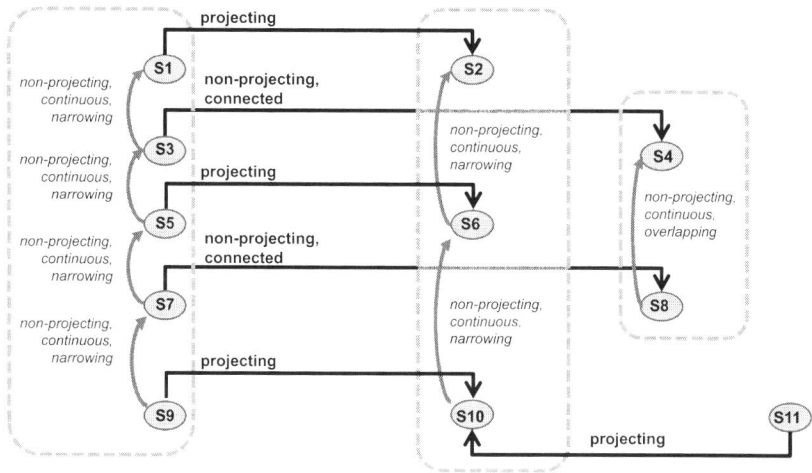

Figure 6.12   Syntagmatic analysis of the extract from Meyer's The Day After *with paradigmatic relationships overlayed*

This net of inter-connections provides a structural and functional unity to the entire fragment. This integrity is both plausible from the perspective of how viewers would actually make sense of the segment and well-grounded empirically in that we have described quite precisely how the audiovisual information in the film itself signals the structure that emerges. The overall interconnected syntagmatic and paradigmatic structure is then shown in Figure 6.12. Here the hypotactic paradigmatic hypotactic relations are shown in a lighter, italic font, and the cross-track paratactic relations are shown larger in bold. Here we can see that the basic multitrack syntagmatic organisation provides a kind of scaffold over which the paradigmatic relations provide more detail.

The construction of textual patterns and 'higher-order' organisations over the bare temporal sequence of shots shows one of the fundamental ways in which the repeated selection of conjunctive relations as a film unfolds gives rise to complex structural configurations building on the one-dimensional flow of shots on screen. Here it is particularly important to emphasise that this interpretation is constructed from the constraints imposed by the system network and the syntagmatic specification. Such incremental construction of 'larger-scale' structures is not provided by less formal characterisations of what is occurring in such segments, precisely because those interpretations are not channelled sufficiently tightly into possible discourse strategies.

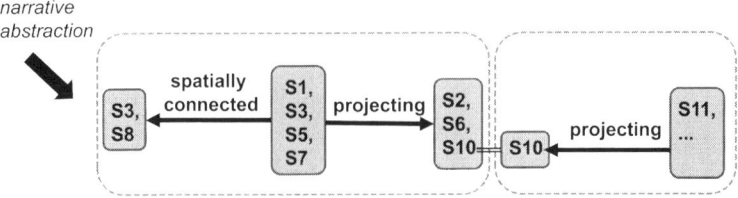

Figure 6.13   *Abstracted narrative relationships in the extract from Meyer's* The Day After

Grouping sequences together on the basis of dependency and PROJEC-TION status then naturally gives rise to structural consequences of the kind shown here. This naturally supports many levels of narrative 'abstraction' as the analysis moves from individual shots to collections of shots, and so on. A graphical view of the generalised narrative 'abstraction' concerning what is occurring in our current example is suggested in Figure 6.13. Here we can clearly see the role discourse structure plays in bundling together groups of shots so that relationships can be drawn between the bundles as a whole rather than the individual component elements.

Such connections are commonly drawn upon in film analysis—as in, for example, Raymond Bellour's classic analysis of the 'Bodega Bay' sequence from Alfred Hitchcock's *The Birds* (1963), in which the shots depicting the first journey of the main female character Melanie Daniels (Tippi Hedren) across the bay are grouped together as "a strict binary alternation governed by a simple process: Melanie seeing/what Melanie sees" (Bellour, 2000a: 50). Similar is Edward Branigan's account of *continuing POV*, described as "simple two-shot POV structures ... repeated in chains" (Branigan, 1975: 63) in order to provide a sustained viewpoint "implicating the viewer in the experience" of the character.

In our example here, the essential binding nature of a coherence-building principle is also provided by projection—however, we will see in the chapter following a generalisation of this notion of coherence-building that allows us to explore richer narrative structures for all kinds of alternations.

When combined with increasingly detailed syntagmatic constraints, alternation of this kind therefore allows the construction of correspondingly complex filmic structures *without* any need to posit anything like a 'grammar'. This dynamic construction of discourse structure is then indeed quite parallel to the construction of discourse structures in verbal language as we have been suggesting throughout.

6.5   Summary and Conclusions

In this chapter we have introduced the basic paradigmatic options available to the dynamic image flow semiotic mode of film. We have motivated

	grande syntagmatique	*grande paradigmatique*
2	parallel syntagma	contrast, internal, specific
3	bracket syntagma	similar, internal, generic
4	descriptive syntagma	extending, classification, specific
5	alternating syntagma	contrast, external, specific
6	scene	extending, continuous, specific
7	episodic	similar, external, specific
8	ordinary	extending, ellipsis, specific

Table 6.2   Correspondence between Metz and the paradigmatic account presented here

these options and illustrated their use in the construction of higher-order structures that provide plausible degrees of narrative abstraction on the basis of the information actually appearing in the films analysed.

The network for filmic logical relations we have provided differs substantially from that for conjunctive relations as proposed for language (Martin, 1992) and taken over for film in several respects by van Leeuwen (1991). As suggested above, this is due to the much richer semiotic base offered by the film medium. Each shot necessarily includes a wealth of spatial-temporal information from the content portion associated with that unit—this is then very different to the situation in verbal language.

The correspondence between the categories of this *grande paradigmatique* and those of Metz is summarised in Table 6.2. The correspondences with the accounts of Colin, van Leeuwen and others follows directly from the inclusion of their categories as portions of the network as indicated by the dashed boxes in Figure 6.7. The network naturally generates very many more possible relationships than the eight of the *grande syntagmatique*, however, and so it will be interesting to consider the various gaps that are revealed as research continues.

Our claim is that all of the possible combinations covered by the network occur in filmic sequences: but this is obviously an empirical issue and may lead to changes in the network when more data, i.e., films, have been treated in its terms. It may also be the case that dependencies between feature choices are revealed: for example, that external comparisons always require diegetic selections. This may also lead to changes in the network. And, as inherent in our account of semiotic modes as historically situated achievements, the network as given may well need to vary when addressing films from specific time periods and is certain to change as films develop further.

The most important step that we have taken here, however, is to reach a classification of possibilities that is fine-grained enough to support explicit testing against data. As the lengthy debates following the *grande syntagmatique* have shown, this was not the case with Metz's original proposal. In order to carry out empirical work of the kind we envisage, it is necessary to formulate more precise characterisations of just what possibilities are supported and which not; this is just what our description provides. It now remains to provide the last round of formal specification where we return to the syntagmatic organisation in order to constrain the analysis delivered for the discourse stratum of this semiotic mode still further. This is the task we undertake in the next chapter.

Further Reading

A good overview and collection of pointers to **coherence relations** as developed within linguistics, particularly from a cognitive orientation, is given by Knott et al. (2001). These may provide a basis for some more generic cognitively motivated accounts of conjunctive relations that could hold across distinct semiotic modes.

Further discussions and examples of the role of the *grande paradigmatique* as a part of the discourse semantics of film can be found in Bateman (2007). We have also now made more use of the non-structural connections described by **multimodal cohesion** in motivating our paradigmatic analyses. Models of multimodal cohesion were originally developed in van Leeuwen (2005*a*); Royce (2007); Liu and O'Halloran (2009). For the application of this notion particularly to film, see Tseng (2008); Janney (2010); Tseng and Bateman (2010). An important feature of multimodal cohesion is that relations may be constructed freely across very different kinds of units, e.g., between image and sound, which offers important resources for understanding multimodal synergies of the kinds commonly found in film.

At several points there are points where a useful bridge can be drawn between paradigmatic accounts and analyses undertaken with **narratology**. For discussion of other narratological constructs and their application to film, as well as extensive literature reviews, see Kuhn (2009, 2011) and Verstraten (2009)—as well as the other references in the *Further Reading* section of Chapter 4.

The necessity of recognising distinct **diegetic levels** in film has also long been noted, typically realised in narrative strategies such as the 'film-in-film'. Hartmann (2007) points to this as a now standard strategy for beginning films. For further discussion of moving *between* diegetic levels, i.e., *metalepsis* in narratological terms, see Herman (1997), Nelles (1997), Wolf (2005) and Pier (2010).

7 The syntagmatic organisation of film

> *"Unless a film contains obviously intrusive camera work—flashing lights, rapid montage, striking camera angles—we have difficulty believing that there may be problems in interpreting film comparable to the problems we find in fully understanding the other arts. Because we have gotten so much from a film at first viewing, we often balk at any insistence that the understanding of certain canons, methods, and traditions will help us understand more. But we resist especially because films seem so real and therefore so self-sufficient, without need of any critical interloper to explain them to us." (Braudy, 1976: 20)*

In this chapter we turn to the detailed presentation of our proposed methods for decomposing film structurally, i.e., how we deal with the syntagmatic axis of filmic organisation. As motivated above, the strategy we adopt for this task employs a 'document'-based view of the filmic artefacts that we are analysing; the kinds of structural organisations currently being developed for describing arbitrarily complex 'documents'—including those involving temporal and spatial combinations of materials—offer us a secure foundation that also relates well to current standardisation efforts for film and other audiovisual media.

We begin by refining the basic sketch of syntagmatic organisation given previously to the point that it becomes strong enough for supporting detailed analysis. Without such a foundation, analyses even of the basic structure of a film tend to be subject to a range of variation due by and large to a lack of clear criteria for segmentation. In our document-based approach, we therefore make explicit many of the motivations by which those analysing films have previously made their decisions in any case. The definitions we provide go further, however, so as to guide us through cases for which, without precise definitions, it would be difficult to formulate intersubjectively reliable analyses.

We have seen in earlier chapters several of the organising principles standing behind such analyses, including temporal relations, spatial relations, mental and perceptual projection and so on. These were gathered together and summarised in the form of the *grande paradigmatique* proposed in the previous chapter. Now we ground these distinctions firmly in the syntagmatic organisation of film by providing further definitions that constrain the document structures possible. As explained above, we consider a filmic document structure to consist of a collection of organised content that is rendered appropriately via a *layouting process* for display in some output medium. It is then in the relationship between the *logical* perspective and the *layout* perspective that we situate many of the basic mechanisms of filmic interpretation. Our concern in this chapter is to develop additional constraints on this foundation that progressively isolate distinctive forms of filmic organisation. As we proceed, we will also identify those places in the account where bridges between the syntagmatic document view and the discourse view function to channel activities of interpretation.

The constraints we uncover will need to be sufficiently precise as to enable clear and unambiguous application. This is not to say that films always have unique 'readings'—several conditions may be met simultaneously by any particular film segment. Moreover, different groups of viewers may attend to different aspects of the film they are seeing. In both cases we may therefore need to produce differently organised cinematographic documents. The filmic organisations we propose are then always to be understood as showing what follows *as long as* certain boundary conditions are met. Our definitions will make these boundary conditions explicit whenever relevant.

Our first task for this part of the account is to set out some basic definitions that are necessary for describing any filmic document. We then provide a re-characterisation of the Metzian categories, showing how the finer-grained definitions we provide serve to resolve many of the difficulties in application raised by Metz's original account. For ease of reference back to Metz's description, we will again follow Metz and use several examples from Jacques Rozier's *Adieu Philippine* (1962) just as we did in our introduction to Metz's account in Chapter 4. Here again it is worth noting that it would be useful for the reader not only to have seen this film, but also to have to hand Metz's syntagma-by-syntagma analysis of the film as presented in Metz (1974*a*: Chapter 6, 149–176).

7.1 Basic properties of the cinematographic document

In Chapter 5 (§5.4) we gave our first definitions for restricting the kinds of properties that a cinematographic document must exhibit. The structures supported by these definitions were, however, rather simple: essentially any series of shots following one another in a chain would suffice—this clearly offers an insufficient foundation for narrative construction. The four broad syntagmatic dependency types we defined for illustrating paradigmatic organisation (cf. Figures 6.4 and 6.5) then suggested informally how such chains might come to carry more specific and complex structures. That is: the individual elements of the logical structure are not simply placed one after the other in succession because that is all the medium can support—which would be a kind of 'blind linearity'; instead, this sequentiality has itself been taken over during the development of the semiotic modes of film in order to serve the requirements of diverse discourse structures, narrative organisation among them. The resulting configurations carry paradigmatic distinctions and further, more abstract, discourse organisations building on them.

Our goal now is to progressively develop tighter definitions that impose the necessary further organisation more formally. This organisation must in turn support the construction of discourse configurations sufficiently complex for the expressive demands placed upon the medium. We begin with definitions that allow us systematically to *classify* elements appearing in a film. Metz used the term **segment** to characterise any analytic extract for which a classification was to be sought (cf. Metz, 1974a: 123). A 'segment' is therefore a film extract, for which a specific classification has not yet been achieved. We also adopt this usage here.

In addition, we note again that we are dealing with documents that both depict states of affairs that unfold over time—the diegetic world of the film—and which *themselves* unfold over time—the 'document time'. A layouted structure within a cinematographic document thus commits to a temporally ordered presentation of its layout elements. This is then different to documents for which, informally, the term 'layout' is more commonly used in a static sense. With a document theoretic account it is natural to generalise across these cases. Furthermore, the attribution of diegetic space and time to elements in the cinematographic document is always coupled with sets of *observers*: that is, as also emphasised previously (cf. §5.3), we build the interpretive role of observers into the framework at a foundational level. In one of our next examples, we will show just how crucial this is both for following analyses and for avoiding interpretative deadlocks between different 'viewings' of a film.

As we have defined above, the result of the layouting process is a layout structure. A layouting process can then very generally be seen as grouping together elements from the logical structure in order to form a layout structure. We can accordingly consider a filmic segment as, very generally, some particular grouping of elements brought about by a layouting process. This allows us to remain quite agnostic concerning the particular 'size' of unit that we are considering—we will be describing organisations both of shots and of higher-order structures below.

A layouting process then, by virtue of its grouping together of elements, 'partitions' the elements it operates over: that is, rather than having just a chain of elements of some kind, typically shots, a layouting process says which elements belong together and which do not. Combining segments and our document-view, we can state that:

Definition 7.1 *A* **segment** *in a cinematographic document is a non-empty ordered set selected from all of the temporally ordered shots produced from a given layouting process.*

The construction of additional filmic structure is then defined in terms of more specific logical and layout segmentation as we shall now see.

It is useful to relate the above definition back to the possibilities for decomposing documents we saw set out by Martínez (2002*a*) in Figure 2.6. There is, for example, no requirement that the segments in our definition are strictly contiguous in the layout: that is, we can naturally consider *discontinuous* segments; this will be important below because this is one respect in which film syntagmatic organisation is quite different to that of natural language. This is no doubt supported by the fact that it is much easier to 'index' individual shots as being associated with different space-time regions in film than it is to index the more abstract grammatical constituents within linguistic constructions. The rich information particularly in the visual array provides almost instant access to a diversity of organising features that can then be drawn on in the construction of complex discourse structures.

A further point of difference at least to linguistic syntactic structure is the frequent occurrence of *overlap* between segments—although, interestingly we *do* find such constructions in linguistic *discourse* organisation: as illustrated, for example, in Martin's (1992: 263) discussion of 'sandwich' structures at the discourse level looking both to the 'left' and to the 'right'. For reasons that will become clear as we proceed, we term this filmic phenomenon **fusion**.

In Chapter 4 (§ 4.2) above, we introduced aspects of Metz's analysis of Jacques Rozier's *Adieu Philippine* (1962). Here we take this further and focus on the first two segments of the film since these offer a ready illustration of the fusion phenomenon. Metz considered these two segments to belong to very different syntagma types. Segment 2, as we discussed earlier (cf. Figure 4.3), is an ordinary scene and is, therefore, chronological; Segment 1, however, Metz analysed as a bracket syntagma, i.e., an achronological succession of shots which together depict typical elements of a particular reality or world-view in order that that view is exemplified visually. In the present case, the shots of the syntagma collectively 'exemplify' the concept of a busy TV studio.

This analysis appears quite appropriate since Segment 1, at first glance, does communicate bustling recording studio activity without any apparent narrative development. Strengthening this interpretation is the fact that the segment is also part of the titles sequence of the film, with the names of the actors appearing in overlay over the images. Metz suggests that it is only when the main character Michel is instructed to fetch something from outside the studio that he becomes individuated by his participation in the dialogue and by subsequently being tracked by the camera. Only then is it reconstructible for an observer that Michel is a principal point of focus for the film; this is cemented further by Segment 2, which begins solely concerned with Michel. In Figure 7.1 we present the first segment graphically, including both shot durations and some further annotations that we will return to below.

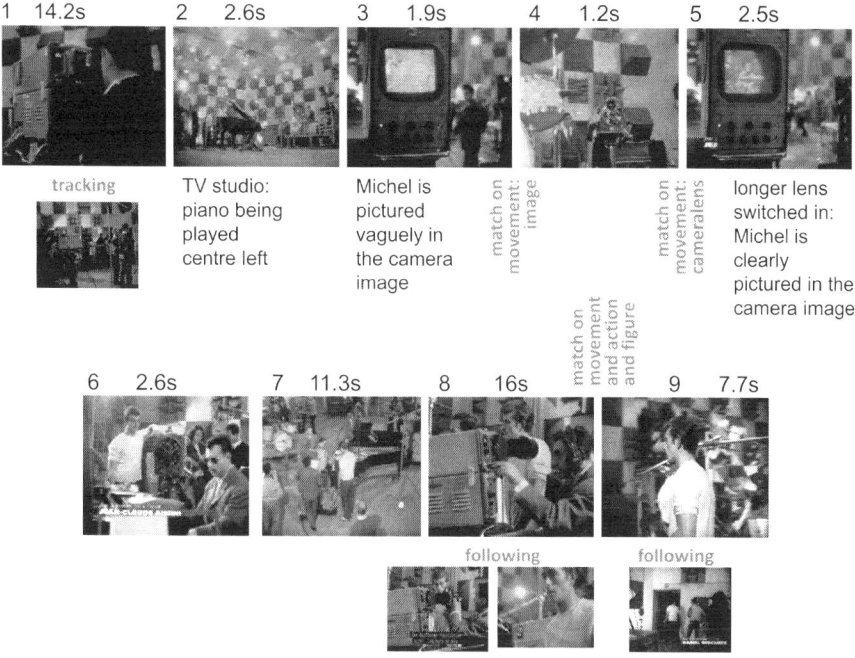

Figure 7.1   Segment 1 of Jacques Rozier's Adieu Philippine *(1962)*

Metz raises the difficulty here that there appear to be equal grounds for also including the shots where Michel is told to fetch a new pair of headphones by a camera operator (Shots 8 and 9 in Segment 1 in the figure) as part of Segment 2. Within Segment 1, these shots continue the presentation of bustling TV studio activity; but, as part of Segment 2, the shots just as well show Michel's journey from the camera to the studio door to the corridor outside and out of the building. Metz's solution is to suggest that these shots (actually Metz only identifies one shot here: it may be that the prints differ or that the slight jump cut between shots 8 and 9 was considered irrelevant) actually belong to both segments (Metz, 1974*a*: 150). The segments would therefore 'overlap'.

Rather than weaken our notion of segments in this way, we instead treat such situations formally as involving what we will call the *fusion* of two technically distinct elements within a single shot—i.e., we envisage a 'virtual' doubling up of an element. Notationally, we will indicate such doubling for a film shot 'E' by separating the shot into two overlapping but formally distinct elements: E^- and E^+. Thus, as far as the logical structure is concerned, we have an element which ends the first segment, and which is to be classified according to the definitional requirements of its corresponding syntagma, and a separate element beginning the second segment, which must meet correspondingly the definitional requirements of *that* syntagma. These two elements are formally fused within the layouting process so as to be realised in a single shot.

Our definition for fusion is then accordingly:

Definition 7.2 *A given shot in a cinematographic document is a* **fusion** *for some layouting process and some given set of observers, when:*

1. *two segments both containing the given shot exist that can be classified as representing distinct events by all observers, and*
2. *the given shot is the sole intersection of the sets of shots in these segments for the given layouting process.*

We can turn any document with fusions into a corresponding **fusion-free** document for the purposes of further analysis by simply expanding the fused shots so as to create non-overlapping partitions for the segments involved. The created 'subshots' are then, in the case of reliable spatiotemporal measurement that we assume here, necessarily continuous in time and space. This allows us to simplify our definitions below considerably, while also maintaining the overall thrust of Metz's account within a more formally defined framework.

While this resolves the difficulty of having to enforce a potentially arbitrary boundary between two segments, for a complete treatment of what is happening in Segments 1 and 2 we are not quite out of the woods. Problematic is the fact that the main character, Michel, is actually often visible within the first segment acting as a cable assistant carrying out minor tasks within the overall bustle of recording studio activity. Thus, when a viewer sees the film a *second* time, it may well be clear from the outset that the main male character of the film is being shown even in this first segment. This reduces substantially any grounds we might have assumed for a clear separation between Segments 1 and 2. It is then awkward to analyse the two segments as Metz does as a simple succession of two distinct syntagmas.

In order to treat this problem we will need substantially more of our syntagmatic account in place. We will, therefore, return to this problem at the end of the chapter after having set out the framework as a whole.

7.2   Monochronicity

The syntagmatic classification of the 'morphological' structure of a cinematographic document must first be carried out for the parts given by that document's logical structure. In particular, we will consider syntagmas as particular classifications of sufficiently complex sub-trees of the logical structure—each such sub-tree should contain at least one intermediate organising node between the root and the leaves of the document logical structure tree that captures its 'unity' in some sense. We specify this more formally thus:

Definition 7.3 *A* **syntagma** *classifies such partial trees of the logical structure of a document which contain at least one composite logical object and which a layouting process renders in at least one segment.*

Following this definition, we will now speak of the *segments of a syntagma*. This can be abbreviated as the 'shots of a syntagma' when these shots belong to one of the syntagma's segments. The *purpose* of a classification according to one syntagma rather than another is then to bring additional constraints to bear on the necessary properties of the sub-trees so classified. This will be used below to impose specific structures on the logical trees that are permitted, which will in turn guide interpretation.

To begin refining the account, we consider again briefly the simplest possible case: the non-structured document as discussed in Chapter 5. According to the Metzian *grande syntagmatique*, there are two possible classifications for such a structure: either as an *insert* or as a *sequence shot*. The former we have considered briefly in the previous chapter and will return to below; the latter provides a convenient starting point for considering syntagmatic organisations of all kinds. However, for reasons that will shortly become clear, we will no longer talk of 'sequence shot', preferring instead the term **scene shot**; this has been discussed as a syntagmatic category in its own right under the term *Planszene* in the characterisation provided in German by Schmidt and Strauch (2002) and we follow their account here, developing it further where necessary.

A scene shot occurs when a given layouting process allocates a single shot to a scene and no other syntagmatic classification can be found. In general, the scene shot leaves no doubt about the temporal unfolding of its content: i.e., as described in Section 5.3, we assume that the audiovisual content associated with our logical document object is a *reliable measurement*. The segment thus constructs a timeline that is 'homomorphic' to that of what it depicts as regards to temporal order—i.e., temporal precedence relations are preserved across the two domains: the content portion and its presentation.[1] The presentation may be varied by speeding or slowing diegetic time within the shot, but more complex variations (cf. Wolf, 2006) are still rare at this point in the historical development of film.

We use the term 'scene shot' in order to bring out the strong similarity between such single shot scenes and multiple shot scenes—essentially the same conditions hold for both. If we carry the temporal simplicity of the scene shot over to a segment involving *two* shots, however, then

---

[1] A **homomorphism** is a mathematical construct indicating in general that some structural properties involving a given operation are preserved across two domains. For us here, it means that if two content portions show events that occur in some order then the depictions of those content portions within shots or segments will be displayed in the layouted document/film in that order.

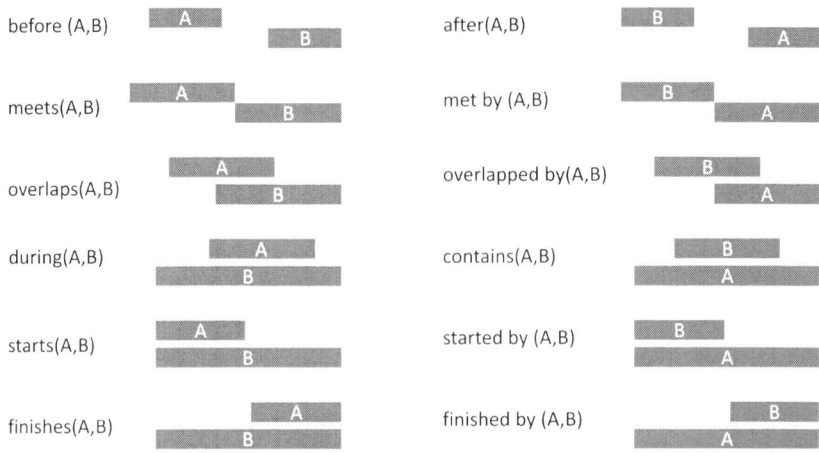

Figure 7.2   The base relations of Allen's temporal logic (excluding equal) shown over pairs of temporal intervals, A and B; time is taken to run from left-to-right across the page within each column

an observer has to make some estimation of the spatiotemporal world 'slices' being depicted—itself an abductive, i.e., defeasible, interpretation necessary for subsequent discourse processing—and then use this information to characterise the relationship between the segments (cf. §5.4). The temporal relation induced may be either absolute or relative. In the absolute case, the segments would need to show some clock or similar measuring device; the more usual case, in which an observer can posit with some confidence that the second shot is a little later than the first but without knowing *exactly* how much later, is relative.

To describe these possible temporal relationships more specifically, we adopt one of the standard formalisations developed for temporal relationships: Allen's (1984) temporal logic (or *Interval Algebra*). This logic provides a set of basic temporal relations that together capture all the various ways in which temporal intervals can be related to one another. These relations are called the **base relations** of the logic and cover situations where intervals strictly precede (BEFORE) or, its inverse, follow (AFTER) one another, meet at a point (MEETS and its inverse MET-BY), overlap one another (OVERLAPS and its inverse OVERLAPPED-BY), start or finish another interval (STARTS and its inverse STARTED-BY, FINISHES and its inverse FINISHED-BY), are strictly included within another (DURING and its inverse CONTAINS), or are equal (EQUAL). The logic thus has 13 base relations. We show the alternatives graphically in Figure 7.2.

One obvious advantage of adopting such a framework is that we can be sure that we have 'exhausted' the space of possibilities. In most descriptions of filmic temporal relations previously presented, including accounts that have specifically concerned themselves with temporality (e.g., Burch, 1973; Gaudreault, 1983), it is striking that some of the theoretically possible relations are omitted. This is because these other relations are, indeed, very rare or even unobserved in film; but this does not seem to us to be a sufficient reason for ruling them out *a priori*. Before Christopher Nolan's *Memento* (2000), for example, the utility of the inverse of the MEETS relation for film may not have been considered self-evident. The Allen relation set is also that now assumed in more formalised approaches to temporal documents, such as the MPEG-7 standard mentioned in Chapter 2.

Using these relations, we can define for some set of observations obtained by an observer by interpretation of audiovisual portions that:

Definition 7.4 *A sub-tree of the logical structure of a document is* **chronological** *for some set of observers when the associated set of content portions can be assigned diegetic times which can all be related pairwise according to a temporal relation taken from* BEFORE, MEETS, OVERLAPS, DURING, STARTS, FINISHES, EQUAL *and their inverses.*

On the basis of this definition, we can then define the particular case of *monochronic document structures* as follows; these will provide a basic building block for many kinds of discourse organisation below:

Definition 7.5 *A sub-tree of the logical structure of a document is* **monochronic** *for some observer set when:*

1. *it is* chronological *for that observer set (→Def 7.4), and*
2. *all observers from the observer set take the* same temporal relation *to hold throughout.*

We term a filmic segment **monochronic** when it can be seen under some layouting process as the image of a monochronic sub-tree of the logical structure. As usual, when observers disagree about the relationships that hold, then we must treat them as considering distinct document structures; in the present case, *for those observers* the document would not be monochronic.

7.3 Monospatial monochronicity

With these definitions in place, we can now provide definitions that cover the majority of syntagmatic categories defined by Metz; this renders them significantly more reliable in their application and will support our definition of more complex structures below. For the development of this syntagmatic analysis, the following distinct cases are centrally relevant:

1. diegetic ordering of segments 'without gaps' (as in a Metzian *scene*),
2. diegetic ordering of segments 'with gaps' (as in a Metzian *ordinary sequence*),

3. diegetic overlap,
4. no temporal relationship.

The first three cases can be explicitly represented using Allen's basic temporal relations, in particular by MEETS, BEFORE and OVERLAPS respectively. In the final case, however, we need to assume a more complex relationship between the information being portrayed and its filmic realisation—for example, that the document consists of several chronologically unrelated components. This can then be included within our account by first decomposing the document down to its chronological parts and then applying the remaining three situations to each of these in turn. Thus we need first of all only to provide definitions which incorporate the first three types; the fourth type can then be built on top of these. We return to the non-chronological case in the final section of this chapter.

7.3.1   The Metzian scene

The *scene* is considered here to be recognizable by an observer if it is possible for that observer to carry out a substitution test of the following sort. If the observer can perform a thought experiment in which the putative scene can be designed as a single audiovisually reliable shot, i.e., can play the scene out as a shot in a spatially-unified context, then there is good evidence to accept that a scene is on hand.

This has the following theoretical motivation. The scene shot is naturally closely related to Metz's *scene*. The scene shot and the scene have in common that their temporal succession is continuous. In a scene shot the camera by and large follows object trajectories; however, in a scene we find predominantly discontinuous changes of camera positions, with one important boundary condition: the spatial integrity of the scene needs to be maintained by virtue of the material shown. If this spatial integrity is only maintained by acts of inference on the part of the observer, i.e., is only 'conceptualised' or reconstructed by an observer on the basis of inference or expectation, we consider this insufficient for current purposes to yield a 'scene'. Thus, we attempt to remain as close as possible to concrete measurement data (e.g., in particular, in film images) in order to provide the foundation we need for empirical investigation.

This is naturally quite a strong restriction. We use it to rule out as much freedom of interpretation as possible without doing violence to what is being analysed. We discuss the kind of spatial construction that relies on leaps of inference on the part of the viewer further below. For the present, our aim is to make our scheme of analysis as robust, objective and reproducible as possible.

More formally, then, we can define a scene as classifying a sub-tree of the logical structure where the following conditions hold. First the sub-tree must allocate at least two shots as content portions. Second, it must be possible for an observer to construct both a unified spatial field for all the spatial contributions of the shots involved and a unified temporal duration for all temporal contributions of the shots involved. Third, there must be a layouting process by which the order created by the sequence of shots and the temporal unfolding of the depicted content are homomorphic. And fourth, there can be no further shot in the document that meets the previous conditions and which is allocated to a basic logical object outside this sub-tree. This last condition expresses an implicit maximality criterion: scenes are maximal because the inclusion of a further shot to a scene is not permitted to result in anything but a scene.

Figure 7.3 shows a graphical representation of a minimal scene. This graphic assumes that the allocated diegetic world-times pick out temporal intervals which meet in the desired sense; this is the minimal condition applied by many observers. It is also possible, however, to remain conformant with our definition above and to construct more complex temporal relationships—for example, certain degrees of overlap would also be possible as long as an overall perception of continuity is not impaired. This leads to the following definition:

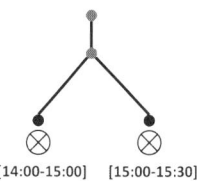

[14:00-15:00]   [15:00-15:30]

Figure 7.3   A simplest scene

Definition 7.6 *A sub-tree of the logical structure of a cinematographic document to which at least two shots are assigned as content portions is a **scene** for some set of observers when:*

1. *the diegetic spaces of all shots assigned to the sub-tree can be conceptualised by all observers as being connected,*
2. *the diegetic times portrayed in the shots can be conceptualised by all observers as connected,*
3. *a layouting process exists such that the created order of shots and their diegetic succession can be seen as homomorphic by all observers—i.e., the shots are displayed in an order that corresponds to the unfolding of events in the 'narrative' or diegetic world,*
4. *no further shot exists meeting the conditions (1)–(3).*

Since films can be constructed so as to provide the necessary points of 'visual overlap' in a variety of ways and are by no means restricted to repetition, there are several possible operationalisations that we might consider for both the temporal and spatial 'connectedness' required here. For example, on the one hand a possible operationalisation of the conceptualisation of temporal connectedness would be an interpolation-free mapping (i.e., no 'gaps') of the shots of a segment to a connected interval of 'world-time'; i.e., MEETS and OVERLAPS in Allen's terms as noted above. On the other hand, a conceptualisation of spatial connectedness can be provided drawing on general work on the representation of space, including qualitative spatial representations and such notions as *cognitive maps* developed within approaches to spatial cognition and also increasingly used in studies of narrative (cf. Ryan, 2003; Levin and Wang, 2009).

Although there are many more possibilities for describing space than there are for describing time, we will for present purposes work with an analogously simple set of spatial relationships: those of Randell et al.'s (1992) *Region Connection Calculus*. This includes base relations of spatial overlap, touching, containment and disjointness. More complex spatial relations can be included as needed, however—we do not need to commit for current purposes to any particular view of 'filmic space' (see *Further Reading*).

We can highlight the challenges raised by spatial organisation and its filmic representation by considering the standard example of filming a shared meal—here the presence of the table can be used as a springboard for joining a series of shots together as spatially connected. A collection of regions connected in this way can naturally support an observer in building up a map of the spatial relationships involved; a theoretical discussion of one such case is given in the treatment of a segment from Joseph L. Mankiewicz's *The Barefoot Contessa* (1954) presented by Colin (1995*a*), in which successive shots first show individuals sitting around a table in a nightclub without first revealing their relative spatial relationships.

A further illustration of our definitions and new classifications of syntagmas in action is offered by another two segments from near the beginning of *Adieu Philippine*, Segments 3 and 4. In Section 4.2 in Chapter 4 above, we discussed Segment 3 and its segmentation with respect to the preceding segment. After its introduction by means of a sudden close-up of a jukebox with no reference to what has gone before, Segment 3 continues with a three-way dialogue in a café between the main characters of the film, Michel, Juliette and Liliane. For current purposes what is particularly interesting about Segment 3 is that, as Metz describes it, a single extraneous shot is inserted *in the middle* of the conversation. This insert shows Michel sitting idly in the television studio as the real work is done by others. Its positioning within the conversation of Segment 3 is motivated by the dialogue: the insert comes just as Michel states that his contribution is vital to the functioning of the TV studio where he works and so comments ironically on Michel's claims of grandeur in the world of television.

Metz classifies this additional shot as an autonomous segment, falling under his category of a 'displaced diegetic insert' (see Figure 4.1 above); this single shot is what Metz labels as Segment 4. The segmentation follows as a necessary result of the *grande syntagmatique* definitions: the insert is clearly from the 'world' of the story (and so is diegetic), but is unrelated temporally with the scene surrounding it and so must be segmented as Metz proposes. However, while this is strictly speaking correct according to Metz's account, we can now employ our definitions in order to examine this situation more closely and to arrive at a tighter and, we believe, more revealing analysis.

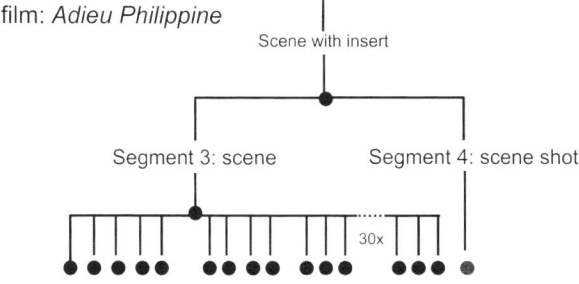

Figure 7.4   Logical structure of Segments 3 and 4 of Adieu Philippine

We show the logical structure that our account allows for this fragment of the film graphically in Figure 7.4; the spacing between shots and other units in the tree shown in the figure is intended only to improve readability and is not otherwise significant. The root of the logical structure (not visible in the figure) corresponds to the entire film. Under this root there are a number of aggregated segments, including *one that combines Segments 3 and 4 into a single composite element*. This is where our description begins to go beyond Metz's account since we can make explicit film structures over and above a straightforward chain of syntagma following syntagma.

Within this combining element, there are then 40 shots distributed across two immediate sub-elements of logical structure. Segment 3 corresponds to the content portion of the conversation in the café, whereas Segment 4 corresponds to Michel's work environment, i.e., the TV studio. In this logical structure there are then 8 shots before the insert, 30 following, as well as the further introductory shot at the beginning showing the jukebox (i.e., Jukebox+8+insert+30 = 40).

Before proceeding further, however, we must first confirm that this rendition of the film is indeed an appropriate structuring according to our definitions since so far we have just asserted this without checking in detail. First, the thought experiment described above for the recognition of scenes applies without problem to the shots constituting Segment 3 and so it is at least informally plausible. Then, running through the conditions of Definition 7.6, the various shots can indeed be conceptualised as being spatially connected by virtue of their placement around the table in the café, the times are connected as the conversation proceeds, and the order of display of the shots corresponds with the times of the events depicted. Therefore we must analyse the conversation between Michel, Liliane and Juliette as a scene in the sense defined even though this scene is interrupted by the insert constituting Segment 4.

With respect to their narrative function, inserts in general place the temporal development of the story 'on hold' so that, following the insert, the narration continues where it left off as if no time had elapsed. This is also the case here. In terms of the *layout structure*, therefore, we can show the organisation of these two segments more appropriately as suggested in Figure 7.5. This brings out both the logical dependency and constituency relationships and the interwoven layouting of content portions as actually takes place in the film.

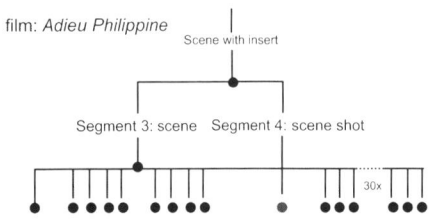

Figure 7.5   *Logical structure of Segments 3 and 4 of* Adieu Philippine *shown reflecting the results of the layouting process*

We can see with this example, therefore, how our definitions allow the construction of deeper hierarchical segmentations for cinematographic documents. It is then possible to build segment trees and not just lists of segments as provided in the original Metzian account. Although Metz did consider it possible for a syntagma, in the present case a scene, to be interrupted by another—this is, after all, the very function of 'inserts'—this was not integrated into a general account of filmic structure. Indeed, the rather weak specification provided by Metz appears to us only to be unproblematic for cases of non-diegetic and displaced inserts. Otherwise the criteria for segmenting scenes are weakened too far and it is no longer sufficiently clear where divisions should or should not be made.

7.3.2   The Metzian sequence

The scene as just introduced is differentiated fundamentally from the weaker requirements of a *sequence*. The sequence does not insist on temporal connectedness—in fact, Metz explicitly rules out a temporal connection in the case of sequences. This leads directly to the following definition.

Definition 7.7 *A sub-tree of the logical structure of a cinematographic document to which at least two shots are assigned as content portions is a **sequence** for some set of observers when:*

1. *the diegetic spaces of all shots assigned to the sub-tree can be conceptualised by all observers as being connected,*
2. *the diegetic times portrayed in the shots* cannot *be conceptualised by all observers as connected,*
3. *a layouting process exists such that the created order of shots and their diegetic succession can be seen as homomorphic by all observers,*
4. *no further shot exists meeting the conditions (1)–(3).*

This formal definition echoes that for scenes above apart from the temporal conditions. For a sequence, there has to be at least one temporal gap. Moreover, in contrast to the case with scenes, it is possible from the definition for a sequence to 'contain' a scene as a sub-element: this provides another glimpse of more deeply embedded filmic structure—we will see many more cases of this phenomenon below.

This definition of sequence achieves a similarly strict notion to that adopted for the scene: it is, for example, not allowed that the filmic portrayal of an entrance to a restaurant and taking a place at a table can be classified as a sequence at all if the spatial relationship between start point and end point is not carried by a series of anchors in the depicted audiovisual content making the relationships explicit—such as, e.g., points shown on the way to the table. For such situations to be classified as sequences, we can require minimally that, over all of the shots of the segment, each pair of shots shows identifiable spatial anchors that allow their spatial relations to be constructed. Taken together, they then form measurement points that warrant the construction of a single space—i.e., in total the recording can be conceptualised as 'measurements' of a connected space.

It is worth noting at this point that our definitions for both temporal and spatial classifications of the logical document structure have quite deliberately avoided any notion of 'actions' or 'activities'. They are accordingly less restrictive than definitions that explicitly rely on activities and therefore have a broader extensional coverage. We are first of all concerned with obtaining classifications that are based as closely as possible on what is actually portrayed in the information presented without further dramaturgical commitments; viewer interpretations of what is occurring are placed subsequent to this. The segments that we succeed in classifying following our definitions here then serve as the interface to the paradigmatic analysis described in the previous chapter.

As a consequence, these definitions now deviate considerably from Metz's intuition that one can omit the requirement of spatial connectedness and instead rely on the unity of complex activities (with potential omission of 'unimportant' details) in order to define sequences. We are more cautious in this respect precisely because such an appeal to 'unity of activities' opens up considerable possibilities for divergent analyses. We will see below that the entire topic of considering units of activities for syntagmatic classification only becomes relevant for us in our consideration of *non-basic syntagmas.* The strong spatio-temporal connectivity requirements involved here differentiate sequences from what we will term *narrative series* below, where further constraints for determining the connectedness of units in addition to that directly discernable in the image data must be applied.

7.3.3   Basic Narrative Syntagmas

Schmidt and Strauch (2002) argue in detail that, for narrative films, the syntagmas of **scene shot**, **scene** and **sequence** provide a fully sufficient foundation for constructing more complex structure. Here we adopt this position for filmic discourse structures in general and accordingly term these three syntagmas, the **basic narrative syntagma**s; i.e.:

Definition 7.8 *A syntagma is a* **basic narrative syntagma** *if it is either a* scene shot, *a scene (→Def 7.6) or a sequence (→Def 7.7).*

For the classification of simple cinematographic documents basic narrative syntagmas are all that is required. By 'simple' here we mean *narratively* simple—i.e., a document consisting of just these three basic categories is considered **narratively basic**. The cinematographic document is then a straightforward tree with a maximum depth of four: the root, the series of composite elements corresponding to each basic syntagma of the film, possible scenes included within sequences, and the shots themselves (as content portions). The basic syntagmas thus begin to provide more content constraints for our simplest filmic organisations discussed in Section 5.1 above, and in particular those of our broad syntagmatic dependency types 1–3 as introduced in Section 6.2.

Such organisations are reminiscent of Metz's argument that film is *syntagmatically* simple but paradigmatically complex (cf., e.g., Metz, 1974a: 67–68): a variety of relationships might be found between basic syntagmas on the basis of the paradigmatic relations that we set out in the previous chapter. However, we also suggested in that chapter that it is natural for more complex structures to 'emerge' from the paradigmatic description. And this is where our view of basic syntagmas takes the analysis a step further. All more complex narrative filmic units result from *hierarchalisation* to form higher-order structures; Metz himself considered this possibility but did not include it within his categorisation scheme.

Despite their simplicity, we should note here that in many applications of moving images the construction of such 'narratively basic' artefacts is the *only allowable* 'narrative style': for example, in video surveillance, medical imaging, etc. less restrictive montage would be considered inappropriate or even misleading. The narrational triviality of such documents is based on the fact that it is only space-time that delivers integrity conditions and so, beneath the document logical root, only one level of composite logical objects is necessary. Other genres may exhibit other properties; Carl Plantinga, for example, suggests that documentaries make a far more free use of spatial and temporal connection (Plantinga, 1997). Our goal here, therefore, is to provide an account capable of making such differences explicit; we are not claiming exhaustiveness in one single leap.

More complex narrative units, to which we now turn, are in general constructed by imposing an organisational hierarchy 'on top of' the basic syntagmas and it is this hierarchy that opens up the possibility of serving more complex narrative needs. Regardless of this complexity, however, the claim made here is that the basic syntagmas will, under normal circumstances, always be recognised as such by viewers and be grouped together accordingly. This grouping ranges from a basic functioning of the perceptual system to the simplest narrative inferences and forms the most fundamental interpretative operations within the semiotic modes of film.

7.4   Narrative hierarchalisation

We described in Chapter 5 above how we consider the material substrate of film to commit to particular 'slices' of space-time: this was the notion underlying reliable audiovisual measurement. The availability of such slices allows our account to make statements that involve relative places and times. We now use this as an anchor point for building further levels of narrative structure into cinematographic documents.

We can conceive of the additional document logical structure required for narrative in terms of the introduction of further levels of montage. With this we leave the area of the basic syntagmas introduced in the previous section where the logical structure has a single level of dependents beneath the root. With non-simple narrative, we find the kind of organisation suggested in Figure 7.6, where we see two levels of composite logical objects in the tree. This adds considerably to the range of meanings that can be made.

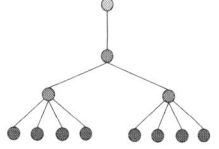

Figure 7.6

Narrative hierarchy

The second montage level may, for example, also be accepted *syntagmatically* by a set of observers as being chronological. For this, it is necessary for a minimal temporal order to hold between the constituting syntagmas of the first montage level. We can again define conditions that must hold for the construction of such complex narrative structures; we term these structures **narrative series**.

These conditions may be summarised in a preliminary form thus—we will discuss the conditions and refine them slightly as we proceed:

> **Definition (preliminary)** *For the syntagmatic classification of a sub-tree of the logical structure of a cinematographic document by an observer set as a (first order)* **narrative series***, it is necessarily the case that:*
>
> 1. *the root of this sub-tree must contain at least two logical objects as descendents,*
> 2. *all of these descendents may be classified as basic filmic syntagmas—i.e., there are maximally three (or four if scenes occur within sequences) levels of 'montage' involved,*
> 3. *in each of the segments belonging to these descendents there must be a segment, which for the observer has a temporal relationship to at least one segment in at least one of the other relevant descendents, and*
> 4. *the observer cannot conceptualise the diegetic spaces of these descendents as connected.*

In the tree structure depicted in Figure 7.6, for example, the root of the tree is the only node of the second montage level (condition 1) and the spatial diegesis in the content portions associated with the left-hand four nodes and the spatial diegesis of the content portions of the right-hand four nodes must at no point allow an observer conceptualisation in which the spaces are connected (condition 4), otherwise the two sub-trees could be collapsed into a single sequence.

The first two conditions of this definition provide the basic structural complexity required. The third ensures that we are dealing with some kind of chronological structure. The fourth then makes sure that it is not possible to provide a false classification of a basic syntagma on its own as a 'narrative series'—a basic syntagma would insist on spatial connection, which condition (4) explicitly rules out.

These basic requirements deliver a foundation sufficiently broad for considerable narrative analysis. The temporal relationships involved are constrained as follows. Since all of the basic filmic syntagmas that are embedded in a narrative series (i.e., scene shot, scene or sequence) enforce a complete chronological ordering on their respective segments, the question can be raised as to which temporal relation these for their part may have to one another. Two extreme cases are conceivable:

- within every segment there is just one shot which shows a temporal relation with a shot outside the 'home' segment (i.e., its own), or
- all shots from all of the segments allow themselves to be placed along a time line, establishing a chronological order over them.

We allow everything between these two extremes as long as the document remains monochronic for the given set of observers: that is, the narrative series will generally move the story onward in time—we do not yet deal here with more complex organisations in terms of projection, flashbacks, flashforwards, alternative timelines and the like; we return to some more complex cases below.

In practice, it is often unproblematic to divide narrative series from one another. For human observers there must therefore be narrative integrity conditions, analogous to the space-time continuity in a scene, which allow us to make such segmentations. The classification of such narrative invariants naturally goes beyond purely time or space-related abstractions and so cannot in all cases be handled by an account of filmic syntagmatic organisation alone. Nevertheless, there are some regularly occurring filmic possibilities for which it is useful to provide a detailed syntagmatic account: these may be considered cases of filmic constructions (cf. Bateman, 2009) which have passed over into the discourse organisation of film and, for which, corresponding syntagmatic organisations can be usefully posited.

One such variant involves narratives that are readily intelligible even without spatial integrity—a prime example of which occurs in filmed telephone dialogues. A filmic dialogue without spatial co-presence of the interactants requires a monochronological syntagma of a type that we can loosely label for now as 'change of location with continuing time'.

Following this kind of filmic construction in detail will allow us to extend our syntagmatic classification possibilities considerably. Also, as we shall see, it is here that contact is made with our fourth basic syntagmatic dependency type, multitracking (cf. §6.2).

7.4.1   Polyspatial narration: the Metzian approach

According to Metz, the 'alternating syntagma' is the category with which any representation of two or more distinct trains of events in distinct places should be classified (Metz, 1974*a*: 128–129). The precise conditions under which alternating syntagmas can be taken as applying or not were, however, far from watertight in Metz's account and Metz himself pointed to several of the difficulties still requiring resolution (Metz, 1974*a*: 164n). We now develop a more powerful syntagmatic classification in two stages. First we provide an explication of Metz's position concerning this particular aspect of his theory, showing how it is closely centred on the dialogic situation as such; second, we broaden this to cover associated forms of narration in general.

Metz also introduces his 'alternate' (or narrative) syntagma (cf. Figure 4.1) by means of the classic illustration of the telephone call. A telephone call typically involves at least two participants and two *distinct internally-connected* spatial regions. We omit cases where the telephone call is being made with mobile telephones of some kind, which could then introduce an arbitrary number of further spatial regions. Metz distinguishes four distinct ways in which such a simple telephone call situation might be portrayed filmically (Metz, 1974*a*: 160–161). These are, using the original terms of the *grande syntagmatique*:

- a sequence—which is rarely used since it would fragment the conversation by leaving temporal gaps,
- a scene without insertions—whereby only one of the participants appears on the screen,
- a scene with insertions—whereby one of the participants is portrayed as central and shots involving the other participant are offered as inserts,
- an alternating syntagma—whereby the shots of both participants appear equally balanced or varying with no clear preference for one participant rather than the other.

Although now differing somewhat from Metz's original account, our definitions of basic syntagmas given above are still broadly compatible with the first three variants—decisive is solely the assumption of continuous space-time regions, which are only broken into distinct temporal intervals in the case of the sequence.

The fourth option is, however, quite different. With a clear decomposition into turns, the situation with two participants calls for at least two *sequences* in order to portray the two speech situations of the distinct speakers, with temporal gaps naturally introduced whenever the film switches to the 'other' speaker. When we have precisely two sequences, the spatial configuration of the speech situations is actually again as suggested in Figure 7.6 concerning narrative hierarchalisation above. All of the conditions in our definition for a narrative series apply and so combining these spatial regions also requires us to recognise here a particular type of narrative series. In this case, however, the layouting process presents the logical document objects in a special way—rather than having one sequence followed by another as suggested in Figure 7.6, here the layouting process 'shuffles' the sequences together respecting the more fine-grained temporal ordering of the individual document objects involved.

Nothing of course now prevents us from extending this situation to any number of telephone participants acting together in a conference call. In general we can describe this extended situation of a narrative series constituted by some number n of sequences as an 'n-partitioned set' of shots analogous to our depiction of multitracking in Figure 6.5 of the previous chapter. It is useful to describe this property in its own right and so we reformulate the first part of our earlier preliminary definition as follows:

Definition 7.9 *A sub-tree of the logical structure in a cinematographic document is syntagmatically* **spatially partitionable** *for a set of observers if:*

1. *at least two shots are present in the sub-tree as content portions,*
2. *for these shots, a partition can be found that divides them into at least two collections of shots (the 'partition sets' resulting from the partition) such that each associated logical substructure can be classified with a basic narrative syntagma (→Def 7.8).*

We term a filmic segment 'spatially partitionable' when it can be seen under some layouting process as the image of a spatially partitionable sub-tree of the logical structure.

If then in addition to being partitionable, temporal relations hold, then we have a more satisfactory definition of a first-order narrative series and can replace our former preliminary definition with the following:

Definition 7.10 *For the syntagmatic classification of a sub-tree of the logical structure in a cinematographic document as a (first order)* **narrative series**, *it is necessary that:*

1. *the sub-tree is spatially partitionable into two or more sets (→Def 7.9),*
2. *in each set, it is possible for the observer to find a shot that bears some temporal relationship with at least one shot of another (distinct) set.*

The final condition here is necessary because the first point alone would also be applicable to filmic examples for two sets of temporally unrelated shots, which Metz treats as cases of parallel syntagmas—i.e., achronological. The last condition is the only condition that ensures that the individual partitioned sets of shots share an (albeit weak) temporal relationship and that a single narrative can therefore be seen to unfold. If the basic narrative syntagma involved is always a *sequence*, then we refer to the syntagma as **sequentially partitionable**.

Examining this definition, we can see that the original starting point with a dialogic situation has now actually retreated entirely into the background. This characterisation is no longer specific to dialogue at all. Whenever we have a change in location and a possibility of attributing a temporal relationship between the space-time slices depicted, then we have a basis for inducing a narrative series. There are then several distinct kinds of such narrative series. Probably the simplest is that of the **itinerary**, where a character in a film proceeds from locale to locale, without there necessarily being any identifying feature across spatial settings apart from their linking as successive 'stations' on the figure's journey. This involves structures carrying paradigmatic selections from the region of 'elliptical' temporal and 'non-contiguous' spatial areas of the paradigmatic system—in particular, *prolongation* (cf. Figure 6.7).

This then offers one way in which predominantly paratactically related segments, i.e., segments falling under our second broad syntagmatic dependency type, can be grouped into larger structures. These structures are based on properties holding in the diegetic world depicted (i.e., 'external' in terms of our *grande paradigmatique*) and expectations that may have been constructed only in the narrative. We will encounter further examples of this below.

7.4.2   Polyspatial alternation

Our general definition of narrative series now also provides the basis for considering the situation when particular locales *reoccur*: i.e., 'alternation' of various kinds and not just itineraries or telephone dialogues.

For this, we begin with two disjoint (i.e., non-overlapping) spatio-temporal regions and consider particular sequences of shots as possible layouts provided for a document exhibiting the logical structure given in Figure 7.6 above. We can succinctly characterise any such sequence of shots as a two-column table showing the individual shots, numbered consecutively to show their order of presentation, and with columns standing for single spatiotemporal regions. An example of such as table is shown on the left-hand side of Table 7.1. Within this particular example layout, we see three groups of shots for the first space-time region Space-Time$_1$ and also three groups for the second region Space-Time$_2$. When the film is shown in the order in which the shots have been numbered, there are then five corresponding *changes* in location depicted; this is suggested in the graph on the right-hand side of Table 7.1.

Space-Time$_1$	Space-Time$_2$
T_1	
	T_2
	T_3
T_4	
T_5	
	T_6
T_7	
	T_8

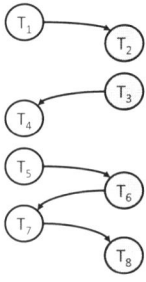

Table 7.1   One layout organisation for a document with the logical structure depicted in Figure 7.6 (left), together with its corresponding transition graph (right)

Segments in film of this kind are often perceived as coherent and the question is when this is the case. Importantly, we can no longer rely on basic perceptual mechanisms of similarity and difference here. Spatial coherence alone is clearly not enough since spatial integrity is explicitly ruled out as a criterion for explaining the coherence of the resulting changes between shot groups. Instead we must look to certain specifiable properties of the jumps across the disjoint space-time regions involved.

We model these spatial jumps by producing for any given layout a **transition graph** of the kind shown on the right in Table 7.1. Transition graphs are often used in film analysis for formally capturing the connectivity between elements of a film according to various criteria (cf. Yeung, Yeo and Liu, 1998; Sidiropoulos, Mezaris, Kompatsiaris, Meinedo and Trancoso, 2009). In our case we use the transition graph to represent the alternation inherent in any spatially partitioned narrative series. The nodes of the graph are taken from the set of all shots; the edges of the graph are taken from the pairs of neighbouring shots in the layout that span different shot partition sets—i.e., different columns in the table. This ensures that the transition graph covers all the spatial jumps present in the portion of the layouts being considered.

In the layout depicted in Table 7.1, the corresponding graph is 'bi-partitioned' in the sense that there are two disjoint corresponding space-time regions involved. In order to establish a coherent reading of this segment, therefore, an observer must reconstruct 'conceptually' some connection. This can only occur by invoking a relationship of some kind that is posited by an observer on the basis of recognised or assumed objects or activities which do not themselves allow the conception of spatial coherence or integrity.

For the case of the bi-partitioned telephone conversation, for example, we might assume a binary relationship 'A and B are telephoning with one another', where A is only in Space-Time$_1$ and B only in Space-Time$_2$.

Conceptualising the alternation then means that for all the *change-pairs* given by the transition graph, the same relation of 'telephoning with' is invoked as part of the knowledge of the observer. This provides the necessary coherence even though the two space-time regions are explicitly constructed as disjoint and as not forming an integrated whole.

We will stipulate that the relations produced in such interpretations are symmetric—or can be made symmetric; so that, for example, from 'A chases B' we make instead 'A chases or is being chased by B'. This allows us to ignore the direction of the 'jump' between shot partition sets and so simplifies the account somewhat. Furthermore, we require that such relations should not be purely spatial since, on the one hand, this is a rather weak basis for building narrative and, on the other, we specified above that the relations should not allow spatial coherence to be inferred because otherwise the segment collapses to a sequence.

We also require by definition at least three changes for an alternating structure to be inferred in the manner described for multitracking structures in Section 6.2 above. This has a certain psychological plausibility in that at least one instantiation of an alternation is necessary in order for an observer to generalise at all and to have sufficient grounds for positing at least some potential relation to hold—e.g., for the telephone conversation case: 'Aha, A and B are telephoning with one another'.

The assumed relation must, however, be invokable across the entire segment in order for the observer to confirm the generalisation assumed and also to understand the segment as alternating. This situation is suggested graphically in Figure 7.7, in which the black arrows are the connections given by the transition graph as before and the gray arrows denote the coherence-building relations hy-

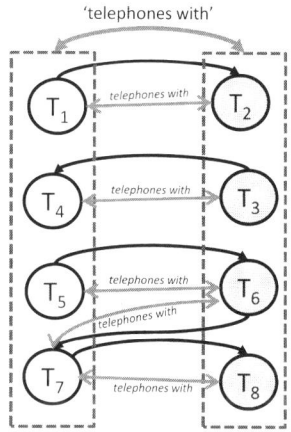

Figure 7.7
Alternation rendered coherent by a common connection

pothesised to hold by the observer. Here, since all the transitions can invoke the same relation, that relation can be 'promoted' to form a relation standing behind the entire alternation; this is indicated by the bold gray arrow at the top of the figure.

In this bi-partitioned case, therefore, an alternation is conceptualisable for an observer if a two-place relation R belongs to (or can be defeasibly inferred for) the observer's knowledge of the portrayed situation with the following properties:

1. R is defined over two sets of entities, one drawn from Space-Time$_1$, the other from Space-Time$_2$,

2. For a given layout, R can be established as holding across all cases of change given in the corresponding transition graph,
3. R is symmetric or, alternatively, a further relation R' can be found or created in the knowledge of the observer with the two preceding properties and such that the disjunction of R and R' forms a symmetric relation replacing R,
4. Space-Time$_1$ and Space-Time$_2$ are not conceptualised by the observer as being spatially connected (otherwise the required polyspatiality would collapse).

With the formulation that the entities over which the relation R is defined belong to two disjoint space-time regions, we have not yet specified how exactly the relation can be made syntagmatically relevant with respect to the film-data and their content portions. In order to make this explicit, we require the following two conditions.

First, we need to be able to refer to regions of space-time as they are given meaning as functionally significant locales by some observer. For this, we assume for present some labelling strategy. This means that we can consider not only the simple 'image data' as recorded but also the processes of diegetic meaning attribution already alluded to in previous chapters— with natural signs we are never faced with raw uninterpreted 'sense data' (cf. §5.2). For example, it is also necessary here to allow interpretations that are associated with objects and activities that are assumed by an observer to be present (i.e., defeasibly inferred) but which may not actually be present in the film-data (for example, by virtue of occlusions).

A good illustration of this is offered by filmed chases. Here it may readily be the case that, in some shots of a chase alternation, the pursuer or pursued might simply not be visible because they are hiding. The shots of such an alternation are then best describable as 'representation of the pursuer' and 'representation of the victim' even when not visually present. In this case, an image of a door can become in addition to just an image of the door, more an indication of 'behind the wooden door stands the pursuer that was seen previously'.

This *qualitative* and *functional* treatment of regions of space-time in terms of their relevance for some ongoing activities is cognitively plausible and supported by a considerable body of literature on the conceptualisation of space (cf. Coventry and Garrod, 2004). Moreover, the *need* to find a consistent common interpretation to hold the shots together establishes strong defeasible hypotheses for interpretation; this indicates how the syntagmatic structures being constructed can play an active role in meaning generation.

The second condition required is relatively self-evident: we must still nevertheless be able to *recognise* the qualitatively described regions on the basis of the image data actually delivered by the shots deployed. Unless this is the case, it is not possible for an observer to relate shots to content portions and the process of interpretation becomes underconstrained (which may, of course, be an intended effect on the part of some film-maker).

Combining all of these considerations leads us to a revised definition and generalisation of the notion of *alternating syntagma* as proposed by Metz. Important here is that we can only speak of an alternation *for a given layout structure* and, therefore, with respect to a corresponding transition graph. Alternation as a classification then only applies to segments, *not* to the logical structure, because it necessarily involves the commitment to a specific layout. This means that alternation is only an observable phenomenon in a cinematographic document and is only weakly dependent on the specific logical structure of the document: the logical structure must of course support the creation of an alternation via the layouting process but does not *itself* include that alternation. This is therefore a further example of a 'second-order' *textual* meaning arising from the way in which material is *presented* rather than its 'content'.

Alternating segments of the type 'change of location with continuously running time' must then, first, be monochronic in order to ensure continuous temporal unfolding for a set of observers and, second, spatially partitioned in order to be anchored 'polyspatially' at several distinct locations. Moreover, within alternating segments, it must be possible for appropriate pairs of space-time components to be related by the observer in order for the necessary coherence-constructing relation to be established by that observer. This coherence may not be based on spatial intersection since otherwise the spatial alternation would not be maintained. Finally, an alternation must have sufficiently many layouted changes, or transitions (at least three), between partition sets.

Bringing all of these together gives the following definition.

Definition 7.11 *A segment in a cinematographic document is* **n-alternating** *with respect to a given layouting process and a set of observers if a partition of the segment exists with n partition sets such that:*

1. *the segment is monochronic for that set of observers (→Def 7.5),*
2. *the segment is spatially partitionable for that set of observers (→Def 7.9),*
3. *for each pair of partition sets, transitions exist for which a specific symmetric relation holds between some member of the first partition set and some member of the second partition set (as defined in the transition graph) for all observers of the observer set and this relation holds for all the transitions between the first and second set—this relation then constitutes the* coherence *for those observers of the alternating shots it relates,*
4. *for all transition pairs between members of the partition, all observers of the observer set conceive the source space-time regions of the members of those pairs to be disjoint,*

> 5. *in the representation according to the given layouting process, there are at least three transitions between the distinct members of each pair of partition sets.*

We will call a 2-alternating segment a **bi-partitioned alternation** and a 3-alternating segment a **tri-partitioned alternation**.

7.5   Alternating dramaturgy and the alternating syntagma

Definition 7.11 opens up an extremely rich variety of possible dramaturgical realisations. Of these we will discuss three possibilities as constructed examples in order to make the implications of the definition clearer and to show it in action. On the way, we will define several further important syntagmatic constructs necessary for building more complex filmic structures. These will lead to the proposal of a definition for an appropriate successor to Metz's alternating syntagma. We then conclude with some further examples, two drawn from *Adieu Philippine* and the other returning to the discussion of the 'button-pushing' sequence from *The Lady from Shanghai* that we began in Section 2.4 above.

7.5.1   Dramaturgical guiding partitions

We have seen that alternations are held together as coherent by the hypothesis of semantic relations. Of particular interest are situations where the same coherence-forming relation holds over more than two sets of partitions. We characterise this in our discussion as follows. We label relations between two partition sets i and j with the expression R_{ij}. We are then interested in cases where two such relations between partition sets, R_{ij} and R_{kl}, either (i) have only one or (ii) no subscript in common.[2] In the first case, we have only one relation of a single 'mediating' space-time region to two or more other space-time regions; in the second case, we have two distinct pairs of space-time regions which are nevertheless related identically. We discuss these two cases separately as follows.

First, let us consider an example where there are two coherence-forming relations holding over exactly three partition sets. This serves to define a 'middle' partition set that is involved in both relations—we suggest this graphically in Figure 7.8(a). Appealing again to the example of a telephone call, here there are three speaking situations realised alternatingly, but an observer cannot conceptualise these as a single telephone call between all participants in their respective source space-time regions. We might find this situation, for example, if the participant represented in the middle locale is using two telephones and is holding two *separate* conversations simultaneously with the others. Examples of such structures can readily be found in film as the situation itself is not particularly uncommon.

---

[2]That is: $R_{ij} = R_{kl}$ where $\{i, j\} \neq \{k, l\}$ and $1 \leq i, j, k, l \leq n$.

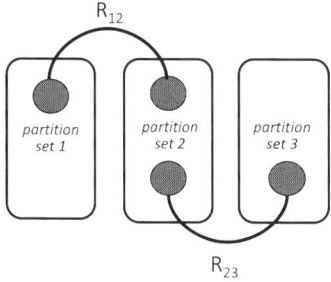

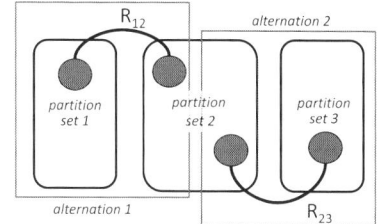

(a) Three space-time regions related by two relations

(b) Two alternations fused with a dramaturgically guiding partition set

Figure 7.8 Partition sets and their interrelations

As a consequence, it is not possible to bind these segments together into a single three-way alternation since it would be necessary to find at least three relations in order to combine them successfully. Nevertheless, the *layout* that is adopted strongly signals that some kind of alternation is in progress, which leads to the construction of more complex structures to accommodate this. In particular, the conditions may be met for forming *two* alternations with one set of shots serving to express participation in both along the lines illustrated in Figure 7.8(b). Within configurations of this kind, we term the middle partition set a **dramaturgically guiding** partition set. We will see several examples of such structures below and in the next chapter.

In the second case, if we continue with a 3-alternating segment and now assume there to be three relations, *all* instances of a coherence-forming relation of telephoning, then we have the conditions necessary for a classical telephone conference with three parties, all of whom are speaking to one another; i.e.:

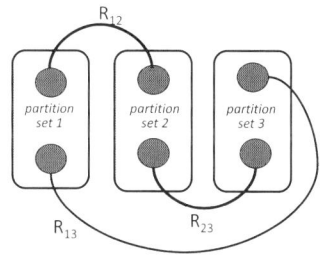

Figure 7.9

Three partition sets related with three equivalent relations

$$R_{12} = R_{23} = R_{13} = \text{telephoning}$$

This is shown graphically in Figure 7.9. In this case, no partition serves a mediating function with respect to any other.

Dramaturgically guiding partition sets serve a variety of functions in film and operate in some respects as the realisation of 'higher-order' comparison or multitracking segments; the precise role played depends on the coherence-building relations that must be hypothesised to meet the definition of alternations. When these relations are similar, then comparison is a logical consequence; if the relations are opposed in some sense, then a contrast may be drawn. Syntagmatically, the organisation of the effected segments clearly signals which portions of a film are to be placed in relation to one another during interpretation. Again, the relations possible are mediated by those provided by our *grande paradigmatique*, particularly those in the region of paratactic contrast and similarity.

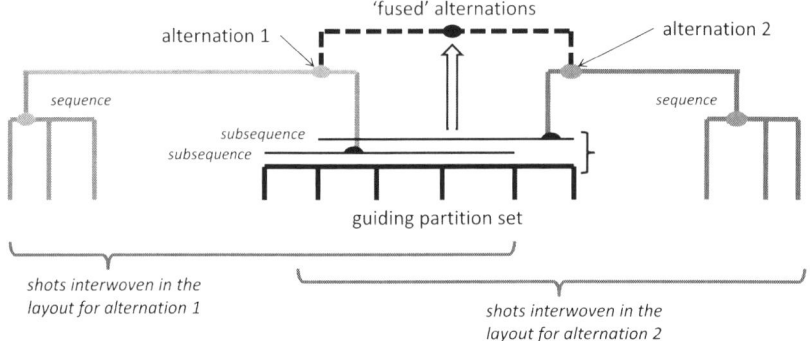

Figure 7.10   Logical document structure showing the mediating role of a dramaturgically guiding partition set

Structurally, this organisation is quite distinctive—we suggest this visually within an augmented document structure diagram in Figure 7.10. The collection of shots forming the dramaturgically guiding partition set is shown in the middle in black. To both the right and the left of this are two further sequences, shown in shades of gray. Each of these sequences is taken as satisfying the conditions for alternation with some *subsequence* (indicated by the extent of the horizontal lines with half-ovals) from the guiding partition set in the middle. Since there is no maximality condition in the definition of alternation, it is perfectly possible to build alternations from subsequences of longer sequences as is the case for both the alternations shown here. The distinct collections of shots are then shuffled together according to the layouting process as suggested. The existence of the guiding partition set then 'supports' (suggested by the double-lined upwards arrow in the centre) a higher-order segment which fuses the contributing alternations in some sense. The precise functional relationship to be allocated to this fusion then depends on the coherence-relations contributed by the alternations as suggested above.

Let us now go on and consider cases of at least four partition sets and for which the same alternating relationship is conceptualised over two pairs of partition sets; that is: $R_{ij} = R_{kl}$ and there are no intersections of $\{i,j\}$ and $\{k,l\}$ for any of the partition sets. Here we can build substantially more complex patterns. As an example, imagine a script involving the members of two married couples distributed over four distinct places and filmed so that the layout structure depicted in Table 7.2 results.

Imagine further that what is being filmed is as follows. The first pair of shots $\{T_1, T_2\}$ shows the beginning of the conversation for the first couple, and the second pair of shots $\{T_3, T_4\}$ shows the beginning of the conversation for the second couple. The rest of the first couple's conversation then proceeds in shots T_5–T_8 and the second couple's conversation proceeds in shots T_9–T_{12}. What is interesting now is how our definition of alternating segments narrows down the possible syntagmatic interpretations of what is occurring. This is the main work that our definitions perform: by following through how our definitions require filmic structures to be constructed, we are led to particular syntagmatic descriptions in an unambiguous fashion. This is precisely what was missing in Metz's original account and those of his successors.

From our Definition 7.11, then, we know that in the layouting process depicted in Table 7.2 both the shot sequences $\{T_1, T_2, T_5, T_6, T_7, T_8\}$ and $\{T_3, T_4, T_9, T_{10}, T_{11}, T_{12}\}$ are internally themselves 2-alternating segments whose shots obey the conditions for alternation. Both segments are monochronic, spatially partitioned, conceptualisable with an identical relation of 'telephoning with', and spatially disjoint; there are also (more than) three transitions respectively. There is no requirement, however, that the shots are strictly contiguous within the film and this naturally leads on to the construction of *higher-order* alternating structures. Let us complicate our illustrative script one step further to provide an example. If there are some additional commonalities between the *ways in which the conversations are being conducted*, then conditions are provided for a higher order alternation. For example, if in fact the man of the first couple is having an affair with the woman of the second couple and this becomes a topic of heated debate in both telephone conversations, then we might equally apply the conditions of Definition 7.11 for alternation not to individual shots but to entire segments.

To show this, let us call the shot sequence depicting the conversation of the first couple SegPair1 and that of the second couple SegPair2, and divide each of these into two subsegments corresponding to the two openings of the conversations, which we will mark by 'intro', and the rest of the conversations, marked by 'finis'. We can then regroup the layout of Table 7.2 as shown in Table 7.3 by *unifying* the respective space-time regions of the conversations (denoted by set union: '∪'). Now, the 'meta-layout' characterised in Table 7.3 itself can be made to meet the conditions for alternation—in this case by positing coherence-forming relations that are themselves of a higher-order—for example contrast or parallelism with respect to marital discord, fidelity, etc. The further analysis of alternations on the level of segments rather than shots takes us well into the area of *narrative hierarchies*, to which we return below.

SpaceTime$_1$	SpaceTime$_2$	SpaceTime$_3$	SpaceTime$_4$
T_1			
	T_2		
		T_3	
			T_4
T_5			
	T_6		
T_7			
	T_8		
		T_9	
			T_{10}
		T_{11}	
			T_{12}

Table 7.2   One layouted film document for two married couples spread over four places

SpaceTime$_1$ ∪ SpaceTime$_2$	SpaceTime$_3$ ∪ SpaceTime$_4$
$SegPair1_{intro}$	
	$SegPair2_{intro}$
$SegPair1_{finis}$	
	$SegPair2_{finis}$

Table 7.3   Abstracted film organisation for a second-order alternating structure

For now, however, we have demonstrated the central role played by the process of layouting for the construction of alternating structures. The layouting process and its fixing of particular transitions between space-time regions has been decisive for all the cases discussed. Accordingly, we can also build on our definition above for alternating segments (Definition 7.11) and formulate a corresponding constraint for the document logical structure. This then brings our treatment of alternation more in line with the account of basic syntagmas above, where the requirement of the existence of an appropriate layouting process was sufficient and immediately allowed the definition of syntagmas for the logical structure of a document. Such a definition for the logical structure is still missing for alternating structures. We conclude thus:

Definition 7.12 *A sub-tree of the logical structure of a cinematographic document is* **syntagmatically n-alternatable** *for a set of observers if there is a layouting process that produces a corresponding n-alternating segment (→Def 7.11).*

This structure is then our conceptual successor to Metz's alternating syntagma.

7.5.2   Alternation at work

The definitions of alternation provided are somewhat involved and so we will now show how these definitions contribute to interpretation by means of concrete analyses of three further film extracts, two from *Adieu Philippine* and one taking up again our analysis of Orson Welles' *The Lady from Shanghai* (1947) from Chapter 2. These start from the basic workings of alternation to bring about hierarchalisation and then go on to show some consequences of the additional role of dramaturgically guiding sequences within alternations. This will demonstrate how our definitions naturally lead to a treatment of syntagmatic organisation that enables many problematic aspects of Metz's treatment to be avoided. We will see in particular how the constraints on syntagmatic structure prioritise interpretations in an appropriate fashion even though those interpretations are always contingent on the film as actually constructed.

Example: *Adieu Philippine* Segments 21–23

We begin with the segments numbered 21–23 (00:30:33–00:32:00) according to Metz's syntagma-by-syntagma analysis scheme (Metz, 1974a: 159–161). These consist of a long series of tracking shots where Juliette and Liliane are shown walking along a busy Paris shopping street followed by a telephone conversation; the tracking ends when the two go into a telephone box and make a call to Michel (all Segment 21). In the segment following, we have Michel and others at work in the mixing studio of the TV company where Michel is employed (Segment 22). One of the workers answers (it can be assumed) Liliane and Juliette's telephone call and tells Michel to take the call away from the mixing desk, which he does. The layout of the segment is suggested graphically in Figure 7.11; Metz's segmentation is shown below the key frames presented. Metz treats the 'last element' of Segment 21 (entering the telephone box) as simultaneously the first element of Segment 22: we can also assume this to be the case employing our definition of fusion as given above (Definition 7.2).

Problematic with the original Metzian characterisation of Segment 21 and the shots immediately following is that there is no *formal* possibility after this segment has concluded of allowing its 'reprise' as a component of the subsequent telephone dialogue. But this is precisely what happens in the film. Metz is forced to construct another segment, Segment 23, which consists solely of inserts, classified as autonomous shots, of Juliette and Liliane in the telephone box. This is less than satisfactory from the perspective of a syntagmatic analysis because it pulls apart shots that clearly belong together: i.e., the end of the street sequence and the subsequent dialogue turns in the telephone call. 'Free standing' autonomous units in an analysis always leave more work for subsequent interpretation and—our

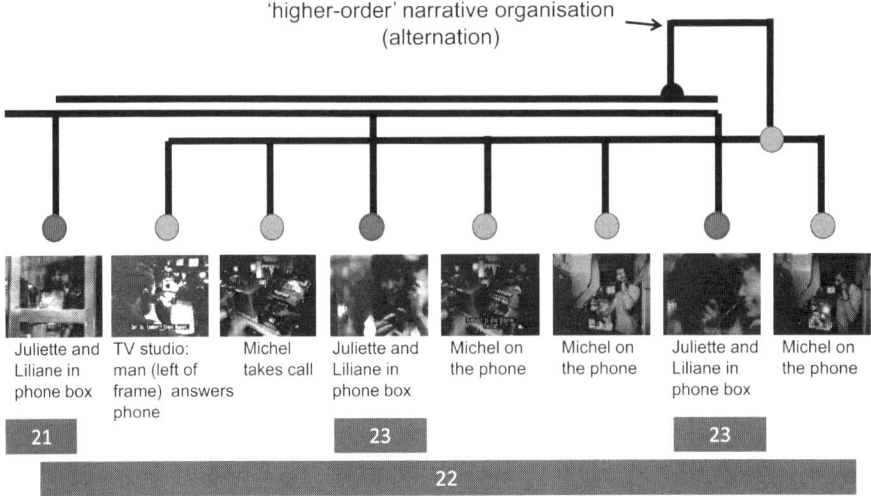

Figure 7.11   Rozier's Adieu Philippine *(00:30:33–00:32:00); Segments 22–23 according to Metz's numbering scheme*

main critique—makes that process of interpretation look less constrained than it really is.[3]

In the first shots of Segment 22 in the TV mixing studio it is clear that the film is portraying a single space-time region and so these can be grouped together syntagmatically following Definition 7.7 as a sequence on the basis of their spatial-temporal integrity. The separate shots in the telephone box of the first 'element' of Segment 21 and of Segment 23 also form a sequence on the same grounds. It is this latter connection that is not captured in Metz's description: the appearance of the inserts of Segment 23 is only related back to Segment 21 in Metz's informal description of the shots, not in the technical account. To go further, we can now apply Definition 7.11 in order to consider the interweaving of these two sequences into an alternation. Given the (uncontroversial) assumption that the two sequences can be related by means of the symmetric, non-spatial relationship of 'telephoning with one another', all of the conditions of the definition are met and we can see the segment corresponding to Metz's Segments 21–23 as a straightforward bi-partitioned alternation. This layout is shown above the key frames in Figure 7.11. Here we can clearly see that members of a sequence do not have to be contiguous as discussed above. The inserts making up Metz's Segment 23 function as a contribution to the 'higher-order' structure shown relating to the two sequences.

---

[3]Metz's description actually talks of these two inserts being 'variations' of a single insert, which is what allows him to place them together as a 'single' segment (Metz, 1974a: 159); we do not follow this line further here however.

Metz seeks to avoid a classification as an alternation in the present case because of the very short duration of the inserts in comparison to the shots in the TV studio. While this is in many respects understandable (and, indeed, relates directly to our discussion of 'deformable' structure in the previous chapter: cf. Figure 6.6), it does not give us license to ignore the implications of the definitions for syntagmatic organisation.

The alternation is present and the usual implications of temporal simultaneity and so on apply; this is not the case if we consider them as unrelated inserts. The strong temporal constraints constructed by the film's organisation need, therefore, to be recognised. The extent to which *other* functions may also be taken up by the briefness and sparsity of the insert durations will have to find a place elsewhere in the account.

Example: *The Lady from Shanghai* 'button-pushing' episode

Turning to our second example, we saw in Chapter 2 above how this famous episode from Orson Welles' *The Lady from Shanghai* (1947) was provisionally analysed in terms of an alternation between three locales: the drawing room in the house of the main female character, Elsa Bannister, the kitchen of the house, and a car (cf. Figure 2.12). We suggested there that an hypothesised notion of causality would be one way of binding the three tracks together and that this would be one explanation for why this episode is discussed so often in the film literature: a non-existent causation (i.e., not-existent in the diegesis) is nevertheless suggested by the way the film is structured. Our appeal to alternation at that point was still informal. Now we can take this several steps further building on the apparatus we have developed.

First, we can check whether the segment is really to be considered as an alternation given the more precise definition now at our disposal. Clearly, the 15 shots making up the segment (cf. Figure 2.8) actually exhibit a rather more complex structure than simple alternation, even a three-way alternation as previously proposed. In the first transition to deal with the progress of the car for example, we have an establishing shot of the outside of the car, a close-up within the car, two point-of-view shots from the perspective of those inside the car, and a cut away to a non-local event (a truck pulling out onto the road that the car is driving along)—and this all within five shots. We are therefore already operating with higher-order narrative organisation and have more on hand than an alternation at the level of individual shots.

For current purposes, however, we will adopt the spatiotemporal granularity used previously in order to identify three sequences as before. Then, focusing on the transitions between locales, it is *not* possible to find a single coherence-building relation for all transitions when considered together as a three-way alternation as our Definition 7.11 would require. In shots 10–13 (repeated for ease of reference in Figure 7.12), there is no relation of

(10) 0.5s　　　(11) 0.5s　　　(12) 0.9s　　　(13) 0.5

Figure 7.12　　*Shots 10–13 from Orson Welles'* The Lady from Shanghai *repeated for ease of reference*

'causing' or 'being caused by' that can usefully be posited between shots 12 and 13. We are therefore forced away from a simple three-way alternation to consider other alternatives.

Following this, there are only a few possible interpretations supported by the fragment. One, which we will not consider further although theoretically a possibility, is that there is simply no further connection drawn between the sequence in the car and that in the kitchen. The car is simply inserted, perhaps showing simultaneity. This might, for example, be an interpretation for viewers who are not following the fragment so closely. Another interpretation, which is more interesting in that it ties up more of the dangling sequences in a unified narrative whole, builds directly on our definition of dramaturgical guiding partition sets. This now allows us to add considerable precision to the analysis.

At least until shot 10 we can consider the shots located in the drawing room to form a sequence that functions as a guiding partition linking two *separate* alternations: one between the drawing room and the kitchen and one between the drawing room and the action around the car. In both cases individual relations of 'causing'/'being caused by' hold. This naturally places the actions of Elsa Bannister even more in the centre of attention than our previous more intuitive account was able to bring out and comes far closer to what that analysis was trying to achieve but lacked the technical means to express. We show this graphically in Figure 7.13 in precisely the same form as we used in our examples in Figure 7.8(b) above.

This configuration follows straightforwardly from our definitions, making the point from Chapter 2 even more strongly that a fixed form of analysis can be both appropriate and beneficial. The analysis also makes it possible for us to include some further 'overtones' in meaning that

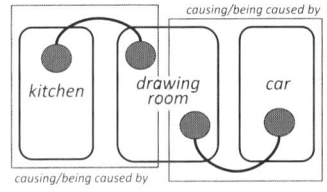

Figure 7.13

The Lady from Shanghai *example represented as two alternations fused with a guiding partition set*

were not available before: for example, the guiding partition set is one way of realising *comparison* or *similarity* between the alternations being related.

This is then developed further as the segment unfolds. The chain of development is brought to a head in the climax following shot 10. Up until shot 10 we have the suggestion of 'causation' and the indirect comparison of caused events induced by the guiding partition just described. Following this shot, however, the guiding partition gives way to a *direct* 'comparison' between the car and the kitchen realised syntagmatically by placing shots with relevant associated content portions directly following one another (shots 12 and 13). In terms of our basic syntagmatic dependency types from the previous chapter, we have here two segments related paratactically. The immediately preceding operation of the guiding partition thus sets up 'comparison or similarity' as highly relevant in the context of interpretation: this then prioritises the relations on offer in the *grande paradigmatique* and provides strong functional motivation for the occurrence of two paratactically-related segments {11,12} and {13,14,15} in order to render the segment coherent.

Although there is still more detail that could be pulled out of this short segment to fully describe its inner workings, the account provided so far is sufficient for current purposes. In Figure 7.14, we present a final graphical rendition of the segment, combining both its high degree of similarity with the cases of guiding partitions discussed above and the direct relationship of comparison exhibited at its end. We have now shown not only that a causal relationship may well be posited between a centrally-involved agent (Mrs. Bannister) and some states of affairs in the (diegetic) world, but also that the consequences of her actions are directly comparable in some way.

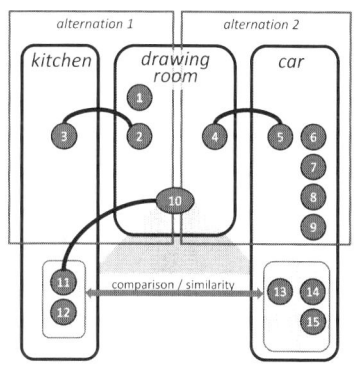

Figure 7.14
The complete The Lady from Shanghai *example*

As before, none of these relationships are directly depicted in the segment—i.e., they do not have 'objective' existence in the world of the story; instead they are invoked interpretations brought about by the syntagmatic organisation of the segment and its suggested paradigmatic relationships. In this way we see a variety of meanings being constructed on top of the basic narrative syntagmas identified, both from a syntagmatic and paradigmatic perspective. Precisely this cross-play between the syntagmatic and the paradigmatic will be one of our main concerns in the detailed example of analysis we present in the next chapter.

Example: *Adieu Philippine* Segment 19

Our next extract for analysis, Segment 19 from *Adieu Philippine* (00:26:51–00:27:59) as discussed by Metz (Metz, 1974*a*: 158–159), shows a further complex example of meaning-making drawing on alternation to create 'higher-order' narrative structures. As before, there are several difficulties to be noted with the original Metzian analysis. The analysis suggests (quite correctly as we shall see) that there are two 'episodes' within the segment at issue and that these episodes "acquire meaning only when taken together". The nature of these episodes and just how they are inter-related is not, however, captured in Metz's formal account and only appears in informal annotations accompanying his proposals for segmentation. Here we will see how our definitions lead directly to the insight that Metz was trying to capture.

Segment 19 begins with two autonomous shots, one in which we see an older woman calling "Juliette!" down some stairs and another where the woman passes across the screen in a different room from left to right and goes to a telephone, saying "Hallo? I'm sorry, she is not there." We then see in the next shot Michel saying "Pity, Goodbye" into a telephone. In the immediately following Segment 20 we jump to a further unrelated location. Here, in a somewhat more complex shot, we see another woman calling out of a bedroom into another room "Liliane! For you!" Liliane asks from off who it is and after the (presumably) mother answers that it is Michel, she comes into the room and takes the phone, lying on a bed; her mother then sits on the bed also. The shots following show the telephone conversation between Michel and Liliane, ending with Michel hanging up the phone and rubbing his hands and Liliane trying out dresses for her evening engagement. Figure 7.15 shows the segment and the shot numbering that we will use in the discussion.

Now, while most of this segment is unproblematic it remains unclear according to the Metzian analysis just how it all hangs together as a single meaningful unit in the narrative. At the beginning of the segment, Michel is looking for a date; by the end of the segment, both Michel and Liliane are preparing for one—the story has been moved on with commentaries on the way concerning the fact that it is more or less by chance that it is Liliane rather than Juliette with whom Michel will spend the evening. We depict the results of the layouting process standing behind the filmic portrayal of these events in Table 7.4, organised around space-time regions as in our discussions above.

Since the allocation of shots to particular locations and times is straightforward, several sequences can be derived immediately following our definitions. Shots $\{T_3, T_5, T_7, T_9\}$ are all visually recognisable as belonging to a single region (labelled 'Michel' in the table), as are the shots $\{T_4, T_6, T_8, T_{10}\}$ (labelled 'Liliane' in the table). The autonomous shots T_1 and T_2 can also be grouped together by virtue of a match on movement

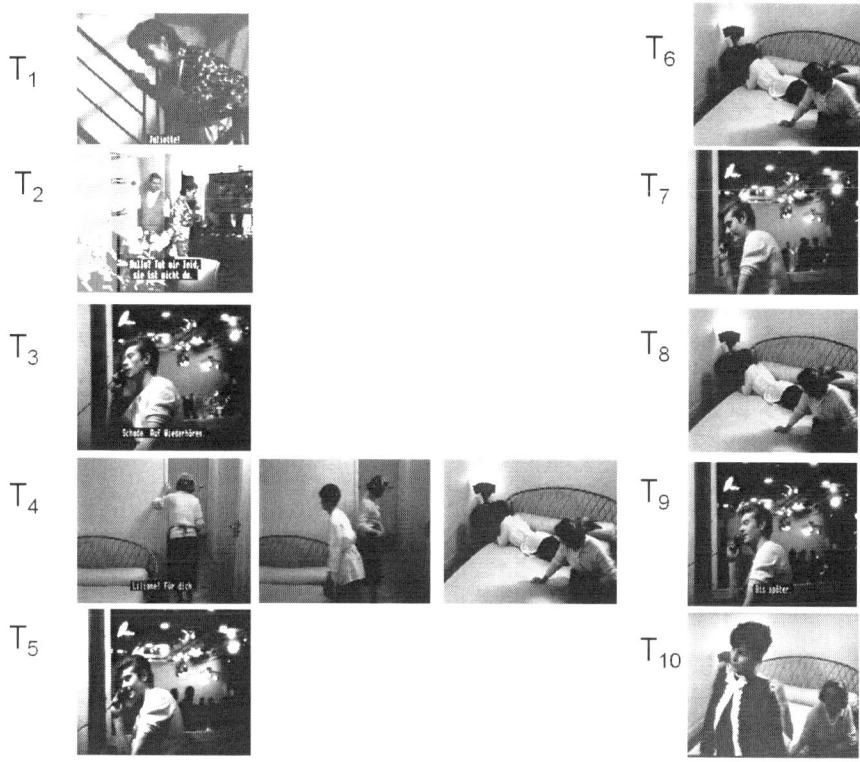

Figure 7.15   Rozier's Adieu Philippine *(00:26:51–00:27:59); Segments 19-20 according to Metz's numbering scheme*

Juliette: SpaceTime$_1$	Juliette: SpaceTime$_2$	Michel: SpaceTime$_3$	Liliane: SpaceTime$_4$
T_1			
	T_2		
		T_3	
			T_4
		T_5	
			T_6
		T_7	
			T_8
		T_9	
			T_{10}

Table 7.4   *Layouted film document for Segment 19 of* Adieu Philippine

of the character shown and continuous sound. Although such groupings are less robust than a visual depiction of the same setting, the continuity achieved between these two initial shots is still difficult for a viewer to ignore. The invited inference is therefore one of immediate temporal succession and spatial prolongation according to our *grande paradigmatique*; syntagmatically we have an itinerary in the sense defined above (§7.4.1). This remains, nevertheless, an hypothesis on the part of an observer and so we are still dealing with two autonomous segments and not a Metzian ordinary sequence or scene.

On the basis of the spatiotemporal information in the layout, it is also clear that the shots following T_2 are strong candidates for an alternation. The distinct sequences of Michel (SpaceTime$_3$) and Liliane (SpaceTime$_4$) are interwoven and thereby form a second telephone conversation. When we form a transition graph from the layout and search for a corresponding non-spatial symmetric relation to bind the sequences together into a coherent alternation as required by our Definition 7.11, however, T_3 is clearly *excluded* since the relationships holding for the other transitions all involve Liliane; in T_3 Michel is still bringing the *first* telephone conversation to a close. Thus, the relationship holding between shots T_2 and T_3 involves Juliette and Michel. In this case, this also corresponds to the space-time regions associated with these shots (SpaceTime$_2$ and SpaceTime$_3$ respectively) and so the following relationship holds:

$$R_{23} = \text{telephoning (\textbf{Juliette}, Michel).}$$

In contrast, the relation holding between the successive pairs of shots beginning with T_4 and T_5 until the end of the fragment instead involves Liliane and Michel. This means that the segment T_3–T_{10} is spatially partitionable (Definition 7.9) and monochronic (Definition 7.5) but does not meet condition (3) of Definition 7.11 for alternation because *there is no relationship* holding between the first transition of the segment: T_3 and T_4. If T_3 is excluded, however, then the remaining segment T_4–T_{10} does meet the necessary condition and an alternation holds. The required coherence relation is then R_{34} over space-time regions 3 (Michel) and 4 (Liliane):

$$R_{34} = \text{telephoning (\textbf{Liliane}, Michel).}$$

With the fragment as constructed, an observer will in all likelihood conclude a causal relationship for the first three shots between the woman's calling for Juliette and Michel's telephone call depicted in T_3. It would therefore be possible for an observer to consider grouping $\{T_1, T_2, T_3\}$ together as a single segment in need of classification. However, any attempt in this direction would violate conditions specified in our definitions above. In particular, our *maximality requirement* for sequences would not be fulfilled since T_3 clearly satisfies the conditions for being a part of the Michel partition set just as do any of the other shots in that sequence; that is, if $\{T_5, T_7, T_9\}$ belong to a sequence then T_3 certainly belongs there as well. Grouping T_3 with T_1 and T_2 thus faces some problems.

This then creates the following tension. On the one hand, our recognition of an alternation for the latter shots works to group shot T_3 separately from shots $\{T_5, T_7, T_9\}$; on the other hand, our definition of sequence and its maximality condition pulls in the other direction so as to include T_3 with these latter shots. In a very real sense, then, which we will now follow up formally, the shot T_3 is being 'pulled apart'. Its dialogue clearly links it back to the preceding brief conversation with Juliette's neighbour, while its spatiotemporal presentation binds it strongly to the subsequent alternation by way of the sequence.

To bring this out further, and to show the key role that T_3 actually plays in constructing a coherent filmic segment from the syntagmatic perspective, we will carry out two thought experiments in which we vary the way in which Rozier solves the narrative challenges he has set himself at this point.

In the first variant let us assume that T_3 is replaced by two shots T_{3-} and T_{3+} (which could more literally be fused within a single shot). In T_{3-} we see again the end of the attempted telephone call to Juliette, but in T_{3+} we add a new dialing situation for the second phone call. Then in the sequence $\{T_{3+}, T_4, \ldots, T_9\}$ we have a complete telephone conversation and we do not have to 'deduce' that this contained the second dialing event.

In the second variant we leave T_3 out completely. We can still conceptualise two telephone calls, but we see from the first only one conversational partner (Juliette's neighbour) in two scene shots without any spatiotemporal information about who she is talking with. We could subsequently deduce that this could have been Michel on the basis of a parallel narrative structuring in the two segments $\{T_1, T_2\}$ and $\{T_4, \ldots, T_9\}$, but the spatiotemporal contextualisation of Michel as assumed conversation partner remains open. This also means that it is not explicitly committed to that the two telephone calls follow immediately one after the other—it could even have been, for example, that Michel called Juliette the (diegetic) evening before. Here then the point would be weakened that Michel turns *immediately* to Liliane under the principle 'if I don't find one, then I'll take the other'. The opportunistic 'hunt' character of the segment, suggested in T_9 even in Michel's gestures (Michel rubs his hands here following his successful 'negotiation' of a date), would be lost.

This interpretation, which is after all decisive for observers' construction of the emotional connection of Michel with the two women—i.e., neither one of the two is particularly preferred over the other—is only guaranteed by the representation of the events with the additional spatiotemporal information that is provided by shot T_3. Therefore the second variant we have discussed is not a real alternative if the necessary information is to be maintained. The first variant also has an 'aesthetic' deficit: in Rozier's version the representation of the beginning parts of both events is constructed in a parallel fashion. Both pointedly omit the dialing 'sub-event' that we have then to deduce from our knowledge of the world. Both begin instead with the intervention of two other women. We have here therefore a case of *ellipsis*, which Metz would have considered as a 'pointed hard montage' or 'montage with effect', contributing to the intended construction of parallelism between the two episodes.

The overall result is then the following. The middle segment $\{T_3, T_5, T_7, T_9\}$ must in any case be considered a sequence by definition. This then functions as a dramaturgically guiding partition set in the sense defined above. This is precisely what we need to combine the two telephone conversations in a coherent whole that also adds considerably more meaning than the conversations would have on their own—just as Metz characterised loosely in his informal description. This guiding sequence forms the backbone of the narration in the entire sequence T_1 - T_{10} and effectively binds the first shot sequence to the second shot sequence as required. In the first telephone call, no contact with intended rendezvous partner Juliette is established; in the second telephone call, contact is established, but with Liliane. The segments $\{T_1, T_2\}$ and $\{T_4, \ldots, T_9\}$ therefore relate to each other as wholes in a very similar fashion to our example with the married couples above. Again, a higher-order narrational purpose is achieved, in the present case at least contrasting failure with success.

This example from *Adieu Philippine* has appealed to the majority of concepts introduced in this chapter for syntagmatic analysis. The distinct diegetic spaces of T_1 and T_2 are brought together by a conceptualised connected movement (an *itinerary*) of an actor within a diegetic neighbourhood; the shots of the segment $\{T_1, T_2, T_3\}$ also belong together as a conceptualised action, although these actually stretch over three diegetic spaces. T_{10} marks a new

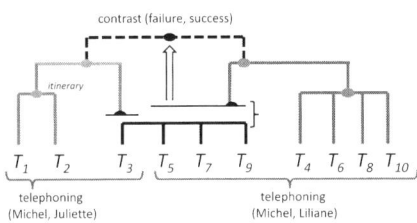

Figure 7.16   Graphical depiction of the operation of shots as a dramaturgically guiding diegetic sequence linking telephone conversations

event portion of the film but also still belongs in the spatial diegesis to $\{T_4, T_6, T_8, T_{10}\}$. Finally, the sequence centering on Michel functions as a guiding partition set that brings the two depicted episodes together into a complete, but contrastive, whole. This fine-grained organisation is suggested graphically in Figure 7.16, represented so as to explicitly show the similarity in structural organisation with our previous cases of dramaturgically guiding partition sets described above.

7.6 Beyond narration

The final kinds of filmic syntagmatic organisations to be addressed in this chapter move us into the regions of the non-narrative syntagmas in Metz's original account. For such syntagmas, the temporal unfolding of the cinematographic document no longer necessarily corresponds in any natural, or iconic, fashion to the unfolding of diegetic time. In a collection of shots within a *descriptive syntagma*, temporal relations of DURING and OVERLAP dominate. Observers may then be able to build a 'temporal container' for the shots related descriptively, but within this the precise inter-relationships of shots are not further specified or decodable. As a consequence, the order of the individual shots as shown can be varied freely without changing the classification or the syntagma as a whole. In essence, the filmic organisation in such cases 'asserts' *co-presence*.

Space precludes us pursuing this area of the syntagmatic organisation in quite as much detail as we have that of chronological syntagmas above. For present purposes, we will restrict the discussion in order to provide a placeholder within the account as a whole; further discussion of non-narrative syntagmas within a document model is offered in Schmidt (2008). We will quite briefly address just two cases of non-narrative syntagmas. The first centres around descriptive syntagmas in which at least some spatial coherence can be relied upon; the second turns to those cases where even spatial coherence is not available.

7.6.1 Description

Our definition of descriptive syntagmas begins with a modification of our treatment of ordinary Metzian scenes above. Returning to the definition offered (Definition 7.6), we see that it is primarily the third condition, i.e., that the shots play out in an order that corresponds to the unfolding of events in the narrative, which anchors such syntagmas in the realm of chronological and narrative syntagmas. We can therefore weaken the temporal conditions while maintaining the others in order to arrive at a workable definition of 'descriptive scenes' as follows:

Definition 7.13 *A sub-tree of the logical structure of a cinematographic document to which at least two shots are assigned as content portions is a* **descriptive scene** *for some set of observers when:*

1. *the diegetic spaces of all shots assigned to the sub-tree can be conceptualised by all observers as being connected,*
2. *the times portrayed in the shots can be conceptualised as falling within a temporal 'container' covering all the time intervals of the involved content portions,*
3. *changing the layouted order of the shots effects neither the temporal container nor the spatial 'container' entailed,*

  4. no further shot exists meeting the conditions (1)–(3).

This then naturally covers cases where we receive a collection of shots illustrating some location, without needing to assume that the showing of the shots follows the unfolding of some purposive activity. The coherence of the segment is given primarily by means of the spatial connectedness: for example, shots from around a room or other locally coherent setting.

In addition, although we state that shots may be freely permutable, there may be further grounds that restrict this in practice—our formal condition applies only to the extent of the spatial and temporal 'containers'. It may well be the case that the effect of a particular segment relies on other non-spatiotemporal grounds in order to be effective, for example building in size or importance for dramatic purpose or maintaining some other ongoing feature holding over the segment. This condition needs, therefore, to be weighed with these other aspects in mind when proceeding with analysis.

With these provisos, the definition at hand gives us the final batch of formal tools required for treating the example with which we began this chapter, Segment 1 from *Adieu Philippine*. There we saw how the assumption of a shot fusing elements from two syntagmas offered a convenient separation between the beginning two syntagmas of the film as required. But it did not solve the problem that Segment 1 of the film appeared to be 'readable' on subsequent viewings of the film not just as an illustration of a busy TV studio.

In fact, if we analyse what is being shown in the first segment more closely, the situation becomes even worse for the Metzian analysis. Not only is Michel present in Segment 1 even from *its second shot*, but also the remaining shots play out *in strict temporal succession*, following Michel's location and activities from shot to shot as he begins by standing near the piano, then helps move a camera and finally is sent to retrieve new headphones by that camera's operator. Moreover, seen *audio*-visually, there is also a strong chronological development since the diegetic music being recorded plays out naturally without jumps.

Michel's actions and their depiction in this segment are then indistinguishable from a segment appropriately classified as a Metzian *chronological* narrative syntagma; a clearly signalled active participant engages in a series of actions that unfold chronologically throughout the segment. This problem relates to the difficulty that several authors have raised, and which we mentioned above during our discussion of the approach of Michel Colin (§4.3.2): defining syntagmas such as the bracket syntagma in such a way that they no longer have any possibility of showing chronological development seems too strong.

Any suggestion that the film does not make this succession of actions on the part of Michel sufficiently visible to be picked up for analysis and is only an artefact of our artificially close viewing is also somewhat problematic.

Michel is the only one in the studio wearing a bright white T-shirt or thin sweater and so stands out visually in almost every shot. He is even portrayed in some shots as the sole subject of camera monitors that appear in the segment. The most prominent case appears in shot 5 (cf. Figure 7.17), nicely motivated by his name credit over-layed beneath ("for the first time on screen: Jean-Claude Aimini"). From the construction of the shots themselves, therefore, it is also difficult to argue that the film is not picking Michel out for special visual 'mention'. This is naturally diametrically opposed to Metz's characterisation:

> "drawing together into a rhythmical entity a number of discontinuous images whose common denominator is simply their ability to suggest a particular atmosphere." (Metz, 1974a: 150)

Figure 7.17
Michel appearing in a camera monitor in Segment 1, shot 5 of Adieu Philippine

The close analysis would seem to call for a Metzian ordinary *scene* from shot 2 up until the end of Segment 2 (cf. Figure 4.3 above); there are actually no grounds within Metz's definitions for coming to a different conclusion.

And, yet, there is a sense in which Metz's classification *does* need to be considered. There is unarguably an impression that the segment does communicate a sense of bustling TV activity over and above any other information that might be obtained from it and so we need to do some justice to both perspectives on what is going on. Metz's analysis was no doubt guided by his 'feeling' of what would be appropriate for the film segment at hand and the looseness of his definitions allowed him to 'bend' them just sufficiently to motivate his desired bracket classification. This phenomenon is by no means rare in film analysis: it is in practice not uncommon to find the boundaries between categories of analysis pushed to fit one analysis result rather than another. It is precisely to make such shaping of analyses to fit desired results more difficult that we are seeking a more formal account.

This situation then provides us with an ideal real-life example of our requirement that analyses of artefacts as complex as film *include consideration of the observer*. For the first-time viewer of *Adieu Philippine* who is just beginning to focus on the film as the credits rush by, it may well be the case that Michel is not picked out and that the segment has passed before anything apart from the impression of a busy TV studio has been formed—i.e., the segment is a bracket syntagma as Metz claims. For the second-time viewer, who sees Michel in shot 2, we still want to maintain the sense that one function of the segment is to suggest a busy TV studio even when Michel's actions are being followed. For viewers in between, who might notice Michel as an individual in the film only when he takes his time leaving the studio (shot 9), or only when he is spoken to (shot 8), or when he puts one foot out to help move the camera (shot 7) and so on, we need to allow the flexibility not to have to claim that such viewers have misunderstood the film or have missed the segment boundary. The film *constructs* a fluid segment boundary and that is the filmic organisation that we need to capture.

What we actually have in the present case, therefore, is a dense inter-weave of forward and backward references that cannot be entirely handled within a syntagmatic analysis defined as Metz attempted. The Metzian classification of the first segment by means of a bracket syntagma as an achronological syntagma is only valid if one also makes the following strong assumption: the shots belonging to the syntagma, including the 'last' shots, are aggregated from the perspective of an exemplificatory (cf. §6.3) reference style *without a consideration of temporal relations* and are decoupled from the rest of the (temporally unfolding) diegesis. This means that the logical content can well possess a chronological flavour, but the syntagma selected is not appealing to this—that is, the film 'does not commit' to this.

That the achronological attribution is in some sense accurate can be shown by means of a thought experiment in which the actor playing Michel is replaced by another for the duration of the segment (or even, for a hard test, is replaced by a different actor in each shot). Although this would destroy a number of cohesive 'reference chains' (Tseng, 2008) within the opening sequence, as well as the motivation for the positioning of the credits, it would otherwise do little damage for the narrative structure and comprehension of the film. In this sense, then, Metz was quite justified in his analysis.

A better treatment would be, however, an extension of the framework to combine chronological and exemplificatory syntagmas so as to be able to say that Segment 1 is both chronological *and* exemplificatory: then, even an observer who sees Michel from his first appearance will still be justified in taking away from Segment 1 the message that we have just seen an example of a busy TV studio. If an observer notices certain occurrences of Michel but fails to see the integrated action (which is quite possible, since the camera angles change rather rapidly and the duration of shots is short), sense to the whole is still given by the evident shared location of the studio. This classification of the segment then meets our conditions for a descriptive scene, which comes closest to the classification that Metz intended.

In order to reconcile these conflicting perspectives, our final proposal for a treatment of the case at hand further integrates several parts of our overall framework. We have described both the situation where an observer recognises that Michel is active throughout and the situation where an observer only receives an impression of a busy TV studio. The former is a

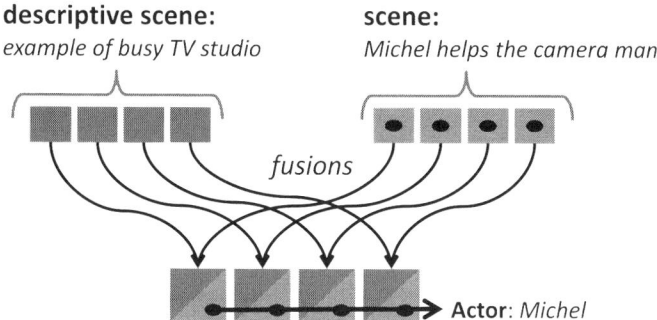

Figure 7.18   Creating more complex shots by coordinate fusions of syntagmas

normal scene according to our definitions; the latter is a descriptive scene as introduced above. Since the definitions already make reference to the interpretative work of observers, the existence of two possible syntagma classifications is not in itself a problem. More interesting is the fact that the film probably intends *both* of these possibilities to hold—that is, we need to make sure that our characterisation of the film is not so partial that it forces one or the other of these possible classifications out of the picture.

To describe this state of affairs, we can explore extensions of our notion of fusion. In general, fusion can be seen as holding when a shot in a film is associated with a content portion that is responding to different motivations simultaneously. Now we can consider the situation where a content portion may combine information sufficient for giving an example of a busy TV studio *and* information describing the action of a particular protagonist. By these means we can envisage a situation in which we have *both* a descriptive scene and a regular scene as depicted graphically in Figure 7.18; this extends the cases of varieties of filmic realisation summarised in Figure 5.11 above, establishing the possibility of motivating *internal* shot details discoursally.

The more an observer sees only the cues appropriate for the descriptive scene, the more this interpretation is placed in the foreground; the more cues for the ordinary scene are seen, then the more this interpretation is foregrounded. Both alternatives are, however, made available by the design of the film and there is nothing to rule out their simultaneous relevance within the segment.

This naturally opens up a considerable range of expressive possibilities that we will not be able to delve into any more deeply here. Regardless of the complexity opened up, however, we still see the definitions of the syntagmas and their paradigmatic internal organisation and inter-relationships as playing the central role in unravelling the film interpretations that can apply. The only difference is that there may simply be more than one syntagmatic classification holding at the same time, again due to the richness of the material substrate on offer within film and its capability of carrying several semiotic organisations at once.

7.6.2   Non-spatial, non-temporal film segments

Finally, we turn to the cases where even spatial coherence is not available and nevertheless the film segments constructed remain intelligible. A general account of film must also be in a position to support syntagmas of this kind. These form the more general case discussed by Metz under *bracket syntagmas*, including views that may in themselves, i.e., visually and in terms of their content, have *no* necessary features in common. Placing them together within a syntagmatic unit is then what asserts their connectedness.

This interpretation may be supported by selecting shots where some connection may readily be hypothesised by viewers, but this is certainly not necessary; the grounds for connection may also be provided externally to the visual presentations—for example, in a filmic fragment where one character announces: "here are some things I did on my holidays" and following this we receive a collection of quite diverse shots. This makes another connection with our broad syntagmatic dependency type 2, paratactically related shot series.

The conditions binding such shots together cannot, therefore, be specified in advance, or even as belonging to some established domain of relations (such as the spatial relations of the descriptive scene case). Current knowledge allows us only to state that we are dealing here with filmic realisations of *ad hoc* categories (cf. Barsalou, 1983): that is categories that are formed 'on the fly' for some purpose. Such purposes in the filmic document can be drawn from a variety of sources, ranging from the narrative development assumed to be motivating the design of the document to particular statements of purpose (both explicit and implicit) intradiegetically within the world of the portrayed events. However, just as with chronological syntagmas, the syntagmatic organisation provides the overall structural scaffold within which the paradigmatic options then provide the necessary channel to appropriate *kinds* of world knowledge that might be relevant.

We have characterised some of these options already in our description of the paradigmatic options in the previous chapter. For example, if a character looks thoughtful and the next collection of shots shows apparently random objects, then we may assume that we have a variant of a descriptive syntagma that is anchored into the narrative by virtue of some kind of *projection*: perhaps the character is remembering the objects, or assembling them in the mind's eye for some future purpose. The precise relationship will not be signalled syntagmatically: it can only be derived by defeasible hypothesis building drawing on what is known from the film and the world. The syntagmatic organisation *does* 'assert', however, that there is some coherence-building to be done, as well as demarcating precisely the basis and extent for this work in the filmic material.

The next step is to remove even the assumption that there is a temporally bounded container for the shots grouped together in the syntagma. Whenever we move to a different diegetic realm, for example, during a mental projection, then the temporal relationships between the events or objects shown may not even be definable. We need, therefore, to weaken this condition also. In essence, what remains is analogous to the underlying condition for alternation discussed above, the viewer must be able to hypothesise an *aggregation condition* that gives coherence to the segment. Without this, its unity collapses and the viewer is faced simply with a collection of unrelated fragments.

Such aggregation conditions may involve relations such as examples of X, subtypes of X, instances of X, showing similarities to X, used for the purpose of X, and so on. Fixing a relation that holds for the observed scenes is then the 'contextualisation' effort that an observer needs to bring to bear in the interpretation, again in a precisely analogous way to the contextualisation of semantic expressions within verbal language discourse (cf. Asher and Lascarides 2003 and Chapter 2). This then leads to the definition of arbitrary aggregation principles for content portions in documents which need no longer be necessarily cinematographic—this is clearly a task for future research and must be considered beyond the scope of our current concerns.

7.7   Summary and Conclusions

We have now presented a formal specification of the syntagmatic axis of chronological cinematographic documents that allows us to pursue analysis in a more robust and reproducible fashion than has been possible hitherto.

For Metz, syntagmas were simply arrayed one after the other and so, even though he spoke at various points of more complex structures, the account remained sketchy. It was then difficult to decide on the basis of the Metzian definitions on a classification doing adequate justice to more complex organisations that a film might exhibit. In his analysis of *Adieu Philippine*, for example, Metz is left with 83 autonomous units, each classified according to the *grande syntagmatique*—but how these units themselves cohere into a larger organisation of the narrative of the film as a whole is not explained. By grouping elements according to our definitions into higher order structures as we have illustrated here, we provide more opportunities for expressing important relationships holding between segments in a film and a principled mechanism for combining segments into hierarchies of narrative organisation. In short, we have begun to provide a bridge between detailed shot-by-shot accounts and more dramaturgically-motivated decompositions of films into acts, episodes and scenes as often pursued in less formal approaches to film analysis.

There are, naturally, many more phenomena to be uncovered here and we have little doubt that substantial extension of our framework will prove necessary as more data are considered. We see the current development therefore very much as a foothold on the steep path of filmic analysis. It remains to explore the framework's application and to evaluate its performance with respect to the support it provides for the characterisation of filmic meaning and the construction of more abstract interpretations of films. Although much of this work is for the future, in the chapter following we provide one further extended illustration of all aspects of our framework at work, showing in detail how the definitions combine to focus and constrain possible analyses in the case of a single film.

Further reading

Many of the details of the **syntagmatic organisation** developed in this chapter are set out more formally together with further examples in the series of articles published in German as Schmidt and Strauch (2002), Schmidt (2004) and Schmidt (2008); the latter discusses in far more detail the syntagmatic treatment of description and perception segments in film as well as some of the document-theoretic foundations.

We have mentioned some of the approaches that have attempted to extend the *grande syntagmatique* structurally at various points in the discussion here and in previous chapters; the most significant of these, however, have been Fledelius (1978), Möller-Naß (1986) and Colin (1995*b*).

For more on the now extensive range of **qualitative treatments of space**, see Bateman and Farrar (2004) and the many references given there. The connections of this work with the now almost equally extensive treatments of space within film research (cf. Khouloki, 2007; Sierek, 2009; Schmidt, 2010) has yet to be explored, although Levin and Wang (2009) take some first steps.

8 Combining syntagmatic and paradigmatic analysis: a detailed example

> *"There can be no question of trying to fix the film in a single reading, a coherent 'interpretation'...: the purpose of the present analysis is merely to suggest the mechanism of the film, its functioning, its system, the terms of its production."* (Heath, 1975b: 95)

In the chapters preceding we have set out a detailed analytic framework for the close analysis of film. This framework combines new understandings of how to specify and explore paradigmatic relationships in film and how to specify and explore syntagmatic configurations of filmic units. We have given examples of how this works for individual parts of the framework as they were introduced. In this chapter we take this further by providing an almost exhaustive analysis of an extensive filmic fragment, showing exactly how the constructs we have proposed are applied in practice.

A central aspect of this approach will be seen to be the *interaction* of the paradigmatic and the syntagmatic descriptions. The paradigmatic axis provides a set of relations that must be applied element-by-element to a film as it unfolds; this suggests particular syntagmatic configurations that may apply. The syntagmatic axis then provides the precise definitional conditions that need to hold for each syntagmatic configuration. This may then rule out some of the possibilities raised paradigmatically and require revision. Analysis is thus an ongoing cycle of exploration, from paradigmatic to syntagmatic and back again, making use of how the two axes mutually constrain one another. An analysis is completed when we have covered an entire target film fragment *both* paradigmatically and syntagmatically, respecting all of the constraints both within and across axes on the way.

Descriptions of this kind quickly become very detailed and so we have made our selection on the basis of length and relative complexity. We analyse the early silent film *The Girl and her Trust* (1912) produced under the direction of D. W. Griffith by American Biograph, with Dorothy Bernard and Wilfred Lucas in the main roles of Grace and Jack respectively. The film is around 15 minutes long and consists of 140 shots taken from 35 different camera positions. The restriction to a silent film will also help us concentrate for present purposes on the image track and the information that we are drawing from this; analysis can, however, naturally be extended to include information from the soundtrack as we have done with many of our examples in previous chapters.

Even though the film is short and restricted in many ways, it is by no means trivial. As we shall see, it already makes use of a considerable range of filmic meaning-making devices, some of these working in the way they would nowadays, some looking distinctly different. We give a reasonably detailed account of the fragments we focus on for analysis but nevertheless consider viewing the film both prior to reading the present chapter and when following the analysis through as indispensable (see *Further Reading*). We will not be able to present all the analyses undertaken here in equal detail, nor will be able to consider the entire film. The detail of the descriptions we do provide should, however, on the one hand, be specific enough to indicate how that analysis proceeds further and, on the other, already cover the most complex parts of the film. For example, we do not consider the final 'chase' sequence of the film as this has already been discussed in the literature (for instance by Edward Branigan as we describe below) and, in terms of our framework, is in any case relatively straightforward.

We also omit here any discussion of the many problems of a practical nature that confront serious studies of films from this period—questions, for example, of whether the version we analyse is the 'original' and so on will not be considered. Although this is essential for arguments concerning the historical development of film, it plays no significant role for our present task of showing our method of analysis at work.

The length of *The Girl and her Trust* brings it within the limits where an exhaustive analysis is possible. In contrast, the present state of the art still renders analyses at this level of detail for full-length feature films prohibitively time-consuming and, indeed, often unnecessary for useful analysis. Over long stretches of the majority of films, a combined syntagmatic-paradigmatic discourse analysis of the kind we have developed runs smoothly without facing problematic issues—for the purpose of further analysis, therefore, providing all the 'detail behind the scenes' in the style of the close analytic reading that we provide here would be overkill. Nevertheless, in the move towards more empirically-oriented film research that has been our aim throughout this book, the fine-grained analysis shown has important advantages: first, whenever analysis is *not* straightforward, our framework often raises the questions necessary to make progress; and second, we consider the precision that we pursue for the definition of filmic categories necessary in order to support the *automatic* construction of segmentations of this kind—we believe that we have now understood at least basic narrative cinematographic documents sufficiently well that automatic analysis at this level of abstraction becomes a realistic goal.

As a consequence, our more general intention here is not to insist that film analysis necessarily be carried out by hand at this level of detail—a position reminiscent of the strict film protocol analyses of early 'film philology' (cf. Kanzog, 1991)—but to work towards a framework in which such analyses can be delivered for subsequent human use by automatic algorithms. The state of the art is still some way away from this latter aim, but the style of analysis we have set out in previous chapters brings us nearer.

Finally, our selection of *The Girl and her Trust* for analysis is also linked to film history and discussions in film studies. As an example of film-making from one of the recognised early masters of the cinematic medium, the film offers a certain 'opening bracket' for all of the analyses we have considered. Griffith is often cited as being if not *the* inventor of many important resources for constructing filmic narrative structure, then at least the director who brought these devices most effectively to the screen, anchoring them within the set of tools film-makers have relied upon ever since. Edward Branigan, for example, has discussed *The Girl and her Trust* as one of his archetypal examples of filmic exposition, using it to characterise several important principles of narrative organisation, such as differential levels of knowledge and cross-cutting (cf. Branigan, 1992: 20–31, 66–71). These and many other techniques, such as point-of-view shots, the 'last minute rescue' alternating narrative structure and continuity editing, have all frequently been traced back to films made by Griffith (see *Further Reading*).

The Girl and her Trust appears to be a re-make or re-working of Griffith's earlier *The Lonedale Operator* (1911). Although Meyer (1971: 111) describes the earlier film as "the most advanced one-reeler of its time", in direct comparison with its successor it takes on more of the qualities of a rough sketch—which shows well how rapidly the conventions and understanding of film technique were developing at that time. In *The Lonedale Operator*, it is comparatively difficult to construct spatial relationships accurately, characters change on-screen direction between shots, there is little inter-action between the various locales constructed, and different states of knowledge are handled almost brusquely—points also alluded to briefly by Salt (1976). Many of the events of *The Lonedale Operator* reappear in modified form in *The Girl and her Trust*, where they display a considerably heightened sense of narrative development.

The earlier film has also been subject to detailed discussion—most particularly in the shot-by-shot analysis provided by Raymond Bellour, in which the extensive role of 'alternation' present in Griffith's films takes pride of place. For Bellour, alternation is a very general principle spanning both cinematic and non-cinematic codes, ranging from visual symmetries and differences through to similarities and differences of general topics and themes. While leading to many insightful observations, Bellour's account is often more suggestive than analytic and Bellour himself states that he was "not concerned ... with an analysis as such—that is, with an underlying logic that would be enlightened by a commentary. Rather, I see the following as an ordered description..." (Bellour 2000c: 262 and Bellour 1990: 360). It is therefore particularly instructive to compare our analysis of

The Girl and her Trust briefly with Bellour's account of *The Lonedale Operator* since our aim is very much one of analysis.

In Bellour's writings generally, the question of units is addressed rather differently to how we have developed it here. In particular, there was an explicit re-orientation to allow the selection of units according to their proposed explanatory relevance at any point rather than due to any preset scheme (e.g. Bellour, 2000*d*: 203). As Gunning, reviewing Bellour, puts it:

> "Bellour uses shot breakdowns ..., but these function partly as a somewhat arbitrary means of marking a place within a film. ... Bellour does not focus our attention on shots as individual elements, but rather as fragments within a system whose true structure is revealed by the play of alternations between shots. ... Patterns of opposition need not take the ready-made segments of the decoupage as their elements, whether shots *or* sequences, but can utilise anything ranging from elements larger than sequences to fragments of shots." (Gunning, 2003: 347/8)

Several authors, including Henderson (1977) and Gunning, suggest that this more 'free-wheeling', dynamic approach to unit selection constitutes an advance because it is more compatible with post-structural analysis—such as that offered for literature by Barthes (1974)—than it is with traditional linguistic or structural semiotic analyses. But this 'practical' flexibility was bought at a considerable theoretical price.

A major criticism of all of such approaches subsequently was the lack of reproducibility in the analytic decisions drawn upon—i.e., there was little guarantee that two analysts would come to segment a film in the same way. We can see this in the fact that the application of Bellour's generic 'principle of alternation' relies crucially upon an observant interpreter deciding on what is relevant and what not. This, although picking out many interesting points, does not itself present a re-usable methodology for approaching films in general.

In contrast, our analysis *does* seek to reveal an 'underlying logic' at work in the film and, as a consequence, is able to bring out the role played by formal alternation in *The Girl and her Trust* in considerable detail. Moreover, our analysis will be seen to follow more or less automatically from the definitions that we have provided in the previous chapters, demonstrating that our approach is tied neither to the specifics of individual films nor to the analyst 'happening' to pick out useful details.

Also relevant here is a further contrast with the description offered by Branigan. Branigan considers the substantial *narrative* complexity of *The Girl and her Trust* in terms of cause-and-effect and the guiding role played by 'narrative schemas'. Such schemas, following a logic of everyday purposes and actions, are assumed to allow the events of a narrative to be followed. This is an example of the general appeal made to cognitive mechanisms that we find in several current styles of film theorising—as set out in our 'map' of film studies in Figure 1.5 in Chapter 1. As we have argued throughout the book, however, we consider it to be the filmic discourse organisation that provides the necessary 'underlying logic'. It is this that plays an essential role in guiding just how narrative can be pieced together. As discussed both by Bellour and by Elsaesser and Barker (1990: 295–296), therefore, it is more the discourse form of Griffith's cross-cutting and alternating that gives rise to the narrative force of the film. Our analysis will bring this process of discourse creation and its guidance of interpretations into particularly sharp relief. We also return to this particular point at the conclusion of this chapter, after we have seen the analysis in full.

8.1   Setting up the story

The film begins as usual for films of that time with a title frame, identifying the production company, and then proceeds to introduce the story with an intertitle frame carrying the message: 'Grace, the telegraph operator, is admired by all' (which we shall label as shot E2). This leads into the first shot of the story in which we see a young woman sitting in a room that could be a telegraph office of the time reading a pamphlet. The cross-modal defeasible discourse inference is naturally that this is Grace, which turns out to be the case.

The first collection of shots serves to combine concisely several story elements and so it is useful to track this carefully employing our analytic scheme. Representative frames from the shots making up what we will consider the 'beginning' of the film are shown in Figure 8.1; the images are to be read from left-to-right and from top to bottom as numbered.

Following our first view of Grace, a young man comes in with a drink and two straws. He gives the drink to Grace in an attempt to get closer to her; in this he is not successful, and she makes him leave the room (E3). Outside he meets the main male character of the film, Jack; they exchange a few words and the first young man leaves (E4). Jack then goes into the telegraph office and, under the pretense of taking a sip of Grace's drink, steals a kiss and is also accordingly sent from the room (E5). Jack stands a while looking dejected in the outside room (E6). In the inner office, Grace looks considerably less angry but then has to start making notes from an incoming telegraph (E7). Jack, still outside, similarly starts some paper work (E8). Grace finishes her notes and then calls Jack (E9). Jack stops writing and goes towards the telegraph office (E10). Inside, Grace shows Jack the message that she has just noted down (E11). An intertitle shows the text "National Bank sending $2000 on No. 7 for Simpson Construction Co." (E12). Jack takes a revolver out of a drawer, to which Grace reacts with displeasure, but he checks the weapon and fills it with bullets taken from the same drawer (E13). The next shot shows a train arriving (E14). Grace and Jack look out of a window of the telegraph office and Jack hastily

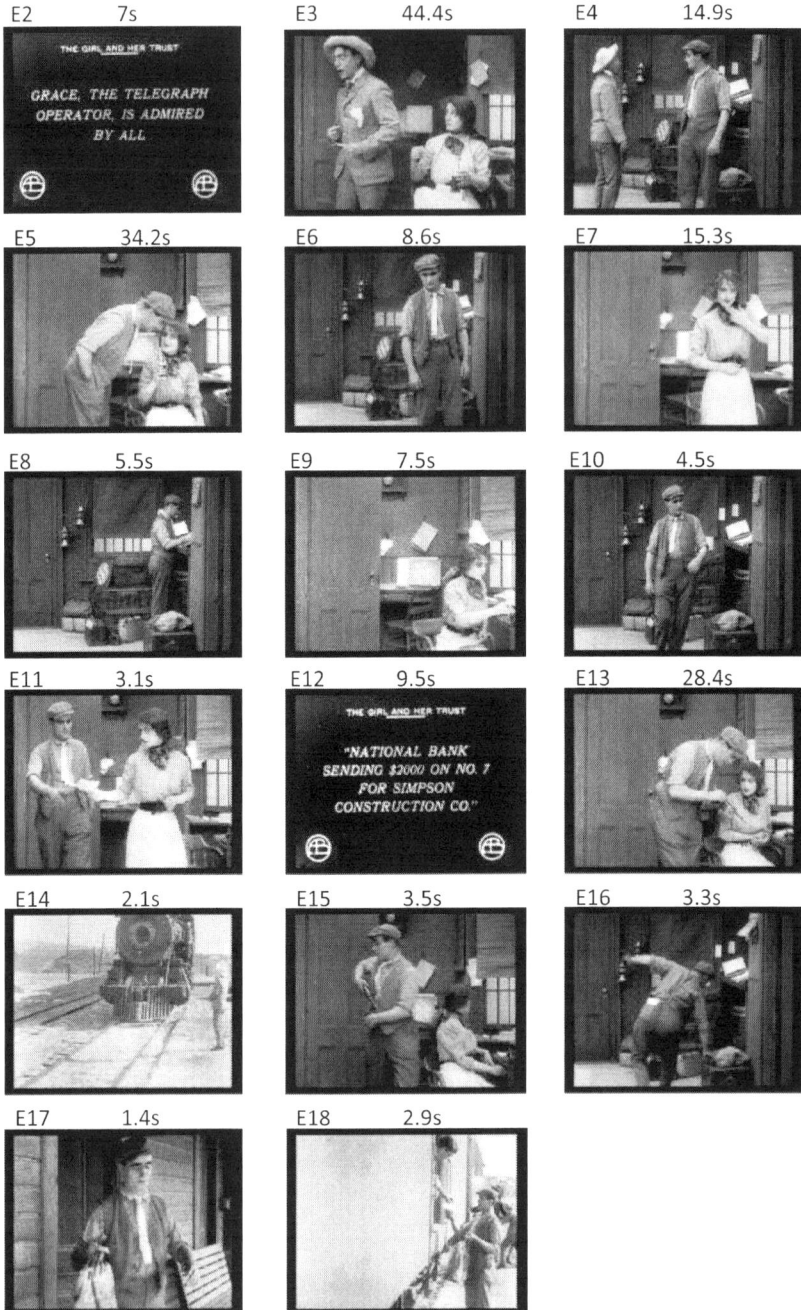

Figure 8.1 Shots E2 to E18 from The Girl and her Trust *(1912, 0:00:07–0:03:24)*

leaves (E15), passes through the outer room where he picks up a bag (E16), and is then shown leaving a wooden building (E17). Finally, Jack comes up to a train and is handed a piece of paper (E18).

Already in this description, we have had to build in interpretations of the film that actually need to come from an analysis rather than being set out in advance. Therefore, following the definitions of possible segments given in the previous chapter and their possible paradigmatic interpretations set out in the chapter before, we now show this process of interpretation in action as it operates shot-by-shot. We will make the description very detailed for this first illustration, explicitly naming the definitions that apply and how these segment and analyse the film. We will relax this somewhat in subsequent sections, but it is important to remember that in the last resort the analysis always has this fine-grained process of cycling through the syntagmatic and paradigmatic axes as its foundation.

To begin, then, E3 gives us a spatio-temporal 'world slice' in which several events are directly provided via perceptual realism. In particular, two characters—one male, one female—are introduced as well as a particular locale. At the end of the shot, the male character moves to the left of the frame. In E4, what appears to be the same character moves from the right of the frame, continuing his trajectory of motion to the left. The setting is clearly a different one: there is no visual overlap with what proceeded. Thus, the viewer is faced with the task of relating E3 and E4. By this time in the history of film, many of the continuity conventions well-known today had already been established but we nevertheless need to follow this through in detail in order to show just what aspects of the semiotic mode of film the mechanisms build upon.

First, the paradigmatic options for the relation between two shots are as given in the *grande paradigmatique* system network of Figure 6.7.[1] We consider the options this provides one-by-one just as illustrated in our examples in Chapter 6; for ease of reference, we also repeat the network at the end of the book. For the shift from E3 to E4, then, there is no evidence of projection at work (this was generally signalled rather clearly in films of this period). For TAXIS, the fact that the motion of a character is continued across the shots suggests that we have a hypotactic relation between shots because of the dependency thus established. In terms of PLANE, we have the most likely defeasible hypotheses of continuous time without any ellipsis, non-contiguous space (because the setting is different), and prolongation (again because of the character's movement which takes us from the old location to the new). It also appears throughout that we

---

[1] Although it may be the case that the paradigmatic options were different in 1912, for the options of concern to us here there appears to be little apparent difference and so we will use the same general classification scheme; it would be an interesting goal in its own right to track the development of paradigmatic options actually provided by film across time, but this is beyond the scope of our present study. Some further remarks on this and further references were given in Chapter 5 above.

are dealing with specific characters identifiable and distinguishable for the purposes of the narrative. The result of this first paradigmatic analysis of the relation between E3 and E4 is then summed up as: no projection, hypotactic, diegetic, event, continuous, non-contiguous, prolongation—i.e., one complete set of maximal paths through the paradigmatic network.

Second, turning to our syntagmatic characterisation, we are looking for a segment which is going to support some specifiable syntagma (Definitions 7.1 and 7.3), otherwise the segment, and its import, remain unclassified. As the extract proceeds, we will be trying to find syntagmatically maximal segments to which syntagmatic classes can be assigned. So far we only have a first indication of possible chronological ordering (Definition 7.4) as this is the *realisation* of the temporal continuity supplied paradigmatically. We may subsequently find that we need to allocate a different relation, but so far this would appear a reasonable defeasible inference.

This shows us one of the important roles played by the paradigmatic description—although there may be many different potential syntagmatic structures to consider by checking whether the conditions given in their definitions hold, the paradigmatic organisation provides a prioritisation of just which definitions to apply. Formally, if we were simply to try and apply all of the definitions from the syntagmatic axis of description to a collection of shots, the number of potential solutions to be checked before finding those that actually apply would be enormous. The paradigmatic relations therefore provide a framework that organises potential solutions according to their contribution to the paradigmatic axis of description—this serves to keep the analysis within useful boundaries. We will see this 'guiding' role of paradigmatic classifications repeatedly throughout the examples in this chapter.

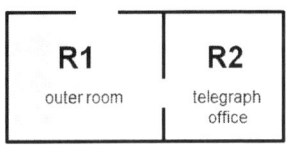

Figure 8.2

Spatial configuration established in shots E3 and E4

We can also note the work of *spatial construction* that the first two shots have already given rise to; we will make detailed use of this in the fine application of our syntagmatic definitions as the analysis proceeds.

The paradigmatic option of prolongation has the effect of requiring an interpretation in which the space being considered is extended; the first setting was the telegraph office (E3) and the second is constructed as an 'immediate neighbour' of the left-hand side of the office (E4). We must also hypothesise a connection relationship between these (through which the characters come and go) and an 'exit' (through which the first man shown leaves). This corresponds to the spatial configuration shown in Figure 8.2; we will add further regions to this as the film proceeds.

Continuing with the segment, shot E5 is then linked to shot E4 in a manner similar to how shot E4 was linked to E3, although in the reverse direction. This time it is Jack who goes through the connection between the outer office and the inner office but, in terms of the paradigmatic relationships, little changes. The fact that the settings in E5 and E3 are the same (R2) briefly raises the possibility of a hypotactic embedding; however, since this is quickly countered by the shot following, we will not follow this line of interpretation further here.

Instead, we can now move syntagmatically to the stronger condition of monochronicity (Definition 7.5) because the same temporal relationship now holds across the entire segment so far: {E3, E4, E5}. Shot E6 then parallels E4 in that Jack is now sent from the room and the segment-so-far therefore continues to exhibit monochronicity. And, paradigmatically, over shots E3 to E6 nothing changes—the features that hold continue to be: non-projection, hypotactic, diegetic, event, continuous, non-contiguous and prolongation. Therefore we only receive information that strengthens the hypotheses suggested up to this point and confirmation of syntagmatic monochronicity.

Similar temporal relations continue unbroken until shot E11. Nevertheless, despite the monochronic development, the fragment *does not necessarily* meet the syntagmatic criteria for a filmic *scene* (Definition 7.6)—even though it might have appeared so because of the continuity of the action. To see this we have to consider the definition very strictly. The first two conditions insist on spatial and temporal diegetic 'connectedness'—we link this primarily back to information which is actually *displayed* in the images in order to constrain the analyses that may apply. This is crucial in order to help us away from interpretative analyses and towards analyses that can be based very tightly on the actual 'data' provided by the images in a film and which highlight just where interpretative work *is* required of viewers. In the present case there is no visual overlap between the depicted spaces R1 and R2 and the entire combination is an example of Pudovkin's creative geography (cf. §5.4) carried by the trajectories of the first man and Jack as they go back and forth. This lack of a syntagmatic unit prevents further paradigmatic classification—showing again how the two axes constrain one another.

What we *do* find is that conditions are met for *two sequences* (Definition 7.7). The first sequence is made up of the shots {E3, E5, E7, E9, E11}, the second of shots {E4, E6, E8, E10}. These are then our first candidate basic narrative syntagmas for the opening fragment. Building further on this, we can note that Definition 7.9 holds for shots E3–E11: i.e., the entire collection is spatially partitionable (2-partitionable to be exact) and, for similar reasons, we then have a *narrative series* (Definition 7.10).

Finally, to render the segment maximally coherent, we need to consider whether these sequences can be related. For this we can examine whether the conditions of being an *alternating* syntagma are also satisfied (Definitions 7.11 and 7.12). This is more complex as we have to check whether a common coherence-giving relationship can be found for all transitions between the two contributing sequences. This is the first time that the observer has to move beyond the basic narrative syntagmatic units to consider higher-order structures, which then in turn will become available for carrying further paradigmatic relations.

Between E3 and E11 the shots switch back and forth alternately and so there is a transition to consider between each pair. Between all eight pairs there is a simple relationship of spatial neighbourhood without intersection. This is, according to the definition, insufficient in itself for an alternating syntagma. Between shots E3–E4, E4–E5, E5–E6 and E10–E11, however, we (as 'experienced' observers) can posit an additional relationship of 'paying court to'/'being paid court to'—this is in line with what is occurring in the fragment and, what is more, fits well with the opening intertitle message: "admired by all". In contrast, in E9–E10, in which Grace (in R2) calls to Jack (in R1), there is at best the vestigial 'trajectory' of a verbal exchange, and for the remaining transitions, E6–E7, E7–E8, E8–E9, there is simply no such relationship. This means that it is still open, syntagmatically, how many alternations apply here, given the stable spatial alternation between the representations of R1 und R2.

We then investigate the relevant paradigmatic relationships more closely. In each of the latter transitions, i.e., E6–E7, E7–E8, E8–E9, we no longer have the case of some element or trajectory showing dependence between shots. This indicates that a more appropriate paradigmatic classification would involve a *paratactic* relationship rather than a hypotactic one. The shots in the immediate neighbourhood are then to be seen as independent— apart from the fact that the successive shots are spatiotemporally stable in their presentation. This paratactic classification then opens up new possibilities (cf. Figure 6.7)—in particular the ability to set up contrasts and comparisons. And this indeed appears to capture what is occurring here: within the second alternation bound by the relationships of admiring Grace and Grace being admired, there is a brief interlude where the respective emotional states of Jack and Grace appear to be contrasted or compared.

We might break this down still further to include two minimal points of contrast: E6–E7 showing Jack contemplating the difficulties of relationships and Grace not so disturbed by Jack's stolen kiss after all respectively, and E8–E9 showing Jack and Grace getting back to work respectively (and separately). For current purposes we will not distinguish this level of detail, however, as the precise function is clearly a question of interpretation. Nevertheless, the 'space' for these interpretations is necessarily given by the organisation that our analysis reveals; precisely *these* gaps are opened up rather than others (cf. §2.2). This appears intuitively quite plausible for the current segment.

Next, regardless of whether we distinguish more finely or not, the relationships involved are also to be classified paradigmatically as *internal*—

that is, this is internal to the 'text' organisation and is not given naturally by the diegetic external events of the depicted world which are playing out. As we shall see in a moment, although this is then anchored into the overall structure (in this case a narrative series) by its temporal commitments, it is in addition an 'evaluation' of the events unfolding within the story.

With shot E9, we also have a situation that is similar to the case of inner montage discussed in Section 5.5 above and illustrated graphically in Figure 5.11. That is, the shot can be broken down into several subshots, related by immediate temporal and spatial contiguity. Similar in certain respects to the phenomenon of *fusion* (cf. §7.1 and Definition 7.2), the events shown in the shot are 'pulled apart' by virtue of their participation in two distinct conceptualisations of the observer—conceptualisations motivated directly by the ongoing process of attributing discourse coherence to the unfolding fragment. Leading into the shot we have the playing out of the alternation of contrast that we have just discussed and its corresponding conceptualisation; leading out of the shot, however, is the next action, in which Grace calls Jack back into the telegraph office to read the message that she has just received.

For the purposes of the present chapter, we will use the same notation for inner montage as that introduced in the previous chapter for fusion, although the formal properties of the two phenomena are somewhat different.[2] We therefore analyse shot E9 as a composition of subshots $E9^-$ and $E9^+$; $E9^-$ is the final element of the paratactic contrast or comparison, while $E9^+$ is the continuation of the diegetic alternation begun in E3.

E10 shows the final alternation from space R1 as Jack is called into Grace in R2. E11 is then again a shot playing a double role: $E11^-$ is the last of the alternation between R1 and R2. With $E11^+$, showing Grace's handing of the message to Jack, preparing us for further narrative development. By this time we can also see that the earlier alternation of 'admiring Grace' has ceased to play a role. The story has 'moved on'. Having established Grace's admiration by all and the relationship between Jack and Grace, we are ready to proceed to the main events that will constitute the film's action. We summarise the development seen so far in Figure 8.3

In this figure we can see how the considerations discussed so far all come together to create a growing, coherent discourse structure. The diagram is divided into two components. In the upper part of the diagram, we see the unfolding sequences $\{E3, E5, E9^+, E11^-\}$ and $\{E4, E10\}$. These establish two distinct spatial areas, region R2 and R1 respectively. A coherence-forming relation can be found 'paying court to / being admired by all' and so our definitions establish this as an alternation—indicated in the figure by 'tying' the two sequences together with the topmost structural line. Syntagmatically, this line denotes that an alternation applies. The uppermost

---

[2]In the case of fusion proper, the image data genuinely overlap; with inner montage, segmentation is possible.

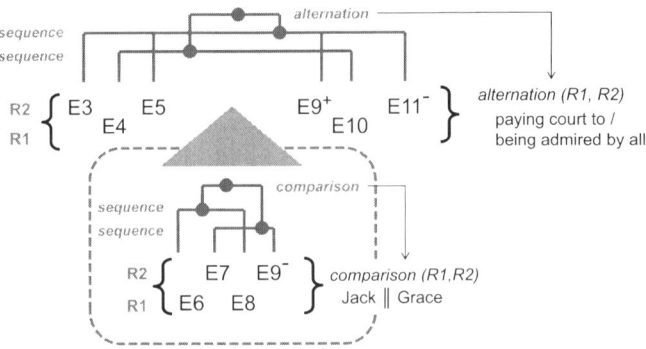

Figure 8.3   Fine-grained filmic structure of shots E3 to E11 of The Girl and her Trust *(1912)*

rightward pointing arrow then links this to the coherence-forming relation assumed and identifies once again the regions being related. In most of the diagrams given below, we will summarise alternations in these terms.

The lower part of the diagram, below the gray triangle, shows the more local establishment of a further alternation formed from two linked alternations. These build again on the two spatial regions R1 and R2 (and are therefore also subsequences of the ongoing R1-sequence and R2-sequence respectively). They are distinguished from the above alternation, however, because a quite different coherence-forming relation appears to apply. This is the comparison between Jack and Grace, indicated again in the figure by the lower rightward pointing arrow. Note that this structure corresponds only to observers who posit the second coherence-forming relation; for observers who miss this, it would be possible that the lower portion of the diagram simply collapses back into the upper sequences and the alternation formed there.

For most of our examples below, we will offer similar structural diagrams of the syntagmatic organisation formed. These will show how the discourse structure is always constructed by the recognition of basic narrative syntagmas (Definition 7.8), which are then grouped to form alternations, itineraries, etc. as required by the image data of the film at hand.

8.2   The message

The events of this next segment precipitate the story taken up in the rest of the film. After Grace has given Jack the note of the telegraph she has just received, we are presented with a very different paradigmatic classification to the surrounding temporal progression—one that is very similar to the example of an *insertion* given in Figure 6.3 above, in which a close-up view of some bank cheques to be paid showed the viewpoint of the characters reading them. The broad paradigmatic classification of such a sequence is hypotactic, embedding, diegetic, *projecting*. The only difference for the current case of the move from E11$^+$ to E12 is that we have a *non-diegetic* insert because the displayed intertitle is not part of the world depicted in the film; questions of space and time are therefore held in abeyance.

The shot E12 nevertheless displays the content of the message received in the world of the film and so is meant to be seen as a projection of the character doing the reading—an interpretation strengthened by the use of quotation marks in the intertitle, in contrast to the commentary intertitle shown in shot E2. This embedded projection can as a consequence also be assimilated within the broader unfolding segment since the two shots bracketing the insert, E11$^+$ and E13, and the insert itself together form a discourse unit for the observer. This unit is then available for the purposes of larger-scale structuring both syntagmatically and paradigmatically.

Shot E13 has a considerable amount of internal structure in its own right and could itself be broken down into several events constituting a scene. For the overall structure, however, it is useful here to consider just two specific sub-events: the first is made up of Jack's actions at least as far as handing back the note that he has read (in order to bracket the insert in E12); the second is constituted by the rest, which then in turn serves to bracket the next insert, E14. E14 shows the arrival of a train and appears without visual forewarning; it could just as easily be the beginning of a new episode in the film. It is only in the shot following, E15, which shows Jack and Grace clearly noticing a noise outside and looking out of a window, that the viewer is invited to construct a connection. Then, paradigmatically, the most likely inference is again a projection.

Branigan (1984: 118) describes the various camera positions and angles as well as the formal permutations available for such projections in considerable detail; the view of the train in E14 is then clearly not a projection in the sense of showing literally what Jack and Grace can see. The train is quite near and is shown from in front and slightly to the right of the tracks. However, the conditions for accepting a projection may well have been different in 1912 since later in the film there is an exactly parallel construction that seems only to be interpretable as a projection.[3] We will

---

[3]We see a number of points where the construction of this film differs from that typical nowadays. For example, the treatment of projection appears rather flexible. One very evident example of this is the following, consisting of shots E101, E102 and E103; here the camera angle of the projected insert in no way corresponds to Grace's point-of-view.

Precisely matching eyelines were evidently not a strong characteristic of early films.

accordingly also take the current shot E14 as showing an object to which both figures at least manifestly react giving the most likely paradigmatic classification as projection. The shot is also, by virtue of no evident visual connection in the image data, to be linked paratactically.

We noted in the previous chapter that it is often not straightforward in film to fix boundaries between segments since segments can 'pre-figure' further segments into which they lead. This is readily supported by the richness of the filmic medium—one can tell the story with certain features of the audiovisual track while other features simultaneously give additional information about what to expect. This can be seen in the present case with E14's showing of the arrival of the train.

On the one hand, this triggers Jack's and Grace's actions in space R2; on the other, it sets up a new space (which we label R4) that acts as the destination of Jack's itinerary which will follow. It is therefore *cohesively* linked with both (cf. *Further Reading*). In our analysis, however, we take the reaction shot interpretation of E14 to be paradigmatically dominant because it is *locally available* as the most likely discourse interpretation. Longer distance relationships between elements are generally to be dispreferred during discourse structure construction. The influence on subsequent interpretation is nevertheless significant since we now have an important piece of additional information about the location of the train: the train tracks are off to the right and somewhere in front of the telegraph office.

E15 is then also most usefully treated as an inner montage since, following Jack and Grace noticing the train, Jack begins a further course of action unrelated to what has been shown previously. He first puts the telegraph message in his pocket (E15$^+$), picks up a bag in the outer office (E16), leaves the building from the same door as the first man earlier, thereby explicitly introducing the new space R3 outside of the office building, walks to the right as we would expect from Jack and Grace's previous glance out of the window (E17), and finally arrives at the train (E18). Paradigmatically, we have diegetic, non-projecting, hypotactic, extending relations with elliptical forward time (since there may be small 'gaps': it is not possible to match the ends and beginnings of these shots *exactly* as would be required for strict continuity) and spatial prolongation. This fills in the previously assumed spatial construction as shown in Figure 8.4. With this assumed space available for connecting shots, we have sufficient grounds for assuming an *itinerary*, but no stronger syntagmatic classification.

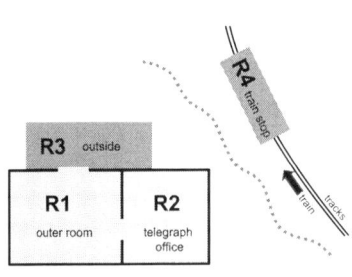

Figure 8.4

Spatial configuration established over the segment E3 to E18

To see this, we can again consider precisely the requirements given in our definitions. For both *scenes* and *sequences* we need to be able to have an explicitly depicted spatial overlap—this is simply not available here. The connection between shots is then held together by information *within* the shots: i.e., Jack as a figure continuing on a trajectory. This is again a cohesive, non-structural connection (cf. §5.5). The reoccurring cohesive element of Jack as actor gives us a paradigmatic bridge and allows us to impose a hypotactic relationship with spatial prolongation, but the disjoint backgrounds prevent this from being classified syntagmatically with our basic syntagmas. We thus link the shots of the trajectory as an itinerary, to show their clear connection, but do not have grounds for a syntagma according to the definitions provided so far.

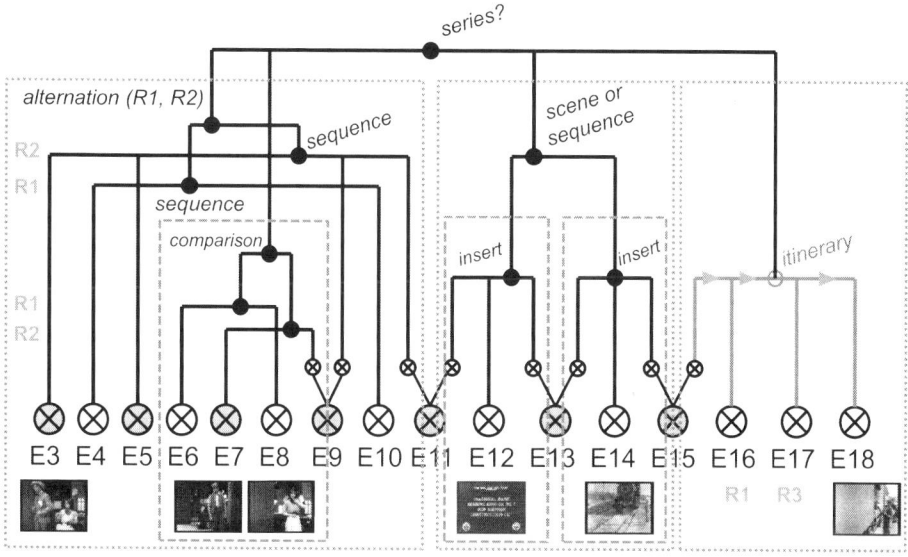

Figure 8.5   *Filmic structure of shots E3 to E18 of* The Girl and her Trust *(1912)*

With this final set of shots in place, we can bring together all of the fragments discussed up until this point; their development is summarised graphically in Figure 8.5. The larger-scale structural elements induced by the discourse organisation are now shown as dashed boxes covering the fragments of film they describe. Thus we can see the alternations discussed above holding over shots E3–E11⁻ in the left-hand side of the figure, with the comparison alternations embedded within the overall alternation between R2 and R1 as shown in more detail in Figure 8.3 above. Following this, shots E11–E15 go on to make up a scene (or sequence, if there are indeed small temporal gaps) primarily playing out within the inner telegraphic office, and shots E15–E18 remain syntagmatically as an itinerary from the office to the train as long as we have no further spatial information. We mark this latter component with a different graphical notation in order to emphasise that the grouping follows paradigmatically but only weakly syntagmatically at this point in the film.

This illustrates how the presence of paradigmatic relations provides a mechanism for building and organising hypotheses concerning filmic coherence even when syntagmatic connections remain unclear. Moreover, because spatial prolongation is hypothesised paradigmatically, this can also be treated as a *defeasibly present* 'fact' capable of being fed back into syntagmatic analysis. That is, if we are entitled to assume that the spaces are connected, then we are also entitled to assume that they form parts of a common larger space. This larger space might then be used to support a scene (or sequence); an example showing an alternation resolving in its final shot to form a scene is discussed in more detail in Schmidt (2004: 297f).

Thus, in the present case, we might assume a 'defeasibly present' syntagma, which a viewer might bear in mind while seeking coherence for the fragment as a whole. Our depiction of this set of shots in the figure using a lighter shade of gray is then also indicative of its less than definite existential status. Nevertheless, if this assumption were to hold, then we also have the working hypothesis that we have managed during film interpretation to put everything together as a *narrative series* (Definition 7.10) as indicated by the top node in the figure (and its accompanying question mark).

To summarise the results of analysis so far, then, we have shown how the shots at the beginning of the film form a tightly interconnected whole. In order to achieve this, we intended to make as little appeal as possible to extrinsic notions of cause-and-effect and common sense logic. This is because it is the discourse organisation of film that guides the operation of such logic and not, as often assumed, the other way round. The ways in which the shots build upon one another within the syntagmatic and paradigmatic axes of the semiotic mode of film thus result in a complex interlinked structure and *only on the basis of this*—including its internal organisation—can further interpretations of narrative intent be sensibly pursued.

8.3   Catching sight of the money

In the next fragments we describe, we encounter several more examples of the filmic portrayal and construction of 'perception'. This plays a central role for the next stages of the story. Key frames of the shots of the first segment to be discussed are shown in Figure 8.6; the fragment begins with the last shot of the previous section, E18, and runs to E24. We see here that the film continues with two 'tramps' arriving on the scene. Later it will transpire that they will attempt to steal the money that we have just learnt is meant to arrive with the train. The fragment shows substantially more of Griffith's filmic skill in the juggling of events, despite the fact that it is only 30 seconds long.

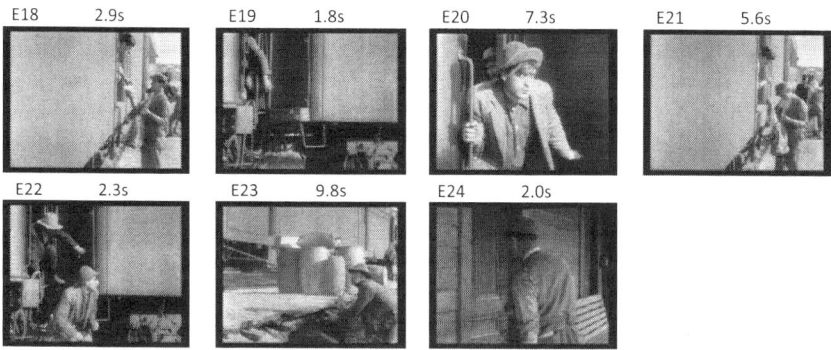

Figure 8.6   The tramps' arrival from The Girl and her Trust *(1912, E18–E24, 0:03:21–0:03:51)*

The segment E18–E21 is particularly interesting in that the first and last shots are taken from the same angle and show Jack talking with someone in the train, giving them a note and receiving something that he deposits into his bag—presumably the money. In the first shot the depicted events are, as we saw previously, the end point on his itinerary from the telegraph office to the area of the train (R4), while in E21 the events are clearly constructed as a *projection* on the part of at least one of the arriving tramps. Taking both shots from the same camera position can, of course, be motivated by the economy of not having to move the camera but, internally to the film discourse, it can also be seen as doing rather more significant work. Repetition of shots is generally strongly suggestive of potential insertion or alternation structures as we shall see.

In the immediate transition from E18 to E19, however, the most likely paradigmatic classification is of continuous time and a neighbouring (i.e., non-distant) place, since we can see the train quite clearly. This provides a little more detail concerning the space R4 around the train and so E19 appears to stand in a hypotactic extending, non-projecting relationship to the shot preceding. In the move to E20, we cut in closer to the train and so have a non-projecting, hypotactic, extending relationship with spatial *inclusion* and *narrowing*. Syntagmatically, E19 and E20 form a *scene*—since we have both a shared spatial environment and continuous time. E21 then returns to E18 as mentioned and so suggests initially that the intermediary shots might be seen paradigmatically as an insert. This would rework the previous hypotactic relationship between E18 and E19 from extending to embedding as generally occurs with the 'correction' of defeasibly asserted previous hypotheses. E20 is then, as noted, classified as a projecting shot since it provides a very plausible position from which to view E21 in the shot following. In E22, however, we return to the position established by

E19. This shows the tramps' next actions—sneaking off the train—and so could equally well suggest that it is the intermediate shots E20 and E21 that form an insert.

The situation here is therefore structurally quite complex since, at first glance, there appear to be two competing insertion structures. First, {E19, E20} may be embedded within {E18 ... E21}; and second, {E20, E21} may be embedded within {E19 ... E22}. This requires us to consider the structural and syntagmatic consequences of our choices more closely. According to the first case, we would have a structural boundary posited *between* shots E20 and E21, whereas the second insertion E20–E21, motivated by projection, would want to group these together. These alternatives and their conflict are depicted graphically in Figure 8.7.

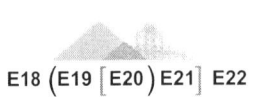

E18 $($E19 $[$E20$)$E21$]$ E22

Figure 8.7

Conflicting 'bracketing' of structure in E18–E22

Although at present we cannot rule out such 'crossing' structures within filmic discourse on theoretical or empirical grounds, their acceptance would certainly complicate the notion of discourse organisation needed and so should not be accepted without good reason.

Treatment of this case in fact provides us with an excellent example of how a more precise treatment of mutually constraining paradigmatic and syntagmatic descriptions can help rule out inappropriate analyses. It will also bring out well some of the fine-grained consequences of adopting particular filmic organisations rather than others.

In general, when we find that there are two competing—that is, in this case, overlapping—candidates for insertions within a fragment, one natural hypothesis to pursue is that there is an alternation at work. If we take as a model an alternating sequence of ABABA...shots, for example, then any collection of three consecutive shots from this sequence appears to embed the shot in the middle: i.e., either ABA or BAB. The formal resolution of the ambiguous role played by shots internal to the sequence is then to separate the sequence into two strands running in parallel. No one strand is then 'embedded' in the other (cf. also the 'fluid' sequences of Figure 6.6 above).

In the present case, this is also supported syntagmatically because the collections of shots {E18, E21, E23} and {E19, E20, E22, E23} each satisfy independently our definition of sequence (Definition 7.7).[4] This means that this fragment filmically *creates* two further 'subregions' within our previously identified space around the train and train tracks. We accordingly label the subregion constructed by the shots showing the tramps R4' and the subregion showing Jack R4''. Each of these subregions then serves as a scaffold providing for further local 'islands' of narrative interest within

---

[4]In the latter case, the sequence may also be decomposed further into two scenes: E19–E20 and E22–E23; cf. Section 7.3.2

the larger-scale development of the film. It is then interesting to see what Griffith does with these as the film unfolds.

Moving on to the definition of an alternating syntagma to see if this can apply (Definition 7.12), however, leaves us with some gaps. At present we have just considered the spatial relationships and this is not sufficient to establish a proper alternation. On the basis of the evidence so far, therefore, we would have grounds for a paradigmatic classification of external contrast plus a suggestion of mutual simultaneity supported by the apparent temporal continuity. This is the situation that would hold if shot E20 were simply to show a close-up of the tramps getting off the train. But Griffith again takes this a stage further.

Shot E20 does not just show the tramps getting off the train—instead, as we described above, we have a clear initial shot of a classical point-of-view segment establishing a paradigmatic relation of projection between shots E20 and E21. Here again, we would want to follow the discourse principle of favouring maximally *local* interpretations over assumptions of more distant dependencies; this means that the projection connection between shots E20 and E21 should be considered the strongest available since these shots are immediate neighbours. This works against placing a structural boundary between the two shots since this would do violence to the paradigmatic interpretation.

This leads to the two alternative schematic structures for this fragment shown in Figure 8.8. In the first alternative, we have the simple multitrack that would support a reading of simultaneity, but little more. In the second alternative, however, the projection relationship forces a further embedding within the sequence E19–E23. Moreover, the embedded insertion is one and the same shot that would otherwise serve as the 'middle' shot of the multitrack strand shown in the first row. This extreme cohesion can therefore be seen as tying the tracks together in a tight relationship of mutual dependency.

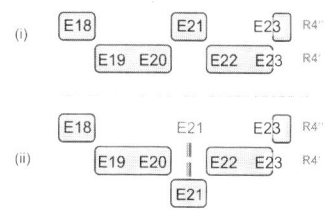

Figure 8.8
Alternate alternations for the segment E18–E23

This also leads naturally to favouring the second analysis over the first because it allows E20 and E21 to remain together structurally linked via an embedding projection. Moreover, the shots surrounding them, i.e., E19–E23, have their own independent sense of unity given by the spatially bounded movement of the tramps in region R4'. In the first analysis, the structural link between E20 and E21 is dissolved by the switching between strands in the multitrack. Considering E22 as closing off its own embedded insertion in E21 is thus clearly a better discourse interpretation. It places the insert containing the projection within a larger-scale embedding, which at that precise point in the film (i.e., during E22) is still 'open'. This larger-scale embedding is then closed when E23 expands the visible space to show us Jack in the background, starting off back the way he came, frame right.

This suggests in turn that E23 may itself in certain respect be treated as a case of inner montage: we then have $E23^-$ finishing (locally) the embedded scene centered on the tramps and $E23^+$ picking up Jack on his now completed mission of collecting the money and beginning his journey back to the telegraph office. This division is suggested in Figure 8.8 by the multiple occurrence of E23 in both strands of the multitrack. Now we can see that it is not the entire shot that occupies both strands: $E23^-$ is in the lower strand and $E23^+$ is in the higher.

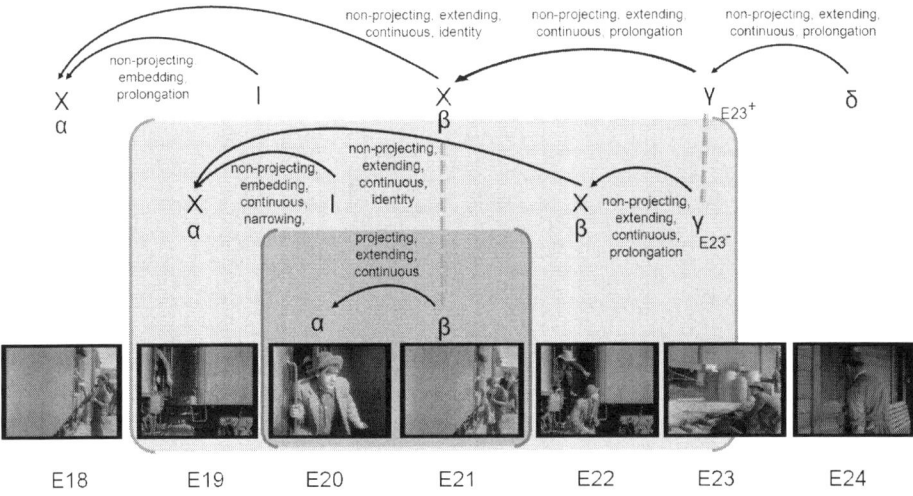

Figure 8.9   *Paradigmatic classification and broad organisation of* The Girl and her Trust *(1912, E18–E24, 0:03:21–0:03:51)*

We can now summarise graphically the *paradigmatic* organisation argued for here as shown in Figure 8.9. This makes the weaving together of structures particularly striking. First, E21 plays a double role as being both the object of perception of the shots first involving the tramps {E19, E20} and a regular continuation of the money-collection sequence begun in E18. This double role is indicated in the figure by showing shot E21 participating in two dependency chains connected by a dashed double vertical line. Second, E23 plays a similar double role; this time bringing together the dependency chain of the tramps' actions and the start of Jack's return itinerary, treated here in terms of inner montage. Shot E24 then brings us again to region R3 outside the telegraph office building, which extends the previous sequence begun as Jack left the building in shot E17.

The answer to the question of whether we have a proper alternation at work here or not is then revealed to be rather more complex than it might first have appeared. As noted above, according to our definition we need a stronger relationship to hold between the sequences realising the strands of our multitrack than a simple spatial connection. This is provided in part by our paradigmatic analysis and the construction of a projection relationship between E20 and E21: the necessary coherence-relation between the sequences is then suggested by the projection and the furtive glances the tramps give in Jack's direction throughout. This relation, i.e., 'observing/being observed by', would allow the satisfaction of all of the conditions necessary for a full-blown alternating syntagma. The subsequences involved are also locally maximal in that by the time shot E24 moves us on to region R3, there is no suggestion of the tramps continued observational presence.

Unfortunately, in another sense, this coherence-forming relation comes 'too late' according to our definition, because it is also required that a sufficient number of alternations in fact occurs: that is, we need at least three transitions between the distinct members of each pair of partition sets (Definition 7.12, Condition 5). This would only work if E23 managed to maintain both the spatial alternation and the coherence-forming relation. This is not straightforwardly the case, however, since here we see Griffith explicitly bringing the two subspaces previously opened up back together. Once this occurs, then our definitions would instead lead to the argument that the subregions R4′ and R4″ are connected and so syntagmatically E18–E23 form a scene (Definition 7.6).

We can take this as a further example of defeasible reasoning at work. Even though the viewer may be building a model of the structure of the film at this point assuming that an alternation is to be pursued, the premature collapse of the distinct spaces must cause this to be revised. This is then similar to the case discussed above for E3–E18, where an alternation was also dissolved as the spatial model constructed by the film grew.

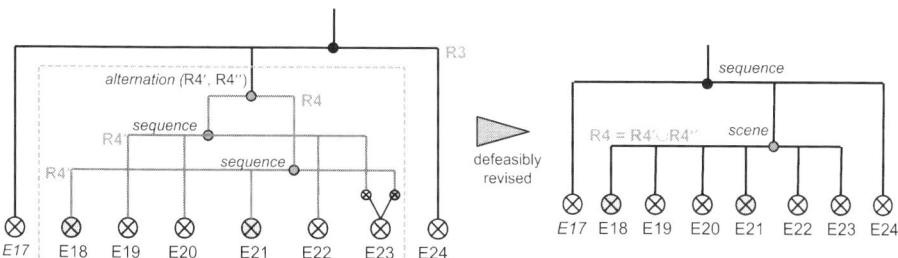

Figure 8.10   *Transitory syntagmatic organisation of* The Girl and her Trust *(1912, E18–E24, 0:03:21–0:03:51) before and after the collapse of the region R4*

The progressive development of the syntagmatic organisation is then as shown in Figure 8.10. On the left hand side, we see an illustrative defeasible hypothesis formed on the basis of an 'observing'/'being observed by'-alternation followed, on the right-hand side, by the situation that holds when the originally distinct spatial regions are unified. The former hypothesis is suggested in order to provide structural support for the ongoing paradigmatic organisation. Taken all together, therefore, the internal requirements of the syntagmatic and paradigmatic analyses show how this fragment employs a potential alternation both to advance the action and to indicate differential states of knowledge in a way supportive of heightened tension. The fragment itself also joins seamlessly at both ends with the initial shot E18 and the next to last shot E23$^+$ since all of these are explicitly located within the spatial region R4 and monochronicity holds throughout. This then again provides an overall syntagmatic unity and continuity to the fragment, binding together what has been established so far while at the same time expertly interweaving new material.

8.4   Casing the joint

In the next fragment, which again involves perception although constructed this time rather differently, the action takes a step further by showing the tramps finding out where the money is being hidden. The key frames of this fragment are shown in Figure 8.11; the fragment continues on immediately after the previous fragment discussed.

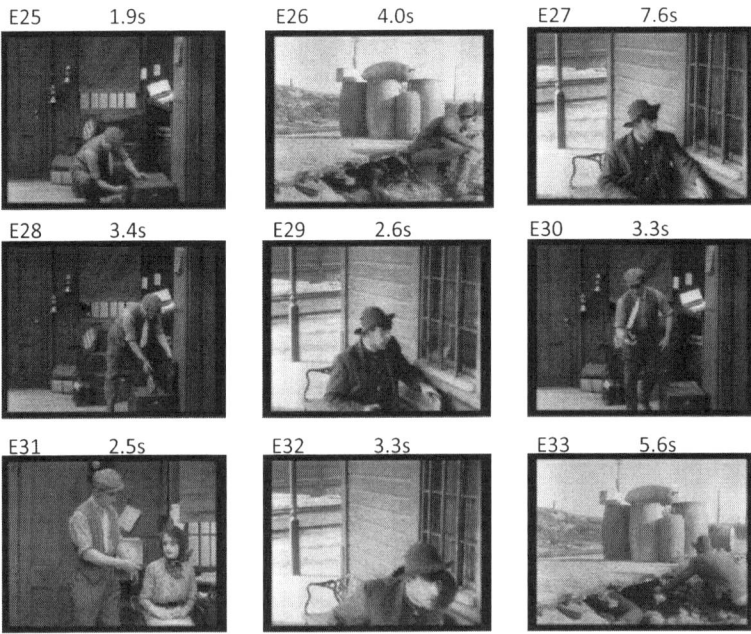

Figure 8.11   The tramps see where the money is located (The Girl and her Trust, *1912, E25–E33, 0:03:53–0:04:27*)

The first shot, E25, therefore continues Jack's return itinerary and shows him back within the outer room of the telegraph building. Here he is seen placing the bag containing the money in a trunk. This means that we can analyse this syntagmatically as picking up and extending the sequence previously established for this spatial region, R1, which was last seen as Jack was leaving the building. The next shot, E26, jumps back to the tramps' hiding place, showing one of them moving off in the direction taken by Jack in shot E24. E27 then shows that tramp sitting furtively on a short bench or chair outside of the telegraph office—thus filling in further spatial information concerning the region outside of the office building. To distinguish these components properly, we re-label the previously introduced 'outside' that Jack passed through in E17 and E24 as R3', and label the new subregion where the tramp is sitting R3".[5]

Paradigmatically, up until this point we have for the tramp the usual relations of an itinerary: no signs of projection, a hypotactic extending relationship due to the cohesive presence of the tramp, and diegetic temporal ellipsis with small gaps and spatial prolongation. Syntagmatically, however, something rather different now happens when compared to the previous fragment because we pass through spatial regions that have already been introduced. Thus, again by the definition of sequence (Definition 7.7), these shots are necessarily *added into* the sequences already established for these spatial locales. This is a consequence of the very strong position given to spatiotemporal connection in all of our definitions of narrative syntagmas. According to these, the syntagmatic classification is *always* attempting to maximise its sequences and scenes in order to provide a structural scaffold for filmic interpretation.

Within, or around, this scaffold, Griffith is then able to construct considerable narrative tension. For example, as in the previous fragment discussed, we have here cases where camera positions are first used neutrally, and then with a perceptual aspect. Thus, shots E25 and E28 both show Jack frontally in the outer room of the building; however shot E28 is framed within shots E27 and E29 showing the tramp looking in through the window (and, indeed, if one looks carefully, a hatted figure can be seen in the window in the background of shot E28—albeit in the 'wrong' corner). There is, however, no evidence of projection in these shots as there is no attempt to reproduce the line of sight of the tramp. The viewer is just 'informed' as part of the information given about this world that the tramp sees what Jack is doing. What precisely the tramp can see and what not is only represented weakly. Thus, presumably E30 is still within the scope of perception of the tramp, whereas E31, which moves back into region R2, the telegraph office proper, presumably is not. E32 and E33 then play

---

[5] Again, this spatial consideration is a *defeasible discourse hypothesis*—subsequently further supported when we 'see' the tramp from inside the building in E28.

out the itinerary of the tramp's coming in the reverse order, showing him leaving the window and rejoining his companion.

This means that structurally the filmic organisation here is in many respects similar to that used previously. Syntagmatically we have the continuation of four sequences, one each corresponding to the spatial regions R1, R4, R3 and R2 respectively. Paradigmatically, we have several paratactically related chains being established, which together lead on to the expectation of a multitracking realisation; in the current case, these cross-cut the syntagmatic sequences, providing points of narrative connection. Thus we have two chains related internally by hypotactic extension: {E25, E28, E30, E31} and {E26, E27, E29, E32, E33}; these sequences as higher-order units in their own right are related paratactically by contrast or comparison.

Considered more finely, however, the syntagmatic constraints impose a further segmentation. Analogously to the previous fragment, woven around the four contributing sequences we have here again local 'islands' of narrative interest created by alternation. In particular, there is a *2-alternating* segment (cf. Definition 7.12) built around events in region R1 and R3″ under the hypothesis of the symmetric coherence relation 'observing/being observed'. We show the corresponding syntagmatic structure in Figure 8.12. Here, as introduced in our discussion of guiding partitions above (cf. §7.5), we represent subsequences of broader sequences participating in their own local constructions by doubling up the horizontal line corresponding to the sequence to indicate just which portion of the sequence is involved.

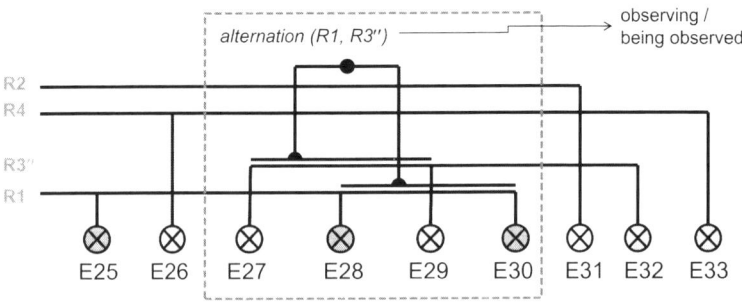

Figure 8.12   Syntagmatic organisation of The Girl and her Trust *(1912, E25–E33, 0:03:53– 0:04:27)*

The links between these sequences are constructed smoothly in the film by the hypotactically realised itineraries remarked upon above: E26–E27 moves us from region R4 to R3″, E32–E33 moves us back again, and E30– E31 takes us from R1 into R2.

8.5   Grace alone

The next fragment brings the first 'act' of the film to a close. The story has been set up—there is money to be stolen, there are tramps to steal it and, as this fragment depicts, Grace is left alone in the telegraph office with no one to help her when the tramps decide to make their move. Key frames of the fragment are shown in Figure 8.13. In the first shots, Jack attempts to have Grace take the revolver so that she can defend herself if necessary; this she refuses to do on the grounds that "Danger? Nothing ever happens here!" (intertitle in shot E36). Jack then leaves in shot E39, crossing over the train tracks (region R4, shot E40) so that the tramps can see him going on his way. Finally, in shot E42, Grace is left alone.

*Figure 8.13   Grace is left alone with the money (*The Girl and her Trust*, 1912, E34–E42, 0:04:27–0:05:32)*

Syntagmatically, this fragment continues the development of the spatial regions that we have seen before. The only new location is shot E41, which shows Jack pausing for thought at an arbitrary point on his way to a further, as yet undisclosed location, which we call R5. Within the fragment, Griffith manages to ramp up the suspense yet again. We can follow this with the paradigmatic description. First, there is a (verbal) projection between E35 and the intertitle in E36, clearly to be attributed to Grace, and a shot-internal depiction of a seeing event between the tramps and Jack in shot E40. E34–E35 are related hypotactically with continuous time showing a double itinerary for Jack and Grace moving from R2 to R1, while E38–E41 are related hypotactically as extensions following Jack on his next itinerary away from the telegraph office. There is also a further paratactic relationship of comparison or contrast between shots E41 and E42, emphasised by strong visual parallelism.

The projection from E35 to E36 would 'normally' be followed by a further variant of E35, i.e., some shot hypotactically extending E35 so that the projection is framed structurally as an insert. Instead, the film cuts back to the tramps in their hiding place near the train tracks, thereby adding a *further* 'insert' commenting ironically on Grace's confident assertion in E36. E35 and E36 need to be combined paradigmatically, as the intertitle is only present in order to make clear what Grace is saying, and so E37 actually stands within the collection of shots E34, E35(E36), E38—in much the same way as Rozier inserted the shot of Michel sitting around doing very little in the television studio just as Michel claims his importance (cf. §7.3.1, *Adieu Philippine*: Metz's Segments 3 and 4).

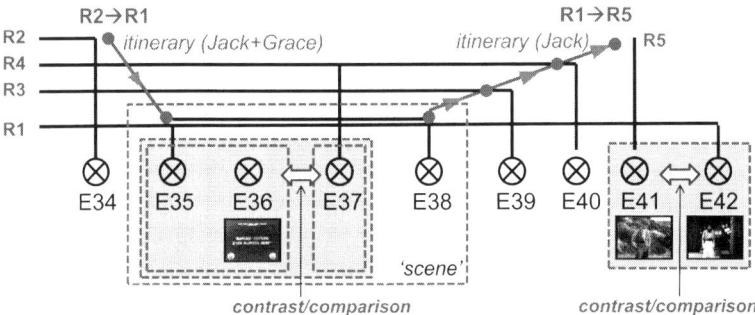

Figure 8.14   *Combined syntagmatic and paradigmatic organisation of* The Girl and her Trust
        (1912, E34–E42, 0:04:27–0:05:32)

However, since these shots clearly have no dependency relationship with the shots preceding, they can only be classified paradigmatically as standing in a paratactic relationship, thus opening up the possibility of internal contrast or comparison—i.e., contrasting Grace's statement about the lack of danger with the evident threat being constructed by the tramps. A similar paradigmatic relationship holds for E41 and E42: comparison/contrast of Jack looking preoccupied and Grace not. Finally, then, E35 with E38 comes close to meeting the syntagmatic conditions for a scene embedded within the R1-sequence more broadly, since we know paradigmatically that the interposed shots can be folded 'out of sight' as far as the narrative development is concerned and that syntagmatically they are in any case 'filtered out'. We show the corresponding combined structure in Figure 8.14, with paradigmatically-motivated organisations depicted in gray as above.

8.6 Spying on Grace

The next fragment is a variation of the previous case, again showing perception from an external, 'objective' perspective. Here we will also see that, although the treatment of spatial relationships is not entirely accurate, the narrative development underway is in any case sufficient to render this unimportant for understanding the film—the inaccuracies might well even go unnoticed. The key frames of the fragment are shown in Figure 8.15.[6]

Figure 8.15   Spying on Grace: The Girl and her Trust *(1912, E43–E54, 0:05:33–0:06:37)*

After Jack has left the office, the tramps explore their options. This is announced with the intertitle of shot E43: 'The tramps' opportunity'. This is no doubt placed at this point, as Branigan (1992: 22) suggests, to signal a new 'episode' in the story since it hardly provides new *content* information

---

[6]E45 is a shot that we take to be misplaced; a full analysis of the film suggests that immediately following shot number 95 of the film would be a more appropriate position.

of its own. However, as we shall see, its precise placement as a structural break at this point is well motivated by the structural organisation of the film, setting up several parallels (and then divergences) with respect to the preceding episode. The two final shots of the previous episode (E41 and E42) also bring about a suitable caesura in the flow of the narrative due to their status as paratactic contrast or comparisons.

The primary organisation of this present fragment was already no doubt already very familiar to audiences when the film was released, just as it is now: we are presented with a situation in which the viewer knows that Grace is being spied on but Grace does not know this—although she quickly comes to suspect the worst before having her suspicions confirmed.

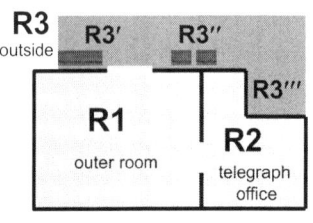

Figure 8.16

Spatial configuration established up until shot E46

In E44 the tramps leave their hiding place, arriving at the telegraph office in E46. This is a part of the outside of the building that we have not seen before; subsequently, in shot E47 from within the building where we see the silhouettes of the tramps through the window, we can further localise the tramps position as outside of the building, directly by the telegraph office. This further subregion of the 'outside' we label as R3'''. This also establishes that the building has a rather more interesting shape than was originally suggested in Figure 8.2 above; we show this in Figure 8.16.

With the tramps located outside and Grace within, the shots following can again be considered from the perspective of our definitions for alternation. This follows straightforwardly under the assumption again of a coherence relation of 'observing/being observed by' binding the partial sequences {E47, E49, E51} and {E46, E48, E50}. This is the kind of alternation described as 'change of location under continuous time' in the previous chapter, supported paradigmatically by the corresponding spatial and temporal diegetic features and the combination of (intra-sequence) hypotactic and (extra-sequence) paratactic relations. The alternation then follows from the transition pairs (R46, E47), (E48, E49), etc. as described in detail in the previous chapter. The alternation over the entire fragment E46–E51 clearly meets the requirements of Definition 7.11.

Since the paradigmatic and syntagmatic organisation here is similar to cases we have seen before, in place of the corresponding diagrams we instead make two comments.

First, differential access to knowledge such as that we see manifested in this alternation has often been singled out as a crucial aspect of narration; in Branigan's words: "Narration is the overall regulation and distribution of knowledge which determines *how* and when the spectator acquires knowledge" (Branigan, 1992: 76, original emphasis). Here we have this constructed in a particularly obvious fashion.

Second, the final shots of our extract raise a further issue: so far the temporal relationships between shots have been considered paradigmatically as either continuous or with non-measurable temporal ellipses, corresponding in our syntagmatic constraints to either MEETS or BEFORE relations. This does not work, however, for shot E52 since here we see the tramps repeating part of an action already seen beginning in shot E50: i.e., running away from the window after having been seen. The strict temporal relationship here is therefore OVERLAPS.

We might consider a variety of motivations for this, ranging from a (from today's perspective) simple continuity mistake to possibilities of providing several illustrative views of the same story event, i.e., a minimal form of descriptive syntagma, or some kind of indication of an episode boundary— i.e., E50 belongs to the spying on Grace and E52, in a sense, begins again with the episode that follows. For an understanding of the story, however, these alternatives make little difference. In any case the tramps have been seen and leave the window. Even the fact that they appear to run in a somewhat implausible direction—*away* from the building, i.e., moving to the right in Figure 8.16—appears to have been of little import. It is to be assumed, therefore, that by this point in the film Griffith has established the spatial relationships and intentions of the participants sufficiently clearly as to make closer reading unnecessary.

8.7   Grace calls for help

The fragment following that just described depicts a further episode where the tramps try and gain access to the building through the main and (apparently) only door to the building. This is the door through which we have previously seen Jack coming and going leading into region R1. The episode begins in shot E54 as just shown, in which the tramps run towards the camera and start pushing the door. In this shot they therefore continue their direction of movement in frame from E52, despite the camera position of E54 being relatively 'behind' that of E52. In E53, Grace having seen the tramps run away, herself runs into the region R1 and tries to keep the main door closed.

The shots subsequent to this show another straightforward alternation between Grace (in R1) and the tramps (in R3). We will therefore omit detailed discussion of this episode. It concludes in shot E57 with Grace giving up her stand at the door and running back into the telegraph office, just managing in shot E58 to lock the door behind her. The fragment beginning with this shot E58 is then the last fragment we analyse in detail. Key frames are shown in Figure 8.17. As we shall see, the organisation of this fragment is quite complex and will bring several more of the principles and definitions that we have introduced in previous chapters into play.

We briefly review the action as before. In E59 one of the tramps investigates the box where the money is while the other attempts to force the door to the inner office. In E60, Grace telegraphs for help, while E61 shows telegraph operators in another office that we have not seen before reading a book and not responding to the telegraph machine. In E62 Grace continues telegraphing and, in E63, the distant telegraph operators finally take note. In E64 Grace continues telegraphing but also reacts to noises from the outer office. E65 shows an intertitle: 'The tramps want the key to the express box'. In E66 the tramps stop attempting to open the locked box and investigate the outer office more closely. In E67 Grace continues telegraphing and in E68 the two distant telegraph operators read the message Grace has sent. In E69 one of the tramps leaves through the front door, the other continues trying to gain access to the inner office. In E70 Grace continues telegraphing. In E71 we then see an outside view of the tramp who had left the building cutting through a telegraph wire plainly visible running through a window to the building. In E72 Grace finishes telegraphing but, glancing forward, evidently sees the actions of the tramp outside shown in E73. In E74 she turns away from the window with a shocked expression and in E75 the distant telegraph operators finally begin to act. Taken all together, this is a complex piece of work demonstrating rather more of the sophisticated alternation that made Griffith famous.

Considered paradigmatically, we have the usual combination of paratactic and hypotactic relations that we have seen at work above. Together these form a web of connections strongly suggesting some kind of multitracking organisation. The question of precisely which tracks are formed and their precise inter-relationships is not, however, answered. For this, we must focus again on the contribution of the syntagmatic organisation and our definitions of possible syntagmas. We will show in detail how the application of our definitions again guides the construction of the individual story tracks and provides the basis for their most likely narrative interpretation.

We begin with the five consecutive shots E60–E64, in which several distinct locations are again brought together. Here we will now build in more detail of our account of 'polyspatial' organisation introduced in Section 7.4.2 of the previous chapter. Among these shots, a new spatial region is introduced into the film, that of the distant telegraph office; we label this region R6.

In the shots {E60, E62, E64} Grace telegraphs for help; this is firstly ignored in E61 and then acknowledged in E63. Visually the shots are designed so that Grace has the source of danger, the tramps, on the left of the frame and the source of possible help, the telegraph, on the right of the frame. The design of the spatial region R6 is complementary to this: here the telegraph operators are in the middle of the frame and

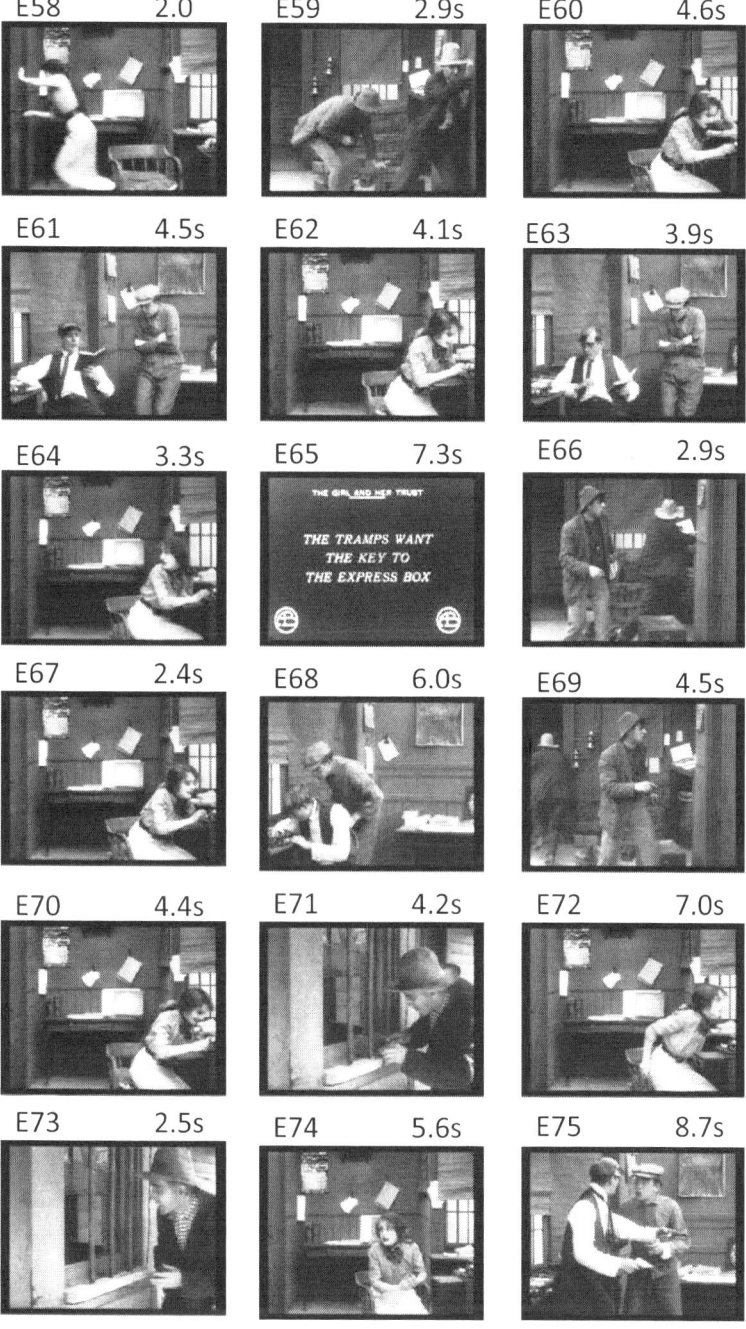

Figure 8.17   Shots E58 to E75 from The Girl and her Trust *(1912, 0:06:44–0:08:05)*

the telegraph device is on the left of the frame. This spatial organisation strongly supports the subsequent unfolding of events as we shall see below.

For the syntagmatic organisation, then, we first explore whether the segment E60–E64 conforms to the definition of being sequentially partitionable (cf. Definition 7.9) and then expand on this, attempting to apply the same definition to the entire fragment at issue.

The definition calls for a set of shots to be partitionable into at least two collections, with each partition itself being classifiable as a sequence. For E60–E64 the definition certainly applies under the assumption that we have two partitions. In fact, the first four shots here also meet the conditions of the definition. This points to a further role for the fifth shot, E64, as taking on a kind of 'bridging' function—Grace continues telegraphing *as* the danger continues to her left. This is cued well by Grace's glancing to the left at this point. This renders the next shot, the intertitle at E65, particularly relevant because it brings the danger of the tramps (and their wanting the key) explicitly into the unfolding story again. Moreover, although this could have been done purely visually with the following E66, which accordingly returns to the tramps at work on the door, it provides information that is not accessible purely from the actions depicted. In particular, the intertitle makes the *motivations* of the tramps explicit—otherwise the specific grounds that the film wishes to construct for the tramps pursuing Grace may not have been clear to an audience. Perhaps for this reason, the placement of intertitle E65 within the narrative structure of the film is by no means as structurally self evident as was the case with the previous intertitle, E43, discussed above.

Returning to the visual action, the shot following the intertitle, E66, allows a further extension of our structure for the film as found so far. In particular, it supports the amalgamation of the sequentially 2-partitionable structure holding over E60–E64 with the preceding {E58, E59} so as to bring about a sequentially *3-partitionable* segment: i.e., a segment spatially anchored in three distinct spatial regions: R1, R2 and R6. We show this in Table 8.1 using a layout table of the form that we introduced in the previous chapter—see Table 7.1 for comparison. Moreover, to aid the following discussion, we also show Grace's 'gaze' activity within the shots, indicating where her attention is directed; this is indicated by the placement of a small eye icon within the corresponding table entries.

The segment E66–E68 visualises the spatial organisation of this tri-partite spatial organisation in miniature. The threat is diegetically 'left' of Grace in the frame; the promise of rescue to the right. Grace turns in E67 away from the threat and in the direction of her rescue. The diegetic location of this rescue is depicted explicitly in E68. As a consequence, we have the following organisation of the spatial relationships involved, corresponding to the split attention that Grace exhibits throughout via her gaze direction:

$$R1 \leftarrow \; \text{👁} \; Grace \; \text{👁} \; \rightarrow R6$$

R1	R2	R6
	👁 E58	
E59		
	E60 👁	
		E61
	E62 👁	
		E63
	👁 E64 👁	
E65: 'The tramps want the key to the express box'		
E66		
	👁 E67 👁	
		E68
E69		
	E70	

Table 8.1   Shots E58–E70 from The Girl and her Trust *as an alternation layouted over three diegetic spatial regions*

It has been known for some time that gaze direction can act as an attention cueing device (Posner, 1980) and so this may well play a role here too. The organisation is repeated in shots E69–E71, although in this case it ends badly for Grace as one of the tramps cuts through the telegraph cable and thereby breaks the connection to R6. The physical breaking of the connection between Grace and the distant telegraph office is also therefore re-constructed abstractly by the deployment of space within the film.

When we consider shot E71 and ask where this is located, it turns out that we have not seen this spatial region before; we label this new portion of the outside space R3''''. Paradigmatically, this may be seen as a spatial prolongation by virtue of the hypotactic extension brought about by the cohesive effect of the same character appearing, but more than this is left unclear. Syntagmatically, however, the existence of E71 as a separate diegetic space within the film is again explicitly constructed within an alternation, in this case that holding over the four shots E70–E73; this also shows the precise spatial relationships involved nicely.

During E71 a viewer is invited to construct the conceptualisation of the spatial details as follows: the tramp outside tries to break through the window in region R3'''' to reach the telegraph office in R2 because the door between R1 and R2 was proving too difficult. But already the direction of Grace's gaze outside in shot E72 and E74 raises spatial questions. The diegetic spatial situation here is different to that constructed before since, in the previous representations of the space outside the building in E46, E48 and E50, there was no telegraph cable to cut through. This then gives us our final extension to the spatial relationships constructed by the film around the telegraph office, as shown in Figure 8.18.

R1	R2	R3''''	R6
	👁 E58		
E59			
	E60 👁		
			E61
	E62 👁		
			E63
	👁 E64 👁		
E65: 'The tramps want the key to the express box'			
E66			
	👁 E67 👁		
			E68
E69			
	E70 👁		
		E71	
	E72 👁		
		E73	
	E74		
			E75⁻

Table 8.2   Shots E58–E75 from The Girl and her Trust *as an alternation layouted over four diegetic spatial regions*

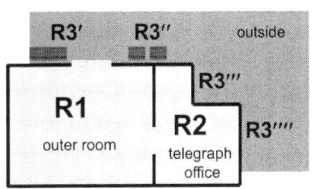

Figure 8.18

Spatial configuration established up until shot E73

This requires at least an update and, in some cases, perhaps a revision of the spatial assumptions an observer may have made up to this point in order to consistently incorporate both the actions of the tramp and the directions in which Grace directs her attention. With this in place, the tramp's breaking of the contact between Grace and the distant telegraph operators is complete: the physical cutting of the cable occurs in a diegetic space (R3'''') which is also directly 'between' Grace (R2) and R6. We now add this latest spatial information into the layout table shown in Table 8.2, extending that given above.

We summarised what happens between E58 and E74 in terms of the story above. The complexity of this constellation of events already suggests that it may be difficult to assimilate all of these shots within a single alternation. For this to work we would according to Definition 7.11 require stable symmetric coherence-assigning semantic relations to hold between each transition pair visible in the table. This is a necessary condition if the entire fragment is to be covered as a 4-partitionable spatial alternation.

Although it would be possible to conceive of an artificial construct of the form:

'informing/being informed by' or 'threatening/being threatened by'

in order to force, formally, a 4-partitionable interpretation to hold with a single relation, we must add an appeal here to some notion of 'naturalness' to rule out such arbitrary constructions. The more 'unnatural' the coherence-assigning semantic relation necessary for an alternation becomes, the more far fetched and difficult we can assume the corresponding interpretation to be *for some set of observers*. In the present case, therefore, we will assume that such a relation is not considered. The next logical option to consider is to explore whether the segment is 3-partitionable. For this to apply, it is necessary again to find a corresponding relation, i.e., a relation relating pairwise three distinct spatial regions and their events and characters. It is, as before, rather difficult to imagine what such a relation might be in the present case.

If we consider the two component relations of our proposed disjunctive relation above, then we reach safer ground. The relationship of threatening appears at first to hold across R1, R3'''' and R2. On closer consideration, however, we see that this in fact induces an aggregation of R1 and R3'''', since these spaces (containing the tramps) stand in relation to Grace in R2 but not to each other: i.e., there is no 'threatening/being threatened by' relationship to be found between R1 and R3''''. For the purposes of syntagmatic construction, therefore, we can hypothesise a binary, i.e., two-place, relation of 'threatening/being threatened by' in order to construct a 2-partitionable sequential alternation over the fragment {**E58**, E59, **E60**, **E62**, **E64**, E66, **E67**, E69, **E70**, E71, **E74**}; we use the bold/non-bold type distinction here to mark the distinct regions involved. This then meets all the requirements of the relevant definitions under the condition that R1 and R3'''' are unified. In addition, we have with the coherence-assigning relation 'informing/being informed by' a similar 2-partitionable sequential alternation holding over the fragment {**E60**, E61, **E62**, E63, **E64**, **E67**, E68, **E70**, **E72**, **E74**, E75$^-$}.

The shots shown in bold in these two alternations are shared and so constitute a fragment meeting our definition of a *guiding partition set* given in Section 7.5 above. This is a sequence that serves to bring together and coordinate two independent but simultaneous activities—we illustrated this with respect to several constructed examples in the previous chapter. This final view of this complex film fragment is then depicted in the layout table shown in Table 8.3.

Here we can see well the filmic construction of a complex constellation of diegetic spaces, which in turn supports the complex interplay of actions being played out in the fragment. The alternation of sending the telegraph message holding between spaces R2 and R6 is highlighted with a bold outline; the alternation of the attempts of the tramps between the outside of the building and R2 is shown with a gray background. Each of these alternations are then, in the terms introduced above, local islands imposing

R1 ∪ R3''''	R2	R6
	◉ E58	
E59		
	E60 ◉	
		E61
	E62 ◉	
		E63
	◉ E64 ◉	
E65: 'The tramps want the key to the express box'		
E66		
	◉ E67 ◉	
		E68
E69		
	E70 ◉	
E71		
	E72 ◉	
E73		
	E74	
		E75⁻

Table 8.3   *Shots E58–E75 from* The Girl and her Trust *as two coordinated alternations layouted over three diegetic spatial regions*

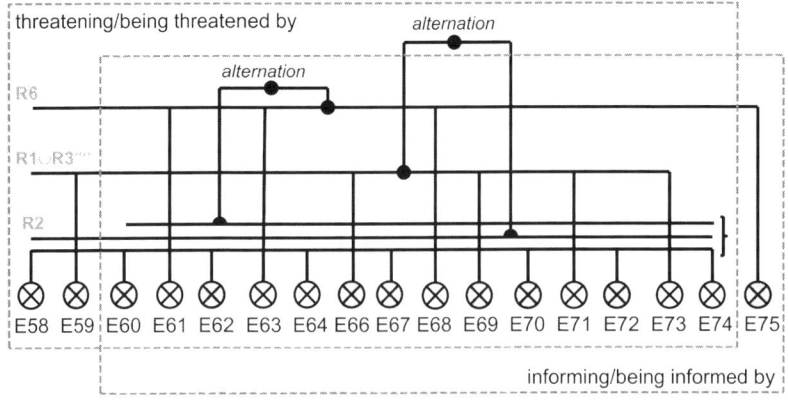

Figure 8.19   *Syntagmatic organisation of shots E58 to E75 from* The Girl and her Trust *(1912, 0:06:44–0:08:05)*

structure on the basic narrative sequences carrying the 'narrative identity' of the shots involved. Although it is here probably somewhat less easy to read due to the overlapping alternations, we also give the same information in Figure 8.19 in the graphical document tree representation that we have used above, both for completeness and for comparison across the two notations. As will be seen, the same organisational information is contained in both.

The last pair of shots E74 and E75$^-$ also round off the fragment, summarising the respective states of knowledge and situations of the participants. In E74, Grace is shown cut off from the outside world and trapped within the innermost space defined within the film, R2. In E75$^-$, however, we see that the external world knows of Grace's predicament—but the telegraph office in R6 is an unknown distance away and, presumably, not in the immediate vicinity. At this point the arc of the story therefore reaches a climax: the remainder of the film, beginning with the 'latter half' of E75, then concerns itself with the swing back towards successful closure, with Grace breaking out of her confinement and proving herself a resourceful and capable opponent (within limits) along the way.

In this last example, therefore, we have again shown with our analysis how filmic discourse organisation and its properties naturally serves to lead viewers to the narrative comprehension intended. We have seen that there is nothing much left to chance here and that the viewer does not need to employ unrestricted common-sense reasoning and sophisticated logics of belief and intentions to follow what is going on. We suggest that the bare 'facts' of what is occurring will be communicated even with a very impoverished understanding of what the tramps are about—precisely because of the discourse organisation that is mobilised.

Space precludes us taking an equally detailed view of the remainder of the film but the last segment has already shown the high point of structural organisation present. The alternations manifested so far continue to the film's end, settling down in the last fragments to the more readily recognisable chase scene already analysed in some detail by Branigan (1992: 20–31, 66–71).

8.8   Summary and Conclusions

For our final words concerning the analysis and the application of our method, we return to Branigan's discussion of the film as a useful point of contrast. Throughout his description, accurate though it may be, explanations are couched in terms of presumed *narrative schemas* and the detailed knowledge of the everyday world that they presume. This is summed up in his description of the workings of the film as follows:

> "Although *The Girl and her Trust* presents events in chronological order and inventories certain actions (e.g., eating, spying, trusting, beating, and kissing),

> we do not perceive the film as a catalogue. The reason, of course, is that the film's events are principally defined through cause and effect (event B *because of* event A; scene Y *because of* scene X)." (Branigan, 1992: 26)

Considering this position from the complementary perspective of discourse semantics serves well to illustrate exactly how the accounts differ.

Branigan, along with many other cognitively-inspired film theorists, considers the process of film interpretation to be one of recognising the actions that are playing out, their reasons and consequences. This is carried out under guidance of a narrative schema, seen as a generic organisation available for understanding narratives in terms of introducing characters and locales, complicating events, repair of the complications, reestablishing equilibrium and so on. Similar accounts of narrative organisation have been around since antiquity, popularised particularly for film by, for example, Vogler (1998). In contrast to this, however, we suggest that the reason that viewers will not see *The Girl and her Trust* simply as a catalogue of events is primarily because of its complex organisation as a filmic document. It is this that provides the necessary hooks both for a viewer to construct narrative and to be carried along *within* that narrative.

If we were to imagine an equivalent film constructed as the result of a single surveillance camera placed over the train station, the effect would be much diminished—although due to the intrinsic 'human interest' of the events depicted, there would still, arguably, be an engaging story at hand. However, the kind of filmic organisation employed by Griffith raises the stakes considerably. Branigan refers to this phenomenon indirectly in terms of the sharing and withholding of knowledge, which is a major function of narrative organisation, but does not place this on the more general foundation of the filmic discourse organisation by which this and many other filmic effects are regularly achieved.

The lack of an account of filmic discourse requires Branigan to look to other potential sources of comprehension. For example:

> "Evaluating relevant contexts in which to evaluate causation is partly a matter of *segmentation*: how is something to be divided into parts that can be seen to interact? To anticipate my answer, I will state that an individual segments an event according to an explicit, or implicit, theory (or theories) of experience." (Branigan, 1992: 28, original emphasis)

While this is true (cf. Zacks and Tversky, 2001; Zacks et al., 2009), it tells us little about the processes at work with *filmic* segmentation of the kind defined here. Indeed, as we have now seen in the fine-grained analysis above, much of the segmentation operating in this film has little to do with how our understanding of the world operates. Such an understanding in no way motivates the very many cuts and individual shots that *pull apart* the, otherwise rather simple, actions being depicted. Branigan sees this aspect of the film as a 'psychological component', which "cannot be defined in strictly material or formal terms" (Branigan, 1992: 29), but this does not do justice at all to just how precisely Griffith's filmic organisation is constructed to work on the viewer.

Branigan proposes that the knowledge of events and their interrelationships guides the search for connections between segments and our account of discourse semantics in Chapter 2 similarly made the point that access to 'contextual knowledge' is critical. We also go further, however, and suggest that it is the filmic discourse organisation that (i) *instructs* viewers concerning which segments are to be created and (ii) strongly *signals* how they are to be brought into relationships with one another. This position is then perhaps closer to observations made by both Elsaesser (1990) and Gunning (1993) concerning the way in which cross-cutting and segmentation open up the door in Griffith's films to almost unlimited diversification and multiplication of narrative strands (see *Further Reading*).

Here, although aspects of knowledge both of the world and of discourse naturally play a role in the understanding of film, it is the specific document discourse semantics that organises access to that knowledge as required by the 'text'—in other words, discourse semantics needs to be done prior to referring to background knowledge in order that access to background knowledge be appropriately guided. The organisation of the filmic document that we have set out here then reveals precisely the segmentation that is available for further interpretation by a viewer, which can be carried out with quite diverse degrees of background knowledge of the culture and of the goals and intents of the characters depicted.

Such variation in background knowledge may result in weakened comprehension of just why characters are doing what they are doing or why events are being presented by the film as significant. As we have emphasised throughout, we consider the observer model holding during the analysis of any particular text to play an essential part. This observer model must be made explicit in order that the sharing out of roles between text and observer is kept under control. Nevertheless, within the semiotic mode of film as we have elaborated it in this book, the segmentation at issue and *its* claims of relative import for events establishes a solid and necessary basis for any such subsequent interpretation.

To conclude the discussion, it is worthwhile considering briefly just what the discourse organisation we have derived in this chapter achieves from a broader formal perspective. Metaphorically speaking, the collection of shots given by any layouted cinematographic document is similar to a deck of playing cards as dealt for some game. Our paradigmatic relations are then used to determine local groupings (such as pairs, three-of-a-kind, flush, etc. as follow from the rules of the particular game being played), while the syntagmatic document analysis makes explicit just what kind of cards are available for play at all (such as hearts, diamonds, clubs and spades).

In *The Girl and her Trust*, then, there are 140 'cards' (i.e., shots) in total. These cards come in four different 'phenotypes': (1) an intertitle showing the title of the film as a whole, (2) a closing intertitle showing the Biograph logo, (3) intertitles showing text insertions (which themselves divide into subtypes according to whether the text is 'quoted' or not), and (4) the shots depicting the perceptually-real moving visual material of the film. Types (1) and (2) each occur only once, at the beginning (E1) and end (E140) of the film respectively. Shots of type (3) occur nine times (in shots E2, E12, E36, E43, E65, E78, E94, E97 and E106). The remaining 129 cards are of type (4). These are distributed across seven distinct diegetic spatial locales, of which we have handled five in detail (R1–R5) and touched on a sixth (R6).

This total of 140 shots could in theory be layouted in 140! (i.e., $140 \times 139 \times 138 \times \ldots \times 2 \times 1$) different ways. This total is reduced somewhat by virtue of the fact that two are fixed in position (E1 and E140); the number of possible layouts is therefore reduced by 140×139, i.e., by almost 20,000. The remaining possible layouts give us 138! potential *The Girl and her Trust* films—i.e., the cards could have been dealt in 138! different ways. Our analysis in the present chapter has been concerned with only a subset of this, the first 75 shots. This means that, excluding the initial intertitle as before, we have provided a *syntagmatic* analysis of the first 74! of the 138! films possible in total. This space of analysis therefore still includes well over 10^{100} possible 'films'—that is, more than 10^{100} different ways of 'dealing the cards'.

These possibilities are not all equally likely, of course, and particularly the principles of *paradigmatic* organisation then impose considerable additional order. Following the definitions we have given in previous chapters, the syntagmatic organisation groups the shots according to basic spatiotemporal properties, fixing the six diegetic locales R1–R6 we have used above. The temporal component of the definitions then provides a means of imposing sequential order on the corresponding shots. Then, on the basis of this, the paradigmatic organisation provides for distinct ways of 'mixing' these sequences together, each bringing with it rather different discourse implications. Particularly in cases where the simplest progression of consecutive time and contiguous space is not followed, we find semantic consequences triggered that are central to the functioning of the narrative.

Each syntagma then presents a unit that may be placed in a relationship with some 'event', or part of an event, that is being depicted within the audiovisual track. In a film such as Griffith's, much of the interest in the events that ensues can be attributed to the way in which events are not allowed to play out in their entirety but are fragmented and re-combined, interweaving in a constant back and forth of mutually conditioning circumstances.

For ease of reference, we now summarise all of the combined syntagmatic and paradigmatic analysis discussed in this chapter in the overview graphic in Figure 8.20. This diagram shows very clearly how collections of shots are combined in order to carry narrative concerns such as progression and simultaneity. Down the left-hand side of the figure we see the syntagmatic groupings as we have discussed them above, including alternations, subsequences and itineraries. For alternations we also show the spatial regions that are involved and the coherence-relation that is assumed for binding the shots together. The rest of the figure shows the individual shots concerned. Although these are of necessity shown only in thumbnail form, they all occur in the tables we have used above when discussing the analyses in detail and so can be referred to there. Here, within each alternation, we also suggest the allocation of shots to spatial regions by offsetting shots spatially on the page. The particular locations used can then be read off from the alternation information on the left of the figure.

We can see from this overview how the basic narrative sequences established syntagmatically serve to set out a frame, or scaffold, across which paradigmatically motivated inter-relationships can be defeasibly assumed. These, together with further syntagmatic constraints concerning alternation and other higher-order syntagmas, impose segmentations on and across the sequences involved. Our analysis therefore characterises quite precisely just how complex filmic organisation emerges from the interplay of syntagmatic and paradigmatic constraints, which has been our primary intention throughout.

Further Reading

The film *The Girl and her Trust* (1912) can be found on DVD in collections such as *D.W. Griffith: Years of Discovery 1909-1913* (2002) and *Landmarks of Early Film, Volume 1* (1997), both from Image Entertainment, as well as on-line, supported by the non-profit Internet Archive and under the Creative Commons Licence 'CC0 1.0 Universal', at http://www.archive.org/details/TheGirlAndHerTrust.

For more on the **influence of D.W. Griffith** on the development of the resources of filmic discourse, see Wees (1973), Wulff (1992), Gunning (1993). For a sustained critique of earlier tendencies to attribute substantial innovation to Griffith, however, see Salt (1976, 1990). For more proposals and discussions of the development of the filmic meaning potential of **early films**, see: Fell (1983), Gaudreault (1988, 1990), Burch (1990), Elsaesser (1990), Doane (2002) and Popple and Kember (2004).

Finally, as noted in both Chapters 6 and 7, further discussion of the **paradigmatic and syntagmatic** modes of analysis we have developed here can be found in Bateman (2007) for the paradigmatic and in Schmidt and Strauch (2002), Schmidt (2004) and Schmidt (2008) for the syntagmatic respectively.

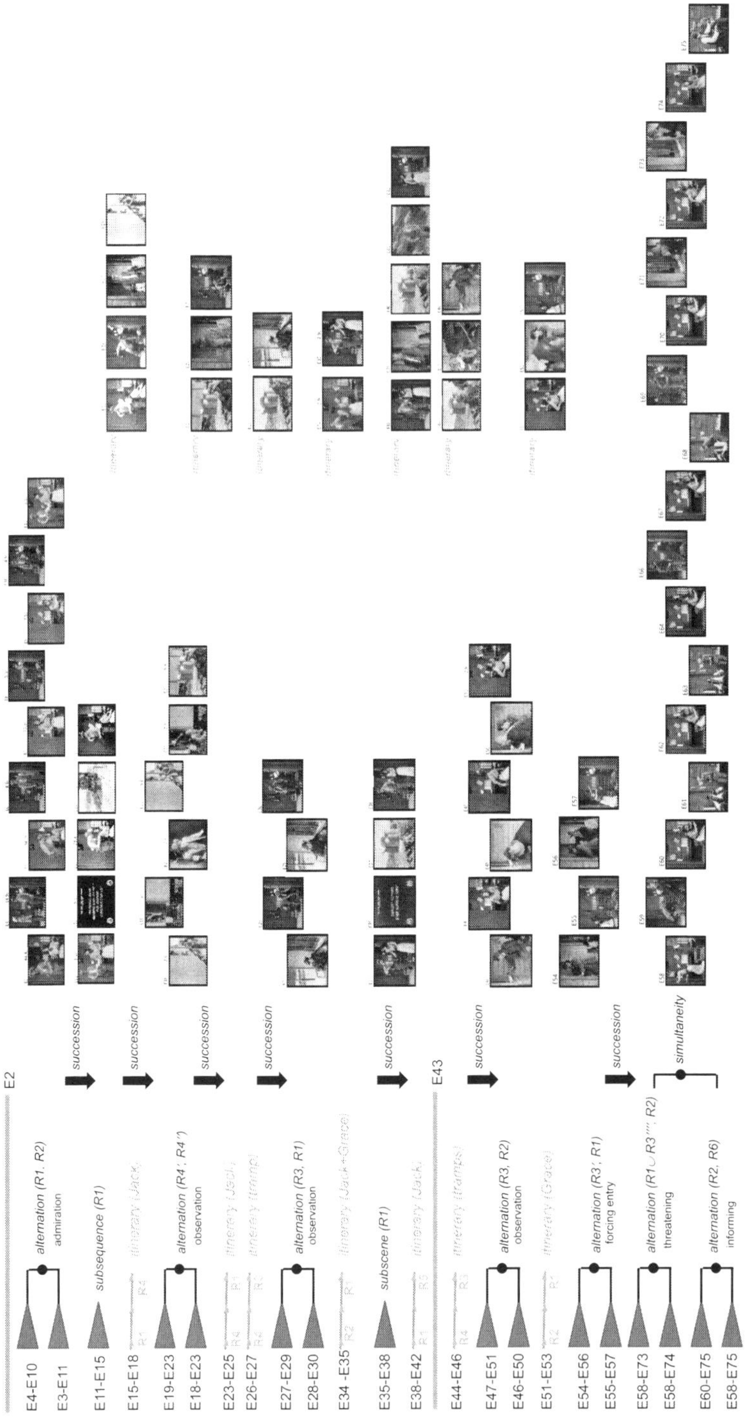

Figure 8.20   Overview of the syntagmatic organisation of shots E3 to E75 from The Girl and her Trust *(1912)*

9 Conclusions and outlook

"Theories thus become instruments, not answers to enigmas, in which we can rest." (James, 2009[1907]: 25)

There can be little doubt that film nowadays forms one, if not the, major transmitter and reinforcer of social values and positions of all kinds and on all sorts of issues. It is therefore more than legitimate to attempt to unravel the workings of film in this regard. Approaches targeting the broader social effects of film generally divide into two methodological areas: first, approaches with a focus on quantitative exploration of media reception and contexts of consumption and production; second, approaches involving discursive interpretation—'discursive', as we set out in Chapter 1, not in the sense of relying on a theoretical understanding of discourse but in the sense of being argued discursively, as an informal style of discussion drawing on a range of interpretation schemes inherited from literature, psychoanalysis, philosophy and so on (cf. our map of the territory in Figure 1.5). Somewhat between the two we can also situate *cultural studies*, which can be pursued both qualitatively and quantitatively (e.g., Berger, 2000; Hammer and Kellner, 2009).

Analyses of all these kinds vary considerably with respect to the attention given to fine-grained detail. Typically there is just too much going on within any literary work, or any film, to permit fine-grained detail to play a central role. Quantitative approaches, therefore, tend to focus less on work-internal organisational aspects, while the methods generally applied in literary-style analyses are of necessity highly selective. Nevertheless, for research where the specific contribution of individual works is in the foreground, the discursive analyses of text/film naturally quickly came to dominate.

But the methods available here have significant limits. Even though many important aspects of a work can be revealed in this way, much is left to the insightfulness of the analyst. The argumentative style is one of first forming hypotheses on the basis of the work as a whole and one's understanding of that work's placement historically and within the work of the author, and then finding support for those hypotheses within the text. We saw a detailed argument of this kind in our discussion of *The Lady from Shanghai* (1947) in Chapter 2. The *partiality* of the selection of 'evidence' within such accounts then exerts a considerable influence on the results (cf. the useful discussion of just this effect by Zöllner, 1989).

This partiality is acerbated whenever the intention is less to explore an artefact 'in its own terms' and more to apply a theoretical framework, a 'style of reading'. This is probably the main reason why this kind of approach to film is criticised in particularly uncompromising terms by David Bordwell, the originator of Neoformalism and *cognitive film theory* (Bordwell, 2009). As he writes:

> "Most theories on offer in film studies ... are not hypothesis driven. They are simply bodies of doctrine (usually not as complex as their baroque presentations make them appear) concerning how society works (usually to the misery of its members) or how the mind works (usually to the unhappiness of its owner). Most of these theories have slender empirical support, but they are immune to testing or refutation because they tend to be vague, equivocal, truistic, or all three at once. They are incorrigible." (Bordwell, 2005: p266)

Incorrigibility and the lack of a way of *testing* hypotheses made concerning films is then the fundamental problem that more empirically-based approaches see themselves as attempting to meet. By restricting opportunities for arbitrary analytic decisions, a close and well specified binding between filmic phenomena and more abstract patterns of meaning defined over those phenomena can be sought. This is our approach to how films mean—and this, of course, leads to substantial challenges of its own.

9.1 Towards empirical investigations of theories of film

A core problem for systematic film analysis and interpretation is still the sheer complexity of the medium. This presents extreme difficulties for the development of reliable schemes of technical description. These difficulties are not in general due to problems of physical measurement or of ascertaining just what is present in the filmic audiovisual material—it is, for example, perfectly possible to measure camera angles more or less precisely, to recognize characters, to extract gaze vectors, to measure brightness and colour distributions, to state how characters are positioned and move with respect to objects and other characters, and so on. The problem is rather one of knowing *which* out of this myriad of variables are going to be significant for an analysis and which not. Carrying out an analysis using these technical details is still today too effort intensive to be considered practical for anything more than very specific and focused analysis of relatively short film sequences.

The current state of the art therefore exhibits a state of affairs in which the possibility of achieving results concerning the social and historical significance of films appears in almost inverse proportion to the level of detail of the analysis. The more fine-grained and detailed an analysis becomes, the harder it is to make contact with broader issues of social significance. Just because one film appears to employ a certain kind of organisation, it is difficult, if not impossible, to scale these results up to general statements of social effectiveness or impact. There is then, as we concluded in Chapter 1, a difficult to reconcile gap between fine-grained analytic approaches on the one hand and approaches of broader social patterns on the other.

We suggested in Chapter 1 that a more up to date view of semiosis and the practice of textual signification might offer ways of overcoming this divide. Within film theory, however, responses to a reconsideration of semiotics are often rather negative. As we have seen, the path that led to this development is an interesting one to follow. Although several researchers from the 1970s and 1980s—such as Raymond Bellour, Thierry Kuntzel, Stephen Heath—produced challenging 'textual' analyses that have had lasting effects on the theory and practice of film analysis, they were already treading on very thin ice. In essence, film was treated as text but it was by no means well understood just what 'text' was, what properties and mechanisms it exhibits, and what descriptive apparatus might be required to deal with it.

As a consequence, the understanding of 'text' incorporated within discursive approaches to film has ended up being rather a simple one, with its own array of problems and inaccuracies; many of these were discussed in detail in Chapter 2. This simple view also 'naturalised' an extended notion of text with respect to film that has since become something of a frozen metaphor: it is seen to have done its work and is now just one of the approaches developed. For some tasks it is considered to add something still; for others, it is treated as a distraction from the real questions of how films function and the search for insightful approaches has moved on.

Against this backdrop, it is telling just how easily a proper engagement with textuality now falls between the cracks—it is so close as to have become invisible. Consider the following recent description of how film works on its recipients taken from an introductory film studies text. Faced with the usual post-structural conundrum of allowing the reader/viewer into the creation of a work and the prospect of as many 'readings' as there are readers, Patrick Phillips writes:

> "With mainstream commercial cinema, three factors work against this diversity of response. First, the audience will have been attracted to the film for broadly similar reasons to do with narrative and genre and star expectations—they will already be in some ways a collective defined by the 'promise' of the film. Second, the film most usually reflects ideological values that are generally accepted as 'common sense' by the majority of the audience. Within a given society people share a very similar constructed sense of some reality, which is sometimes described as a shared social imaginary. Third, the operations of the film will tend towards triggering a processing system that is common to all members of the audience—whether we call this the operation of cognitive processing or the sensory motor mechanism." (Phillips, 2007: 160)

The closest we come to what is actually up for analysis here, the film, is only present, and even then only indirectly, in the third factor: common interpretations are seen to result because the perceptual processing systems of humans are similar. A given film will then trigger that processing system in a similar way for all viewers, and the audience shares genre expectations and ideology.

Within such views, text, i.e., the nature of film as discourse shaping and pre-figuring its own interpretations, has become as good as invisible. Just precisely what is triggered for the 'processing system' and how is assumed as a given rather than, as is necessary, being focused on as a central issue for how films mean. This then leaves inquiries with few reliable methods that can be learned, applied and further extended in the analysis of films.

Symptomatic of this is the overwhelming tendency for introductions to film studies to include a chapter or two (at most) on 'technical' features of film, sometimes described equivalently as 'film language'—set, props, lighting, sound, music, framing, camera movement, editing, etc.—and then to proceed directly to discussion of interpretation, where technical details may be invoked at will in order to *describe* particular aspects of some film but otherwise serve no reliable function.

9.2   Textual logic for multimodal documents

In the meantime, the understanding achieved within linguistics of what it is to be a 'text' has moved on. As set out at length in Chapter 2, the current view of discourse and the functioning of text bears little resemblance to what was on the table when interactions with film studies began. These decisive changes and their implications for the investigation of film have so far found little attention in studies of film and media. Suggestions that textuality should be taken up again are met either with incomprehension on the basis that this is considered already to be done, or with suspicion on the basis that semiotics restricts itself to the Lacan-influenced psychosemiotics of latter Metz or, equally damaging, that such a move makes it impossible to recover *recipient* diversity—if abstract patterns of interpretation follow too closely from the data, then a too simple, traditional account of text appears naturally to marginalise actual recipients and their varied responses.

To work against this state of affairs, we consider a reorientation in film studies to the considerably more refined accounts now available of the phenomenon of textuality an urgent task. Accounts of textuality offer substantial gains for approaching complex semiotic systems such as film—particularly with respect to the promise such accounts bring for combining fine-grained analysis and more abstract social interpretations in a far more systematic fashion than has been achieved previously.

In many respects, this can also be seen as a revitalisation of some quite traditional strands of research that eventually foundered as the limits of the earlier understanding of texts were reached. Jean Mitry, for example, was already much further along in his version of how film works than some current 'text-blind' views; as Dudley Andrew summarises Mitry's position:

> "The cinema as it has existed can best be understood and criticised by an analysis of three levels of signification which should be familiar to us: the realism of the image, the shaping role of narrative, and the higher connotations of a film." (Dudley Andrew, 1976: 231/2)

The higher connotations correspond to ideology and social value as before and the first area activates notions of perception. But the second area replaces often (in non-psychological work) only amorphously specified 'cognitive operations' with an explicitly discoursal phenomenon: 'narrative'. Narrative was taken at that time because of its status as one of the few developed notions of larger-scale textual organisation available. Its function, however, was always essentially textual: it provides an integrating level of organisation that unified the deployment of filmic resources within shots, across shots and over entire films in the service of broader socio-functional communicative (i.e., textual) goals.

We explained in Chapter 2 how narrative is just one manifestation of the more general semiotic phenomenon of textuality, albeit a very significant one for many cultural practices. Shifting attention from narrative as a particular form of textuality to the general notion of textuality itself as a broad principle of discourse semantics reoccurring across semiotic modes then gives us precisely the robust semiotic foundation necessary for approaching the specifics of film. In Chapter 1 we started on this development by drawing attention to a proposed *textual logic* for film—i.e., principles of organisation that are oriented primarily to the structured unfolding of a film as an intendedly interpretable artefact. We contrasted this with the more familiar 'ideational'—i.e., plot, time, space and causality—and 'interpersonal'—i.e., emotion and evaluative—aspects of film, arguing the textual contribution to be crucial for binding the other contributions together.

This focus on fine-grained technical details and formal devices in films as carriers of essentially textual import is not, of course, without its own problems. It is here that we consider it particularly important to develop sufficiently powerful methodological and theoretical frameworks. This cannot be done, however, looking back to older accounts of semiotics or text linguistics. There is little to salvage there for building coherent views of complex multimodal semiotic artefacts such as film. We need instead to move on to sufficiently well developed views of multimodal semiotic artefacts that are open to both cognitive and socio-cultural interpretative concerns.

Chapter 2 accordingly explained the position of textuality within one current socio-semiotic account of language, and Chapter 3 took this as a foothold for constructing a model of semiotic systems that is inherently multimodal. Running through both chapters, we also began importing constructs from document theory in order to arrive at a far more detailed account of the materiality of film and its basic principles of organisation. This allowed us in Chapter 4 to return to the *grande syntagmatique* of Christian Metz and to start re-constructing the model in the light of the advances made since that time in multimodal document-based textuality.

In Chapter 5 we then took this further, spreading the influence of textuality and discourse semantics over further semiotic levels of abstraction. Figure 5.10 showed the relationship we assume between dramaturgically-relevant unities of time, space and action and visual elements expressed in the technical features of film. This effectively brings out more of the particularly narrative concerns that can be described and the supporting foundational mechanisms of document-based textuality as such.

Many further interesting connections remain to be explored here—as in, for example, considerations of the relations between film content and form or between style and plot (cf. Bordwell 1985; Thompson 1986 and, for example, further discussion from a narratological viewpoint in Verstraten 2009: 21–30). The notion of textual logic, of *textuality*, seeks to bring much that has in other approaches been relegated to questions of style and formal 'excess' back into the fold of systematic treatment. From this perspective, a traditional one within the socio-functional perspective we adopt, 'style is functional' (cf. Kress, 1988)—but that function is generally *textual* and not representational.

We have argued that appropriate solutions to the problem of explaining filmic meaning must now be pursued within frameworks that commit to rather more analytic precision than is commonly assumed in film studies. That is, while it is perfectly possible and useful to explore discursively how particular films activate particular kinds of meanings or support particular kinds of interpretations, we believe that explaining the nuts and bolts of filmic meaning-making mechanisms in general needs to go further. And, for this, in Chapters 6 and 7, we defined an elaborated view of the paradigmatic and syntagmatic axes of one basic semiotic mode of film: this account taken as a whole fully integrates our extended approaches drawn from the growing field of 'multimodal linguistics' and modern approaches to multimodal documents.

We consider this linguistically inspired view of semiotics as articulated in these chapters an essential instrument for carrying out the kind of detailed descriptions of filmic artefacts necessary for supporting all manner of subsequent analyses—cognitive and socio-cultural analyses included. Without this level of detail, hypotheses as necessary for psychological investigation are unnecessarily weakened; at the same time, for interpretative, hermeneutic analysis, it is *equally* important that the basis for discussion is made as secure as possible—even when hypotheses are probed by example, the treatment of those examples needs to be as rich as the material warrants, and for film this has not been developed nearly far enough. Prejudices exist on both sides of this divide—the 'scientific' approach has rejected the value of semiotic accounts based on somewhat out-dated views of semiotics; the 'literary' approach has rejected the value of detailed linguistically-inspired decomposition of the documents under study due to lack of reliably usable frameworks. It is in both cases time to move on.

Once we take this step, it becomes possible to reconsider a detailed semiotically-inflected account of the semiotic modes of film. The result is then a fine-grained framework capable of imposing considerable 'textual' constraint on film interpretation. Particularly in our detailed example in Chapter 8, we have seen how it is that, on the basis of 'incoming' shot-to-shot relations, it is possible to construct higher-order structures in a natural way following from an empirically-grounded treatment of the fragments a viewer encounters. And, from these, it is also natural for narrative organisation to emerge given the organisational requirements of the semiotic mode captured in our definitions.

We see this process as operating in a similar fashion across all films. As new shots are encountered, paradigmatic classifications must be sought to relate them to what has occurred. These classifications suggest syntagmatic contributions and these contributions are then themselves subjected to the constraints and definitions of the syntagmatic axis. Satisfying the constraints in turn may lead to the construction of 'higher order' narrative structures which, when successful, serve to bind the elements of a film together into a coherent whole.

Our goal in this book has therefore been to explore the extent to which we can provide a framework that makes visible the more or less immediate *filmic* contributions of a film's organisation to its subsequent interpretations. This is intended as a basic level of filmic organisation that provides a foundation for driving hypothesis formation and understanding. In this sense, then, we have attempted to explain 'how' films mean, for without this level of organisation, a component essential for understanding filmic meanings is surely missing.

We can in conclusion also relate this to comments recently made by David Bordwell in the online essay we quoted from at the beginning of the book. In a critical re-consideration of the account of filmic interpretation presented in Bordwell (1985), he accepts that, in contrast to the earlier position, there is now little evidence that film viewers construct the *fabula*— "the chronological-causal string of events" of an ideational reading—as the actual cognitive memory structures of what they perceive. He concludes:

> "I think that [*Narration in the fiction film* (Bordwell, 1985)] made the valid point that our understanding of narrative is often inferential, and we do flesh out what we're given. But I now think that the inference-making takes place in a very narrow window of time, and it leaves few tangible traces. What is built up in memory as we move through a film is something more approximate, more idiosyncratic, more distorted by strong moments, and more subject to error than the *fabula* that the analyst can draw up." (Bordwell, 2011)

There are many suggestive connections to follow up here.

We explained in Chapter 2 just how the discourse semantics of a semiotic mode takes on the role of guiding inference, of channelling access to contextual and other background knowledge during interpretation. This is also seen as occurring in real-time, as each new discourse element to interpret is encountered—we therefore also have here a necessarily short time-window within which the paradigmatic axis must do its work. We have then concrete hypotheses concerning just what kind of inferences are triggered at each point in the film and why: this will need extensive empirical investigation to know to what extent our account can be maintained.

Some of what stays in memory will no doubt be subject to filmic effects and impact; but *in addition* there will also be the stabilised result of syntagmatic document interpretation. Precisely as we showed in the previous chapter, during the shot-by-shot uptake of film, there may be substantial but transient complex paradigmatic relationships hypothesised which then, as the constraints combine and cohere, collapse into simpler organisations of time and space (cf. Figure 8.10). Our account of film must take both aspects into account. It is to be expected that such transient phenomena will leave measurable traces on film reception as they unfold but, within the current state of the art, such temporally fine-grained recipient studies have barely been performed. This then also represents an exciting area for future research and for more interaction across rather different approaches to film.

Certainly not everyone interested in understanding film will approve of the path we have taken. The kind of argumentation we provide and the details of the framework we develop are avowedly 'formal'. Following the approach we present requires that the reader takes careful note of the definitions we provide in order to apply these as closely as possible to any film material analysed. To the extent that this proves difficult or impossible, our account may well need extension or revision. We see this as one of the most important motivations for adopting this kind of analytic approach at all—by examining just where our definitions fail to fit, we consider research more likely to be able to make improvements, progressively developing a more robust analytic framework for taking our understanding of film further.

Appendix A
Formal definitions used in the book

In this appendix we gather together all the relevant definitions given in the book; their numbering reflects their order of introduction and is the same as used throughout the rest of the book. The first number indicates the chapter, the second number the order of definitions within that chapter. We assume throughout a notion of document as developed discursively in Chapter 2, but omit here a formal definition because there are various positions that could be taken. For those familiar with document modelling within description languages such as XML, replacing the 'text nodes' used there with 'film shots' provides a reasonable analogy for our approach.

Definition 2.1 *A document is termed* **cinematographic** *if,*

1. *each basic document logical object can be assigned to at least one audiovisual content portion of the document,*
2. *a layouting process exists which, for each basic logical object, generates a basic layout object for at least one of the audiovisual content portions associated with that logical object,*
3. *the document is* linearly layoutable *with this layouting process, i.e., the set of content portions can be assigned to a set of basic layout objects that are totally ordered (spatially and/or temporally) by the layouting process.*

Comment: A cinematic document provides the document-theoretic basis for producing filmic meanings. When not stated otherwise, content portions can be taken to be shots.

Definition 5.1 *A document is termed* **structured** *when its logical structure contains at least two descendents (not necessarily immediate) of the document logical root.*

Definition 7.1 *A* **segment** *in a cinematographic document is a non-empty ordered set selected from all of the temporally ordered shots produced from a given layouting process.*

Comment: Throughout the book we use segmental partitions of the set of shots of a cinematographic document, assuming that we have exactly one shot in each layout object. A segmentation of a cinematographic document (or a part of it) is a partition if the set-theoretic union of all segments of the segmentation covers all shots and if there is no shot in two segments.

Definition 7.2 *A given shot in a cinematographic document is a* **fusion** *for some layouting process and some given set of observers, when:*

1. *two segments both containing the given shot exist that can be classified as representing distinct events by all observers, and*
2. *the given shot is the sole intersection of the sets of shots in these segments for the given layouting process.*

Comment: If a cinematographic document for a layout includes a fusion, then it is not partitioned with respect to this layout for a given set of observers. To ensure a complete syntagmatic classification of a document we often treat such situations formally as involving two virtually doubled shots as described in more detail in Section 7.1.

Definition 7.3 *A* **syntagma** *classifies such partial trees of the logical structure of a document which contain at least one composite logical object and which a layouting process renders in at least one segment.*

Definition 7.4 *A sub-tree of the logical structure of a document is* **chronological** *for some set of observers when the associated set of content portions can be assigned diegetic times which can all be related pairwise according to a temporal relation taken from* BEFORE, MEETS, OVERLAPS, DURING, STARTS, FINISHES, EQUAL *and their inverses.*

Comment: A document with a single shot is chronological so long as the associated layouted content portions are assigned a common diegetic time.

Definition 7.5 *A sub-tree of the logical structure of a document is* **monochronic** *for some observer set when:*

1. *it is* chronological *for that observer set (→Def 7.4), and*
2. *all observers from the observer set take the* same temporal relation *to hold throughout.*

Definition 7.6 *A sub-tree of the logical structure of a cinematographic document to which at least two shots are assigned as content portions is a* **scene** *for some set of observers when:*

1. *the diegetic spaces of all shots assigned to the sub-tree can be conceptualised by all observers as being connected,*
2. *the diegetic times portrayed in the shots can be conceptualised by all observers as connected,*
3. *a layouting process exists such that the created order of shots and their diegetic succession can be seen as homomorphic by all observers—i.e., the shots are displayed in an order that corresponds to the unfolding of events in the 'narrative' or diegetic world,*
4. *no further shot exists meeting the conditions (1)–(3).*

Definition 7.7 *A sub-tree of the logical structure of a cinematographic document to which at least two shots are assigned as content portions is a* **sequence** *for some set of observers when:*

1. *the diegetic spaces of all shots assigned to the sub-tree can be conceptualised by all observers as being connected,*
2. *the diegetic times portrayed in the shots cannot be conceptualised by all observers as connected,*
3. *a layouting process exists such that the created order of shots and their diegetic succession can be seen as homomorphic by all observers,*
4. *no further shot exists meeting the conditions (1)–(3).*

Definition 7.8 *A syntagma is a* **basic narrative syntagma** *if it is either a* scene shot, *a* scene *(→Def 7.6) or a* sequence *(→Def 7.7).*

Comment: The *scene shot* was introduced in Section 7.2. It occurs when a given layouting process allocates a single shot to a scene and no other syntagmatic classification can be found.

Definition 7.9 *A sub-tree of the logical structure in a cinematographic document is syntagmatically* **spatially partitionable** *for a set of observers if:*

1. *at least two shots are present in the sub-tree as content portions,*
2. *for these shots, a partition can be found that divides them into at least two collections of shots (the 'partition sets' resulting from the partition) such that each associated logical substructure can be classified with a basic narrative syntagma (→Def 7.8).*

Definition 7.10 *For the syntagmatic classification of a sub-tree of the logical structure in a cinematographic document as a (first order)* **narrative series***, it is necessary that:*

1. *the sub-tree is spatially partitionable into two or more sets (→Def 7.9),*
2. *in each set, it is possible for the observer to find a shot that bears some temporal relationship with at least one shot of another (distinct) set.*

Definition 7.11 *A segment in a cinematographic document is* **n-alternating** *with respect to a given layouting process and a set of observers if a partition of the segment exists with n partition sets such that:*

1. *the segment is monochronic for that set of observers (→Def 7.5),*
2. *the segment is spatially partitionable for that set of observers (→Def 7.9),*
3. *for each pair of partition sets, transitions exist for which a specific symmetric relation holds between some member of the first partition set and some member of the second partition set (as defined in the transition graph) for all observers of the observer set and this relation holds for all the transitions between the first and second set—this relation then constitutes the* coherence *for those observers of the alternating shots it relates,*
4. *for all transition pairs between members of the partition, all observers of the observer set conceive the source space-time regions of the members of those pairs to be disjoint,*
5. *in the representation according to the given layouting process, there are at least three transitions between the distinct members of each pair of partition sets.*

Comment: The *transition graph* is defined in Section 7.4.2.

Definition 7.12 *A sub-tree of the logical structure of a cinematographic document is* **syntagmatically n-alternatable** *for a set of observers if there is a layouting process that produces a corresponding n-alternating segment (→Def 7.11).*

Definition 7.13 *A sub-tree of the logical structure of a cinematographic document to which at least two shots are assigned as content portions is a* **descriptive scene** *for some set of observers when:*

1. *the diegetic spaces of all shots assigned to the sub-tree can be conceptualised by all observers as being connected,*
2. *the times portrayed in the shots can be conceptualised as falling within a temporal 'container' covering all the time intervals of the involved content portions,*
3. *changing the layouted order of the shots effects neither the temporal container nor the spatial 'container' entailed,*
4. *no further shot exists meeting the conditions (1)–(3).*

Filmography

24 (2001–2010). Robert Cochran and Joel Surnow. Imagine Entertainment, USA. (TV series).

About a boy (2002). Chris Weitz and Paul Weitz. Novel: Nick Hornby. Universal Pictures, Studio Canal, Tribeca Productions, Working Title Films, UK / USA / France / Germany.

Adieu Philippine (1962). Jacques Rozier. Rome Paris Films, Euro International Film (EIA), Alpha Productions and Unitec, France / Italy.

A Fistful of dollars (1964). Sergio Leone. Constantin Film Produktion, Jolly Film and Ocean Films, Italy / Spain / W.Germany. Original title: *Per un pugno di dollar*.

Battleship Potemkin (1925). Sergei M. Eisenstein. Goskino, Soviet Union. Original title: *Bronenosets Potyomkin*.

Citizen Kane (1941). Orson Welles. Columbia Pictures Corporation, Mercury Productions, USA.

Eyes Wide Shut (1999). Stanley Kubrik. Novel: Arthur Schnitzler. Hobby Films, Pole Star, Stanley Kubrick Productions, Warner Bros. Pictures, UK / USA.

Fight Club (1999). David Fincher. Writers: Chuck Palahniuk (novel), Jim Uhls (screenplay). Fox 2000 Pictures, Regency Enterprises, Linson Films, Atman Entertainment, Knickerbocker Films and Taurus Film, USA / Germany.

For a few dollars more (1965). Sergio Leone. Produzioni Europee Associati (PEA), Arturo González Producciones Cinematográficas, Constantin Film Produktion, Italy / Spain / W.Germany. Original title: *Per qualche dollaro in più*.

Gigi (1958). Vincente Minnelli. Writers: Alan Jay Lerner (screenplay), Colette (novel). Metro-Goldwyn-Mayer (MGM) and Arthur Freed Production, USA.

Hulk (2003). Ang Lee. Writers: Stan Lee and Jack Kirby. Universal Pictures, Marvel Enterprises, Valhalla Motion Pictures, Good Machine, USA.

Idlewild (2006). Bryan Barber. Atlas Entertainment, Forensic Films, HBO Films, Mosaic Media Group, USA.

In Good Company (2004). Paul Weitz. Universal Pictures and Depth of Field, USA.

La antena (2007). Esteban Sapir. LadobleA, Argentina. English title: *The aerial*.

La Jetée (1962). Chris Marker. Argos Films, France.

L'arrivée d'un train à La Ciotat (1896). Auguste Lumière and Louis Lumière. Lumière, France.

La sortie des usines Lumière (1895). Louis Lumière. Lumière, France.

Last action hero (1993). John McTiernan. Writers: Zak Penn and Adam Leff (story), Shane Black and David Arnott (screenplay). Columbia Pictures Corporation and Oak Productions, USA.

Memento (2000). Christopher Nolan. Writers: Jonathan Nolan (short story: *Memento Mori*), Christopher Nolan (screenplay). Newmarket Capital Group, Team Todd, I Remember Productions, Summit Entertainment, USA.

Monty Python's Flying Circus (1969–1974). Graham Chapman, John Cleese, Terry Gilliam, Eric Idle, Terry Jones and Michael Palin. British Broadcasting Corporation (BBC) and Python (Monty) Pictures, U.K. (TV series).

North by Northwest (1959). Alfred Hitchcock. Writer: Ernest Lehman. Metro-Goldwyn-Mayer, Loew's, USA.

Persona (1966). Ingmar Bergman. Svensk Filmindustri, Sweden.

Purple Rose of Cairo (1985). Woody Allen. Orion Pictures Corporation, USA.

Rope (1948). Alfred Hitchcock. Writers: Patrick Hamilton (play), Hume Cronyn (adaptation), Arthur Laurents (screenplay). Transatlantic Pictures, Warner Bros. Pictures, USA.

Russian Ark (2002). Aleksander Sokurov. The State Hermitage Museum, Hermitage Bridge Studio and the Ministry of Culture of the Russian Federation, Russia / Germany. Original title: *Russkiy kovcheg*.

Sterile Cuckoo (1969). Alan J. Pakula. Writers: John Nichols (novel), Alvin Sargent. Boardwalk Productions, USA.

The Barefoot Contessa (1954). Joseph L. Mankiewicz. Figaro and Transoceanic Film, USA.

The Big Sleep (1946). Howard Hawks. Writers: William Faulkner, Leigh Brackett and Jules Furthman (screenplay). Warner Bros. Pictures, USA.

The Birds (1963). Alfred Hitchcock. Writers: Daphne Du Maurier (story), Evan Hunter (screenplay). Universal Pictures and Alfred J. Hitchcock Productions, USA.

The Bourne Identity (2002). Doug Liman. Novel: Robert Ludlum. Universal Pictures, Kennedy/Marshall Company, Hypnotic, Kalima Productions GmbH & Co. KG, Stillking Films, USA / Germany / Czech Republic.

The Day After (1983). Nicolas Meyer. Writer: Edward Hume. ABC Circle Films, USA. (TV).

The End of the Affair (1999). Neil Jordan. Writers: Graham Greene (novel), Neil Jordan (screenplay). Columbia Pictures Corporation, UK / USA.

The General (1926). Clyde Bruckman and Buster Keaton. Buster Keaton Productions and Joseph M. Schenck Productions, USA.

The Girl and her Trust (1912). D.W. Griffith. Writer: George Hennessy. Biograph Company, USA.

The Good, the Bad and the Ugly (1966). Sergio Leone. Arturo González Producciones Cinematográficas, S.A, Constantin Film Produktion, Produzioni Europee Associati (PEA), Italy / Spain / W.Germany. Original title: *Il buono, il brutto, il cattivo*.

The Lady from Shanghai (1947). Orson Welles. Columbia Pictures Corporation, Mercury Productions, USA.

The Lonedale Operator (1911). D.W. Griffith. Writer: Mack Sennett. Biograph Company, USA.

The Marriage of Maria Braun (1979). Rainer Werner Fassbinder. Albatros Filmproduktion, Fengler Films, Filmverlag der Autoren, Tango Film, Trio Film and Westdeutscher Rundfunk (WDR), West Germany. Original title: *Die Ehe von Maria Braun*.

Three colours: Blue (1993). Krzysztof Kieślowski. MK2 Productions, CED Productions, France 3 Cinéma, CAB Productions, Zespol Filmowy "Tor", Canal+, Centre National de la Cinématographie (CNC), Fonds Eurimages du Conseil de l'Europe, France / Poland / Switzerland. Original title: *Trois couleurs: Bleu*.

Timecode (2000). Mike Figgis. Screen Gems and Red Mullet Productions, USA.

Touch of Evil (1958). Orson Welles. Universal International Pictures, USA.

Vertigo (1958). Alfred Hitchcock. Writers: Alec Coppel (screenplay), Samuel A. Taylor (screenplay), Pierre Boileau and Thomas Narcejac (novel "D'Entre Les Morts"). Alfred J. Hitchcock Productions and Paramount Pictures, USA.

Wavelength (1967). Michael Snow. independent, Canada / USA.

Bibliography

Allen, J. F. (1984), 'Towards a General Theory of Action and Time', *Artificial Intelligence* **23**, 123–154.

Allen, M. (2007), Divided interests: split-screen aesthetics in *24*, *in* S. Peacock, ed., 'Reading *24*: TV against the clock', I.B. Taurus, London and New York, pp. 35–48.

Allen, R. and Smith, M., eds (1997), *Film theory and philosophy*, Oxford University Press, Oxford, U.K.

Altman, R. (1999), *Film/Genre*, British Film Institute, London.

Anderson, J. D. (1996), *The Reality of Illusion: An Ecological Approach to Cognitive Film Theory*, Southern Illinois University Press, Carbondale and Edwardsville.

Arijon, D. (1976), *Grammar of the Film Language*, Hastings House, Publishers, New York. Focal Press, Ltd.

Armstrong, P. B. (1990), *Conflicting readings: variety and validity in interpretation*, University of North Carolina Press, Chapel Hill, NC.

Arnheim, R. (1957), *Film as Art*, University of California Press, Berkeley and L.A.

Arnheim, R. (1982), *The power of the center*, University of California Press, Berkeley, CA.

Asher, N. and Lascarides, A. (2003), *Logics of conversation*, Cambridge University Press, Cambridge.

Bacon, H. (2011), 'The extent of mental completion of films', *Projections: Journal for Movies and Mind* **5**(1), 31–50.

Baetens, J. (1993), Revealing traces: a new theory of graphic enunciation, *in* R. Varnum and C. T. Gibbons, eds, 'The language of comics. Words and Images', University Press of Mississippi, Jackson, pp. 145–155.

Bakhtin, M. M. (1986), The problem of speech genres, *in* 'Bakhtin: Speech genres and other late essays', University of Texas Press, Austin, Texas, pp. 60–102. (Translated by V. McGee).

Bal, M. (1985), *Narratology: introduction to the theory of narrative*, University of Toronto Press, Toronto.

Baldry, A. and Thibault, P. J. (2006), *Multimodal Transcription and Text Analysis*, Textbooks and Surveys in Linguistics, Equinox, London and New York.

Barsalou, L. W. (1983), 'Ad hoc categories', *Memory & Cognition* **11**(3), 211–227.

Barthes, R. (1964), *Elements of Semiology*, Jonathan Cape, London. Translated by Annette Lavers and Colin Smith.

Barthes, R. (1974), *S/Z*, Hill and Yang, New York. (Translated by Richard Miller.).

Barthes, R. (1977*a*), *Image – Music – Text*, Fontana Press, London. Translated by Stephen Heath.

Barthes, R. (1977*b*), Introduction to the structural analysis of narratives, *in* 'Image–Music–Text', Fontana, London, pp. 79–124. originally published in French in 1966.

Barthes, R. (1977*c*), The rhetoric of the image, *in* 'Image–Music–Text', Fontana, London, pp. 32–51.

Bartlett, F. (1932), *Remembering*, Cambridge University Press, Cambridge.

Bateman, J. A. (2007), 'Towards a *grande paradigmatique* of film: Christian Metz reloaded', *Semiotica* **167**(1/4), 13 64.

Bateman, J. A. (2008), *Multimodality and Genre: a foundation for the systematic analysis of multimodal documents*, Palgrave Macmillan, London.

Bateman, J. A. (2009), Film and representation: making filmic meaning, *in* W. Wildgen and B. van Heusden, eds, 'Metarepresentation, Self-Organization and Art', European Semiotics, Lang, Bern, pp. 137–162.

Bateman, J. A. (2011), The decomposability of semiotic modes, *in* K. L. O'Halloran and B. A. Smith, eds, 'Multimodal Studies: Multiple Approaches and Domains', Routledge Studies in Multimodality, Routledge, London, pp. 17–38.

Bateman, J. A. and Farrar, S. (2004), Spatial ontology baseline, SFB/TR8 internal report I1-[OntoSpace]: D2, Collaborative Research Center for Spatial Cognition, University of Bremen, Germany.

Bateman, J. A. and Rondhuis, K. J. (1997), "Coherence relations': towards a general specification', *Discourse Processes* **24**, 3–49.

Baudry, J.-L. (1974), 'Ideological effects of the basic cinematographic apparatus', *Film Quarterly* **28**(2), 39–47. translated by Alan Williams.

Bazin, A. (1960), 'The Ontology of the Photographic Image', *Film Quarterly* **13**(4), 4–9. Translated by Hugh Gray.

Bazin, A. (1967), *What is cinema?*, University of California Press, Berkelely.

Bednarek, M. (2010), *The language of fictional television: Drama and Identity*, Continuum, London.

Bellour, R. (1974), 'The obvious and the code', *Screen* **15**(4), 7–17. Reprinted in Bellour (2000*b*: 69–76).

Bellour, R. (1975), 'The unattainable text', *Screen* **16**(3), 19–28.

Bellour, R. (1990), To alternate / to narrate, *in* T. Elsaesser, ed., 'Early Cinema: space, frame, narrative', BFI Publishing, London, pp. 360–374. First published in English *Australian Journal of Screen Theory* 15/16, 1983. Translated by Inge Pruks.

Bellour, R. (2000*a*), System of a fragment (on *The Birds*), *in* C. Penley, ed., 'The analysis of film', Indiana University Press, Bloomington and Indianopolis, pp. 28–67. Written 1969; translated by Ben Brewster.

Bellour, R. (2000*b*), *The analysis of film*, Indiana University Press, Bloomington and Indianopolis. A collection of essays originally published in French in the 1980s.

Bellour, R. (2000*c*), To alternate / to narrate (on *The Lonedale Operator*), *in* C. Penley, ed., 'The analysis of film', Indiana University Press, Bloomington and Indianopolis, pp. 262–277. First published in English in *Australian Journal of Screen Theory* 15/16, 1983.

Bellour, R. (2000*d*), To segment / to analyze (on *Gigi*), *in* C. Penley, ed., 'The analysis of film', Indiana University Press, Bloomington and Indianopolis, pp. 193–216. Originally published in *Quarterly Review of Film Studies* 1(3), August 1976.

Bellour, R. and Metz, C. (1971), 'Entretien sur la sémiologie du cinéma', *Semiotica* **4**(1), 1–30. Taken from Christian Metz *Essais sur la signification au cinéma II*, 1972, Paris: Klincksieck, Chapter 10.

Benveniste, E. (1966), *Problèmes de linguistique générale*, Gallimard, Paris. Translation available in *Benveniste (1974)*.

Benveniste, E. (1974), *Probleme der allgemeinen Sprachwissenschaft*, Paul List Verlag, München. Translated by Wilhelm Bolle.

Berger, A. A. (2000), *Media and Communication Research Methods: an introduction to qualitative and quantitative approaches*, Sage Publications, Thousand Oaks, CA.

Bertin, J. (1983), *Semiology of graphics*, University of Wisconsin Press, Madison, Wisconsin.

Bordegoni, M., Faconti, G., Maybury, M. T., Rist, T., Ruggieri, S., Trahanias, P. and Wilson, M. (1997), 'A standard reference model for intelligent multimedia presentation systems', *Computer Standards and Interfaces: International Journal on the Development and Application of standards for Computers, Data Communication and Interfaces* **18**(6-7), 477–496.

Bordwell, D. (1982), 'Textual analysis, etc.', *Enclitic* **6**(1), 125–136. Double Issue: International Conference on the textual analysis of film.

Bordwell, D. (1985), *Narration in the fiction film*, University of Wisconsin Press, Madison, WI.

Bordwell, D. (1989), *Making meaning. Inference and rhetoric in the interpretation of cinema*, Harvard University Press, Cambridge, MA.

Bordwell, D. (2005), *Figures traced in light: on cinematic staging*, University of California Press, Berkeley, Los Angeles, London.

Bordwell, D. (2007), *Poetics of Cinema*, Routledge, London, New York.

Bordwell, D. (2009), Cognitive theory, *in* P. Livingston and C. Plantinga, eds, 'The Routledge Companion to Philosophy and Film', Routledge, London and New York, chapter 33, pp. 356–367.

Bordwell, D. (2011), 'Common Sense + Film Theory = Common-Sense Film Theory?', David Bordwell's website on cinema: Essays. May.
http://www.davidbordwell.net/essays/commonsense.php

Bordwell, D. and Thompson, K. (2008), *Film Art: An Introduction. Eighth Edition*, The McGraw-Hill Inc, New York.

Branigan, E. (1975), 'Formal permutations of the point-of-view shot', *Screen* **16**(3), 54–64.

Branigan, E. (1976), 'The space of *Equinox Flower*', *Screen* **17**(2), 74–105.

Branigan, E. (1984), *Point of view in the cinema: a theory of narration and subjectivity in classical film*, number 66 *in* 'Approaches to semiotics', Mouton, Berlin.

Branigan, E. (1986*a*), 'Diegesis and authorship in film', *Iris: revue de théorie de l'image et du son* **7**, 37–54.

Branigan, E. (1986*b*), 'Point of view in the fiction film', *Wide Angle* **8**(3), 4–7.

Branigan, E. (1992), *Narrative comprehension and film*, Routledge, London.

Braudy, L. (1976), *The world in a frame: what we see in films*, Anchor Press / Doubleday, Garden City, New York.

Bremont, C. (1973), *Logique du Récit*, Seuil, Paris.

Buckland, W. (2000), *The Cognitive Semiotics of Film*, Cambridge University Press, Cambridge.

Buckland, W. (2004), Film semiotics, *in* T. Miller and R. Stam, eds, 'A companion to film theory', Blackwell companions in cultural studies, Blackwell, Oxford, pp. 84–104.

Bulterman, D. C. and Rutledge, L. W. (2008), *SMIL 3.0 – Flexible Multimedia for Web, Mobile Device and Daisy Talking Books*, X.media.publishing, 2 edn, Springer, Berlin.

Burch, N. (1969), *Praxis du cinema*, Éditions Gallimard, Paris.

Burch, N. (1973), *Theory of film practice*, Secker and Warburg, London. Translation of *Burch (1969)* by Helen R. Lane.

Burch, N. (1990), *Life to those shadows*, University of California Press, Berkeley and California. Translated and edited by Ben Brewster.

Burke, K. (1945), *A grammar of motives*, Prentice Hall, Inc., London.

Burnett, C. (2008), 'A new look at the concept of style in film: the origins and development of the problem-solution model', *New Review of Film and Television Studies* **6**(2), 127–149.

Cadbury, W. and Poague, L. (1982), *Film Criticism: a Counter Theory*, Iowa State University Press, Ames.

Callenbach, E. (1975), 'Who is Christian Metz and why is everybody saying these awful things about him?', *Film Quarterly* **28**(3), 19.

Carroll, J. M. (1977), 'Linguistics, Psychology, and Cinema Theory', *Semiotica* **20**(1-2), 173–195.

Carroll, J. M. (1980), *Towards a structural psychology of cinema*, number 55 *in* 'Approaches to semiotics', Mouton, The Hague.

Carroll, N. (1974), 'Review of *Film Language*', *Film comment* **10**(6), 61–63.

Carroll, N. (1995), 'Critical study Kendall L. Walton: Mimesis As Make-Believe', *The Philosophical Quarterly* **45**(178), 93–99.

Carroll, N. (1996a), *Theorizing the moving image*, Cambridge University Press, Cambridge, chapter XXII. Cognitivism, Contemporary Film Theory and Method: a response to Warren Buckland, pp. 321–335.

Carroll, N. (1996b), *Theorizing the moving image*, Cambridge University Press, Cambridge, chapter IV. Defining the moving image, pp. 49–74.

Carroll, N. (1996c), Towards an ontology of the moving image, *in* C. A. Freeland and T. E. Wartenberg, eds, 'Philosophy and Film', Routledge, London, pp. 68–85.

Casetti, F. (1998), *Inside the Gaze: The Fiction Film and Its Spectator*, Indiana University Press, Bloomington. translated by Nell Andrew with Charles O'Brien.

Cavell, S. (1980), *The world viewed: reflections on the ontology of film*, Harvard University Press, Cambridge, MA.

Cegarra, M. (1973), 'Cinema and semiology', *Screen* **14**, 129–187. Reprinted from *Cinéthique* 7/8, 1970.

Chandler, D. (2002), *Semiotics: The Basics*, Routledge, London and New York.

Chateau, D. (1976), 'Vers un modèle génératif du discours filmique', *Humanisme et entreprise* **99**, 1–10. Neuilly.

Chatman, S. (1978), *Story and discourse: narrative structure in fiction and film*, Cornell University Press, Ithaca and London.

Chatman, S. (1992), What novels can do that films can't (and vice versa), *in* G. Mast, M. Cohen and L. Braudy, eds, 'Film theory and criticsm: introductory readings', 3rd edn, Oxford University Press, pp. 403–419. Originally appeared in *Critical Inquiry*, **8**, 1980.

Chaudrini, S. (2006), *Feminist film theories. Laura Mulvey, Kaja Silverman, Terese de Lauretis, Barbara Creed*, Routlege, London and New York.

Chomsky, N. (1966), *Cartesian Linguistics: a chapter in the history of rationalist thought*, Harper and Row Pub. Inc.

Cohen, A. J. (2004), How music influences the interpretation of film and video: approaches from experimental psychology, *in* 'Perspectives in Systematic Musicology', number 12 *in* 'Selected Reports in Ethnomusicology', UCLA Press, Los Angeles, pp. 15–36.

Cohen-Séat, G. (1948), 'Le discourse filmique', *Revue Internationale de Filmologie* **5**, 37–48.

Colin, M. (1985), *Langue, film, discours : prolégomènes à une sémiologie générative du film*, Klincksieck, Paris.

Colin, M. (1989a), 'A 'Generative Semiology' of film: To what end?', *Iris: revue de théorie de l'image et du son* **9**, 159–169.

Colin, M. (1989b), 'La Grande Syntagmatique revisitée', *Actes Sémiotiques* **1**, 1–49.

Colin, M. (1995*a*), Film semiology as a cognitive science, *in* W. Buckland, ed., 'From film spectator: from sign to mind', Film culture in transition, Amsterdam University Press, pp. 86–110.

Colin, M. (1995*b*), The grande syntagmatique revisited, *in* W. Buckland, ed., 'From film spectator: from sign to mind', Film culture in transition, Amsterdam University Press, pp. 45–85. Translation of *Colin (1989b)* by Claudine Tourniaire.

Coventry, K. R. and Garrod, S. C. (2004), *Saying, seeing and acting. The psychological semantics of spatial prepositions*, Essays in Cognitive Psychology series, Psychology Press, Hove, UK.

Cowie, P. (1973), *The cinema of Orson Welles*, A.S. Barnes and Company /The Trinity Press, South Brunswick and New York / London.

Currie, G. (1995), *Image and mind: film, philosophy and cognitive science*, Cambridge University Press, Cambridge, U.K.

Currie, G. (1996), Film, reality and illusion, *in* D. Bordwell and N. Carroll, eds, 'Posttheory: reconstructing film studies', University of Wisconsin Press, Madison, Wisconsin, pp. 325–344.

Currie, G. (1997), The film theory that never was: a nervous manifesto, *in* R. Allen and M. Smith, eds, 'Film theory and philosophy', Oxford University Press, Oxford, U.K., pp. 42–59.

Currie, G. (2010), *Narratives and narrators: a philosophy of stories*, Oxford University Press, Oxford, U.K.

Cutting, J. (2005), Perceiving Scenes in Film and in the World, *in* J. Anderson and B. Anderson, eds, 'Moving Image Theory: Ecological Considerations', Southern Illinois University Press, pp. 9–27.

Cutting, J. E., DeLong, J. E. and Nothelfer, C. E. (2010), 'Attention and the evolution of Hollywood film', *Psychological Science* 21(3), 432–439.

Davis, D. (1974), *The grammar of television production*, Barrie, Jenkins, London.

de Beaugrande, R. (1980), *Text, Discourse, and Process: Toward a Multidisciplinary Science of Texts*, Vol. IV of *Advances in Discourse Processes*, Ablex, Norwood, N. J.

de Beaugrande, R. and Dressler, W. U. (1981), *Introduction to Text Linguistics*, Longman, London.

De Grauwe, S. (2003), 'The possibility of minimal units in the filmic image', *Image and Narrative* 7. Online magazine of the visual narrative.
http://www.imageandnarrative.be

Deleuze, G. (1986), *Cinema 1: The movement-image*, The Athlone Press, London. (Translated by Hugh Tomlinson and Barbara Haberjam.).

Doane, M. A. (2002), *The emergence of cinematic time: modernity, contingency, the archive*, Harvard University Press, Cambridge, MA and London, England.

Dudley Andrew, J. (1976), *The major film theories: an introduction*, Oxford University Press, Oxford.

Eco, U. (1972), *Einführung in die Semiotik*, Fink, München.

Eco, U. (1976), Articulations of the cinematic code, *in* B. Nichols, ed., 'Movies and methods: an anthology', University of California Press, Berkeley, pp. 592–607.

Eisenstein, S. (1963), *Film form: Essays in Film Theory*, Dennis Dobson, London.

Elleström, L. (2010), The modalities of media: a model for understanding intermedial relations, *in* L. Elleström, ed., 'Media Borders, Multimodality and Intermediality', Palgrave Macmillan, Basingstoke, pp. 11–50.

Elsaesser, T. and Barker, A. (1990), The continuity system: Griffith and beyond. Introduction, *in* T. Elsaesser, ed., 'Early Cinema: space, frame, narrative', BFI

Publishing, London, pp. 293–317.

Elsaesser, T., ed. (1990), *Early Cinema: space, frame, narrative*, BFI Publishing, London. edited with Adam Barker.

Engelhardt, Y. (2007), 'Syntactic structures in graphics', *Image: Zeitschrift für interdisziplinäre Bildwissenschaft* **5**, 23–35. Special issue: Computational Visualistics and Picture Morphology; edited by Jörg R.J. Schirra.

Ezra, E. (2000), *Georges Méliès*, Manchester University Press, Manchester.

Fann, K. T. (1970), *Peirce's theory of abduction*, Nijhoff, The Hague.

Fauconnier, G. and Turner, M. (2003), *The Way We Think: Conceptual Blending and the Mind's Hidden Complexities*, Basic Books, New York.

Fell, J. L., ed. (1983), *Film before Griffith*, University of California Press, Berkeley and Los Angeles.

Fledelius, K. (1978), Syntagmatic film analysis: with special reference to historical research, *in* 'Untersuchung zur Syntax des Films: 1', number 8 *in* 'PAPMAKS', Münsteraner Arbeitskreis for Semiotik e.V., Münster, pp. 32–68.

Fludernik, M. (2009), *Introduction to narratology*, Routledge, London.

Forceville, C. J. (2006), Non-verbal and multimodal metaphor as a cognitivist framework: agendas for research, *in* G. Kristiansen, M. Achard, R. Dirven and F. R. de Mendoza Ibanez, eds, 'Cognitive Linguistics: Current Applications and Future Perspectives', Mouton de Gruyter, Berlin/New York, pp. 379–402.

Forceville, C. J. (2007), 'Book Review: *Multimodal Transcription and Text Analysis: A Multimedia Toolkit and Coursebook* by Anthony Baldry and Paul J. Thibault', *Journal of Pragmatics* **39**, 1235–1238.

Freadman, A. (1986), Structuralist uses of Peirce: Jakobson, Metz et al., *in* T. Threadgold, E. A. Grosz, G. Kress and M. A. K. Halliday, eds, 'Semiotics – language – ideology', number 3 *in* 'Sydney Studies in Society and Culture', Sydney Association for Studies in Society and Culture, Sydney, pp. 93–124.

Garwood, I. (2008), 'Sound and space in the split-screen movie', *Refractory: a journal of Entertainment Media* **14**.
http://blogs.arts.unimelb.edu.au/refractory/category/
browse-past-volumes/volume-14/

Gaudreault, A. (1983), Temporality and narrativity in early cinema, 1895–1908, *in* J. L. Fell, ed., 'Film before Griffith', University of California Press, Berkeley and Los Angeles, pp. 311–329.

Gaudreault, A. (1988), *Du litteraire au filmique: System du récit*, Meridiens Klincksieck, Paris. Translated as Gaudreault (2009).

Gaudreault, A. (1990), Detours in film narrative: the development of cross-cutting, *in* T. Elsaesser, ed., 'Early Cinema: space, frame, narrative', BFI Publishing, London, pp. 133–152. originally published in *Cinema Journal*, 19(1), 1979. Translated by Charles Musser and Martin Sopocy.

Gaudreault, A. (2009), *From Plato to Lumière. Narration and Monstration in Literature and Cinema*, University of Toronto Press, Toronto.

Gaudreault, A. and Marion, P. (1994), 'Dieu est l'auteur des documentaires...', *Cinémas. Journal of film studies. Revue d'études cinématographiques* **2**, 11–26.

Gaut, B. (2010), *A philosophy of cinema art*, Cambridge University Press, Cambridge.

Genette, G. (1980), *Narrative discourse*, Cornell University Press, Ithaca, NY. Translated by Jane E. Lewin.

Gibson, J. (1977), The theory of affordances, *in* R.Shaw and J.Brandsford, eds, 'Perceiving, Acting, and Knowing: Toward and Ecological Psychology', Erlbaum,

Hillsdale, NJ, pp. 62–82.

Giddens, A. (1984), *The constitution of society: outline of the theory of structuration*, Polity Press, Cambridge.

Goguen, J. (1999), An introduction to algebraic semiotics, with applications to user interface design, *in* C. Nehaniv, ed., 'Computation for metaphors, analogy and agents', number 1562 *in* 'LNAI', Springer, Berlin, pp. 242–291.

Gombrich, E. (1959), *Art and Illusion: A Study in the Psychology of Pictorial Representation*, Phaidon Press, London.

Goodman, N. (1969), *Languages of Art. An approach the a theory of symbols*, Oxford University Press, London.

Graesser, A., Singer, M. and Trabasso, T. (1994), 'Constructing inferences during narrative text comprehension', *Psychological Review* **101**, 371–395.

Graham, M. (1981), 'The inaccessibility of *The Lady from Shanghai*', *Film Criticism* **5**(3), 21–37.

Greimas, A.-J. (1972), Elemente einer narrativen Grammatik, *in* H. Blumensath, ed., 'Strukturalismus in der Literaturwissenschaft', Kiepenheuer & Witsch, Köln, pp. 47–67. übersetzt von Irmela und Jochen Rehbein.

Greimas, A.-J. (1983), *Structural semantics: an attempt at a method*, University of Nebraska Press, Lincoln and London. Originally published as *Sémantique structurale: Recherche de mèthode* (Librarie Larousse, 1966); translated by Daniele McDowell, Ronald Schleifer and Alan Velie.

Grodal, T. (2009), *Embodied Visions: Evolution, Emotions, Culture, and Film*, Oxford University Press, Oxford.

Groupe μ (1992), *Traité du signe visuel*, Editions du Seuil, Paris.

Gunning, T. (1993), *D.W. Griffith and the Origins of American Narrative Film: The Early Years at Biograph*, University of Illinois Press, Champaign, IL.

Gunning, T. (2003), 'Review Article. The work of film analysis: Systems, fragments, alternation', *Semiotica* **144**(1-4), 343–357.

Hackenberg, A. (2004), *Filmverstehen als kognitiv-emotionaler Prozess. Zum Instruktionscharakter filmischer Darstellungen und dessen Bedeutung für die Medienrezeptionsforschung*, Logos.

Hall, E. T. (1968), 'Proxemics', *Current Anthropology* **9**(2/3), 83–108.

Halliday, M. A. K. (1975), *Learning How to Mean: explorations in the development of language*, Edward Arnold, London.

Halliday, M. A. K. (1978), *Language as social semiotic*, Edward Arnold, London.

Halliday, M. A. K. and Hasan, R. (1976), *Cohesion in English*, Longman, London.

Halliday, M. A. K. and Matthiessen, C. M. I. M. (2004), *An Introduction to Functional Grammar*, 3rd edn, Edward Arnold, London.

Hammer, R. and Kellner, D., eds (2009), *Media/Cultural Studies: critical approaches*, Peter Lang, New York.

Harrigan, J. A. (2008), Proxemics, kinesics and gaze, *in* J. A. Harrigan, R. Rosenthal and K. R. Scherer, eds, 'The New Handbook of Methods in Nonverbal Behavioral Research', Oxford University Press, Oxford, pp. 137–198.

Hartmann, B. (2007), 'Diegetisieren, Diegese, Diskursuniversum', *montage av. Zeitschrift für Theorie & Geschichte audiovisueller Kommunikation* **16**(2), 53–692.

Hayward, S. (2006), *Cinema Studies: the key concepts*, 3 edn, Routledge, London.

Heath, S. (1973), 'Film/Cinetext/Text', *Screen* **14**, 102–127.

Heath, S. (1975*a*), 'Film and System: terms of analysis; Part I', *Screen* **16**(1), 7–77.

Heath, S. (1975*b*), 'Film and System: terms of analysis; Part II', *Screen* **16**(2), 91–113.

Henderson, B. (1977), 'Segmentation', *Film Quarterly* **31**(1), 57–65.

Herman, D. (1997), 'Towards a formal description of narrative metalepsis', *Journal of Literary Semantics* **26**, 132–152.

Hickethier, K. (2007), *Film und Fernsehanalyse*, 4 edn, J.B. Metzler, Stuttgart / Weimar.

Hjelmslev, L. (1961), *Prolegomena to a theory of language*, University of Wisconsin Press, Madison, Wisconsin. Originally published 1943; Translated by F.J.Whitfield.

Hobbs, R., Frost, R., Davis, A. and Stauffer, J. (1988), 'How first time viewers comprehend editing conventions', *Journal of Communication* **38**(4), 50–60.

Hochberg, J. and Brooks, V. (1978), The Perception of Motion Pictures, *in* M. Friedman and E. Carterette, eds, 'Handbook of Perception', Vol. X, Academic Press, New York.

Hochberg, J. and Brooks, V. (1996), Movies in the mind's eye, *in* D. Bordwell and N. Carroll, eds, 'Post-theory: reconstructing film studies', University of Wisconsin Press, Madison, Wisconsin, pp. 368–387.

Hodge, R. and Kress, G. (1988), *Social Semiotics*, Polity Press, Cambridge, England.

Holman, T. (1997), *Sound for film and television*, Focal Press, Boston.

Ingarden, R. (1989), *Ontology of the Work of Art: The musical work, the picture, the architectural work, the film*, Ohio University Press, Athens. translated by Raymond Meyer and J.T. Goldwait.

Iser, W. (1978), *The act of reading: a theory of aesthetic response*, John Hopkins University Press, Baltimore.

James, W. (2009[1907]), *Pragmatism. A New Name for Some Old Ways of Thinking*, The Echo Library, Teddington, Middlesex. Also published by Harvard University Press, Cambridge, MA, 1979.

Janney, R. W. (2010), Film discourse cohesion, *in* C. R. Hoffmann, ed., 'Narrative Revisited. Telling a story in the age of new media', number 199 *in* 'Pragmatics and Beyond', John Benjamins, Amsterdam, pp. 245–266.

Jewitt, C. and Kress, G. (2003), *Multimodal literacy*, number 4 *in* 'New literacies and digital epistemologies', P. Lang, Frankfurt a.M. / New York.

Joost, G. (2008), *Bild-Sprache: Die audio-visuelle Rhetorik des Films*, transcript – Verlag für Kommunikation, Kultur und soziale Praxis, Bielefeld.

Joyce, M. (2007), The Soviet montage cinema of the 1920s, *in* J. Nelmes, ed., 'Introduction to Film Studies', 4th edn, Routledge, London, chapter 15, pp. 364–397.

Kamp, H. and Reyle, U. (1993), *From discourse to logic: introduction to modeltheoretic semantics of natural language, formal logic and discourse representation theory*, Kluwer Academic Publishers, London, Boston, Dordrecht. Studies in Linguistics and Philosophy, Volume 42.

Kanzog, K., ed. (1991), *Einführung in die Filmphilologie*, number 4 *in* 'diskurs film: Münchener Beiträge zur Filmphilologie', Verlegergemeinschaft Schaudig/Bauer/Ledig, München.

Kawin, B. F. (1978), *Mindscreen: Bergman, Godard, and First-Person Film*, Princeton University Press, Princeton, N.J.

Kawin, B. F. (1992), *How movies work*, University of California Press, Berkeley / Los Angeles / London.

Keppler, A. and Seel, M. (2002), 'Über den Status filmischer Genres', *montage av. Zeitschrift für Theorie & Geschichte audiovisueller Kommunikation* **11**(2), 59–68.

Khouloki, R. (2007), *Der filmische Raum. Konstruktion, Wahrnehmung, Bedeutung*, Bertz + Fischer.

Kim, J.-H. (2009), 'The post-medium condition and the explosion of cinema', *Screen* **50**(1), 114–123.

Knott, A., Sanders, T. and Oberlander, J. (2001), 'Levels of representations in discourse relations', *Cognitive Linguistics* **12**(3), 197–209.

Koch, C. H. (1970), Understanding Film as Process of Change: A metalanguage for the study of film developed and applied to Ingmar Bergman's *Persona* and Alan J. Pakula's *The Sterile Cuckoo*, PhD thesis, University of Iowa, Iowa. UMI Microform, Ann Arbor, MI.

Korte, H. (2004), *Einführung in die Systematische Filmanalyse. Ein Arbeitsbuch*, 3 edn, Erich Schmidt Verlag, Berlin.

Kozloff, S. (2000), *Overhearing film dialogue*, Univ. of California Press, Berkeley.
http://www.loc.gov/catdir/bios/ucal052/99046452.html

Kracauer, S. (1993[1927]), 'Photography', *Critical Inquiry* **19**(3), 421–436. Translated by Thomas Y. Levin; first published in the *Frankfurter Zeitung*, 1927.

Krampen, M. (2010), Code, *in* T. A. Sebeok and M. Danesi, eds, 'Encyclopedic dictionary of semoitics', 3 edn, Vol. 1, Mouton de Gruyter, Berlin, pp. 127–135.

Krauss, R. E. (1999), 'Reinventing the medium', *Critical Inquiry* **25**(2), 289–305.

Kress, G. (1988), Textual matters: the social effectiveness of style, *in* D. Birch and M. O'Toole, eds, 'Functions of Style', Pinter, London.

Kress, G. (2000), Multimodality, *in* M. Kalantzis and B. Cope, eds, 'Multiliteracies: Literacy Learning and the Design of Social Futures', Routledge, London, chapter 9, pp. 182–202.

Kress, G. (2009), What is mode?, *in* C. Jewitt, ed., 'The Routledge Handbook of multimodal analysis', Routledge, London, pp. 54–67.

Kress, G. (2010), *Multimodality: a social semiotic approach to contemporary communication*, Routledge, London.

Kress, G., Jewitt, C., Ogborn, J. and Tsatsarelis, C. (2000), *Multimodal teaching and learning*, Continuum, London.

Kress, G. and van Leeuwen, T. (1996), *Reading Images: the grammar of visual design*, Routledge, London and New York.

Kress, G. and van Leeuwen, T. (2001), *Multimodal discourse: the modes and media of contemporary communication*, Arnold, London.

Kress, G. and van Leeuwen, T. (2002), 'Colour as a semiotic mode: notes for a grammar of colour', *Visual Communication* **1**(3).

Kress, G. and van Leeuwen, T. (2006), *Reading Images: the grammar of visual design*, 2 edn, Routledge, London and New York.

Kuchenbuch, T. (2005), *Filmanalyse: Theorien. Methoden. Kritik*, number 2648 *in* 'UTB', 2 edn, Böhlau Verlag, Wien / Köln / Weimar.

Kuhn, M. (2009), Film Narratology: Who Tells? Who Shows? Who Focalizes? Narrative Mediation in Self-Reflexive Fiction Films, *in* P. Hühn, W. Schmid and J. Schönert, eds, 'Point of View, Perspective, Focalization: Modeling Mediation in Narrative', de Gruyter, Berlin / New York, pp. 259–278.

Kuhn, M. (2011), *Filmnarratologie. Ein erzähltheoretisches Analysemodell*, number 26 *in* 'Narratologia / Contributions to Narrative Theory', de Gruyter, Berlin and New York.

Labov, W. (2001), *Principles of linguistic change, Volume 2: social factors*, Blackwell, Oxford.

Lacey, N. (2000), *Narrative and genre: key concepts in media studies*, Palgrave, New York.

Laetz, B. and Lopes, D. M. (2009), Genre, *in* P. Livingston and C. Plantinga, eds, 'The Routledge Companion to Philosophy and Film', Routledge, London and New York, chapter 14, pp. 152–161.

Lapsley, R. and Westlake, M. (2006), *Film theory: an introduction*, 2nd edn, Manchester University Press, Manchester and New York.

Lemke, J. L. (1991), Text production and dynamic text semantics, *in* E. Ventola, ed., 'Functional and systemic linguistics: approaches and uses', Mouton de Gruyter, Berlin, pp. 23–38.

Lemke, J. L. (1998), Multiplying meaning: visual and verbal semiotics in scientific text, *in* J. Martin and R. Veel, eds, 'Reading science: critical and functional perspectives on discourses of science', Routledge, London, pp. 87–113.

Lemke, J. L. (2000), 'Across the scales of time: artefacts, activities and meanings in ecosocial systems', *Mind, Culture, and Activity* **7**(4), 273–290.

Levin, D. T. and Wang, C. (2009), 'Spatial representation in cognitive science and film', *Projections* **3**, 24–52.
http://www.ingentaconnect.com/content/berghahn/proj/2009/
00000003/00000001/art00003

Levinson, J. (1990), *Music, art and metaphysics. Essays in philosophical aesthetics*, Cornell University Press, Ithaca, NY and London.

Liptay, F. (2006), Leerstellen im Film. Zum Wechselspiel von Bild und Einbildung, *in* T. Koebner and T. Meder, eds, 'Bildtheorie und Film', edition text+kritik, München, pp. 108–134.

Liu, Y. and O'Halloran, K. L. (2009), 'Intersemiotic texture: analyzing cohesive devices between language and images', *Social Semiotics* **19**(4), 367–388.

Livingston, P. (1997), Cinematic authorship, *in* R. Allen and M. Smith, eds, 'Film theory and philosophy', Oxford University Press, Oxford, U.K., pp. 132–148.

Livingston, P. and Plantinga, C., eds (2009), *The Routledge Companion to Philosophy and Film*, Routledge, London and New York.

Machin, D. (2009), Multimodality and theories of the visual, *in* C. Jewitt, ed., 'The Routledge Handbook of multimodal analysis', Routledge, London, pp. 181–190.

Magliano, J., Dijkstra, K. and Zwaan, R. (1996), 'Generating predictive inferences while viewing a movie', *Discourse Processes* **22**, 199–224.

Martin, J. R. (1983), Conjunction: the logic of English text, *in* J. S. Petöfi and E. Sözer, eds, 'Micro and macro connexity of discourse', number 45 *in* 'Papers in Textlinguistics', Helmut Buske Verlag, Hamburg, pp. 1–72.

Martin, J. R. (1992), *English text: systems and structure*, Benjamins, Amsterdam.

Martin, J. R. (2011), Multimodal semiotics: Theoretical challenges, *in* S. Dreyfus, S. Hood and M. Stenglin, eds, 'Semiotic Margins: reclaiming meaning', Continuum, London, pp. 243–270.

Martin, J. R. and Rose, D. (2003), *Working with discourse: meaning beyond the clause*, Continuum, London and New York.

Martin, J. R. and Rose, D. (2007), *Genre relations: mapping culture*, Equinox, London and New York.

Martinec, R. and Salway, A. (2005), 'A system for image-text relations in new (and old) media', *Visual Communication* **4**(3), 337–371.

Martínez, J. M. (2002*a*), *ISO/IEC JTC1/SC29/WG11, Coding of moving pictures and audio, N4980, MPEG7 Overview*, ISO.

http://www.chiariglione.org/mpeg/standards/mpeg-7/mpeg-7.htm

Martínez, J. M. (2002*b*), 'MPEG-7 overview of MPEG-7 description tools, part 2', *IEEE Multimedia* **9**(3), 83–93.

Martínez, J. M., Koenen, R. and Pereira, F. (2002), 'MPEG-7 the generic multimedia content description standard, part 1', *IEEE Multimedia* **9**(2), 78–87.

Martinez, M. and Scheffel, M. (1999), *Einführung in die Erzähltheorie*, Beck, München.

McCloud, S. (1994), *Understanding comics: the invisible art*, HarperPerennial, New York.

Metz, C. (1966), 'La grande syntagmatique du film narratif', *Communications* **8**, 120–124. Recherches sémiologiques: l'analyse structurale du récit.

Metz, C. (1972*a*), *Essais sur la signification au cinéma, Volume 2*, Klincksieck, Paris.

Metz, C. (1972*b*), 'Ponctuations et démarcations dans le film de diégèse', *Cahiers du cinéma* pp. 63–78. Reprinted in *Essais sur la signification au cinéma*, Volume 2, Paris: Klincksieck, 1972, pp. 111–137.

Metz, C. (1973), 'Methodological Propositions for the Analysis of Film', *Screen* **14**(1–2), 89–101. Translated by Diana Matias; original French article from 1968 reprinted in Metz (1972*a*: pp97-110).

Metz, C. (1974*a*), *Film language: a semiotics of the cinema*, Oxford University Press and Chicago University Press, Oxford and Chicago. Translated by Michael Taylor.

Metz, C. (1974*b*), *Film language: a semiotics of the cinema*, Oxford University Press and Chicago University Press, Oxford and Chicago, chapter Problems of denotation in the fiction film, pp. 108–146. Translated by Michael Taylor. Originally published in French in 1968.

Metz, C. (1974*c*), *Film language: a semiotics of the cinema*, Oxford University Press and Chicago University Press, Oxford and Chicago, chapter The cinema: language or language system?, pp. 31–91. Translated by Michael Taylor.

Metz, C. (1974*d*), *Language and Cinema*, number 26 *in* 'Approaches to Semiotics', Mouton, The Hague. Translated by Donna Jean Umiker-Sebeok.

Meyer, R. J. (1971), The films of David Wark Griffith: The development of themes and techniques in forty-two of his films, *in* H. M. Geduld, ed., 'Focus on D. W. Griffith', Prentice-Hall, Eaglewood Cliffs, N.J.

Mitchell, W. (1994), *Picture Theory: Essays on verbal and visual representation*, University of Chicago Press, Chicago.

Mitchell, W. (2005), 'There are no visual media', *Journal of visual culture* **4**(2), 257–266.

Mitchell, W. (2007), There are no visual media, *in* O. Grau, ed., 'Media Art Histories', MIT Press, Cambridge, MA, pp. 395–406.

Mitry, J. (1998[1963]), *The Aesthetics and Psychology of Cinema*, The Athlone Press, London. Translated by Christopher King.

Möller, K.-D. (1978), Schichten des Filmbildes und Ebenen des Films, *in* 'Die Einstellung als Größe einer Filmsemiotik', number 7 *in* 'papmaks', MAKS (Münsteraner Arbeitskreis for Semiotik) Publikationen, Münster, pp. 37–81.

Möller-Naß, K.-D. (1986), *Filmsprache: eine kritische Theoriegeschichte*, MAKS (Münsteraner Arbeitskreis for Semiotik) Publikationen, Münster.

Monaco, J. (2000), *How to read a film: movies, media, multimedia*, 3rd edn, Oxford University Press, Oxford, U.K.

Monaco, J. (2009), *How to read a film: movies, media and beyond*, 30th anniversary edition edn, Oxford University Press, Oxford, U.K.

Morris, C. W. (1938), *Foundations of the Theory of Signs*, University of Chicago Press, Chicago.

Müller, M. G. (2007), 'What is visual communication? Past and future of an emerging field of communication research', *Studies in Communication Sciences* **7**(2), 7–34.

Münsterberg, H. (2001[1916]), *Hugo Münsterberg on Film: The Photoplay - A Psychological Study and Other Writings*, Routledge. Edited by Allan Langdale.

Naremore, J. (1978), *The magic world of Orson Welles*, Oxford University Press, London and New York.

Nelles, W. (1997), *Frameworks: narrative levels and embedded narrative*, Lang, Frankfurt a.M. / New York.

Nelmes, J. (2007*a*), Gender and film, *in* J. Nelmes, ed., 'Introduction to Film Studies', 4th edn, Routledge, London, chapter 10, pp. 220–251.

Nelmes, J., ed. (2007*b*), *Introduction to Film Studies*, 4th edn, Routledge, London.

Nichols, B. (1975), 'Style, grammar and the movies', *Film Quarterly* **28**(3), 33–49.

Norris, S. (2004), *Analyzing Multimodal Interaction: a Methodological Framework*, Routledge, London and New York.

Nöth, W. (1995*a*), *Handbook of Semiotics*, Indiana University Press, Bloomington.

Nöth, W. (1995*b*), *Handbook of Semiotics*, Indiana University Press, Bloomington, chapter Communication and Semiosis, pp. 168–180.

Ochs, E. (1979), Transcription as Theory, *in* E. Ochs and B. B. Schieffelin, eds, 'Developmental Pragmatics', Academic Press, New York, pp. 43–72.

Oeler, K. (2009), *A grammar of murder: Violent scenes and film form*, The University of Chicago Press, Chicago.

O'Halloran, K. L. (1999), 'Interdependence, Interaction and Metaphor in Multisemiotic Texts', *Social Semiotics* **9**(3), 317–354.

O'Halloran, K. L. (2008), 'Systemic Functional-Multimodal Discourse Analysis (SF-MDA): Constructing Ideational Meaning using Language and Visual Imagery', *Visual Communication* **7**(4), 443–475.

Ong, W. J. (1982), *Orality and literacy : the technologizing of the word*, Methuen, London.

O'Toole, M. (1994), *The language of displayed art*, Leicester University Press (Pinter), London.

Oviatt, S. L. (1999), 'Ten myths of multimodal interaction', *Communications of the ACM* **42**(11), 74–81.

Paech, J. (1988), *Literatur und Film*, Metzler, Stuttgart.

Palmer, R. (1989), Bakhtinian translinguistics and film criticism: the dialogical image?, *in* R. Palmer, ed., 'The cinematic text: methods and approaches', AMS Press, New York, pp. 303–341.

Panofsky, E. (1967), *Studies in Iconology: Humanistic Themes in the Art of the Renaissance*, 2 edn, Harper & Row, New York.

Panofsky, E. (1995), Style and medium in the motion pictures, *in* I. Lavin, ed., 'Three essays on style', MIT Press, Cambridge, Massachusetts, pp. 91–126. Originally published in *Critique*, **1**(3): 5–28 (1947).

Panofsky, E. (2004), Style and medium in the motion pictures, *in* L. Braudy and M. Cohen, eds, 'Film Theory and Criticism', sixth edn, Oxford University Press, Oxford. Originally published in *Critique*, **1**(3): 5–28 (1947).

Peirce, C. S. (1931-1958), *Collected Papers of Charles Sanders Peirce*, The Belknap Press of Harvard University Press, Cambridge, MA.

Penley, C., ed. (1988), *Feminism and Film Theory*, Routledge and British Film Institute Publishing, London.

Persson, P. (2003), *Understanding cinema*, Cambridge University Press, Cambridge.

Peters, J. M. L. (1981), *Pictorial signs and the language of film*, Rodopi, Amsterdam.

Phillips, P. (2007), Spectator, audience and response, *in* J. Nelmes, ed., 'Introduction to Film Studies', 4th edn, Routledge, London, chapter 7, pp. 143–171.

Pier, J. (2010), Metalepsis, *in* P. Hühn, J. Pier, W. Schmid and J. Schönert, eds, 'The living handbook of narratology', Hamburg University Press, Hamburg. last accessed: 22 Mar 2011].
  hup.sub.uni-hamburg.de/lhn/index.php?title=Metalepsis&oldid=802

Pippin, R. B. (2011), 'Agency and fate in Orson Welles's *The Lady from Shanghai*', *Critical Inquiry* **37**(2), 214–244.

Plantinga, C. R. (1997), *Rhetoric and representation in nonfiction film*, Cambridge University Press, Cambridge.

Plantinga, C. and Smith, G. M. (1999), Introduction, *in* C. Plantinga and G. M. Smith, eds, 'Passionate views: film, cognition, and emotion', The John Hopkins University Press, Baltimore and London, pp. 1–17.

Popple, S. and Kember, J. (2004), *Early cinema: from factory gate to dream factory*, Wallflower Press, London.

Porter, M. J. (1982), 'The *grande syntagmatique*: A methodology for analysis of the montage structure of television narratives', *Southern Communication Journal* **47**(3), 330–341.

Posner, M. I. (1980), 'Orienting of attention', *Quarterly Journal of Experimental Psychology* **32**(1), 3–25.

Prince, G. (1973), *A grammar of stories*, Mouton, The Hague.

Prince, S. (1993), 'The discourse of pictures: iconicity and film studies', *Film Quarterly* **47**(1), 16–28.

Prince, S. (1996), 'True lies: Perceptual realism, digital images, and film theory', *Film Quarterly* **49**(3), 27–37.

Prince, S. (2007), *Movies and meaning: An introduction to film*, 4th ed. edn, Pearson Allyn and Bacon, Boston, MA.

Pudovkin, V. I. (1926), *Film technique and film acting: the cinema writings of V. I. Pudovkin*, Bonanza Books, New York. Translated by Ivor Montagu. Republished by Sims Press, 2007.

Radell, K. M. (1992), 'Orson Welles: the semiotics of focalization in *The Lady from Shanghai*', *The Journal of Narrative Technique* **22**(2), 97–104.

Randell, D., Cui, Z. and Cohn, A. (1992), A spatial logic based on regions and connection, *in* 'Proceedings of the 3rd. International Conference on Knowledge Representation and Reasoning', Morgan Kaufmann, San Mateo, pp. 165–176.

Rasmussen, R. (2006), *Orson Welles. Six films analyzed, scene by scene*, McFarland & Company, Inc., Jefferson, North Carolina, and London.

Rauh, R. (1987), *Sprache im Film: Die Kombination von Wort und Bild im Spielfilm*, Film- und fernsehwissenschaftliche Arbeiten, MAkS-Publ., Münster.

Reddy, M. (1979), The Conduit Metaphor, *in* A. Ortony, ed., 'Metaphor and Thought', Cambridge University Press, Cambridge.

Reisz, K. and Millar, G. (1953), *The Technique of Film Editing*, Focal Press, London.

Reisz, K. and Millar, G. (1968), *The Technique of Film Editing*, Focal Press, London. 2nd edition.

Rieser, K. (2007), For your eyes only: some thoughts on the descriptive in film, *in* W. Wolf and W. Bernhart, eds, 'Description in Literature and Other Media', number 2 *in* 'Studies in Intermediality', Rodopi, Amsterdam, pp. 215–238.

Rimmon-Kenan, S. (2002), *Narrative fiction: contemporary poetics*, 2 edn, Routledge, London.

Roth, L. (1983), *Film semiotics, Metz, and Leone's trilogy*, Garland Publishing, New York.

Royce, T. D. (2007), Intersemiotic Complementarity: A Framework for Multimodal Discourse Analysis, *in* T. D. Royce and W. L. Bowcher, eds, 'New Directions in the Analysis of Multimodal Discourse', Lawrence Erlbaum Associates, pp. 63–110.

Ryan, M. and Kellner, D. (1988), *Camera Politica: The poetics and ideology of contemporary Hollywood film*, Indiana University Press, Bloomington.

Ryan, M.-L. (1992), 'Possible worlds in recent literary theory', *Style* **26**(4), 528–553.

Ryan, M.-L. (2003), Cognitive maps and the construction of narrative space, *in* D. Herman, ed., 'Narrative Theory and the Cognitive Sciences', CLSI, Stanford, CA, pp. 214–242.

Sachs-Hombach, K. (2006), Elemente einer philosophischen Bildtheorie des Films, *in* T. Koebner and T. Meder, eds, 'Bildtheorie und Film', edition text+kritik, München, pp. 158–175.

Salt, B. (1976), 'The early development of film form', *Film form* **1**(1), 91ff. Page citations taken from the version reprinted in Fell (1983: 284–298); a further version appears in Salt (2007: 24–34).

Salt, B. (1990), Film form 1900–1906, *in* T. Elsaesser, ed., 'Early Cinema. Space, frame, narrative', BFI Publishing, pp. 31–44. Originally published in *Sight and Sound* (Summer, 1978).

Salt, B. (2007), *Moving Into Pictures: More on Film History, Style, and Analysis*, Starword, London.

Sandro, P. (1985), Signification in the cinema, *in* B. Nichols, ed., 'Movies and methods: Volume II, an anthology', University of California Press, Berkeley and Los Angeles, CA, pp. 391–407.

Saussure, F. (1959[1915]), *Course in General Linguistics*, McGraw-Hill and the Philosophical Library, Inc., New York / Toronto / London. Edited by Charles Bally and Albert Sechehaye, in collaboration with Albert Riedlinger; Translated by Wade Baskin.

Schank, R. C. and Abelson, R. P. (1977), *Scripts, Plans, Goals and Understanding*, Lawrence Erlbaum Associates, Hillsdale, New Jersey.

Scharf, I. (2008), *Nation and identity in the New German Cinema*, Routledge, New York and London.

Schmidt, K.-H. (2004), 'Zur chronologischen Syntagmatik von Bewegtbilddaten (II): Polyspatiale Alternanz', *Kodikas/Code: Ars Semeiotica* **27**(3-4), 255–283.

Schmidt, K.-H. (2008), 'Zur chronologischen Syntagmatik von Bewegtbilddaten (III): Deskriptive Syntagmen', *Kodikas/Code: Ars Semeiotica* **31**(3–4), 217–270.

Schmidt, K.-H. and Strauch, T. (2002), 'Zur chronologischen Syntagmatik von Bewegtbilddaten', *Kodikas/Code: Ars Semeiotica* **25**(1-2), 65–96.

Schmidt, O. (2010), 'Die räumliche Wahrnehmung von Wirklichkeit. Drei Anmerkungen zum Verhälthnis von filmischer Repräsentation und Zuschauer', *Rabbit Eye – Zeitschrift für Filmforschung* **2**, 28–53.
http://www.rabbiteye.de

Schriver, K. A. (1997), *Dynamics in document design: creating texts for readers*, John Wiley and Sons, New York.

Schwan, S. and Ildirar, S. (2010), 'Watching film for the first time : How adult viewers interpret perceptual discontinuities in film', *Psychological Science* .
http://pss.sagepub.com/content/early/2010/05/28/0956797610372632

Sessions, R. (1960), 'Problems and issues facing the composer today', *The Musical Quarterly* **46**(2), 159–171.

Sharff, S. (1982), *The elements of cinema: towards a theory of cinesthetic impact*, Columbia University Press, New York.

Sidiropoulos, P., Mezaris, V., Kompatsiaris, I., Meinedo, H. and Trancoso, I. (2009), Multi-modal scene segmentation using scene transition graphs, *in* 'Proceeding MM '09 Proceedings of the 17th ACM international conference on Multimedia', ACM, ACM, New York, NY, USA, pp. 665–668.
http://doi.acm.org/10.1145/1631272.1631383

Siegrist, H. (1986), *Textsemantik des Spielfilms: Zum Ausdruckpotential der kinematographischen Formen und Techniken*, number 19 *in* 'Medien in Forschung + Unterricht: Serie A', Niemeyer, Tübingen.

Sierek, K. (2009), Filmwissenschaft, *in* 'Raumwissenschaften', Suhrkamp, Frankfurt am Main, pp. 125–141.

Smith, G. M. (1999), Local emotions, global moods, and film structure, *in* C. Plantinga and G. M. Smith, eds, 'Passionate views: film, cognition, and emotion', The John Hopkins University Press, Baltimore and London, chapter 5, pp. 103–126.

Smith, M. (1995), *Engaging Characters: Fiction, Emotion, and the Cinema*, Oxford University Press, Oxford.

Smith, M. and Wartenberg, T., eds (2006), *Thinking Through Cinema. Film as Philosophy*, Blackwell, Oxford.

Smith, R., Anderson, D. R. and Fischer, C. (1985), 'Young children's comprehension of montage', *Child Development* **56**, 962–971.

Smith, T. J. (2010), Film (cinema) perception, *in* E. B. Goldstein, ed., 'The Sage Encyclopedia of Perception', Sage Publications, Thousand Oaks, CA.

Smith, T. J. and Henderson, J. M. (2008), 'Edit blindness: The relationship between attention and global change blindness in dynamic scenes', *Journal of Eye Movement Research* **2**(2)(6), 1–17.

Sobchack, V. (1992), *The address of the eye: a phenomenology of film experience*, Princeton University Press, Princeton.

Souriau, E. (1951), 'La structure de l'univers filmique et le vocabulaire de la filmologie', *Revue Internationale de Filmologie* **7/8**, 231–240.

Sperber, D. and Wilson, D. (1995), *Relevance: communication and cognition*, 2 edn, Blackwell, Oxford.

Spottiswoode, R. (1935), *A grammar of the film: an analysis of film technique*, Faber and Faber, London.

Stam, R. (1989), Film and language: from Metz to Bakhtin, *in* R. Palmer, ed., 'The cinematic text: methods and approaches', AMS Press, New York, pp. 277–302.

Stam, R. (2000), *Film Theory: An Introduction*, Blackwell Publishing Limited, London.

Stam, R., Burgoyne, R. and Fliterman-Lewis, S. (1992), *New vocabularies in film semiotics: structuralism, post structuralism and beyond*, Routlege, London and New York.

Stöckl, H. (2004), In between modes: language and image in printed media, *in* E. Ventola, C. Charles and M. Kaltenbacher, eds, 'Perspectives on Multimodality', John Benjamins, Amsterdam, pp. 9–30.

Suckfüll, M. (2000), 'Filmanalysis and psychophysiology: effects of moments of impact and protagonists', *Media Psychology* **2**(3), 269–301.

Suckfüll, M. and Scharkow, M. (2009), 'Modes of reception for fictional films', *Communications* **34**(4), 361–384.

Sweeney, K. W. (2009), Medium, *in* P. Livingston and C. Plantinga, eds, 'The Routledge Companion to Philosophy and Film', Routledge, London and New York, chapter 16, pp. 173–183.

Tan, E. (1996), *Emotion and the Structure of Narrative Film. Film as an Emotion Machine*, Lawrence Erlbaum, Mahwah, N.J.

Taverniers, M. (2008), 'Hjelmslev's semiotic model of language: an exegesis', *Semiotica* **171**(1/4), 367–394.

Taverniers, M. (2011), 'The syntax-semantics interface in systemic functional grammar: Halliday's interpretation of the Hjelmslevian model of stratification', *Journal of Pragmatics* **43**(4), 1100–1126.

Telotte, J. (1984), 'Narration, Desire and a Lady from Shanghai', *South Atlantic Review* **49**(1), 56–71.

Thibault, P. J. (2006), *Brain, mind and the signifying body: an ecosocial semiotic theory*, Continuum, London.

Thompson, E., Noë, A. and Pessoa, L. (1999), Perceptual completion: a case study in phenomenology and cognitive science, *in* J. Petitot, F. Varela, B. Pachoud and J.-M. Roy, eds, 'Naturalizing phenomenonlogy: Issues in contemporary phenonomenlogy and cognitive science', Stanford University Press, Stanford, CA, pp. 161–195.

Thompson, K. (1986), The concept of cinematic excess, *in* P. Rosen, ed., 'Narrative, apparatus, ideology: a film theory reader', Columbia University Press, New York, pp. 130–142.

Thompson, K. (1988), *Breaking the Glass Armor : Neoformalist Film Analysis*, Princeton University Press., Princeton, NJ.

Thompson, R. and Bowen, C. (2009*a*), *Grammar of the shot*, 2 edn, Focal Press, Amsterdam.

Thompson, R. and Bowen, C. J. (2009*b*), *Grammar of the edit*, 2 edn, Focal Press, Amsterdam.

Thornham, S., Bassett, C. and Marris, P., eds (2009), *Media Studies: a reader*, 3 edn, Edinburgh University Press, Edinburgh.

Todorov, T. (1990), Reading as construction, *in* 'Genres in discourse', Cambridge University Press, Cambridge, pp. 39–49. Originally appearing as 'La Lecture comme construction.' Poétique 24 (1975): 417-425; translated by Catharine Porter.

Tomasello, M. (2005), *Constructing a language : a usage-based theory of language acquisition*, Harvard University Press, Cambridge, MA.

Tseng, C. (2008), Cohesive harmony in filmic text, *in* L. Unsworth, ed., 'Multimodal Semiotics: Functional Analysis in Contexts of Education', Continuum, London, pp. 87–104.

Tseng, C. and Bateman, J. A. (2010), Chain and choice in filmic narrative: an analysis of multimodal narrative construction in *The Fountain*, *in* C. R. Hoffmann, ed., 'Narrative Revisited. Telling a story in the age of new media', number 199 *in* 'Pragmatics and Beyond', John Benjamins, Amsterdam, pp. 213–244.

Tufte, E. R. (1983), *The visual display of quantitative information*, Graphics Press, Cheshire, Connecticut.

Turim, M. (1989), *Flashbacks in film: memory and history*, Routledge, London.

van Leeuwen, T. (1991), 'Conjunctive structure in documentary film and television', *Continuum: journal of media and cultural studies* **5**(1), 76–114.

van Leeuwen, T. (1996), Moving English: the visual language of film, *in* S. Goodman and D. Graddol, eds, 'Redesigning English: new texts, new identities', Routledge and the Open University, London and New York, chapter 2, Reading B, pp. 81–105.

van Leeuwen, T. (2005*a*), *Introducing social semiotics*, Routledge, London.

van Leeuwen, T. (2005*b*), Multimodality, genre and design, *in* S. Norris and R. Jones, eds, 'Discourse in Action – Introducing Mediated Discourse Analysis', Routledge, London, pp. 73–94.

Verstraten, P. (2009), *Film narratology*, Toronto University Press, Toronto. Translated by Stefan Van Der Lecq.

Vogler, C. (1998), *The Writer's Journey: Mythic Structure for Writers*, Michael Wiese Productions, Studio City, CA.

Wahlster, W., ed. (2006), *SmartKom: Foundations of Multimodal Dialogue Systems*, Cognitive Technologies, Springer, Heidelberg, Berlin.

Walton, K. L. (1984), 'Transparent pictures: On the nature of photographic realism', *Critical Inquiry* **11**(2), 246–277.

Walton, K. L. (1997), On pictures and photographs: objections answered, *in* R. Allen and M. Smith, eds, 'Film theory and philosophy', Oxford University Press, Oxford, U.K., pp. 60–75.

Wees, W. C. (1973), 'Dickens, Griffith and Eisenstein: Form and Image in Literature and Film', *The Humanities Association Review/La Revue de l'Association des Humanités* **24**, 266–276.

West, A. (1982), 'A textual analysis of *Lady from Shanghai*', *Enclitic* **6**(1), 90–98. Double Issue: International Conference on the textual analysis of film.

Wilson, G. M. (1986), *Narration in light: Studies in cinematic point of view*, John Hopkins University Press, Baltimore and London.

Wilson, G. M. (1995), Morals for method, *in* C. A. Freeland and T. E. Wartenberg, eds, 'Philosophy and Film', Routlege, New York and London, pp. 49–67.

Wilson, G. M. (1997), On film narrative and narrative meaning, *in* R. Allen and M. Smith, eds, 'Film theory and philosophy', Oxford University Press, Oxford, U.K., pp. 221–238.

Wirth, U. (2005), 'Abductive reasoning in Peirce's and Davidson's account of interpretation', *Semiotica* **153**(1), 199–208.

Wolf, M. J. P. (2006), 'Space, time, frame, cinema: exploring the possibilities of spatiotemporal effects', *New Review of Film and Television Studies* **4**(3), 167–181. http://dx.doi.org/10.1080/17400300600981876

Wolf, W. (2005), Metalepsis as a transgeneric and transmedial phenomenon: a case study of the possibilities of 'exporting' narratological concepts, *in* J. C. Meister, T. Kindt, W. Schermus and M. Stein, eds, 'Narrative Beyond Literary Criticism', De Gruyter, Berlin, pp. 83–107.

Wolf, W. (2007), Description as a transmedial mode of representation: general features and possibilities of realization in painting, fiction and music, *in* W. Wolf and W. Bernhart, eds, 'Description in Literature and Other Media', number 2 *in* 'Studies in Intermediality', Rodopi, Amsterdam, pp. 1–90.

Wolf, W. and Bernhart, W., eds (2007), *Description in Literature and Other Media*, number 2 *in* 'Studies in Intermediality', Rodopi, Amsterdam and New York.

Wollen, P. (1998), *Signs and meaning in the cinema*, 4th revised and enlarged edn, bfi Publishing, London.

Wulff, H. J. (1991), 'Split screen: Erste Überlegungen zur semantischen Analyse des filmischen Mehrfachbildes', *Kodikas/Code: Ars Semeiotica* **14**(3–4), 281–290.

Wulff, H. J. (1992), 'Raum und Handlung. Zur Analyse textueller Funktionen des Raums am Beispiel von Griffiths A WOMAN SCORNED', *montage av. Zeitschrift für Theorie & Geschichte audiovisueller Kommunikation* **1**(1), 91–112.

Wulff, H. J. (2007), 'Schichtenbau und Prozesshaftigkeit des Diegetischen: Zwei Anmerkungen', *montage av. Zeitschrift für Theorie & Geschichte audiovisueller Kommunikation* **16**(2), 39–51.

Wuss, P. (1990), 'Narration and the film structures for three learning phases', *Poetics* **19**, 549–570.

Wuss, P. (1993), *Filmanalyse und Psychologie*, Edition Sigma, Berlin.

Wuss, P. (2009), *Cinematic narration and its psychological impact: functions of cognition, emotion and play*, Cambridge Scholars, Newcastle.

Yeung, M., Yeo, B.-L. and Liu, B. (1998), 'Segmentation of video by clustering and graph analysis', *Journal of Computational Vision and Image Understanding* **71**(1), 94–109.

Zacks, J. M. and Magliano, J. P. (2011), Film, narrative and cognitive neuroscience, *in* D. Melcher and F. Bacci, eds, 'Art and the Senses', Oxford University Press, New York.

Zacks, J. M., Speer, N. K. and Reynolds, J. R. (2009), 'Segmentation in reading and film comprehension', *Journal of Experimental Psychology* **138**, 307–327.

Zacks, J. M., Tversky, B. and Iyer, G. (2001), 'Perceiving, remembering and communicating structure in events', *Journal of Experimental Psychology* **130**, 29–58.

Zacks, J. and Tversky, B. (2001), 'Event structure in perception and conception', *Psychological Bulletin* **127**(1), 3–21.

Zettl, H. (1973), *Sight, sound, motion: Applied media aesthetics*, Wadsworth, Belmont, CA.

Zöllner, K. (1989), *"As you can see in the text..." which passages do literary scholars quote and interpret in "Gulliver's Travels"*, number 19 *in* 'Askpekte der englischen Geistes- und Kulturgeschichte', Peter Lang, Frankfurt am Main.

Index of Works Cited

24 (2001–2010), 50

A Fistful of dollars (1964), 112
About a boy (2002), 107
Adieu Philippine (1962), 109, 111, 116, 124, 128, 179 198, 200, 227, 232, 270
Allen and Smith (1997), 26
Allen (1984), 204
Allen (2007), 50
Altman (1999), 34
Anderson (1996), 140, 143, 150, 152
Arijon (1976), 25
Armstrong (1990), 68
Arnheim (1957), 87
Arnheim (1982), 138
Asher and Lascarides (2003), 42, 44, 48, 243

Bacon (2011), 48
Baetens (1993), 164
Bakhtin (1986), 92
Baldry and Thibault (2006), 169
Bal (1985), 128
Barsalou (1983), 242
Barthes (1964), 84
Barthes (1974), 248
Barthes (1977a), 32, 74, 158
Barthes (1977b), 155, 164
Barthes (1977c), 145
Bartlett (1932), 4
Bateman and Farrar (2004), 244
Bateman and Rondhuis (1997), 74
Bateman (2007), 122, 128, 178, 196, 285, 301
Bateman (2008), 74, 164, 165
Bateman (2009), 169, 214
Bateman (2011), 78, 94, 97, 98, 133, 165
Battleship Potemkin (1925), 160
Baudry (1974), 21, 38, 101
Bazin (1960), 145
Bazin (1967), 120
Bednarek (2010), 144
Bellour and Metz (1971), 142
Bellour (1974), 159
Bellour (1975), 26
Bellour (1990), 247
Bellour (2000a), 194
Bellour (2000b), 115
Bellour (2000c), 247
Bellour (2000d), 99, 113, 157, 158, 176, 248
Benveniste (1966), 27
Benveniste (1974)
Berger (2000), 287
Bertin (1983), 33

Bordegoni et al. (1997), 98
Bordwell and Thompson (2008), 4, 12, 14, 17, 25
Bordwell (1982), 80, 148, 164
Bordwell (1985), 4, 12, 20, 60, 118, 146, 160, 292, 293
Bordwell (1989), 2, 12, 22, 34, 70, 71
Bordwell (2005), 3, 34, 40, 47, 143, 157, 288
Bordwell (2007), 4, 22, 144
Bordwell (2009), 22, 140, 288
Bordwell (2011), 293
Branigan (1975), 169, 194
Branigan (1976), 15
Branigan (1984), 18, 46, 80, 100, 169, 179, 257
Branigan (1986a), 140
Branigan (1986b), 169, 189
Branigan (1992), 4, 62, 247, 271, 273, 281, 282
Braudy (1976), 197
Bremont (1973), 140, 164
Buckland (2000), 24, 46, 119, 166
Buckland (2004), 135, 136
Bulterman and Rutledge (2008), 74
Burch (1969)
Burch (1973), 87, 89, 180, 205
Burch (1990), 285
Burke (1945), 140
Burnett (2008), 74

Cadbury and Poague (1982), 27
Callenbach (1975), 99
Carroll (1974), 111, 113
Carroll (1977), 119
Carroll (1980), 46, 119
Carroll (1995), 140
Carroll (1996a), 41
Carroll (1996b), 132, 133, 140
Carroll (1996c), 97
Casetti (1998), 1
Cavell (1980), 26, 76, 77, 164
Cegarra (1973), 113
Chandler (2002), 29, 73
Chateau (1976), 46
Chatman (1978), 47, 55
Chatman (1992), 118, 162
Chaudrini (2006), 26
Chomsky (1966), 35
Citizen Kane (1941), 107
Cohen-Séat (1948), 33, 73
Cohen (2004), 92
Colin (1985), 73, 75
Colin (1989a), 73
Colin (1989b), 125, 304

Subject and Name Index

Figure 6.7
(repeated omitting references).

Our extension of the *grande paradigmatique* for film originally motivated in Bateman (2007) and motivated at length in Chapter 6.

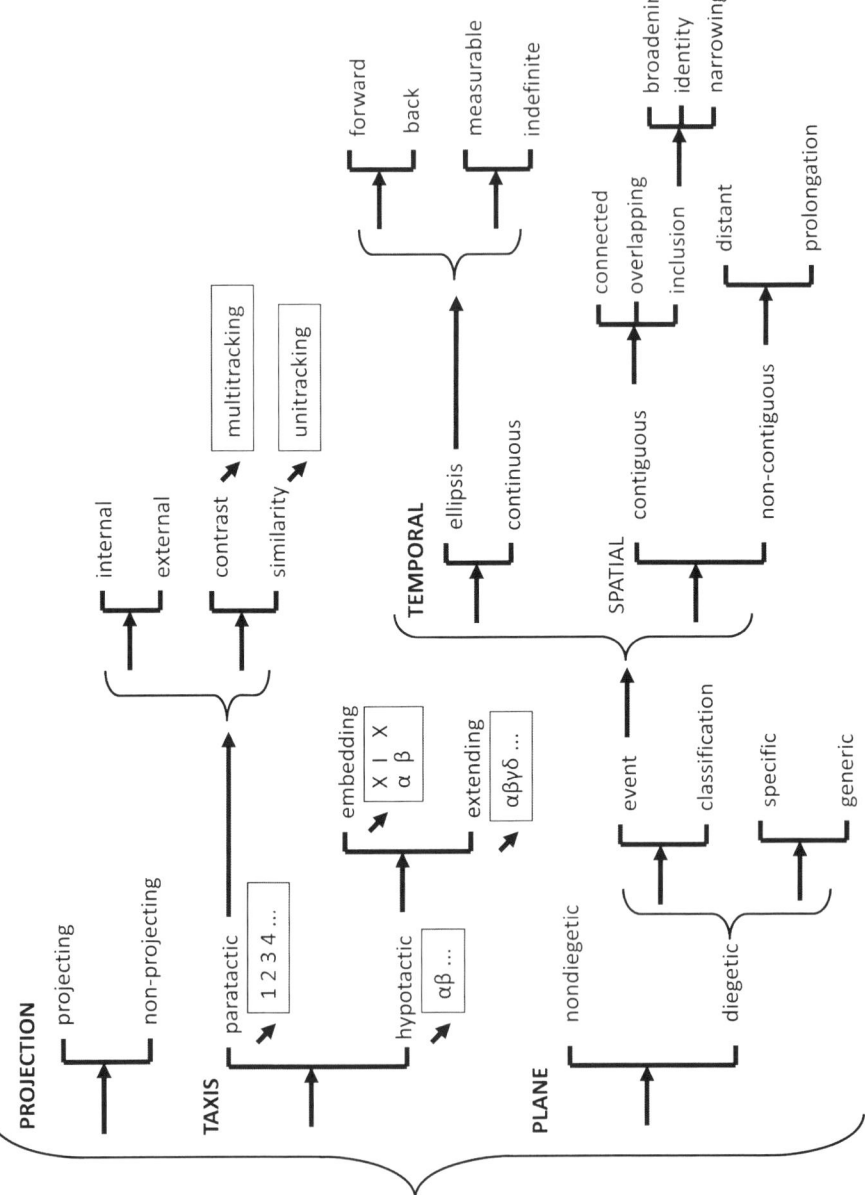

13187633R00191

Printed in Poland
by Amazon Fulfillment
Poland Sp. z o.o., Wrocław